Systems Programming in Unix/Linux

K. C. Wang

Systems Programming in Unix/Linux

 Springer

K. C. Wang
School of Electrical Engineering
Washington State University
Pullman, WA, USA

ISBN 978-3-030-06429-7   ISBN 978-3-319-92429-8   (eBook)
https://doi.org/10.1007/978-3-319-92429-8

This Springer imprint is published by the registered company Springer Nature Switzerland AG
The registered company address is: Gewerbestrasse 11, 6330 Cham, Switzerland

Dedicated to
Cindy

Preface

Systems programming is an indispensable part of Computer Science and Computer Engineering education. System programming courses in Computer Science/Engineering curriculums play two important roles. First, it provides students with a wide range of knowledge about computer system software and advanced programming skills, allowing them to interface with operating system kernel, perform file operations and network programming, and make efficient use of system resources to develop application programs. Second, it prepares students with needed background to pursue advanced studies in Computer Science/Engineering, such as operating systems, embedded systems, database systems, data mining, artificial intelligence, computer networks, and distributed and parallel computing. Due to its importance, systems programming in Unix/Linux has been a popular subject matter in CS/CE education and also for self-study by advanced programmers. As a result, there are a tremendous number of books and online articles in this area. Despite these, I still find it difficult to choose a suitable book for the Systems Programming course I teach at WSU. For many years, I had to use my own class notes and programming assignments in the course. After careful thinking, I have decided to put together the materials into a book form.

The purpose of this book is to provide a suitable platform for teaching and learning the theory and practice of systems programming. Unlike most other books, this book covers systems programming topics in greater depth and it stresses programming practice. It uses a series of programming projects to let students apply their acquired knowledge and programming skills to develop practical and useful programs. The book is intended as a textbook in technical-oriented systems programming courses. It contains detailed example programs with complete source code, making it suitable for self-study also.

Undertaking this book project has proved to be another very demanding and time-consuming endeavor. While preparing the manuscripts for publication, I have been blessed with the encouragement and help from many people. I would like to take this opportunity to thank all of them. I want to especially thank Yan Zhang for his help in preparing figures for the book and proofreading the manuscript.

Special thanks go to Cindy for her continuing support and inspirations, which have made this book possible. Above all, I would like to thank my family for bearing with me with endless excuses of being busy all the time.

Sample solutions of programming projects in the book are available for download at http://wang.eecs.wsu.edu/~kcw. For source code, please contact the author by email.

Pullman, WA, USA   K. C. Wang
April, 2018

Contents

About the Author

K. C. Wang received the BSEE degree from National Taiwan University in 1960 and the PhD degree in Electrical Engineering from Northwestern University, Evanston, IL, in 1965. He is currently a professor in the School of Electrical Engineering and Computer Science at Washington State University. His academic interests are in operating systems, distributed systems, and parallel computing.

Introduction

Abstract

This chapter presents an introduction to the book. It describes the book's scope, intended audience and its suitability as a textbook in Computer Science/Engineering curriculums. It presents a brief history of Unix, which includes early versions of Unix at Bell Labs, AT&T System V and other developments of Unix, such as BSD, HP UX, IBM AIX and Sun/Solaris Unix. It describes the development of Linux and various Linux distributions, which include Debian, Ubuntu, Mint, Red Hat and Slackware. It lists both the hardware platforms and virtual machines for Linux. It shows how to install Ubuntu Linux to both VirtualBox and Vmware virtual machines inside the Microsoft Windows. It explains the startup sequence of Linux, from booting the Linux kernel to user login and command execution. It describes the Unix/Linux file system organization, file types and commonly used Unix/Linux commands. Lastly, it describes system administration tasks for users to manage and maintain their Linux systems.

1.1   About This Book

This book is about systems programming in the Unix/Linux (Thompson and Ritchie 1974, 1978; Bach 1986; Linux 2017) environment. It covers all the essential components of Unix/Linux, which include process management, concurrent programming, timer and time service, file systems, network programming and MySQL database system. In addition to covering the functionalities of Unix/Linux, it stresses on programming practice. It uses programming exercises and realistic programming projects to allow students to practice systems programming with hands-on experiences.

1.2   Roles of Systems Programming

Systems programming is an indispensable part of Computer Science and Computer Engineering education. System programming courses in Computer Science/Engineering curriculums serve two main purposes. First, it provides students with a wide range of knowledge about computer system software and advanced programming skills, allowing them to interface with operating system kernel, make efficient use of system resources to develop application software. Second, it prepares students with the needed background to pursue advanced studies in Computer Science/Engineering, such as operating systems, embedded systems, database systems, data mining, artificial intelligence, computer networks, network security, distributed and parallel computing.

1.3   Objectives of This Book

This book is intended to achieve the following objectives.

1.3.1   Strengthen Students Programming Background

Computer Science/Engineering students usually take introductory programming courses in their first or second year. Such courses typically cover basic programming in C, C++ or Java. Due to time limitations, these courses can only cover the basic syntax of a programming language, data types, simple program structures and using library functions for I/O. Students coming out of such course are rather weak in programming skills due to a lack of sufficient practices. For instance, they usually do not know much about the software tools, the steps of program development and run-time environment of program executions. The first object of this book is to provide students with the needed background and skills to do advanced programming. This book covers program development steps in detail. These include assembler, compiler, linker, link library, executable file contents, program execution image, function call conventions, parameter passing schemes, local variables, stack frames, link C program with assembly code, program termination and exception handling. In addition, it also shows how to use Makefiles to manage large programming projects and how to debug program executions by GDB.

1.3.2   Applications of Dynamic Data Structures

Most elementary data structure courses cover the concepts of link lists, queues, stacks and trees, etc. but they rarely show where and how are these dynamic data structures used in practice. This book covers these topics in detail. These include C structures, pointers, link lists and trees. It uses programming exercises and programming projects to let the students apply dynamic data structures in real life. Case in point: a programming exercise is for the students to display the stack contents of a program with many levels of function calls, allowing them to see the function calling sequence, passed parameters, local variables and stack frames. Another programming exercise is to let students implement a printf-like function with varying parameters, which requires them to apply parameter passing schemes to access varying parameters on stack. Yet another programming exercise is to print the partitions of a disk, in which the extended partitions form a "link list" in the disk, but not by the conventional pointers as they learned in programming languages. A programming project is to implement a binary tree to simulate the Unix/Linux file system tree, which supports pwd, ls, cd, mkdir, rmdir, creat, rm operations as in a real file system. Besides using dynamic data structures, the programming project allows them to apply a wide range of programming techniques, such as string tokenization, search for nodes in a tree, insert and delete tree nodes, etc. It also allows them to apply binary tree traversal algorithms to save binary trees as files and reconstruct binary trees from saved files.

1.3.3   Process Concept and Process Management

The major focus of systems programming is the abstract notion of processes, which is rather hard to grasp. This book uses a simple C program together with a piece of assembly code to let students see real processes in action. The program implements a multitasking environment to simulate process operations in an OS kernel. It allows the students to create processes, schedule processes by priority, run different processes by context switching, maintain process relations by a binary tree, use sleep and wakeup to implement wait for child process termination, etc. This concrete example makes it much easier for students to understand processes and process management functions. Then it covers process management in Unix/Linux in detail, which includes fork(), exit(), wait() and change process execution image by exec(). It also covers I/O redirection and pipes. It uses a programming project to let the students implement a sh simulator for command execution. The sh simulator behaves exactly the same as the bash of Linux. It can execute all Unix/Linux commands with I/O redirections, as well as compound commands connected by pipes.

1.3.4   Concurrent Programming

Parallel computing is the future of computing. It is imperative to introduce parallel computing and concurrent programming to CS/CE students at an early stage. This book covers parallel computing and concurrent programming. It explains the concept of threads and their advantages over processes. It covers Pthreads (Pthreads 2017) programming in detail. It explains the various kinds of threads synchronization tools, such as threads join, mutex lock, condition variables, semaphores and barriers. It demonstrates applications of threads by practical examples, which include matrix computation, quicksort and solving system of linear equations by concurrent threads. It also introduces the concepts of race conditions, critical regions, deadlock and deadlock prevention schemes. In addition to using Pthreads, it uses a programming project to let students experiment with user-level threads, implement threads synchronization tools and practice concurrent programming by user-level threads.

1.3.5   Timer and Time Functions

Timer and time functions are essential to process management and file systems. This book covers the principle of hardware timers, timer interrupts and time service function in Unix/Linux in detail. It shows how to use interval timers and timer generated signals in systems programming. In addition, it uses a programming project to let students implement interval timer support for concurrent tasks.

1.3.6   Signals, Signal Processing and IPC

Signals and signal processing are keys to understanding program exceptions and Inter-Process Communication (IPC). This book covers signals, signal processing and IPC in Unix/Linux. It explains signal origins, signal delivery and processing in the OS kernel and the relation between signals and exceptions. It shows how to install signal catchers to handle program exceptions in user mode. It uses a programming project to let students use Linux signals and pipes to implement an IPC mechanism for concurrent tasks to exchange messages.

1.3.7 File system

Besides process management, file system is the second major component of an operating system. This book provides an in depth coverage of file systems. It describes file operations at different levels and explains their relationships. These include storage devices, file system support in Unix/Linux kernel, system calls for file operations, library I/O functions, user commands and sh scripts. It uses a series of programming exercises to let the students implement a complete EXT2 file system that is totally Linux compatible. These not only allow the students to have a thorough understanding of file operations but also provide them with the unique experience of writing a complete file system. Another programming project is to implement and compare the performances of different I/O buffer management algorithms. The simulation system supports I/O operations between processes and disk controllers. It allows the students to practice I/O programming, interrupts processing and synchronization between processes and I/O devices.

1.3.8 TCP/IP and Network Programming

Network programming is the third major component of an operating system. This book covers TCP/IP protocols, socket API, UDP and TCP programming using sockets and the server-client model in network computing. A programming project is for the students to implement a server-client based system for remote file operations across the Internet. As of now, WWW and Internet services have become an indispensable part of daily lives. It is essential to introduce CS/CE students to this technology. This book covers HTTP and Web programming in detail. It allows the students to configure the HTTPD server on their Linux machines to support HTTP programming. It shows how to use HTML for static Web pages and PHP to create dynamic Web pages. It covers the MySQL database system, shows how to create and manage databases in both command and batch modes and interface MySQL with both C and PHP. A programming project is for the students to implement a Web server to support file operations by HTTP forms and dynamic Web pages using CGI programming.

1.4 Intended Audience

This book is intended as a textbook for systems programming courses in technically oriented Computer Science/Engineering curriculums that emphasize both theory and programming practice. The book contains many detailed working example programs with complete source code. It is also suitable for self-study by advanced programmers and computer enthusiasts.

1.5 Unique Features of This Book

This book has many unique features which distinguishes it from other books.

1. This book is self-contained. It includes all the foundation and background information for studying systems programming. These include program development steps, program execution and termination, function call conventions, run-time stack usage and link C programs with assembly code. It also covers C structures, pointers and dynamic data structures, such as link lists, queues and binary trees. It shows applications of dynamic data structures in system programming.

2. It uses a simple multitasking system to introduce and illustrate the abstract notion of processes. The multitasking system allows students to create processes, schedule and run different processes by context switching, implement process synchronization mechanisms, control and observe process executions. This unique approach allows the students to have a concrete feeling and better understanding of process operations in real operating systems.

3. It describes the origin and roles of processes in Unix/Linux in detail, from system booting to INIT process, daemon processes, login processes and the user sh process. It describes the execution environment of user processes, such as stdin, stdout, stderr file streams and environment variables. It also explains how does the sh process execute user commands.

4. It covers process management functions in Unix/Linux in detail. These include fork(), exit(), wait (), changing process execution image by exec(), I/O redirection and pipes. Moreover, it allows the students to apply these concepts and programming techniques to implement a sh simulator for command execution. The sh simulator behaves exactly the same as the standard bash of Linux. It supports executions of simple commands with I/O redirections, as well as compound commands connected by pipes.

5. It introduces parallel computing and concurrent programming. It covers Pthreads programming by detailed examples, which include matrix computation, quicksort and solving systems of linear equations by concurrent threads, and it demonstrate the use of threads synchronization tools of join, mutex lock, condition variables and barriers. It also introduces the important concepts and problems in concurrent programming, such as race conditions, critical regions, deadlock and deadlock prevention schemes. In addition, it allows the students to experiment with user-level threads, design and implement threads synchronizing tools, such as threads join, mutex lock, semaphores and demonstrate the capabilities of user-level threads by concurrent programs. These allow the students to have a deeper understanding how threads work in Linux.

6. It covers timers and time service functions in detail. It also allows the reader to implement interval timers for concurrent tasks in a multitasking system.

7. It presents a unified treatment of interrupts and signals, treating signals as interrupts to processes, similar to interrupts to a CPU. It explains signal sources, signal types, signal generation and signal processing in great detail. It shows how to install signal catchers to allow processes to handle signals in user mode. It discusses how to use signals for IPC and other IPC mechanisms in Linux. It uses a programming project to let the students use Linux signals and pipes to implement an IPC mechanism for tasks to exchange messages in a multitasking system.

8. It organizes file operations into a hierarchy of different levels, ranging from storage devices, file system support in Unix/Linux kernel, system calls for file operations, library I/O functions, user commands and sh scripts. This hierarchical view provides the reader with a complete picture of file operations. It covers file operations at the various levels in detail and explains their relationships. It shows how to use system calls to develop file operation commands, such as ls for listing directory and file information, cat for displaying file contents and cp for copying files.

9. It uses a programming project to lead the students to implement a complete EXT2 file system. The programming project has been used in the CS360, System Programming course, at Washington State University for many years, and it has proved to be very successful. It provides students with the unique experience of writing a complete file system that not only works but is also totally Linux compatible. This is perhaps the most unique feature of this book.

10. It covers TCP/IP protocols, socket API, UDP and TCP programming using sockets and the server-client model in network programming. It uses a programming project to let the students implement a server-client based system for remote file operations across the Internet. It also covers HTTP and Web programming in detail. It shows how to configure the Linux HTTPD server to support HTTP

programming, and how to use PHP to create dynamic Web pages. It uses a programming project to let the students implement a Web server to support file operations via HTTP forms and dynamic Web pages using CGI programming.

11. It emphasizes on programming practice. Throughout the book, it illustrates system programming techniques by complete and concrete example programs. Above all, it uses a series of programming projects to let students practice system programming. The programming projects include

(1) Implement a binary tree to simulate the Unix/Linux file system tree for file operations (Chap. 2).

(2) Implement a sh simulator for command executions, including I/O redirections and pipes (Chap. 3).

(3) Implement user-level threads, threads synchronization and concurrent programming (Chap. 4).

(4) Implement interval timers for concurrent tasks in a multitasking system (Chap. 5).

(5) Use Linux signals and pipes to implement an IPC mechanism for concurrent task to exchange messages (Chap. 6).

(6) Convert file pathname to file's INODE in an EXT2 file system (Chap. 7).

(7) Recursive file copy by system calls (Chap. 8).

(8) Implement a printf-like function for formatted printing using only the basic operation of putchar() (Chap. 9).

(9) Recursive file copy using sh functions and sh scripts (Chap. 10).

(10) Implement a complete and Linux compatible EXT2 file system (Chap. 11).

(11) Implement and compare I/O buffer management algorithms in an I/O system simulator (Chap. 12).

(12) Implement a file server and clients on the Internet (Chap. 13).

(13) Implement a file server using HTTP forms and dynamic Web pages by CGI programming (Chap. 13).

Among the programming projects, (1)–(3), (6)–(9), (12)–(13) are standard programming assignments of the CS360 course at Washington State University. (10) has been the class project of the CS360 course for many years. Many of the programming projects, e.g. (12)–(13) and especially the file system project (10), require the students to form two-person teams, allowing them to acquire and practice the skills of communication and cooperation with peers in a team-oriented working environment.

1.6   Use This Book As Textbook in Systems Programming Courses

This book is suitable as a textbook for systems programming courses in technically oriented Computer Science/Engineering curriculums that emphasize both theory and practice. A one-semester course based on this book may include the following topics.

1. Introduction to Unix/Linux (Chap. 1)
2. Programming background (Chap. 2).
3. Process management in Unix/Linux (Chap. 3)
4. Concurrent programming (Parts of Chap. 4)
5. Timer and time Service functions (Parts of Chap. 5)
6. Signals and signal processing (Chap. 6)

7. File operation levels (Chap. 7)
8. File system support in OS kernel and system calls for file operations (Chap. 8)
9. I/O library functions and file operation commands (Chap. 9)
10. Sh programming and sh scripts for file operations (Chap. 10)
11. Implementation of EXT2 file system (Chap. 11)
12. TCP/IP and network programming, HTTP and Web programming (Chap. 13).
13. Introduction to MySQL database system (Parts of Chap. 14).

The problems section of each chapter contains questions designed to review the concepts and principles presented in the chapter. Many problems are suitable as programming projects to let students gain more experience and skills in systems programming.

Most materials of this book have been used and tested in the Systems Programming course, CS360, in EECS at Washington State University. The course has been the backbone of both Computer Science and Computer Engineering programs in EECS at WSU. The current CS360 course syllabus, class notes and programming assignments are available for review and scrutiny at

http://www.eecs.wsu.edu/~cs360

The course project is to lead students to implement a complete EXT2 file system that is totally Linux compatible. The programming project has proved to be the most successful part of the CS360 course, with excellent feedbacks from both industrial employers and academic institutions.

1.7 Other Reference Books

Due to its importance, systems programming in Unix/Linux has been a popular subject matter in CS/CE education and also for self-study by advanced programmers. As a result, there are a tremendous number of books and online articles in this area. Some of these books are listed in the reference section (Curry 1996; Haviland et al. 1998; Kerrisk 2010; Love 2013; Robbins and Robbins 2003; Rochkind 2008; Stevens and Rago 2013). Many of these books are excellent programmer's guides, which are suitable as additional reference books.

1.8 Introduction to Unix

Unix (Thompson and Ritchie 1974, 1978) is a general purpose operating system. It was developed by Ken Thompson and Dennis Ritchie on the PDP-11 minicomputers at Bell Labs in the early 70s. In 1975, Bell Labs released Unix to the general public. Initial recipients of this Unix system were mostly universities and non-profit institutions. It was known as the **V6 Unix.** This early version of Unix, together with the classic book on the C programming language (Kernighan and Ritchie 1988) started the Unix revolution on Operating Systems, with long-lasting effects even to this day.

1.8.1 AT&T Unix

Development of Unix at AT&T continued throughout the 1980s, cumulating in the release of the **AT&T System V** Unix (Unix System V 2017), which has been the representative Unix of AT&T.

System V Unix was a uniprocessor (single CPU) system. It was extended to multiprocessor versions in the late 80s (Bach 1986).

1.8.2 Berkeley Unix

Berkeley Unix (Leffler et al. 1989, 1996) refers to a set of variants of the Unix operating system developed by the Berkeley Software Distribution **(BSD)** at the University of California, Berkeley, from 1977 to 1985. The most significant contributions of BSD Unix are implementation of the TCP/IP suite and the socket interface, which are incorporated into almost all other operating systems as a standard means of networking, which has helped the tremendous growth of the Internet in the 90s. In addition, BSD Unix advocates open source from the beginning, which stimulated further porting and development of BSD Unix. Later releases of BSD Unix provided a basis for several open source development projects, which include FreeBSD (McKusick et al. 2004), OpenBSD and NetBSD, etc. that are still ongoing to this day.

1.8.3 HP Unix

HP-UX (HP-UX 2017) is Hewlett Packard's proprietary implementation of the Unix operating system, first released in 1984. Recent versions of HP-UX support the HP 9000 series computer systems, based on the PA-RISC processor architecture, and HP Integrity systems, based on Intel's Itanium. The unique features of HP-UX include a built-in logical volume manager for large file systems and access control lists as an alternative to the standard rwx file permissions of Unix.

1.8.4 IBM Unix

AIX (IBM AIX 2017) is a series of proprietary Unix operating systems developed by IBM for several of its computer platforms. Originally released for the IBM 6150 RISC workstation, AIX now supports or has supported a wide variety of hardware platforms, including the IBM RS/6000 series and later POWER and PowerPC-based systems, IBM System I, System/370 mainframes, PS/2 personal computers, and the Apple Network Server. AIX is based on UNIX System V with BSD4.3-compatible extensions.

1.8.5 Sun Unix

Solaris (Solaris 2017) is a Unix operating system originally developed by Sun Microsystems (Sun OS 2017). Since January 2010, it was renamed Oracle Solaris. Solaris is known for its scalability, especially on SPARC systems. Solaris supports SPARC-based and x86-based workstations and servers from Oracle and other vendors.

As can be seen, most Unix systems are proprietary and tied to specific hardware platforms. An average person may not have access to these systems. This present a challenge to readers who wishes to practice systems programming in the Unix environment. For this reason, we shall use Linux as the platform for programming exercises and practice.

1.9   Introduction to Linux

Linux (Linux 2017) is a Unix-like system. It started as an experimental kernel for the Intel x86 based PCs by Linus Torvalds in 1991. Subsequently, it was developed by a group of people world-wide. A big milestone of Linux occurred in the late 90s when it combined with **GNU** (Stallman 2017) by incorporating many GNU software, such as the GCC compiler, GNU Emacs editor and bash, etc. which greatly facilitated the further development of Linux. Not long after that, Linux implemented the TCP/IP suite to access the Internet and ported X11 (X-windows) to support GUI, making it a complete OS.

Linux includes many features of other Unix systems. In some sense, it represents a union of the most popular Unix systems. To a large extent, Linux is POSIX compliant. Linux has been ported to many hardware architectures, such as Motorola, SPARC and ARM, etc. The predominate Linux platform is still the Intel x86 based PCs, including both desktops and laptops, which are widely available. Also, Linux is free and easy to install, which makes it popular with computer science students.

1.10   Linux Versions

The development of Linux kernel is under the strict supervision of the Linux kernel development group. All Linux kernels are the same except for different release versions. However, depending on distributions, Linux has many different versions, which may differ in distribution packages, user interface and service functions. The following lists some of the most popular versions of Linux distributions.

1.10.1   Debian Linux

Debian is a Linux distribution that emphasizes on free software. It supports many hardware platforms. Debian distributions use the .deb package format and the dpkg package manager and its front ends.

1.10.2   Ubuntu Linux

Ubuntu is a Linux distribution based on Debian. Ubuntu is designed to have regular releases, a consistent user experience and commercial support on both desktops and servers. Ubuntu Linux has several official distributions. These Ubuntu variants simply install a set of packages different from the original Ubuntu. Since they draw additional packages and updates from the same repositories as Ubuntu, the same set of software is available in all of them.

1.10.3   Linux Mint

Linux Mint is a community-driven Linux distribution based on Debian and Ubuntu. According to Linux Mint, it strives to be a "modern, elegant and comfortable operating system which is both powerful and easy to use". Linux Mint provides full out-of-the-box multimedia support by including some proprietary software, and it comes bundled with a variety of free and open-source applications. For this reason, it was welcomed by many beginner Linux users.

1.10.4 RPM-Based Linux

Red Hat Linux and SUSE Linux were the original major distributions that used the RPM file format, which is still used in several package management systems. Both Red Hat and SUSE Linux divided into commercial and community-supported distributions. For example, Red Hat Linux provides a community-supported distribution sponsored by Red Hat called Fedora, and a commercially supported distribution called Red Hat Enterprise Linux, whereas SUSE divided into openSUSE and SUSE Linux Enterprise

1.10.5 Slackware Linux

Slackware Linux is known as a highly customizable distribution that stresses on ease of maintenance and reliability over cutting-edge software and automated tools. Slackware Linux is considered as a distribution for advanced Linux users. It allows users to choose Linux system components to install and configure the installed system, allowing them to learn the inner workings of the Linux operating system.

1.11 Linux Hardware Platforms

Linux was originally designed for the Intel x86 based PCs. Earlier versions of Linux run on Intel x86 based PCs in 32-bit protected mode. It is now available in both 32-bit and 64-bit modes. In addition to the Intel x86, Linux has bee ported to many other computer architectures, which include MC6800 of Motorola, MIP, SPARC, PowerPC and recently ARM. But the predominant hardware platform of Linux is still the Intel x86 based PCs, although ARM based Linux for embedded systems are gaining popularity rapidly.

1.12 Linux on Virtual Machines

Presently, most Intel x86 based PCs are equipped with Microsoft Windows, e.g. Windows 7, 8 or 10, as the default operating system. It is fairly easy to install Linux alongside Windows on the same PC and use dual-boot to boot up either Windows or Linux when the PC starts. However, most users are reluctant to do so due to either technical difficulty or preference to stay in the Windows environment. A common practice is to install and run Linux on a virtual machine inside the Windows host. In the following, we shall show how to install and run Linux on virtual machines inside the Microsoft Windows 10.

1.12.1 VirtualBox

VirtualBox (VirtualBox 2017) is a powerful x86 and AMD64/Intel64 virtualization product of Oracle. VirtualBox runs on Windows, Linux, Macintosh, and Solaris hosts. It supports a large number of guest operating systems, including Windows (NT 4.0, 2000, XP, Vista, Windows 7, Windows 8, Windows 10) and Linux (2.4, 2.6, 3.x and 4.x), Solaris and OpenSolaris, OS/2, and OpenBSD. To install virtualBox on Windows 10, follow these steps.

(1). Download VirtualBox.

At the VirtualBox website, **http://download.virtualbox.org,** you will find links to VirtualBox binaries and its source code. For Windows hosts, the VirtualBox binary is

VirtualBox-5.1.12-112440-win.exe

In addition, you should also download the

VirtualBox 5.1.12 Oracle VM VirtualBox Extension Pack

which provides support for USB 2.0 and USB 3.0 devices, VirtualBox RDP, disk encryption, NVMe and PXE boot for Intel cards.

(2). Install VirtualBox

After downloading the **VirtualBox-5.1.12-112440-win.exe** file, double click on the file name to run it, which will install the VirtualBox VM under Windows 10. It also creates an Oracle VM VirtualBox icon on the desktop.

(3). Create a VirtualBox Virtual Machine

Start up the VirtualBox. An initial VM window will appear, as shown in Fig. 1.1.

Choose the New button to create a new VM with 1024 MB memory and a virtual disk of 12GB.

(4). Install Ubuntu 14.04 to VirtualBox VM

Insert the Ubuntu 14.04 install DVD to a DVD drive. Start up the VM, which will boot up from the DVD to install Ubuntu 14.04 to the VM.

(5). Adjust Display Size

For some unknown reason, when Ubuntu first starts up, the screen size will be stuck at the 640 × 480 resolution. To change the display resolution, open a terminal and enter the command line **xdiagnose**. On the X Diagnostic settings window, enable all the options under **Debug,** which consist of

Extra graphic debug message
Display boot messages
Enable automatic crash bug reporting

Although none of these options seems to be related to the screen resolution, it does change the resolution to 1024 × 768 for a normal Ubuntu display screen. Figure 1.2 shows the screen of Ubuntu on the VirtualBox VM.

Fig. 1.1 VirtualBox VM Window

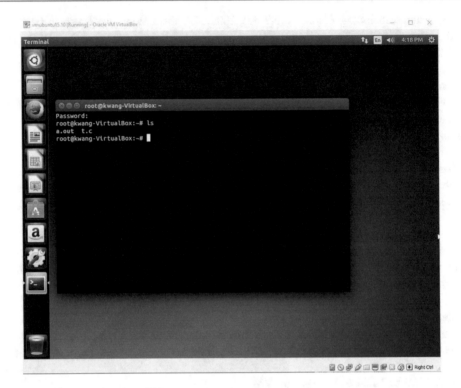

Fig. 1.2 Ubuntu Linux on VirtualBox VM

(6). Test C programming under Ubuntu

Ubuntu 14.04 has the gcc package installed. After installing Ubuntu, the user may create C source files, compile them and run the C programs. If the user needs emacs, install it by

sudo apt-get install emacs

Emacs provides an Integrated Development Environment (IDE) for text-edit, compile C programs and run the resulting binary executables under GDB. We shall cover and demonstrate the emacs IDE in Chap. 2.

1.12.2   VMware

VMware is another popular VM for x86 based PCs. The full versions of VMware, which include VM servers, are not free, but VMware Workstation Players, which are sufficient for simple VM tasks, are free.

(1). Install VMware Player on Windows 10

The reader may get VMware Workstation Player from VMware's download site. After downloading, double click on the file name to run it, which will install VMware and create a VMware Workstation icon on the Desktop. Click on the icon to start up the VMware VM, which displays a VMware VM window, as shown in Fig. 1.3.

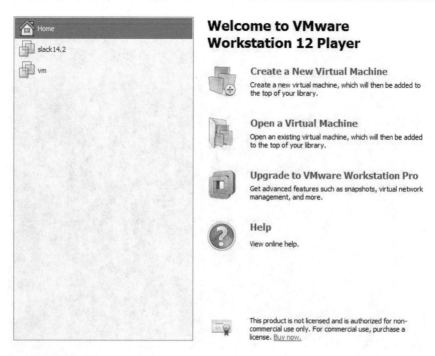

Fig. 1.3 VMware VM Window

(2). Install Ubuntu 15.10 on VMware VM

To install Ubuntu 15.10 on the VMware VM, follow the following steps.

1. Download Ubuntu 15.10 install DVD image; burn it to a DVD disc.
2. Download Vmware Workstation Player 12 exe file for Windows 10.
3. Install Vmware Player.
4. Start up Vmware Player

   Choose: Create a new virtual machine;

   Choose: Installer disc: DVD RW Drive (D:)

   => insert the installer disc until it is ready to install

   Then, enter Next

   Choose: Linux

   Version: ubuntu

   Virtual machine name: change to a suitable name, e.g. ubuntu

   Vmware will create a VM with 20GB disk size, 1GB memory, etc.

   Choose Finish to finish creating the new VM

   Next Screen: Choose: play virtual machine to start the VM.

   The VM will boot from the Ubuntu install DVD to install Ubuntu.

5. Run C Program under Ubuntu Linux

Figure 1.4 shows the startup screen of Ubuntu and running a C program under Ubuntu.

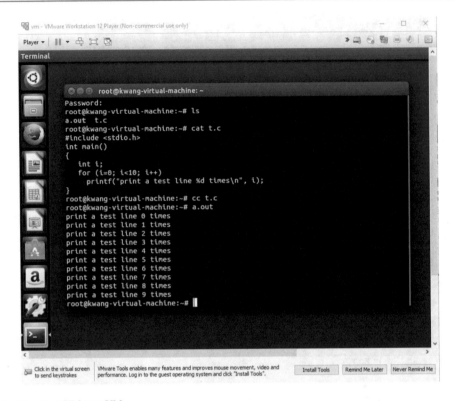

Fig. 1.4 Ubuntu on VMware VM

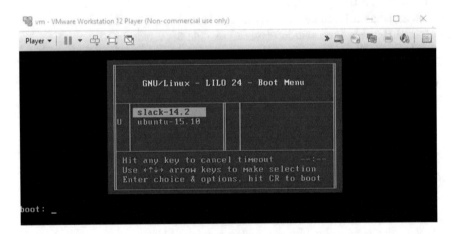

Fig. 1.5 Dual-Boot Window of Slackware and Ubuntu Linux

1.12.3   Dual Boot Slackware and Ubuntu Linux

It seems that free VMware Player only supports 32-bit VMs. The install steps are identical to above except the installer disc is the Slackware14.2 install DVD. After installing both Slackware 14.2 and Ubuntu 15.10, set up LILO to boot up either system when the VM starts up. If the reader installs Slackware first followed by installing Ubuntu, Ubuntu will recognize Slackware and configure GRUB for dual boot. The following figure shows the dual-boot menu of LILO (Fig. 1.5).

1.13   Use Linux

1.13.1   Linux kernel image

In a typical Linux system, Linux kernel images are in the /boot directory. Bootable Linux kernel images are named as

vmlinuz-generic-VERSION_NUMBER
initrd as the initial ramdisk image for the Linux kernel.

A bootable Linux kernel image is composed of three pieces:

| BOOT | SETUP | linux kernel |

BOOT is a 512-byte booter for booting early versions of Linux from floppy disk images. It is no longer used for Linux booting but it contains some parameters for SETUP to use. SETUP is a piece of 16-bit and 32-bit assembly code, which provides transition from the 16-bit mode to 32-bit protected mode during booting. Linux kernel is the actual kernel image of Linux. It is in compressed form but it has a piece of decompressing code at beginning, which decompresses the Linux kernel image and relocates it to high memory.

1.13.2   Linux Booters

The Linux kernel can be booted up by several different boot-loaders. The most popular Linux boot-loaders are GRUB and LILO. Alternatively, the HD booter of (Wang 2015) can also be used to boot up Linux.

1.13.3   Linux Booting

During booting, the Linux boot-loader first locates the Linux kernel image (file). Then it loads

BOOT+SETUP to 0×90000 in real mode memory
Linux kernel to 1MB in high memory.

For generic Linux kernel images, it also loads an initial ramdisk image, initrd, to high memory. Then it transfers control to run SETUP code at 0×902000, which starts up the Linux kernel. When the Linux kernel first starts up, it runs on initrd as a temporary root file system. The Linux kernel executes a sh script, which directs the kernel to load the needed modules for the real root device. When the real root device is activated and ready, the kernel abandons the initial ramdisk and mounts the real root device as the root file system, thus completing a two-phase booting of the Linux kernel.

1.13.4   Linux Run-levels

The Linux kernel starts up in the single user mode. It mimics the run-levels of System V Unix to run in multi-user mode. Then it creates and run the INIT process P1, which creates the various daemon processes and also terminal processes for users to login. Then the INIT process waits for any child process to terminate.

1.13.5   Login Process

Each login process opens three file streams, stdin for input, stdout for output and stderr for error output, on its terminal. Then it waits for users to login. On Linux systems using X-windows as user interface, the X-window server usually acts as an interface for users to login. After a user login, the (pseudo) terminals belong to the user by default.

1.13.6   Command Executions

After login, the user process typically executes the command interpreter sh, which prompts the user for commands to execute. Some special commands, such as cd (change directory), exit, logout, &, are performed by sh directly. Non-special commands are usually executable files. For a non-special command, sh forks a child process and waits for the child to terminate. The child process changes its execution image to the file and executes the new image. When the child process terminates, it wakes up the parent sh, which prompts for another command, etc. In addition to simple commands, sh also supports I/O redirections and compound commands connected by pipes. In addition to built-in commands, the user may develop programs, compile-link them into binary executable files and run the programs as commands.

1.14   Use Ubuntu Linux

1.14.1   Ubuntu Versions

Among the different versions of Linux, we recommend **Ubuntu Linux** 15.10 or later for the following reasons.

(1) It is very easy to install. It can be installed online if the user has connection to the Internet.
(2) It is very easy to install additional software packages by
        sudo apt-get install PACKAGE
(3) It is updated and improved regularly with new releases.
(4) It has a large user base, with many problems and solutions posted in discussion forums online.
(5) It provides easy connections to wireless networks and access to the Internet.

1.14.2   Special Features of Ubuntu Linux

Here are some helps on how to use the Ubuntu Linux.

(1) When installing Ubuntu on a desktop or laptop computer, it will ask for a user name and a password to create a user account with a default home directory /home/username. When Ubuntu boots up, it immediately runs in the environment of the user because it already has the default user logged in automatically. Enter **Control-Alter-T** to open a pseudo-terminal. Right click the **Term** icon and choose "**lock to launcher**" to lock the Term icon in the menu bar. Subsequently, launch new terminals by choosing the **terminal->new terminal** on the menu bar. Each new terminal runs a sh for the user to execute commands.

(2) For security reasons, the user is an **ordinary user**, not the root or **superuser**. In order to run any privileged commands, the user must enter

```
sudo command
```

which will verify the user's password first.

(3) The user's **PATH** environment variable setting usually does not include the user's current directory. In order to run programs in the current directory, the user must enter **./a.out** every time. For convenience, the users should change the PATH setting to include the current directory. In the user's home directory, create a **.bashrc** file containing

```
PATH=$PATH:./
```

Every time the user opens a pseudo-terminal, sh will execute the .bashrc file first to set PATH to include the current working directory ./

(4) Many users may have installed 64-bit Ubuntu Linux. Some of the programming exercises and assignments in this book are intended for 32-bit machines. In 64-bit Linux, use

```
gcc -m32 t.c # compile t.c into 32-bit code
```

to generate 32-bit code. If the 64-bit Linux does not take the **-m32** option, the user must install additional support for gcc to generate 32-bit code.

(5) Ubuntu provides an excellent GUI user interface. Many users are so accustomed to the GUI that they tend to rely on it too much, often wasting time by repeatedly dragging and clicking the pointing device. In systems programming, the user should also learn how to use command lines and sh scripts, which are much more general and powerful than GUI.

(6) Nowadays, most users can connect to computer networks. Ubuntu supports both wired and wireless connections to networks. When Ubuntu runs on a PC/laptop with wireless hardware, it displays a wireless icon on top and it allows wireless connections by a simple user interface. Open the wireless icon. It will show a list of available wireless networks near by. Select a network and open the **Edit Connections** submenu to edit the connection file by entering the required login name and password. Close the Edit submenu. Ubuntu will try to login to the selected wireless network automatically.

```
                    |--> bin   (common commands)
                    |--> boot  (kernel images)
                    |--> dev   (special files)
                    |--> etc   (system maintenance file)
                    |--> home  (user home directories)
        / ---> |--> lib   (link libraries)
                    |--> proc  (system information pseudo file system)
                    |--> sbin  (superuser commands)
                    |                    |--> bin       (commands)
                    |--> tmp         |--> include   (header files)
                    |                    |--> lib       (libraries)
                    |--> usr ----->|--> local
                    |                    |--> man       (man pages)
                                        |--> X11       (X-Windows)
```

Fig. 1.6 Unix/Linux File System Tree

1.15   Unix/Linux File System Organization

The Unix/Linux file system is organized as a tree, which is shown (sideway) in Fig. 1.6.

Unix/Linux considers everything that can store or provide information as a file. In a general sense, each node of the file system tree is a FILE. In Unix/Linux, files have the following types.

1.15.1   File Types

(1). Directory files: A directory may contain other directories and (non-directory) files.

(2). Non-directory files: Non-directory files are either REGULAR or SPECIAL files, which can only be leaf-nodes in the file system tree. Non-directory files can be classified further as

(2).1 REGULAR files: Regular files are also called ORDINARY files. They contain either ordinary text or executable binary code.

(2).2 SPECIAL files: Special files are entries in the /dev directory. They represent I/O devices, which are further classified as

CHAR special files: I/O by chars, e.g. /dev/tty0, /dev/pts/1, etc.
BLOCK special files: I/O by blocks, e.g. /dev/had, /dev/sda, etc.
Other types such as network (socket) special files, named pipes, etc.

(3). Symbolic LINK files: These are Regular files whose contents are pathnames of other files. As such, they act as pointers to other files. As an example, the Linux command

```
ln -s aVeryLongFileName myLink
```

creates a symbolic link file, mylink, which points to aVeryLongFileName. Access to myLink will be redirected to the actual file aVeryLongFileName.

1.15.2   File Pathnames

The root node of a Unix/Linux file system tree, symbolized by /, is called the **root directory** or simply the root. Each node of the file system tree is specified by a **pathname** of the form

```
/a/b/c/d     OR     a/b/c/d
```

A pathname is **ABSOLUTE** if it begins with a /. Otherwise, it is **RELATIVE** to the **Current Working Directory (CWD)** of the process. When a user login to Unix/Linux, the CWD is set to the user's HOME directory. The CWD can be changed by the cd (change directory) command. The pwd command prints the absolute pathname of the CWD.

1.15.3   Unix/Linux Commands

When using an operating system, the user must learn how to use the system commands. The following lists the most often used commands in Unix/Linux.

ls: ls dirname: list the contents of CWD or a directory
cd dirname: change directory
pwd: print absolute pathname of CWD
touch filename: change filename timestamp (create file if it does not exist)
cat filename: display file contents
cp src dest: copy files
mv src dest: move or rename files
mkdir dirname: create directory
rmdir dirname: remove (empty) directory
rm filename: remove or delete file
ln oldfile newfile: create links between files
find: search for files
grep: search file for lines containing a pattern
ssh: login to remote hosts
gzip filename: compress filename to .gz file
gunzip file.gz: uncompress .gz file
tar –zcvf file.tgz . : create compressed tar file from current directory
tar -zxvf file.tgz . : extract files from .tgz file
man: display online manual pages
zip file.zip filenames : compress files to .zip file
unzip file.zip : uncompress .zip file

1.15.4   Linux Man Pages

Linux maintains online man (manual) pages in the standard /usr/man/directory. In Ubuntu Linux, it is in /usr/share/man directory. The man pages are organized into several different categories, denoted by man1, man2, etc.

```
/usr/man/
        |-- man1: commonly used commands: ls, cat, mkdir ...., etc.
        |-- man2: system calls
        |-- man3: library functions: strtok, strcat, basename, dirname
        etc.
```

All the man pages are compressed .gz files. They contain text describing how to use the command with input parameters and options. **man** is a program, which reads man page files and displays their contents in a user friendly format. Here are some examples of using man pages.

man ls   : show man page of ls in man1
man 2 open   : show man page of open in man2
man strtok   : show man page of strtok in man 3, etc.
man 3 dirname : show dirname in man3, NOT that of man1

Whenever needed, the reader should consult the man pages for how to use a specific Linux command. Many of the so called Unix/Linux systems programming books are essentially condensed versions of the Unix/Linux man pages.

1.16   Ubuntu Linux System Administration

1.16.1   User Accounts

As in all Linux, user accounts are maintained in the **/etc/passwd** file, which is owned by the superuser but readable by anyone. Each user has a line in the /etc/passwd file of the form

loginName:x:gid:uid:usefInfo:homeDir:initialProgram

where the second field x indicates checking user password. Encrypted user passwords are maintained in the **/etc/shadow** file. Each line of the **shadow** file contains the encrypted user password, followed by optional aging limit information, such as expiration date and time, etc. When a user tries to login with a login name and password, Linux will check both the /etc/passwd and /etc/shadow files to authenticate the user. After a user login successfully, the login process becomes the user process by acquiring the user's gid and uid, changes directory to the user's homeDir and executes the listed initialProgram, which is usually the command interpreter sh.

1.16.2   Add New User

This may be a pathological case for most users who run Ubuntu Linux on their personal PCs or laptops. But let's assume that the reader may want to add a family member to use the same computer but as a different user. As in all Linux, Ubuntu supports an **adduser** command, which can be run as

sudo adduer username

It adds a new user by creating an account and also a default home directory /home/username for the new user. Henceforth, Ubuntu will display a list of user names in its "About The Computer" menu. The new user may login to the system by selecting the new username.

1.16.3 The sudo Command

For security reasons, the **root** or **superuser** account is disabled in Ubuntu, which prevents anyone from login as the root user (well, not quite; there is a way but I won't disclose it). **sudo** ("superuser do") allows a user to execute a command as another user, usually the superuser. It temporarily elevates the user process to the superuser privilege while executing a command. When the command execution finishes, the user process reverts back to its original privilege level. In order to be able to use sudo, the user's name must be in the **/etc/sudoers** file. To allow a user to issue sudo, simply add a line to sudoers files, as in

```
username ALL(ALL)    ALL
```

However, the /etc/sudoers file has a very rigid format. Any syntax error in the file could breech the system security. Linux recommends editing the file only by the special command **visudo**, which invokes the vi editor but with checking and validation.

1.17 Summary

This chapter presents an introduction to the book. It describes the book's scope, intended audience and its suitability as textbook in Computer Science/Engineering curriculums. It presents a brief history of Unix, which includes early versions of Unix at Bell Labs, AT&T System V and other developments of Unix, such as BSD, HP UX, IBM AIX and Sun/Solaris Unix. It describes the development of Linux and various Linux distributions, which include Debian, Ubuntu, Mint, Red Hat and Slackware. It lists both the hardware platforms and virtual machines for Linux. It shows how to install Ubuntu Linux to both VirtualBox and Vmware virtual machines inside the Microsoft Windows. It explains the startup sequence of Linux, from booting the Linux kernel to user login and command execution. It describes the Linux file system organization, file types and commonly used Unix/Linux commands. Lastly, it describes some system administration tasks for users to manage and maintain their Linux systems.

References

Bach M., "The Design of the UNIX Operating System", Prentice-Hall, 1986
Curry, David A., Unix Systems Programming for SRV4, O'Reilly, 1996.
Haviland, Keith, Gray, Dian, Salama, Ben, Unix System Programming, Second Edition, Addison-Wesley, 1998.
HP-UX, http://www.operating-system.org/betriebssystem/_english/bs-hpux.htm, 2017
IBM AIX, https://www.ibm.com/power/operating-systems/aix, 2017
Kernighan, B.W., Ritchie D.M, "The C Programming Language" 2nd Edition, 1988
Kerrisk, Michael, The Linux Programming Interface: A Linux and UNIX System Programming Handbook, 1st Edition, No Starch Press Inc, 2010.
Leffler, S.J., McKusick, M. K, Karels, M. J. Quarterman, J., "The Design and Implementation of the 4.3BSD UNIX Operating System", Addison Wesley, 1989
Leffler, S.J., McKusick, M. K, Karels, M. J. Quarterman, J., "The Design and Implementation of the 4.4BSD UNIX Operating System", Addison Wesley, 1996

Linux, https://en.wikipedia.org/wiki/Linux , 2017

Love, Robert, Linux System Programming: Talking Directly to the Kernel and C Library, 2nd Edition, O'Reilly, 2013.

McKusick, M. K, Karels, Neville-Neil, G.V., "The Design and Implementation of the FreeBSD Operating System", Addison Wesley, 2004

Robbins Kay, Robbins, Steve, UNIX Systems Programming: Communication, Concurrency and Threads: Communication, Concurrency and Threads, 2nd Edition, Prentice Hall, 2003.

Pthreads: https://computing.llnl.gov/tutorials/pthreads, 2017

Rochkind, Marc J., Advanced UNIX Programming, 2nd Edition, Addison-Wesley, 2008.

Stallman, R., Linux and the GNU System, 2017

Stevens, W. Richard, Rago, Stephan A., Advanced Programming in the UNIX Environment, 3rd Edition, Addison-Wesley, 2013.

Solaris, http://www.operating-system.org/betriebssystem/_english/bs-solaris.htm, 2017

Sun OS, https://en.wikipedia.org/wiki/SunOS, 2017

Thompson, K., Ritchie, D. M., "The UNIX Time-Sharing System", CACM., Vol. 17, No.7, pp. 365-375, 1974.

Thompson, K., Ritchie, D.M.; "The UNIX Time-Sharing System", Bell System Tech. J. Vol. 57, No.6, pp. 1905–1929, 1978

Unix System V, https://en.wikipedia.org/wiki/UNIX_System V, 2017

VirtualBox, https://www.virtualbox.org, 2017

Wang, K. C., Design and Implementation of the MTX Operating System, Springer International Publishing AG, 2015

Programming Background

2

Abstract

This chapter covers the background information needed for systems programming. It introduces several GUI based text editors, such as vim, gedit and EMACS, to allow readers to edit files. It shows how to use the EMACS editor in both command and GUI mode to edit, compile and execute C programs. It explains program development steps. These include the compile-link steps of GCC, static and dynamic linking, format and contents of binary executable files, program execution and termination. It explains function call conventions and run-time stack usage in detail. These include parameter passing, local variables and stack frames. It also shows how to link C programs with assembly code. It covers the GNU make facility and shows how to write Makefiles by examples. It shows how to use the GDB debugger to debug C programs. It points out the common errors in C programs and suggests ways to prevent such errors during program development. Then it covers advanced programming techniques. It describes structures and pointer in C. It covers link lists and list processing by detailed examples. It covers binary trees and tree traversal algorithms. The chapter cumulates with a programming project, which is for the reader to implement a binary tree to simulate operations in the Unix/Linux file system tree. The project starts with a single root directory node. It supports mkdir, rmdir, creat, rm, cd, pwd, ls operations, saving the file system tree as a file and restoring the file system tree from saved file. The project allows the reader to apply and practice the programming techniques of tokenizing strings, parsing user commands and using function pointers to invoke functions for command processing.

2.1   Text Editors in Linux

2.1.1   Vim

Vim (Linux Vi and Vim Editor 2017) is the standard built-in editor of Linux. It is an improved version of the original default Vi editor of Unix. Unlike most other editors, vim has 3 different operating modes, which are

. **Command mode:** for entering commands
. **Insert mode:** for entering and editing text
. **Last-line mode:** for saving files and exit

© Springer International Publishing AG, part of Springer Nature 2018

K. C. Wang, *Systems Programming in Unix/Linux*, https://doi.org/10.1007/978-3-319-92429-8_2

When vim starts, it is in the default **Command mode**, in which most keys denote special commands. Examples of command keys for moving the cursor are

h: move cursor one char to the left;	**l: move cursor one char to the right**
j: move cursor down one line;	**k: move cursor up one line**

When using vim inside X-window, cursor movements can also be done by arrow keys. To enter text for editing, the user must switch vim into **Insert mode** by entering either the **i** (insert) or **a** (append) command:

i: switch to Insert mode to insert text;
a: switch to Insert mode to append text

To exit Insert mode, press the **ESC key** one or more times. While in Command mode, enter the **:** key to enter the **Last-line mode**, which is for saving texts as files or exit vim:

:w write (save) file
:q exit vim
:wq save and exit
:q! force exit without saving changes

Although many Unix users are used to the different operating modes of vim, others may find it somewhat unnatural and inconvenient to use as compared with other Graphic User Interface **(GUI)** based editors. The following editors belong to what is commonly known as What You See Is What You Get **(WYSIWYG)** type of editors. In a WYSIWYG editor, a user may enter text, move the cursor by arrow keys, just like in regular typing. Commands are usually formed by entering a special **meta key**, together with, or followed by, a letter key sequence. For example,

Control-C: abort or exit,
Control-K: delete line into a buffer,
Control-Y: yank or paste from buffer contents
Control-S: save edited text, etc.

Since there is no mode switching necessary, most users, especially beginners, prefer WYSUWYG type editors over vim.

2.1.2   Gedit

Gedit is the default text editor of the **GNOME** desktop environment. It is the default editor of Ubuntu, as well as other Linux that uses the GNOME GUI user interface. It includes tools for editing both source code and structured text such as markup languages.

2.1.3   Emacs

Emacs (GNU Emacs 2015) is a powerful text editor, which runs on many different platforms. The most popular version of Emacs is **GNU Emacs**, which is available in most Linux distributions.

All the above editors support direct inputs and editing of text in full screen mode. They also support search by keywords and replace strings by new text. To use these editors, the user only needs to learn a few basics, such as how to start up the editor, input text for editing, save edited texts as files and then exit the editor.

Depending on the Unix/Linux distribution, some of the editors may not be installed by default. For example, **Ubuntu** Linux usually comes with **gedit, nano** and **vim**, but not **emacs**. One nice feature of Ubuntu is that, when a user tries to run a command that is not installed, it will remind the user to install it. As an example, if a user enters

```
emacs filename
```

Ubuntu will display a message saying "The program emacs is currently not installed. You can install it by typing apt-get install emacs". Similarly, the user may install other missing software packages by the **apt-get** command.

2.2   Use Text Editors

All text editors are designed to perform the same task, which is to allow users to input texts, edit them and save the edited texts as files. As noted above, there are many different text editors. Which text editor to use is a matter of personal preference. Most Linux users seem to prefer either **gedit** or **emacs** due to their GUI interface and ease to use. Between the two, we strongly recommend emacs. The following shows some simple examples of using emacs to create text files.

2.2.1   Use Emacs

First, from a pseudo terminal of X-windows, enter the command line

```
emacs [FILENAME]                    # [ ] means optonal
```

to invoke the emacs editor with an optional file name, e.g. t.c. This will start up emacs in a separate window as show in Fig. 2.1. On top of the emacs window is a menu bar, each of which can be opened to show additional commands, which the user can invoke by clicking on the menu icons. To begin with, we shall not use the menu bar and focus on the simple task of creating a C program source file. When emacs starts, if the file t.c already exists, it will open the file and load its contents into a buffer for editing. Otherwise, it will show an empty buffer, ready for user inputs. Fig. 2.1 shows the user input lines. Emacs recognizes any .c file as source file for C programs. It will indent the lines in accordance with the C code line conventions, e.g. it will match each left { with a right }with proper indentations automatically. In fact, it can even detect incomplete C statements and show improper indentations to alert the user of possible syntax errors in the C source lines.

After creating a source file, enter the meta key sequence **Control-x-c** to save the file and exit. If the buffer contains modified and unsaved text, it will prompt the user to save file, as shown on the bottom line of Fig. 2.2. Entering y will save the file and exit emacs. Alternatively, the user may also click the **Save icon** on the menu bar to save and exit.

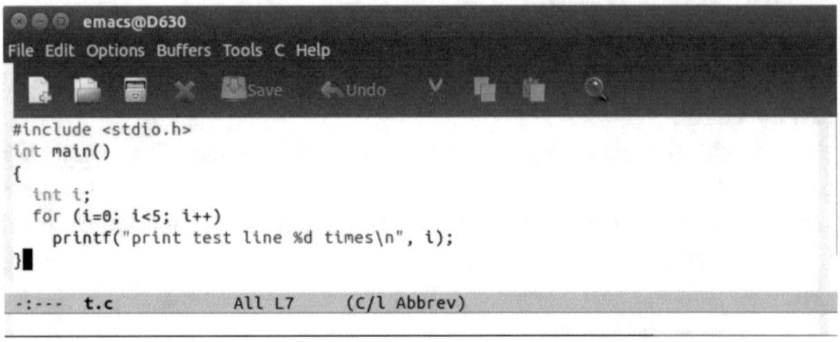

Fig. 2.1 Use emacs 1

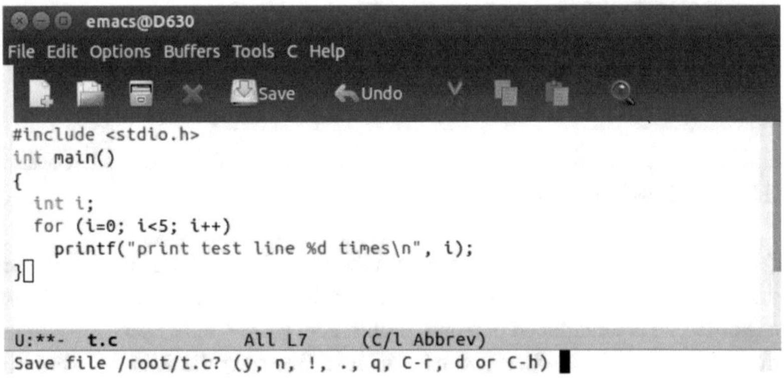

Fig. 2.2 Use emacs 2

2.2.2   Emacs Menus

At the top of the emacs window is a menu bar, which includes the icons

File   Edit Options Buffers Tools   C   Help

The **File** menu supports the operations of open file, insert file and save files. It also supports printing
   the editing buffer, open new windows and new frames.
The **Edit** menu supports search and replace operations.
The **Options** menu supports functions to configure emacs operations.
The **Buffers** menu supports selection and display of buffers.
The **Tools** menu supports compilation of source code, execution of binary executables and debugging.
The **C** menu supports customized editing for C source code.
The **Help** menu provides support for emacs usage, such as a simple emacs tutorial.

As usual, clicking on a menu item will display a table of submenus, allowing the user to choose
individual operations. Instead of commands, the user may also use the emacs menu bar to do text
editing, such as undo last operation, cut and past, save file and exit, etc.

2.2.3   IDE of Emacs

Emacs is more than a text editor. It provides an Integrated Development Environment (**IDE**) for
software development, which include compile C programs, run executable images and debugging

program executions by **GDB**. We shall illustrate the IDE capability of emacs in the next section on program development.

2.3 Program Development

2.3.1 Program Development Steps

The steps of developing an executable program are as follows.

(1). Create source files: Use a text editor, such as gedit or emacs, to create one or more source files of a program. In systems programming, the most important programming languages are C and assembly. We begin with C programs first.

Standard comment lines in C comprises matched pairs of /* and */. In addition to the standard comments, we shall also use // to denote comment lines in C code for convenience. Assume that t1.c and t2.c are the source files of a C program.

```
/********************** t1.c file ***************************/
int g = 100;                // initialized global variable
int h;                      // uninitialized global variable
static int s;               // static global variable

main(int argc, char *argv[ ]) // main function
{
  int a = 1; int b;         // automatic local variables
  static int c = 3;         // static local variable
  b = 2;
  c = mysum(a,b);           // call mysum(), passing a, b
  printf("sum=%d\n", c);    // call printf()
}
/********************** t2.c file ***************************/
extern int g;               // extern global variable
int mysum(int x, int y)     // function heading
{
   return x + y + g;
}
```

2.3.2 Variables in C

Variables in C programs can be classified as **global, local, static, automatic** and **registers**, etc. as shown in Fig. 2.3.

Global variables are defined outside of any function. **Local variables** are defined inside functions. Global variables are unique and have only one copy. **Static globals** are visible only to the file in which they are defined. **Non-static globals** are visible to all the files of the same program. Global variables can be initialized or uninitialized. Initialized globals are assigned values at compile time. Uninitialized globals are cleared to 0 when the program execution starts. Local variables are visible only to the function in which they are defined. By default, local variables are **automatic**; they come into existence

```
                                  |- non-static-|
                      |- global-|             |- initialized or uninitialized
                      |         |- static ----|
         Variables -  |
                      |- local -|- register---|- in CPU register (if possible)
                                 |- automatic -|- allocated on stack
                                 |- static ----|- initialized or uninitialized
```

Fig. 2.3 Variables in C

Fig. 2.4 Program
development steps

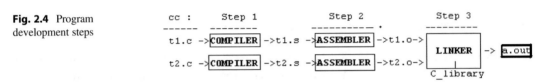

when the function is entered and they logically disappear when the function exits. For **register variables**, the compiler tries to allocate them in CPU registers. Since automatic local variables do not have any allocated memory space until the function is entered, they cannot be initialized at compile time. **Static local variables** are permanent and unique, which can be initialized. In addition, C also supports **volatile variables**, which are used as memory-mapped I/O locations or global variables that are accessed by interrupt handlers or multiple execution threads. The volatile keyword prevents the C compiler from optimizing the code that operates on such variables.

In the above t1.c file, g is an initialized global, h is an uninitialized global and s is a static global. Both g and h are visible to the entire program but s is visible only in the t1.c file. So t2.c can reference g by declaring it as extern, but it cannot reference s because s is visible only in t1.c. In the main() function, the local variables a, b are automatic and c is static. Although the local variable a is defined as int a = 1, this is not an initialization because a does not yet exist at compile time. The generated code will assign the value 1 to the current copy of a when main() is actually entered.

2.3.3   Compile-Link in GCC

(2). Use gcc to convert the source files into a binary executable, as in

```
        gcc  t1.c  t2.c
```

which generates a binary executable file named a.out. In Linux, cc is linked to gcc, so they are the same.

(3). What's gcc? **gcc** is a program, which consists of three major steps, as shown in Fig. 2.4.

Step 1. Convert C source files to assembly code files: The first step of cc is to invoke the C COMPILER, which translates .c files into .s files containing **assembly code** of the target machine. The C compiler itself has several phases, such as preprocessing, lexical analysis, parsing and code generations, etc, but the reader may ignore such details here.

Step 2. Convert assembly Code to **OBJECT code**: Every computer has its own set of machine instructions. Users may write programs in an assembly language for a specific machine. An ASSEMBLER is a program, which translates assembly code into machine code in binary form. The resulting .o files are called OBJECT code. The second step of cc is to invoke the ASSEMBLER to translate .s files to .o files. Each .o file consists of

. a header containing sizes of CODE, DATA and BSS sections
. a CODE section containing machine instructions
. a DATA section containing initialized global and initialized static local variables
. a BSS section containing uninitialized global and uninitialized static local variables
. relocation information for pointers in CODE and offsets in DATA and BSS
. a Symbol Table containing non-static globals, function names and their attributes.

Step 3: LINKING: A program may consist of several .o files, which are dependent on one another. In addition, the .o files may call C library functions, e.g. printf(), which are not present in the source files. The last step of cc is to invoke the LINKER, which combines all the .o files and the needed library functions into a single binary executable file. More specifically, the LINKER does the following:

. Combine all the CODE sections of the .o files into a single Code section. For C programs, the combined Code section begins with the default C startup code **crt0.o**, which calls main(). This is why every C program must have a unique main() function.

. Combine all the DATA sections into a single Data section. The combined Data section contains only initialized globals and initialized static locals.

. Combine all the BSS sections into a single bss section.

. Use the relocation information in the .o files to adjust pointers in the combined Code section and offsets in the combined Data and bss sections.

. Use the Symbol Tables to resolve cross references among the individual .o files. For instance, when the compiler sees c = mysum(a, b) in t1.c, it does not know where mysum is. So it leaves a blank (0) in t1.o as the entry address of mysum but records in the symbol table that the blank must be replaced with the entry address of mysum. When the linker puts t1.o and t2.o together, it knows where mysum is in the combined Code section. It simply replaces the blank in t1.o with the entry address of mysum. Similarly for other cross referenced symbols. Since static globals are not in the symbol table, they are unavailable to the linker. Any attempt to reference static globals from different files will generate a cross reference error. Similarly, if the .o files refer to any undefined symbols or function names, the linker will also generate cross reference errors. If all the cross references can be resolved successfully, the linker writes the resulting combined file as a.out, which is the binary executable file.

2.3.4   Static vs. Dynamic Linking

There are two ways to create a binary executable, known as **static linking** and **dynamic linking.** In static linking, which uses a **static library**, the linker includes all the needed library function code and data into a.out. This makes a.out complete and self-contained but usually very large. In dynamic linking, which uses a **shared library**, the library functions are not included in a.out but calls to such functions are recorded in a.out as directives. When execute a dynamically linked a.out file, the operating system loads both a.out and the shared library into memory and makes the loaded library code accessible to a.out during execution. The main advantages of dynamic linking are:

. The size of every a.out is reduced.
. Many executing programs may share the same library functions in memory.
. Modifying library functions does not need to re-compile the source files again.

Libraries used for dynamic linking are known as **Dynamic Linking Libraries (DLLs)**. They are called **Shared Libraries** (.so files) in Linux. Dynamically loaded (DL) libraries are shared libraries which are loaded only when they are needed. DL libraries are useful as plug-ins and dynamically loaded modules.

2.3.5   Executable File Format

Although the default binary executable is named a.out, the actual file format may vary. Most C compilers and linkers can generate executable files in several different formats, which include

(1) **Flat binary executable**: A flat binary executable file consists only of executable code and initialized data. It is intended to be loaded into memory in its entirety for execution directly. For example, bootable operating system images are usually flat binary executables, which simplifies the boot-loader.
(2) **a.out executable file**: A traditional a.out file consists of a header, followed by code, data and bss sections. Details of the a.out file format will be shown in the next section.
(3) **ELF executable file**: An Executable and Linking Format **(ELF)** (Youngdale 1995) file consists of one or more program sections. Each program section can be loaded to a specific memory address. In Linux, the default binary executables are ELF files, which are better suited to dynamic linking.

2.3.6   Contents of a.out File

For the sake of simplicity, we consider the traditional a.out files first. ELF executables will be covered in later chapters. An a.out file consists of the following sections:

(1) header: the header contains loading information and sizes of the a.out file, where
    tsize = size of Code section;
    dsize = size of Data section containing initialized globals and static locals;
    bsize = size of bss section containing uninitialized globals and static locals;
    total_size = total size of a.out to load.
(2) **Code Section**: also called the **Text section**, which contains executable code of the program. It begins with the standard C startup code **crt0.o**, which calls main().
(3) **Data Section**: The Data section contains initialized global and static data.
(4) **Symbol table**: optional, needed only for run-time debugging.

Note that the **bss section**, which contains uninitialized global and static local variables, is not in the a. out file. Only its size is recorded in the a.out file header. Also, automatic local variables are not in a.out. Figure 2.5 shows the layout of an a.out file.

In Fig. 2.5, _brk is a symbolic mark indicating the end of the bss section. The total loading size of a. out is usually equal to _brk, i.e. equal to tsize+dsize+bsize. If desired, _brk can be set to a higher value for a larger loading size. The extra memory space above the bss section is the **HEAP** area for dynamic memory allocation during execution.

Fig. 2.5 Contents of a.out file

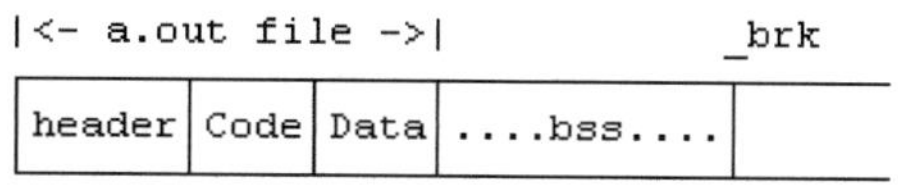

```
      |<- a.out file ->|              _brk

       header Code Data ....bss....
```

2.3.7   Program Execution

Under a Unix-like operating system, the **sh** command line

```
        a.out one two three
```

executes a.out with the token strings as **command-line parameters**. To execute the command, sh forks a child process and waits for the child to terminate. When the child process runs, it uses a.out to create a new execution image by the following steps.

(1) Read the header of a.out to determine the total memory size needed, which includes the size of a stack space:

```
        TotalSize = _brk + stackSize
```

where stackSize is usually a default value chosen by the OS kernel for the program to start. There is no way of knowing how much stack space a program will ever need. For example, the trivial C program

```
        main(){ main(); }
```

will generate a segmentation fault due to **stack overflow** on any computer. So the usual approach of an OS kernel is to use a default initial stack size for the program to start and tries to deal with possible stack overflow later during run-time.

(2) It allocates a memory area of TotalSize for the execution image. Conceptually, we may assume that the allocated memory area is a single piece of contiguous memory. It loads the Code and Data sections of a.out into the memory area, with the stack area at the high address end. It clears the bss section to 0, so that all uninitialized globals and static locals begin with the initial value 0. During execution, the stack grows downward toward low address.

(3) Then it abandons the old image and begins to execute the new image, which is shown in Fig. 2.6.

In Fig. 2.6, _brk at the end of the bss section is the program's initial "break" mark and _splimit is the stack size limit. The Heap area between bss and Stack is used by the C library functions malloc()/free() for dynamic memory allocation in the execution image. When a.out is first loaded, _brk and _splimit may coincide, so that the initial Heap size is zero. During execution, the process may use the brk (address) or sbrk(size) system call to change _brk to a higher address, thereby increasing the Heap size. Alternatively, malloc() may call brk() or sbrk() implicitly to expand the Heap size. During execution, a stack overflow occurs if the program tries to extend the stack pointer below _splimit. On machines with memory protection, this will be detected by the memory management hardware as an error, which traps the process to the OS kernel. Subject to a maximal size limit, the OS kernel may grow the stack by allocating additional memory in the process address space, allowing the execution to continue. A stack

Fig. 2.6 Execution image

```
                              |              | O's | _brk  | _splimit
Low Address  | Code | Data | bss | Heap | Stack | High Address
```

overflow is fatal if the stack cannot be grown any further. On machines without suitable hardware support, detecting and handling stack overflow must be implement in software.

(4). Execution begins from crt0.o, which calls main(), passing as parameters argc and argv to main(), which can be written as

int main(int argc, char *argv[ ]) { .... }

where argc = number of command line parameters and each argv[ ] entry points to a corresponding command line parameter string.

2.3.8   Program Termination

A process executing a.out may terminate in two possible ways.

(1). Normal Termination: If the program executes successfully, main() eventually returns to crt0.o, which calls the library function exit(0) to terminate the process. The exit(value) function does some clean-up work first, such as flush stdout, close I/O streams, etc. Then it issues an _exit(value) **system call,** which causes the process to enter the OS kernel to terminate. A 0 exit value usually means normal termination. If desired, a process may call exit(value) directly without going back to crt0.o. Even more drastically, a process may issue an _exit(value) system call to terminate immediately without doing the clean-up work first. When a process terminates in kernel, it records the value in the _exit(value) system call as the exit status in the process structure, notifies its parent and becomes a ZOMBIE. The parent process can find the ZOMBIE child, get its pid and exit status by the system call

pid = wait(int *status);

which also releases the ZMOBIE child process structure as FREE, allowing it to be reused for another process.

(2). Abnormal Termination: While executing a.out the process may encounter an error condition, such as invalid address, illegal instruction, privilege violation, etc. which is recognized by the CPU as an **exception**. When a process encounters an exception, it is forced into the OS kernel by a trap. The kernel's trap handler converts the trap error type to a magic number, called a **SIGNAL**, and delivers the signal to the process, causing it to terminate. In this case, the exit status of the ZOMBIE process is the signal number, and we may say that the process has terminated abnormally. In addition to trap errors, signals may also originate from hardware or from other processes. For example, pressing the Control_C key generates a hardware interrupt, which sends the number 2 signal SIGINT to all processes on that terminal, causing them to terminate. Alternatively, a user may use the command

kill -s signal_number pid   # signal_number = 1 to 31

to send a signal to a target process identified by pid. For most signal numbers, the default action of a process is to terminate. Signals and signal handling will be covered later in Chap. 6.

2.4   Function Call in C

Next, we consider the run-time behavior of a.out during execution. The run-time behavior of a program stems mainly from function calls. The following discussions apply to running C programs on 32-bit Intel x86 processors. On these machines, the C compiler generated code passes parameters on the stack in function calls. During execution, it uses a special CPU register (ebp) to point at the stack frame of the current executing function.

2.4.1   Run-Time Stack Usage in 32-Bit GCC

Consider the following C program, which consists of a main() function shown on the left-hand side, which calls a sub() function shown on the right-hand side.

```
------------------------------------------------------------
   main()                     |    int sub(int x, int y)
   {                          |    {
     int a, b, c;             |      int u, v;
     a = 1; b = 2; c = 3;     |      u = 4; v = 5;
     c = sub(a, b);           |      return x+y+u+v;
     printf("c=%d\n", c);     |    }
   }                          |
------------------------------------------------------------
```

(1) When executing a.out, a process image is created in memory, which looks (logically) like the diagram shown in Fig. 2.7, where Data includes both initialized data and bss.
(2) Every CPU has the following registers or equivalent, where the entries in parentheses denote registers of the x86 CPU:
PC (IP): point to next instruction to be executed by the CPU.
SP (SP): point to top of stack.
FP (BP): point to the stack frame of current active function.
Return Value Register (AX): register for function return value.
(3) In every C program, main() is called by the C startup code crt0.o. When crt0.o calls main(), it pushes the return address (the current PC register) onto stack and replaces PC with the entry address of main(), causing the CPU to enter main(). For convenience, we shall show the stack contents from left to right. When control enters main(), the stack contains the saved return PC on top, as shown in Fig. 2.8, in which XXX denotes the stack contents before crt0.o calls main(), and SP points to the saved return PC from where crt0.o calls main().
(4) Upon entry, the compiled code of every C function does the following:
. push FP onto stack # this saves the CPU's FP register on stack.
. let FP point at the saved FP # establish stack frame
. shift SP downward to allocate space for automatic local variables on stack
. the compiled code may shift SP farther down to allocate some temporary working space on the stack, denoted by temps.

```
Low Address   | Code | Data | Heap| Stack |  High Address
```

Fig. 2.7 Process execution image

```
High Address          ------------>          Low Address
        ---------------------------------------------------
        XXXX|PC|
        -------|-----------------------------------------
               SP
```

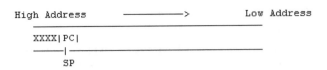

Fig. 2.8 Stack contents in function call

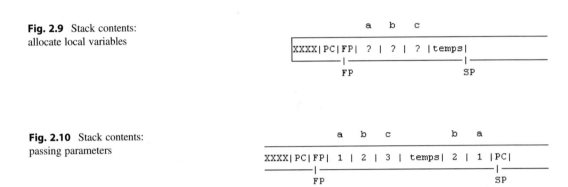

Fig. 2.9 Stack contents: allocate local variables

```
                a    b    c
------------------------------------------------
XXXX|PC|FP| ?  | ?  | ?  |temps|
----------|-------------------|------------------
          FP                  SP
```

Fig. 2.10 Stack contents: passing parameters

```
            a    b    c          b    a
--------------------------------------------------------
XXXX|PC|FP| 1  | 2  | 3  | temps| 2  | 1  |PC|
----------|----------------------------------|-----------
          FP                                 SP
```

For this example, there are 3 automatic local variables, int a, b, c, each of sizeof(int) = 4 bytes. After entering main(), the stack contents becomes as shown in Fig. 2.9, in which the spaces of a, b, c are allocated but their contents are yet undefined.

(5) Then the CPU starts to execute the code a=1; b=2; c=3; which put the values 1, 2, 3 into the memory locations of a, b, c, respectively. Assume that sizeof(int) is 4 bytes. The locations of a, b, c are at -4, -8, -12 bytes from where FP points at. These are expressed as -4(FP), -8(FP), -12(FP) in assembly code, where FP is the stack frame pointer. For example, in 32-bit Linux the assembly code for b=2 in C is

```
movl   $2, -8(%ebp)        # b=2 in C
```

where $2 means the value of 2 and %ebp is the ebp register.

(6) main() calls sub() by c = sub(a, b); The compiled code of the function call consists of
. Push parameters in reverse order, i.e. push values of b=2 and a=1 into stack.
. Call sub, which pushes the current PC onto stack and replaces PC with the entry address of sub, causing the CPU to enter sub().
When control first enters sub(), the stack contains a return address at the top, preceded by the parameters, a, b, of the caller, as shown in Fig. 2.10.

(7) Since sub() is written in C, it actions are exactly the same as that of main(), i.e. it
. Push FP and let FP point at the saved FP;
. Shift SP downward to allocate space for local variables u, v.
. The compiled code may shift SP farther down for some temp space on stack.
The stack contents becomes as shown in Fig. 2.11.

Fig. 2.11 Stack contents
of called function

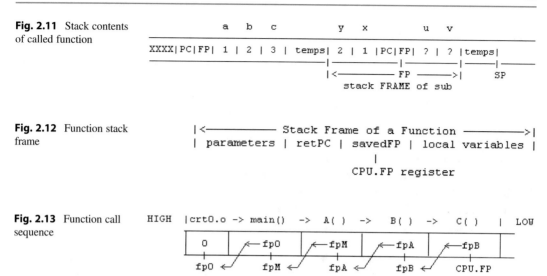

Fig. 2.12 Function stack
frame

Fig. 2.13 Function call
sequence

2.4.2   Stack Frames

While execution is inside a function, such as sub(), it can only access global variables, parameters passed in by the caller and local variables, but nothing else. Global and static local variables are in the combined Data section, which can be referenced by a fixed base register. Parameters and automatic locals have different copies on each invocation of the function. So the problem is: how to reference parameters and automatic locals? For this example, the parameters a, b, which correspond to the arguments x, y, are at 8(FP) and 12(FP). Similarly, the automatic local variables u, v are at -4(FP) and -8(FP). The stack area visible to a function, i.e. parameters and automatic locals, is called the **Stack Frame** of a function, like a frame of movie to a person. Thus, FP is called the **Stack Frame Pointer.** To a function, the stack frame looks like the following (Fig. 2.12).

From the above discussions, the reader should be able to deduce what would happen if we have a sequence of function calls, e.g.

```
crt0.o --> main() --> A(par_a) --> B(par_b) --> C(par_c)
```

For each function call, the stack would grow (toward low address) one more frame for the called function. The frame at the stack top is the stack frame of the current executing function, which is pointed by the CPU's frame pointer. The saved FP points (backward) to the frame of its caller, whose saved FP points back at the caller's caller, etc. Thus, the function call sequence is maintained in the stack as a link list, as shown in Fig. 2.13.

By convention, the CPU's FP = 0 when crt0.o is entered from the OS kernel. So the stack frame link list ends with a 0. When a function returns, its stack frame is deallocated and the stack shrinks back.

2.4.3   Return From Function Call

When sub() executes the C statement **return x+y+u+v**, it evaluates the expression and puts the resulting value in the return value register (AX). Then it deallocates the local variables by

Fig. 2.14 Stack contents
with reversed allocation
scheme

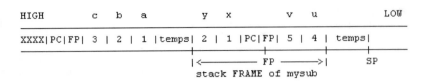

.copy FP into SP;   # SP now points to the saved FP in stack.

.pop stack into FP; # this restores FP, which now points to the caller's stack frame,

              # leaving the return PC on the stack top.

(On the x86 CPU, the above operations are equivalent to the **leave** instruction).

.Then, it executes the RET instruction, which pops the stack top into PC register, causing the CPU to execute from the saved return address of the caller.

(8) Upon return, the caller function catches the return value in the return register (AX). Then it cleans the parameters a, b, from the stack (by adding 8 to SP). This restores the stack to the original situation before the function call. Then it continues to execute the next instruction.

It is noted that some compilers, e.g. GCC Version 4, allocate automatic local variables in increasing address order. For instance, int a, b; implies (address of a) < (address of b). With this kind of allocation scheme, the stack contents may look like the following (Fig. 2.14).

In this case, automatic local variables are also allocated in "reverse order", which makes them consistent with the parameter order, but the concept and usage of stack frames remain the same.

2.4.4   Long Jump

In a sequence of function calls, such as

```
main() --> A() --> B()-->C();
```

when a called function finishes, it normally returns to the calling function, e.g. C() returns to B(), which returns to A(), etc. It is also possible to return directly to an earlier function in the calling sequence by a long jump. The following program demonstrates long jump in Unix/Linux.

```
/** longjump.c file: demonstrate long jump in Linux **/
#include <stdio.h>
#include <setjmp.h>
jmp_buf env;        // for saving longjmp environment

int main()
{
  int r, a=100;
  printf("call setjmp to save environment\n");
  if ((r=setjmp(env)) == 0){
    A();
    printf("normal return\n");
  }
```

```
      else
         printf("back to main() via long jump, r=%d a=%d\n", r, a);
  }

  int A()
  {   printf("enter A()\n");
      B();
      printf("exit A()\n");
  }

  int B()
  {
    printf("enter B()\n");
    printf("long jump? (y|n) ");
    if (getchar()=='y')
       longjmp(env, 1234);
    printf("exit B()\n");
  }
```

In the longjump program, **setjmp()** saves the current execution environment in a jmp_buf structure and returns 0. The program proceeds to call A(), which calls B(). While in the function B(), if the user chooses not to return by long jump, the functions will show the normal return sequence. If the user chooses to return by **longjmp(env, value)**, execution will return to the last saved environment with a nonzero value. In this case, it causes B() to return to main() directly, bypassing A(). The principle of long jump is very simple. When a function finishes, it returns by the (callerPC, callerFP) in the current stack frame, as shown in Fig. 2.15.

If we replace (callerPC, callerFP) with (savedPC, savedFP) of an earlier function in the calling sequence, execution would return to that function directly. In addition to the (savedPC, savedFP), **setjmp()** may also save CPU's general registers and the original SP, so that **longjmp()** can restore the complete environment of the returned function. Long jump can be used to abort a function in a calling sequence, causing execution to resume from a known environment saved earlier. Although rarely used in user mode programs, it is a common technique in systems programming. For example, it may be used in a signal catcher to bypass a user mode function that caused an exception or trap error. We shall demonstrate this technique later in Chap. 6 on signals and signal processing.

2.4.5   Run-Time Stack Usage in 64-Bit GCC

In 64-bit mode, the CPU registers are expanded to rax, rbx, rcx, rdx, rbp, rsp, rsi, rdi, r8 to r15, all 64-bit wide. The function call convention differs slightly from 32-bit mode. When calling a function, the first 6 parameters are passed in rdi, rsi, rdx, rcx, r8, r9, in that order. Any extra parameters are passed through the stack as they are in 32-bit mode. Upon entry, a called function first establishes the stack frame (using rbp) as usual. Then it may shift the stack pointer (rsp) downward for local variables and working spaces on the stack. The GCC compiler generated code may keep the stack pointer fixed,

Fig. 2.15 Function return
frame

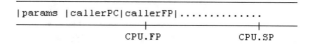

with a default reserved **Red Zone** stack area of 128 bytes, while execution is inside a function, making it possible to access stack contents by using rsp as the base register. However, the GCC compiler generated code still uses the stack frame pointer rbp to access both parameters and locals. We illustrate the function call convention in 64-bit mode by an example.

Example: Function Call Convention in 64-Bit Mode

(1) The following t.c file contains a main() function in C, which defines 9 local int (32-bit) variables, a to i. It calls a sub() function with 8 int parameters.

```
/*********   t.c file ********/
#include <stdio.h>
int sub(int a, int b, int c, int d, int e, int f, int g, int h)
{
  int u, v, w;
  u = 9;
  v = 10;
  w = 11;
  return a+g+u+v; // use first and extra parameter, locals
}


int main()
{
  int a, b, c, d, e, f, g, h, i;
  a = 1;
  b = 2;
  c = 3;
  d = 4;
  e = 5;
  f = 6;
  g = 7;
  h = 8;
  i = sub(a,b,c,d,e,f,g,h);
}
```

(2) Under 64-bit Linux, compile t.c to generate a t.s file in 64-bit assembly by

```
        gcc -S t.c  # generate t.s file
```

Then edit the t.s file to delete the nonessential lines generated by the compiler and add comments to explain the code actions. The following shows the simplified t.s file with added comment lines.

```
#------------ t.s file generated by 64-bit GCC compiler -------------
        .globl  sub
sub:                # int sub(int a,b,c,d,e,f,g,h)

# first 6 parameters a,  b,  c,  d,  e,  f are in registers
#                    rdi,rsi,rdx,rcx,r8d,r9d
# 2 extra parameters g,h are on stack.
```

```
# Upon entry, stack top contains g, h
#       ---------------------------------
#       ......| h | g | PC |    LOW address
#       --------------|------------------
#                     rsp
```

 # establish stack frame
```
        pushq   %rbp
        movq    %rsp, %rbp
```
```
# no need to shift rsp down because each function has a 128 bytes
# reserved stack area.
# rsp will be shifted down if function define more locals
```

 # save first 6 parameters in registers on stack
```
        movl    %edi, -20(%rbp) # a
        movl    %esi, -24(%rbp) # b
        movl    %edx, -28(%rbp) # C
        movl    %ecx, -32(%rbp) # d
        movl    %r8d, -36(%rbp) # e
        movl    %r9d, -40(%rbp) # f
```

 # access locals u, v, w at rbp -4 to -12
```
        movl    $9,    -4(%rbp)
        movl    $10,   -8(%rbp)
        movl    $11, -12(%rbp)
```

 # compute x + g + u + v:
```
        movl    -20(%rbp), %edx    # saved a on stack
        movl    16(%rbp), %eax     # g at 16(rbp)
        addl    %eax, %edx
        movl    -4(%rbp), %eax     # u at -4(rbp)
        addl    %eax, %edx
        movl    -8(%rbp), %eax     # v at -8(rbp)
        addl    %edx, %eax
```

 # did not shift rsp down, so just popQ to restore rbp
```
        popq    %rbp
        ret
```

```
#====== main function code in assembly ======
        .globl        main
main:
```
 # establish stack frame
```
        pushq   %rbp
        movq    %rsp, %rbp
```

 # shit rsp down 48 bytes for locals
```
        subq    $48, %rsp
```

```
# locals are at rbp -4 to -32
        movl    $1,   -4(%rbp)     # a=1
        movl    $2,   -8(%rbp)     # b=2
        movl    $3,  -12(%rbp)     # c=3
        movl    $4,  -16(%rbp)     # d=4
        movl    $5,  -20(%rbp)     # e=5
        movl    $6,  -24(%rbp)     # f=6
        movl    $7,  -28(%rbp)     # g=7
        movl    $8,  -32(%rbp)     # h=8


# call sub(a,b,c,d,e,f,g,h): first 6 parameters in registers
        movl    -24(%rbp), %r9d  # f in r9
        movl    -20(%rbp), %r8d  # e in r8
        movl    -16(%rbp), %ecx  # d in ecx
        movl    -12(%rbp), %edx  # c in edx
        movl     -8(%rbp), %esi  # b in esi
        movl     -4(%rbp), %eax  # a in eax but will be in edi
# push 2 extra parameters h,g on stack
        movl    -32(%rbp), %edi  # int h in edi
        pushq   %rdi             # pushQ rdi ; only low 32-bits = h
        movl    -28(%rbp), %edi  # int g in edi
        pushq   %rdi             # pushQ rdi ; low 32-bits = g

        movl    %eax, %edi       # parameter a in edi
        call    sub              # call sub(a,b,c,d,e,f,g,h)

        addq    $16, %rsp        # pop stack: h,g, 16 bytes
        movl    %eax, -36(%rbp)  # i = sub return value in eax

        movl    $0, %eax         # return 0 to crt0.o
        leave
        ret

# GCC compiler version 5.3.0
        .ident   "GCC: (GNU) 5.3.0"
```

2.5   Link C Program with Assembly Code

In systems programming, it is often necessary to access and control the hardware, such as CPU registers and I/O port locations, etc. In these situations, assembly code becomes necessary. It is therefore important to know how to link C programs with assembly code.

2.5.1   Programming in Assembly

(1) C code to Assembly Code

```
/************* a.c file ******************/
#include <stdio.h>

extern int B();

int A(int x, int y)
{
  int d, e, f;
  d = 4; e = 5; f = 6;
  f = B(d,e);
}


======= compile a.c file into 32-bit assembly code ======
cc -m32 -S a.c ===> a.s file


==================================================
        .text
        .globl A
A:
        pushl    %ebp
        movl     %esp, %ebp

        subl     $24, %esp
        movl     $4, -12(%ebp)    # d=4
        movl     $5,  -8(%ebp)    # e=5
        movl     $6,  -4(%ebp)    # f=6

        subl     $8, %esp
        pushl    -8(%ebp)         # push e
        pushl    -12(%ebp)        # push d
        call     B

        addl     $16, %esp        # clean stack
        movl     %eax, -4(%ebp)   # f=return value in AX

        leave
        ret


=======================================================
```

Explanations of the Assembly Code

The assembly code generated by GCC consists of three parts:

(1). Entry: also called the **prolog**, which establishes stack frame, allocates local variables and working space on stack

(2). Function body, which performs the function task with return value in AX register

(3). Exit: also called the **epilog**, which deallocates stack space and return to caller

The GCC generated assembly code are explained below, along with the stack contents

```
A:                                      # A() start code location
```
(1). Entry Code:
```
        pushl   %ebp
        movl    %esp, %ebp              # establish stack frame
```

The entry code first saves FP (%bp) on stack and let FP point at the saved FP of the caller. The stack contents become

```
            SP
---------|-------------------------- LOW address
 xxx  |PC|FP|
---------|--------------------------
          FP


        subl    $24, %esp
```

Then it shift SP downward 24 bytes to allocate space for locals variables and working area.

(2). Function Body Code:
```
        movl    $4, -20(%ebp)   // d=4
        movl    $5, -16(%ebp)   // e=5
        movl    $6, -12(%ebp)   // f=6
```

While inside a function, FP points at a fixed location and acts as a base register for accessing local variables, as well as parameters. As can be seen, the 3 locals d, e, f, each 4 bytes long, are at the byte offsets -20, -16, -12 from FP. After assigning values to the local variables, the stack contents become

```
            SP  ---   -24  ---->  SP
             |                     |
---------- -4  -8 -12 -16 -20 -24|------------------- LOW address
 xxx  |PC|FP|? |? |  6 |  5 |  4 |?  |
---------|---------f---e---d----|-------------------
          FP

# call B(d,e): push parameters d, e in reverse order:

        subl    $8, %esp        # create 8 bytes TEMP slots on stack
        pushl   -16(%ebp)       # push e
        pushl   -20(%ebp)       # push d

                                            SP
-------------|-4 -8 -12 -16 -20 -24|- TEMP -|-------|--- LOW address
 xxx  |retPC|FP|? |? |  6 | 5 |  4 |?  | ??| ?? | e | d |
---------|---------f---e---d----|-------------------
           FP
```

```
        call     B                        # B() will grow stack to the RIGHT

# when B() returns:
        addl     $16, %esp        # clean stack
        movl     %eax, -4(%ebp)   # f = return value in AX
```

(3). Exit Code:
```
#       leave
          movl     %ebp, %esp     # SAME as leave
          popl     %ebp


          ret                     # pop retPC on stack top into PC
```

2.5.2   Implement Functions in Assembly

Example 1: Get CPU registers. Since these functions are simple, they do not need to establish and deallocate stack frames.

```
#============== s.s file ===============
        .global get_esp, get_ebp
get_esp:
        movl     %esp, %eax
        ret
get_ebp:
        movl     %ebp, %eax
        ret
#=====================================

int main()
{
   int ebp, esp;
   ebp = get_ebp();
   esp = get_esp();
   printf("ebp=%8x   esp=%8x\n", ebp, esp);
}
```

Example 2: Assume int mysum(int x, int y) returns the sum of x and y. Write mysum() function in ASSEMBLY. Since the function must use its parameters to compute the sum, we show the entry, function body and exit parts of the function code.

```
# =========== mysum.s file ===========================
        .text                    # Code section
        .global mysum, printf    # globals: export mysum, import printf
mysum:
```

```
# (1) Entry:(establish stack frame)

        pushl %ebp
        movl  %esp, %ebp

# Caller has pushed y, x on stack, which looks like the following
#           12   8    4    0
#------------------------------------------------------
#          | y | x |retPC| ebp|
#---------------------------|----------------------
#                          ebp

# (2): Function Body Code of mysum: compute x+y in AX register
        movl  8(%ebp), %eax     # AX = x
        addl  12(%ebp), %eax    # AX += y

# (3) Exit Code: (deallocate stack space and return)
        movl  %ebp, %esp
        pop   %ebp
        ret
# =========== end of mysum.s file ==========================

int main()  # driver program to test mysum() function
{
  int a,b,c;
  a = 123; b = 456;
  c = mysum(a, b);
  printf("c=%d\n", c);    // c should be 579
}
```

2.5.3   Call C functions from Assembly

Example 3: Access global variables and call printf()

```
int a, b;
int main()
{
   a = 100; b = 200;
   sub();
}

#========== Assembly Code file ================
        .text
        .global sub, a, b, printf
sub:
        pushl   %ebp
        movl    %esp, %ebp
```

```
        pushl    b
        pushl    a
        pushl    $fmt         # push VALUE (address) of fmt
        call     printf       # printf(fmt, a, b);
        addl     $12, %esp

        movl     %ebp, %esp
        popl     %ebp
        ret

        .data
fmt:    .asciz   "a=%d  b=%d\n"
#====================================
```

2.6   Link Library

A link library contains precompiled object code. During linking, the linker uses the link library to complete the linking process. In Linux, there are two kinds of link libraries; **static link library** for static linking, and **dynamic link library** for dynamic linking. In this section, we show how to create and use link libraries in Linux.

Assume that we have a function

```
// musum.c file
int mysum(int x, int y){ return x + y; }
```

We would like to create a link library containing the object code of the mysum() function, which can be called from different C programs, e.g.

```
// t.c file
int main()
{
    int sum = mysum(123,456);
}
```

2.6.1   Static Link Library

The following steps show how to create and use a static link library.

```
(1). gcc  -c  mysum.c           # compile mysum.c into mysum.o
(2). ar  rcs  libmylib.a  mysum.o  # create static link library with member
                                       mysum.o
(3). gcc  -static  t.c  -L. -lmylib # static compile-link t.c with libmylib.a
                                       as link library
(4). a.out                      # run a.out as usual
```

In the compile-link step (4), -L. specifies the library path (current directory), and -l specifies the library. Note that the library (mylib) is specified without the prefex lib, as well as the suffix .a

2.6.2 Dynamic Link Library

The following steps show how to create and use a dynamic link library.

```
(1). gcc  -c  -fPIC  mysum.c          # compile to Position Independent
                                        Code mysum.o
(2). gcc -shared  -o libmylib.so  mysum.o  # create shared libmylib.so with
                                        mysum.o
(3). gcc  t.c  -L.  -lmylib           # generate a.out using shared library
                                        libmylib.so
(4). export LD_LIBRARY_PATH=./        # to run a.out, must export
                                        LD_LIBRARY=./
(5). a.out                            #  run a.out. ld will load libmylib.so
```

In both cases, if the library is not in the current directory, simply change the –L. option and set the LD_LIBRARY_PATH to point to the directory containing the library. Alternatively, the user may also place the library in a standard lib directory, e.g. /lib or /usr/lib and run ldconfig to configure the dynamic link library path. The reader may consult Linux ldconfig (man 8) for details.

2.7 Makefile

So far, we have used individual gcc commands to compile-link the source files of C programs. For convenience, we may also use a **sh script** which includes all the commands. These schemes have a major drawback. If we only change a few of the source files, the sh commands or script would still compile all the source files, including those that are not modified, which is unnecessary and time-consuming. A better way is to use the Unix/Linux **make** facility (GNU make 2008). make is a program, which reads a **makefile**, or **Makefile** in that order, to do the compile-link automatically and selectively. This section covers the basics of makefiles and shows their usage by examples.

2.7.1 Makefile Format

A make file consists of a set of **targets, dependencies** and **rules. A target** is usually a file to be created or updated, but it may also be a directive to, or a label to be referenced by, the make program. A target depends on a set of source files, object files or even other targets, which are described in a **Dependency List. Rules** are the necessary commands to build the target by using the Dependency List. Figure 2.16 shows the format of a makefile.

2.7.2 The make Program

When the **make** program reads a makefile, it determines which targets to build by comparing the timestamps of source files in the Dependency List. If any dependency has a newer timestamp since last

Fig. 2.16 Makefile format

Target	Dependency List
target:	file1 file2 ... fileN
	Rules
\<tab\>	command1
\<tab\>	command2
\<tab\>	other command

build, **make** will execute the rule associated with the target. Assume that we have a C program consisting of three source files:

```
(1). type.h file:          // header file
     int mysum(int x, int y)   // types, constants, etc

(2). mysum.c file:          // function in C
     #include <stdio.h>
     #incldue "type.h"
     int mysum(int x, int y)
     {
         return x+y;
     }

(3). t.c file:              // main() in C
     #include <stdio.h>
     #include "type.h"
     int main()
     {
         int sum = mysum(123,456);
         printf("sum = %d\n", sum);
     }
```

Normally, we would use the sh command

```
gcc -o myt main.c mysum.c
```

to generate a binary executable named **myt**. In the following, we shall demonstrate compile-link of C programs by using makefiles.

2.7.3   Makefile Examples

Makefile Example 1

(1). Create a makefile named mk1 containing:

```
myt: type.h t.c mysum.c        # target: dependency list
     gcc -o myt t.c mysum.c    # rule: line MUST begin with a TAB
```

The resulting executable file name, myt in this example, usually matches that of the target name. This allows make to decide whether or not to build the target again later by comparing its timestamp against those in the dependency list.

(2). Run make using mk1 as the makefile: **make** normally uses the default makefile or Makefile, whichever is present in the current directory. It can be directed to use a different makefile by the –f flag, as in

```
make -f mk1
```

make will build the target file myt and show the command execution as

```
gcc -o myt  t.c  mysum.c
```

(3). Run the make command again. It will show the message

```
make: 'myt' is up to date
```

In this case, make does not build the target again since none of the files has changed since last build.

(4). On the other hand, make will execute the rule command again if any of the files in the dependency list has changed. A simple way to modify a file is by the **touch** command, which changes the timestamp of the file. So if we enter the sh commands

```
touch type.h     // or touch *.h, touch *.c, etc.
make -f mk1
```

make will recompile-link the source files to generate a new myt file

(5). If we delete some of the file names from the dependency list, make will not execute the rule command even if such files are changed. The reader may try this to verify it.

As can be seen, mk1 is a very simple makfile, which is not much different than sh commands. But we can refine makefiles to make them more flexible and general.

Makefile Example 2: Macros in Makefile

(1). Create a makefile named mk2 containing:

```
CC = gcc                  # define CC as gcc
CFLAGS = -Wall            # define CLAGS as flags to gcc
OBJS = t.o mysum.o        # define Object code files
INCLUDE = -Ipath          # define path as an INCLUDE directory

myt: type.h $(OBJS)       # target: dependency: type.h and .o files
        $(CC) $(CFLAGS) -o t $(OBJS) $(INCLUDE)
```

In a makefile, macro defined symbols are replaced with their values by $(symbol), e.g. $(CC) is replaced with gcc, $(CFLAGS) is replaced with –Wall, etc. For each .o file in the dependency list, make will compile the corresponding .c file into .o file first. However, this works only for .c files. Since all the .c files depend on .h files, we have to explicitly include type.h (or any other .h files) in the dependency list also. Alternatively, we may define additional targets to specify the dependency of .o files on .h files, as in

```
t.o:      t.c type.h       # t.o depend on t.c and type.h
      gcc -c t.c
mysum.o:  mysum.c type.h   # mysum.o depend type.h
      gcc -c mysum.c
```

If we add the above targets to a makefile, any changes in either .c files or type.h will trigger make to recompile the .c files. This works fine if the number of .c files is small. It can be very tedious if the number of .c files is large. So there are better ways to include .h files in the dependency list, which will be shown later.

(3). Run make using mk2 as the makefile:

```
make -f mk2
```

(4). Run the resulting binary executable myt as before.

The simple makefiles of Examples 1 and 2 are sufficient for compile-link most small C programs. The following shows some additional features and capabilities of makefiles.

Makefile Example 3: Make Target by Name
When make runs on a makefile, it normally tries to build the **first target** in the makefile. The behavior of make can be changed by specifying a target name, which causes make to build the specific named target. As an example, consider the makefile named mk3, in which the new features are highlighted in **bold face** letters.

```
# ----------------- mk3 file -------------------
CC = gcc             # define CC as gcc
CFLAGS = -Wall       # define CLAGS as flags to gcc
OBJS = t.o mysum.o   # define Object code files
INCLUDE = -Ipath     # define path as an INCLUDE directory

all: myt install     # build all listed targets: myt, install

myt: t.o mysum.o     # target: dependency list of .o files
      $(CC) $(CFLAGS) -o myt $(OBJS) $(INCLUDE)

t.o:    t.c  type.h  #  t.o depend on t.c and type.h
      gcc -c t.c
mysum.o: mysum.c type.h #  mysum.o depend mysum.c and type.h
      gcc -c mysum.c

install: myt         # depend on myt: make will build myt first
      echo install myt to /usr/local/bin
      sudo mv myt /usr/local/bin/  # install myt to /usr/local/bin/
```

```
run:     install           # depend on install, which depend on myt
         echo run executable image myt
         myt || /bin/true  # no make error 10 if main() return non-zero

clean:
         rm -f *.o 2> /dev/null          # rm all *.o files
         sudo rm -f /usr/local/bin/myt   # rm myt
```

The reader may test the mk3 file by entering the following **make** commands:

```
(1). make [all] -f mk3    # build all targets: myt and install
(2). make install -f mk3  # build target myt and install myt
(3). make run -f mk3      # run /usr/local/bin/myt
(4). make clean -f mk3    # remove all listed files
```

Makefile Variables: Makefiles support variables. In a makefile, **%** is a wildcard variable similar to *
in sh. A makefile may also contain **automatic variables**, which are set by make after a rule is matched.
They provide access to elements from the target and dependency lists so that the user does not have to
explicitly specify any filenames. They are very useful for defining general pattern rules. The following
lists some of the automatic variables of make.

$@ : name of current target.
$< : name of first dependency
$^ : names of all dependencies
$* : name of current dependency without extension
$? : list of dependencies changed more recently than current target.

In addition, make also supports **suffix rules,** which are not targets but directives to the make program.
We illustrate make variables and suffix rules by an example.

In a C program, .c files usually depend on all .h files. If any of the .h files is changed, all .c files must
be re-compiled again. To ensure this, we may define a dependency list containing all the .h files and
specify a target in a makefile as

```
DEPS = type.h          # list ALL needed .h files
%.o: %.c $(DEPS)       # for all .o files: if its .c or .h file changed
        $(CC) -c -o $@ # compile corresponding .c file again
```

In the above target, %.o stands for all .o files and $@ is set to the current target name, i.e. the current .o
file name. This avoids defining separate targets for individual .o files.

Makefile Example 4: Use make variables and suffix rules

```
# ---------- mk4 file -------------
CC = gcc
CFLAGS = -I.
OBJS = t.o mysum.o
AS = as     # assume we have .s files in assembly also
DEPS = type.h           # list all .h files in DEPS
```

```
.s.o: # for each fname.o, assemble fname.s into fname.o
         $(AS) -o $< -o $@  # -o $@ REQUIRED for .s files

.c.o: # for each fname.o, compile fname.c into fname.o
         $(CC) -c $< -o $@  # -o $@ optional for .c files

%.o:  %.c $(DEPS) # for all .o files: if its .c or .h file changed
         $(CC) -c -o $@ $<  # compile corresponding .c file again

myt: $(OBJS)
         $(CC) $(CFLAGS) -o $@ $^
```

In the makefile mk4, the lines .s.o: and .c.o: are not targets but directives to the make program by the **suffix rule.** These rules specify that, for each .o file, there should be a corresponding .s or .c file to build if their timestamps differ, i.e. if the .s or .c file has changed. In all the target rules, $@ means the current target, $< means the first file in the dependency list and $^ means all files in the dependency list. For example, in the rule of the myt target, -o $@ specifies that the output file name is the current target, which is myt. $^ means it includes all the files in the dependency list, i.e. both t.o and mysum.o. If we change $^ to $< and touch all the .c files, make would generate an "undefined reference to mysum" error. This is because $< specifies only the first file (t.o) in the dependency list, make would only recompile t.c but not mysum.c, resulting a linking error due to missing mysum.o file. As can be seen from the example, we may use make variables to write very general and compact makefiles. The downside is that such makefiles are rather hard to understand, especially for beginning programmers.

Makfiles in Subdirectories

A large C programming project usually consists of tens or hundreds of source files. For ease of maintenance, the source files are usually organized into different levels of directories, each with its own makefile. It's fairly easy to let make go into a subdirectory to execute the local makefile in that directory by the command

```
(cd DIR; $(MAKE))   OR   cd DIR && $(MAKE)
```

After executing the local makefile in a subdirectory, control returns to the current directory form where make continues. We illustrate this advanced capability of make by a real example.

Makefile Example 5: PMTX System Makefiles

PMTX (Wang 2015) is a Unix-like operating system designed for the Intel x86 architecture in 32-bit protect mode. It uses 32-bit GCC assembler, compiler and linker to generate the PMTX kernel image. The source files of PMTX are organized in three subdirectories:

Kernel : PMTX kernel files; a few GCC assembly files, mostly in C
Fs   : file system source files; all in C
Driver : device driver source files; all in C

The compile-link steps are specified by Makefiles in different directories. The top level makefile in the PMTX source directory is very simple. It first cleans up the directories. Then it goes into the Kernel subdirectory to execute a Makefile in the Kernel directory. The Kernel Makefile first generates .o files for both .s and .c files in Kernel. Then it directs make to go into the Driver and Fs subdirectories to generate .o file by executing their local Makfiles. Finally, it links all the .o files to a kernel image file. The following shows the various Makefiles of the PMTX system.

```
#------------- PMTX Top level Makefile -------------
all: pmtx_kernel

pmtx_kernel:
        make clean
        cd Kernel && $(MAKE)


clean: # rm mtx_kerenl, *.o file in all directories

#------------- PMTX Kernel Makefile ----------------
AS = as -Iinclude
CC = gcc
LD = ld
CPP = gcc -E -nostdinc
CFLAGS = -W -nostdlib -Wno-long-long -I include -fomit-frame-pointer

KERNEL_OBJS = entry.o init.o t.o ts.o traps.o trapc.o queue.o \
fork.o exec.o wait.o io.o syscall.o loader.o pipe.o mes.o signal.o \
threads.o sbrk.o mtxlib.o

K_ADDR=0x80100000      # kernel start virtual address

all: kernel

.s.o:   # build each .o if its .s file has changed
        ${AS} -a $< -o $*.o > $*.map


pmtx_kernel: $(KERNEL_OBJS)      # kernel target: depend on all OBJs
        cd ../Driver && $(MAKE) # cd to Driver, run local Makefile
        cd ../Fs && $(MAKE)      # cd to Fs/,    run local Makefile

# link all .o files with entry=pm_entry, start VA=0x80100000
        ${LD} --oformat binary -Map k.map -N -e pm_entry \
            -Ttext ${K_ADDR} -o $@ \
              ${KERNEL_OBJS} ../DRIVER/*.o ../FS/*.o
clean:
        rm -f *.map *.o
        rm -f ../DRIVER.*.map ../DRIVER/*.o
        rm -f ../FS/*.map ../FS/*.o
```

The PMTX kernel makefile first generates .o files from all .s (assembly) files. Then it generates other .o files from .c files by the dependency lists in **KERNEL_OBJ**. Then it goes into **Driver** and **Fs** directories to execute the local makefiles, which generate .o files in these directories. Finally, it links all the .o files to generate the pmtx_kernel image file, which is the PMTX OS kernel. In contrast, since all files in **Fs** and **Driver** are in C, their Makefiles only compile .c files to .o files, so there are no .s or ld related targets and rules.

```
#------------ PMTX Driver Makefile ----------------
CC=gcc
CPP=gcc -E -nostdinc
CFLAGS=-W -nostdlib -Wno-long-long -I include -fomit-frame-pointer

DRIVER_OBJS = timer.o pv.o vid.o kbd.o fd.o hd.o serial.o pr.o atapi.o
driverobj: ${DRIVER_OBJS}

#------------ PMTX Fs Makefile ------------------
CC=gcc
CPP=gcc -E -nostdinc
CFLAGS=-W -nostdlib -Wno-long-long -I include -fomit-frame-pointer

FS_OBJS = fs.o buffer.o util.o mount_root.o alloc_dealloc.o \
          mkdir_creat.o cd_pwd.o rmdir.o link_unlink.o stat.o touch.o \
          open_close.o read.o write.o dev.o mount_umount.o
fsobj:   ${FS_OBJS}
#-------------- End of Makefile ------------------
```

2.8   The GDB Debugger

The GNU Debugger **(GDB)** (Debugging with GDB 2002; GDB 2017) is an interactive debugger, which can debug programs written in C, C++ and several other languages. In Linux, the command **man gdb** displays the manual pages of gdb, which provides a brief description of how to use GDB. The reader may find more detailed information on GDB in the listed references. In this section, we shall cover GDB basics and show how to use GDB to debug C programs in the Integrated Development Environment (IDE) of EMACS under X-windows, which is available in all Linux systems. Since the Graphic User Interface (GUI) part of different Linux distributions may differ, the following discussions are specific to Ubuntu Linux Version 15.10 or later, but it should also be applicable to other Linux distributions, e.g. Slackware Linux 14.2, etc.

2.8.1   Use GDB in Emacs IDE

1. **Source Code:** Under X-window, open a pseudo-terminal. Use EMACS to create a Makefile, as shown below.

Makefile:

```
t: t.c
        gcc -g -o t t.c
```

Then use EMACS to edit a C source file. Since the objective here is to show GDB usage, we shall use a very simple C program.

```
/******** Source file: t.c Code ********/
#include <stdio.h>
int sub();
int g, h;    // globals

int main()
{
  int a, b, c;
  printf("enter main\n");
  a = 1;
  b = 2;
  c = 3;
  g = 123;
  h = 456;
  c = sub(a, b);
  printf("c = %d\n", c);
  printf("main exit\n");
}

int sub(int x, int y)
{
  int u,v;
  printf("enter sub\n");
  u = 4;
  v = 5;
  printf("sub return\n");
  return x+y+u+v+g+h;
}
```

2. **Compile Source Code:** When EMACS is running, it displays a menu and a tool bar at the top of the edit window (Fig. 2.17).

   Each menu can be opened to display a table of submenus. Open EMACS **Tools** menu and select **Compile.** EMACS will show a prompt line at the bottom of the edit window

   ```
       make -k
   ```

and waits for user response. EMACS normally compile-link the source code by a makefile. If the reader already has a makefile in the same directory as shown above, press the Enter key to let EMACS continue. In instead of a makefile, the reader may also enter the command line manually.

Fig. 2.17 EMACS menu and tool bar

Fig. 2.18 GDB menu and
tool bar

```
gcc  -g  -o  t  t.c
```

In order to generate a binary executable for GDB to debug, the **–g** flag is required. With the –g flag, the
GCC compiler-linker will build a symbol table in the binary executable file for GDB to access
variables and functions during execution. Without the **–g** flag, the resulting executable file can not
be debugged by GDB. After compilation finishes, EMACS will show the compile results, including
warning or error messages, if any, in a separate window below the source code window.

3. **Start up GDB:** Open EMACS Tools menu and select Debugger.

EMACS will show a prompt line at the bottom of the edit window and wait for user response.

```
gdb –i=mi  t
```

Press Enter to start up the GDB debugger. GDB will run in the upper window and display a menu and a
tool bar at the top of the EMACS edit window, as shown in Fig. 2.18.

The user may now enter GDB commands to debug the program. For example, to set break points,
enter the GDB commands

```
b main      # set break point at main
b sub       # set break point at sub
b 10        # set break point at line 10 in program
```

When the user enters the Run (r) command (or choose **Run** in the tool bar), GDB will display the
program code in the same GDB window. Other frames/windows can be activated through the submenu
GDB-Frames or **GDB-Windows.** The following steps demonstrate the debugging process by using
both commands and tool bar in the **multi-windows** layout of GDB.

4. **GDB in Multi-Windows:** From the GDB menu, choose **Gud => GDB-MI => Display Other
   Windows,** where => means follow a submenu. GDB will display GDB buffers in different
   windows, as shown in Fig. 2.19.

   Figure 2.19 shows six (6) GDB windows, each displays a specific GDB buffer.

Gud-t: GDB buffer for user commands and GDB messages
t.c: Program source code to show progress of execution
Stack frames: show stack frames of function calling sequence
Local Registers: show local variables in current executing function
Input/output: for program I/O
Breakpoints: display current break points settings

It also shows some of the commonly used GDB commands in a tool bar, e.g. **Run, Continue, Next
line, Step line**, which allows the user to choose an action instead of entering commands.

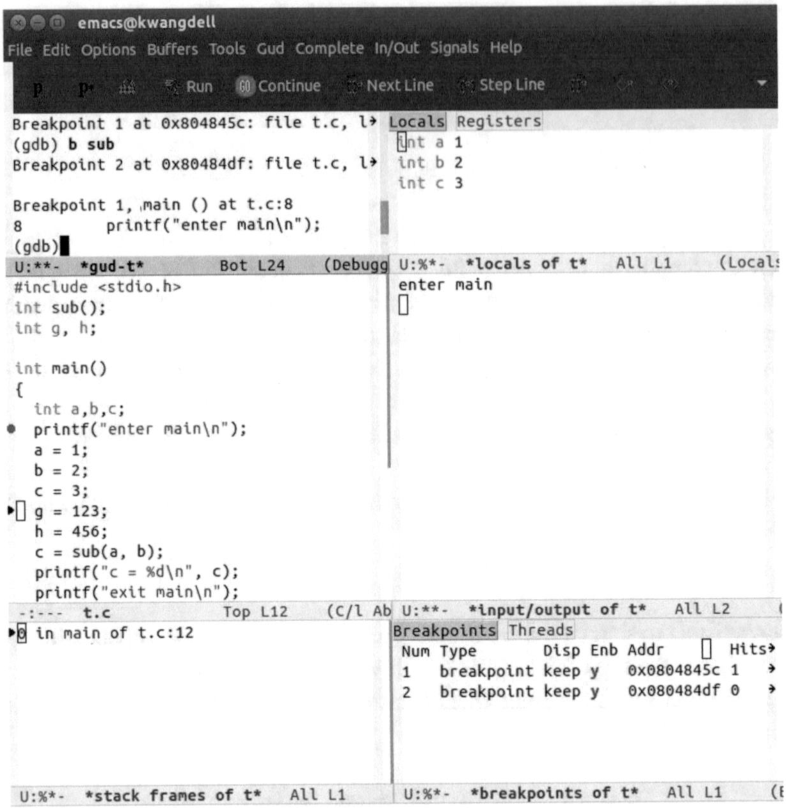

Fig. 2.19 Multi-windows
of GDB

While the program is executing, GDB shows the execution progress by a **dark triangular mark**, which points to the next line of program code to be executed. Execution will stop at each break point, providing a break for the user to interact with GDB. Since we have set main as a break point, execution will stop at main when GDB starts to run. While execution stops at a break point, the user may interact with GDB by entering commands in the GDB window, such as set/clear break points, display/change variables, etc. Then, enter the Continue (c) command or choose **Continue** in the tool bar to continue program execution. Enter Next (n) command or choose **Next line** or **Step line** in the GDB tool bar to execute in single line mode.

Figure 2.19 shows that execution in main() has already completed executing several lines of the program code, and the next line mark is at the statement

$$g = 123;$$

At the moment, the local variables a, b, c are already assigned values, which are shown in the **Locals registers** windows as a=1, b=2, c=3. Global variables are not shown in any window, but the user may enter **Print** (p) commands

```
p g
p h
```

to print the global variables g and h, both of which should still be 0 since they are not assigned any values yet.

Fig. 2.20 Multi-windows of GDB

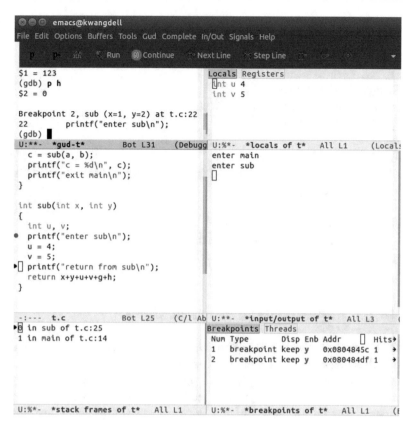

Figure 2.19 also shows the following GDB windows:

. **input/output** window shows the outputs of printf statements of main().
. **stack frames** window shows execution is now inside the main() function.
. **breakpoints** window shows the current breakpoints settings, etc.

This multi-windows layout provides the user with a complete set of information about the status of the executing program.

The user may enter Continue or choose **Continue** in the tool bar to continue the execution. When control reaches the sub() function, it will stop again at the break point. Figure 2.20 shows that the program execution is now inside sub() and the execution already passed the statements before

```
printf("return from sub\n");
```

At this moment, the **Locals Registers** window shows the local variables of sub() as u=4 and v=5. The **input/output** window shows the print results of both main() and sub(). The **Stack frame**s window shows sub() is the top frame and main() is the next frame, which is consistent with the function calling sequence.

(5). Additional GDB Commands: At each break point or while executing in single line mode, the user may enter GDB commands either manually, by the GDB tool bar or by choosing submenu items in the **Gud** menu, which includes all the commands in the GDB tool bar. The following lists some additional GDB commands and their meanings.

Clear Break Points:
   clear line# : clear bp at line#
   clear name : clear bp at function name

Change Variable Values
   set var a=100 : set variable a to 100
   set var b=200 : set b to 200, etc.

Watch Variable Changes:
   watch c : watch for changes in variable c; whenever c changes, it will display its old value and new
         value.

Back trace (bt):
   bt stackFrame# to back trace stack frames

2.8.2   Advices on Using Debugging Tools

GDB is a powerful debugger, which is fairly easy to use. However, the reader should keep in mind that
all debugging tools can only offer limited help. In some cases, even a powerful debugger like the GDB
is of little use. The best approach to program development is to design the program's algorithm
carefully and then write program code in accordance with the algorithm. Many beginning
programmers tend to write program code without any planning, just hoping their program would
work, which most likely would not. When their program fails to work or does not produce the right
results, they would immediately turn to a debugger, trying to trace the program executions to find out
the problem. Relying too much on debugging tools is often counter-productive as it may waste more
time than necessary. In the following, we shall point out some common programming errors and show
how to avoid them in C programs.

2.8.3   Common Errors in C programs

A program in execution may encounter many types of run-time errors, such as illegal instruction,
privilege violation, divide by zero, invalid address, etc. Such errors are recognized by the CPU as
exceptions, which trap the process to the operating system kernel. If the user has not made any
provision to handle such errors, the process will terminate by a signal number, which indicates the
cause of the exception. If the program is written in C, which is executed by a process in user mode,
exceptions such as illegal instruction and privilege violation should never occur. In system programming, programs seldom use divide operations, so divide by zero exceptions are also rare. The
predominate type of run-time errors are due to invalid addresses, which cause memory access
exceptions, resulting in the dreadful and familiar message of segmentation fault. In the following,
we list some of the most probable causes in C programs that lead to memory access exceptions at
run-time.

(1). Uninitialized pointers or pointers with wrong values: Consider the following code segments,
with line numbers for ease of reference.

```
1. int *p;          // global, initial value = 0
   int main()
   {
2.     int *q;       // q is local on stack, can be any value
3.     *p = 1;       // dereference a NULL pointer
4.     *q = 2;       // dereference a pointer with unknown value
   }
```

Line 1 defines a global integer pointer p, which is in the BSS section of the run-time image with an initial value 0. So it's a NULL pointer. Line 3 tries to dereference a NULL pointer, which will cause a segmentation fault.

Line 2 defines a local integer pointer q, which is on the stack, so it can be any value. Line 4 tries to dereference the pointer q, which points at an unknown memory location. If the location is outside of the program's writable memory area, it will cause a segmentation fault due to memory access violation. If the location is within the program's writable memory area, it may not cause an immediate error but it may lead to other errors later due to corrupted data or stack contents. The latter kind of run-time error is extremely difficult to diagnose because the errors may have propagated through the program execution. The following shows the correct ways of using these pointers. Modify the above code segment as shown below.

```
int  x, *p;                 // or  int *p = &x;
int main()
{
    int *q;
    p = &x;                 // let p point at x
    *p = 1;
    q = (int *)malloc(sizeof(int);  // q point at allocate memory
    *q = 2;
}
```

The principle is very simple. When using any pointer, the programmer must ensure the pointer is not NULL or has been set to point to a valid memory address.

(2). Array index out of bounds: In C programs, each array is defined with a finite number of N elements. The index of the array must be in the range of [0, N-1]. If the array index exceeds the range at run-time, it may cause invalid memory access, which either corrupt the program data area or result in a segmentation fault. We illustrate this by an example. Consider the following code segment.

```
   #define N 10
1. int a[N], i; //  An array of N elements, followed by int i
   int main()
   {
2.     for (i=0; i<N; i++)    // index i in range
          a[i] = i+1;         // set a[ ] values = 1 to N
3.     a[N] = 123456789;      // set a[N] to a LARGE value
4.     printf("i = %d\n", i); // print current i value
5.     printf("%d\n", a[i])); // segmentation fault !
   }
```

Line 1 defines an array of N elements, which is followed by the index variable i. Line 2 represents the proper usage of the array index, which is within the bounds [0, N-1]. Line 3.sets a[N] to a large value, which actually changes the variable i because a[N] and i are in the same memory location. Line 4 prints the current value of i, which is no longer N but the large value. Line 5 will most likely to cause a segmentation fault because a[123456789] tries to access a memory location outside of the program's data area.

(3). Improper use of string pointers and char arrays: Many string operation functions in the C library are defined with char * parameters. As a specific example, consider the strcpy() function, which is defined as

```
char * strcpy(char *dest, char *src)
```

It copies a string from src to dest. The Linux man page on strcpy() clearly specifies that the dest string must be large enough to receive the copy. Many programmers, including some 'experienced' graduate students, often overlook the specification and try to use strcpy() as follows.

```
char *s;  // s is a char pointer
strcpy(s, " this is a string");
```

The code segment is wrong because s is not pointing at any memory location with enough space to receive the src string. If s is global, it is a NULL pointer. In this case, strcpy() will cause a segmentation fault immediately. If s is local, it may point to an arbitrary memory location. In this case, strcpy() may not cause an immediate error but it may lead to other errors later due to corrupted memory contents. Such errors are very subtle and difficult to diagnose even with a debugger such as GDB. The correct way of using strcpy() is to ensure dest is NOT just a string pointer but a real memory area with enough space to receive the copied string, as in

```
char s[128];  // s is a char array
strcpy(s, " this is a string");
```

Although the same s variable in both char *s and char s[128] can be used as an address, the reader must beware there is a fundamental difference between them.

(4). The assert macro: Most Unix-like systems, including Linux, support an **assert(condition)** macro, which can be used in C programs to check whether a specified condition is met or not. If the condition expression evaluates to FALSE (0), the program will abort with an error message. As an example, consider the following code segments, in which the mysum() function is designed to return the sum of an integer array (pointed by int *ptr) of n<=128 elements. Since the function is called from other code of a program, which may pass in invalid parameters, we must ensure the pointer ptr is not NULL and the array size n does not exceed the LIMIT. These can be done by including assert() statements at the entry point of a function, as shown below.

```
#define LIMIT 128
int mysum(int *ptr, int n)
{
    int i = 0, sum = 0;
    assert(ptr != NULL);      // assert ptr not NULL
    assert(n <= LIMIT);       // assert n <= LIMIT
    while(i++ < n)
       sum += *ptr++
}
```

When execution enters the mysum() function, if either **assert(condition)** fails, the function will abort with an error message.

(5). Use fprintf() and getchar() in Program Code: When writing C programs, it is often very useful to include fprintf(stderr, message) statements at key places in the program code to display expected results. Since fprintf() to stderr is unbuffered, the printed message or results will show up immediately before the next C statement is executed. If desired, the programmer may also user getchar () to stop the program flow, allowing the user to examine the execution results at that moment before continuing. We cite a simple program task to illustrate the point. A priority queue is a singly link list ordered by priority, with high priority entries in front. Entries with the same priority are ordered First-in-First-out (FIFO). Write an enqueue() function which insert an item into a priority queue by priority.

```c
typedef struct entry{
        struct entry *next;
        char name[64];      // entry name
        int priority;       // entry priority
}ENTRY;

void printQ(ENTRY *queue)    // print queue contents
{
   while(queue){
      printf("[%s %d]-> ", queue->name, queue->priority);
      queue = queue->next;
   }
   printf("\n");
}


void enqueue(ENTRY **queue, ENTRY *p)
{
   ENTRY *q = *queue;
   printQ(q);              // show queue before insertion
   if (q==0 || p->priority > q->priority){ // first in queue
      *queue = p;
      p->next = q;
   }
   else{ // not first in queue; insert to the right spot
      while (q->next && p->priority <= q->priority)
            q = q->next;
      p->next = q->next;
      q->next = p;
   }
   printQ(q);              // show queue after insertion
}
```

In the above example code, if the enqueue() function code is incorrect, it may insert an entry to the wrong spot in the queue, which will cause other program code to fail if they rely on the queue contents being correct. In this case, using either assert() statements or relying on a debugger may offer very little help, since all the pointers are valid and it would be too tedious to trace a long link list in a debugger.

Instead, we print the queue before inserting a new entry and print it again after the insertion. These allow the user to see directly whether or not the queue is maintained correctly. After verifying the code works, the user may comment out the printQ() statements.

2.9   Structures in C

A structure is a composite data type containing a collection of variables or data objects. Structure types in C are defined by the **struct** keyword. Assume that we need a node structure containing the following fields.

next : a pointer to the next node structure;
key : an integer;
name : an array of 64 chars;

Such a structure can be defined as

```
struct node{
    struct node *next;
    int  key;
    char name[64];
};
```

Then, "struct node" can be used as a derived type to define variables of that type, as in

```
struct node x, *nodePtr;
```

These define x as a node structure and nodePtr a node pointer. Alternatively, we may define "struct node" as a derived type by the **typedef** statement in C.

```
typedef struct node{
    struct node *next;
    int  key;
    char name[64];
}NODE;
```

Then, NODE is a derived type, which can be used to define variables of that type, as in

```
NODE x, *nodePtr;
```

The following summarizes the properties of C structures.

(1). When defining a C structure, every field of the structure must have a type already known to the compiler, except for the self-referencing pointers. This is because pointers are always the same size, e.g. 4 bytes in 32-bit architecture. As an example, in the above NODE type, the filed next is a

```
struct node *next;
```

which is correct because the compiler knows **struct node** is a type (despite being incomplete yet) and how many bytes to allocate for the next pointer. In contrast, the following statements

```
typedef struct node{
    NODE *next;       // error
    int  key;
    char name[64];
}NODE;
```

would cause a compile-time error because the compiler does not know what is the NODE type yet, despite next is a pointer.

(2). Each C structure data object is allocated a piece of contiguous memory. The individual fields of a C structure are accessed by using the **. operator**, which identifies a specific field, as in

```
NODE x;    // x is a structure of NODE type
```

Then the individual fields of x are accessed as

x.next; which is a pointer to another NODE type object.
x.key; which is an integer
x.name; which is an array of 64 chars

At run time, each field is accessed as an **offset** from the beginning address of the structure.

(3). The size of a structure can be determined by **sizeof(struct type)**. The C compiler will calculate the size in total number of bytes of the structure. Due to memory alignment constraints, the C compiler may pad some of the fields of a structure with extra bytes. If needed, the user may define C structures with the **PACKED** attribute, which prevents the C compiler from padding the fields with extra bytes, as in

```
typedef struct node{
    struct node *next;
    int  key;
    char name[2];
}__attribute__((packed, aligned(1))) NODE;
```

In this case, the size of the NODE structure will be 10 bytes. Without the packed attribute, it would be 12 bytes because the C compiler would pad the name field with 2 extra bytes, making every NODE object a multiple of 4 bytes for memory alignment.

(4). Assume that NODE x, y; are two structures of the same type. Rather than copying the individual fields of a structure, we can assign x to y by the C statement y = x. The compiler generated code uses the library function memncpy(&y, &x, sizeof(NODE)) to copy the entire structure.

(5). Unions in C is similar to structures. To define a union, simply replace the keyword **struct** with the keyword **union**, as in

```
union node{
    int  *ptr;       // pointer to integer
    int  ID;         // 4-byte integer
    char name[32];   // 32 chars
}x;                  // x is a union of 3 fields
```

Members in unions are accessed in exactly the same way as in structures. The major difference between structures and unions is that, whereas each member in a structure has a unique memory area, all members of a union share the same memory area, which is accessed by the attributes of the individual members. The size of a union is determined by the largest member. For example, in the union x the member name requires 32 bytes. All other members require only 4 bytes each. So the size of the union x is 32 bytes. The following C statements show how to access the individual members of a union.

```
x.ptr = 0x12345678;            // use first 4 bytes of x
x.ID = 12345;                  // use first 4 bytes of x also
strcpy(x.name, "1234567890");  // uses first 11 bytes of x
```

2.9.1   Structure and Pointers

In C, **pointers** are variables which point to other data objects, i.e. they contain the address of other data objects. In C programs, pointers are define with the *** attribute**, as in

```
TYPE *ptr;
```

which defines ptr as a pointer to a TYPE data object, where TYPE can be either a base type or a derived type, such as struct, in C. In C programming, structures are often accessed by pointers to the structures. As an example, assume that NODE is a structure type. The following C statements

```
NODE x, *p;
p = &x;
```

define x as a NODE type data object and p as a pointer to NODE objects. The statement p = &x; assigns the address of x to p, so that p points at the data object x. Then *p denotes the object x, and the members of x can be accessed as

```
(*p).name, (*p).value, (*p).next
```

Alternatively, the C language allows us to reference the members of x by using the "point at" **operator ->**, as in

```
p->name, p->value, p->next;
```

which are more convenient than the . operator. In fact, using the -> operator to access members of structures has become a standard practice in C programming.

2.9.2   Typecast in C

Typecast is a way to convert a variable from one data type to another data type by using the cast operator **(TYPE) variable.** Consider the following code segments.

```
    char *cp, c = 'a';          // c is 1 byte
    int  *ip, i = 0x12345678; // i is 4 bytes

(1). i = c;                 // i = 0x00000061; lowest byte = c
(2). c = i;                 // c = 0x78 (c = lowest byte of i)
(3). cp = (char *)&i;       // typecast to suppress compiler warning
(4). ip = (int *)&c;        // typecast to suppress compiler warning
(5). c = *(char *)ip;       // use ip as a char *
(6). i = *(int *)cp;        // use cp as an int *
```

Lines (1) and (2) do not need typecasting even though the assignments involve different data types. The resulting values of the assignments are shown in the comments. Lines (4) and (5) need typecasting in order to suppress compiler warnings. After the assignments of Lines (4) and (5), *cp is still a byte, which is the lowest byte of the (4-byte) integer i. *ip is an integer = 0x00000061, with the lowest byte = 'c' or 0x 61. Line (6) forces the compiler to use ip as a char *, so *(char *)ip dereferences to a single byte. Line (7) forces the compiler to use cp as an int *, so *(int *)cp dereferences to a 4-byte value, beginning from where cp points at.

Typecasting is especially useful with pointers, which allows the same pointer to point to data objects of different sizes. The following shows a more practical example of typecasting. In an **Ext2/3** file system, the contents of a directory are dir_entries defined as

```
    struct dir_entry{
        int  ino;              // inode number
        int  entry_len;        // entry length in bytes
        int  name_len;         // name_len
        char name[  ]          // name_len chars
    };
```

The contents of a directory consist of a linear list of dir_entries of the form

```
        | ino elen nlen NAME | ino elen nlen NAME | . . .
```

in which the entries are of variable length due to the different name_len of the entries. Assume that char buf[ ] contains a list of dir_entries. The problem is how to traverse the dir_entries in buf[ ]. In order to step through the dir_entires sequentially, we define

```
    struct dir_entry *dp = (struct dir_entry *)buf;  // typecasting
    char *cp = buf;                         // no need for typecasting
    // Use dp to access the current dir_entry;
    // advance dp to next dir_entry:
    cp = += dp->entry_len;       // advance cp by entry_len
    dp = (struct dir_entry *)cp; // pull dp to where cp points at
```

With proper typecasting, the last two lines of C code can be simplified as

```
    dp = (struct dir_entry *)((char *)dp + dp->rlen);
```

which eliminates the need for a char *cp.

2.10   Link List Processing

Structures and pointers are often used to construct and manipulate **dynamic data structures**, such as link lists, queues and trees, etc. The most basic type of dynamic data structures is the link list. In this section, we shall explain the concepts of link list, list operations, and demonstrate list processing by example programs.

2.10.1   Link Lists

Assume that nodes are structures of NODE type, as in

```
typedef struct node{
    struct node *next;   // next node pointer
    int  value;          // ID or key value
    char name[32];       // name field if needed
}NODE;
```

A **(singly) link list** is a data structure consisting of a sequence of nodes, which are linked together by the next pointers of the nodes, i.e. each node's next pointer points to a next node in the list. Link lists are represented by NODE pointers. For example, the following C statements define two link lists, denoted by list and head.

```
    NODE *list, *head;        // define list and head as link lists
```

A link list is empty if it contains no nodes, i.e. an empty link list is just a NULL pointer. In C programming, the symbol **NULL** is defined by the macro (in stddef.h)

```
    #define NULL (void *)0
```

as a pointer with a 0 value. For convenience, we shall use either NULL or 0 to denote the null pointer. Thus, we may initialize link lists as empty by assigning them with null pointers, as in

```
        list = NULL;    // list = null pointer
        head = 0;       // head = null pointer
```

2.10.2   Link List Operations

The most common types of operations on link lists are

Build: initialize and build list with a set of nodes
Traversal: step through the elements of a list
Search: search for an element by key
Insertion: insert new elements into a list
Deletion: delete an existing element from a list
Reorder: reorder a link list by (changed) element key or priority value

In the following, we shall develop C programs to demonstrate list processing.

2.10.3 Build Link List

In many C programming books, dynamic data structures are usually constructed with data objects that are dynamically allocated by the C library function **malloc()**. In these cases, data objects are allocated from the program's **heap** area. This is fine, but some books seem to over emphasize the notion that dynamic data structures must use malloc(), which is false. Unlike static data structures, such as arrays, in which the number of elements is fixed, dynamic data structures consists of data objects that can be modified with ease, such as to insert new data objects, delete existing data objects and reorder the data objects, etc. It has nothing to do with where the data objects are located, which can be in either the program's data area or heap area. We shall clarify and demonstrate this point in the following example programs.

2.10.3.1 Link List in Data Area

Example Program C2.1: This program builds a link list from an array of node structures. The program consists of a type.h header file and a C2.1.c file, which contains the main() function.

(1). **type.h file**: First, we write a type.h file, which includes the standard header files, defines the constant N and the NODE type. The same type.h file will be used as an included file in all list processing example programs.

```
/********** type.h file ***********/
#include <stdio.h>
#include <stdlib.h>
#include <string.h>

#define N 10

typedef struct node{
  struct node *next;
  int  id;
  char name[64];

}NODE;
/******* end of type.h file *******/
```

(2). **C2.1 Program code:** The program constructs a link list and prints the link list.

```
/********************** C2.1.c file **********************/
#include "type.h"

NODE *mylist, node[N]; // in bss section of program run-time image

int printlist(NODE *p) // print list function
{
   while(p){
     printf("[%s %d]->", p->name, p->id);
     p = p->next;
```

```
  }
  printf("NULL\n");
}


int main()
{
  int i;
  NODE *p;
  for (i=0; i<N; i++){
     p = &node[i];
     sprintf(p->name, "%s%d", "node", i); // node0, node1, etc.
     p->id = i;                // used node index as ID
     p->next = p+1;            // node[i].next = &node[i+1];
  }
  node[N-1].next = 0;
  mylist = &node[0];           // mylist points to node[0]
  printlist(mylist);           // print mylist elements
}
```

(4). Explanation of the C2.1.c code

(4).1. Memory location of variables: The following diagram shows the memory location of the variables, which are all in the program's Data area. More precisely, they are in the bss section of the combined program Data area.

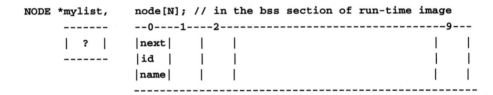

(4).2. The main() function: The main() function builds a link list with node names = "node0" to "node9" and node id values=0 to 9. The link list ends with a null pointer. Note that the list pointer and list elements are all in the array of node[N], which is the program's data area.

(5). Run Results: The reader may compile and run the C2.1 program. It should print the list as

```
    [node0 0]->[ndoe1 1]-> ... [node9 9]->NULL
```


2.10.3.2 Link List in Heap Area

Example C2.2: The next example program, C2.2, builds a link list in the program's **heap area**.

```
/*************** C2.2.c file ****************/
#include "type.h"


NODE *mylist, *node;    // pointers, no NODE area yet


int printlist(NODE *p){ // same as in C2.1 }
```

```
int main()
{
  int i;
  NODE *p;
  node = (NODE *)malloc(N*sizeof(NODE)); // node->N*72 bytes in HEAP
  for (i=0; i < N; i++){
    p = &node[i];            // access each NODE area in HEAP
    sprintf(p->name, "%s%d", "node",i);
    p->id = i;
    p->next = p+1;           // node[i].next = &node[i+1];
  }
  node[N-1].next = 0;
  mylist = &node[0];
  printlist(mylist);
}
```

(1). Memory location of variables: In the C2.2 program, both the variables mylist and node are NODE pointers, which are uninitialized globals. As such they are in the program's bss section, as shown in Fig. 2.21. The program does not have any memory locations for the actual node structures.

NODE *mylist, *node;   // pointers, no NODE area yet

When the program starts, it uses the statement

node = (NODE *)malloc(N*sizeof(NODE));

to allocate N*72 bytes in the program's HEAP area, which will be used as nodes of the list. Since node is a NODE pointer, which points to a memory area containing N adjacent nodes, we may regard the memory area as an array and use node[i] (i=0 to N-1) to access each node element. This is a general principle. Whenever we have a pointer pointing to a memory area containing N adjacent data objects, we may access the memory area as a sequence of array elements. As a further example, assume

int *p = (int *)malloc(N*sizeof(int));

Then the memory area pointed by p can be accessed as *(p + i) or p[i], i=0 to N-1.

Fig. 2.21 Variables in BSS section

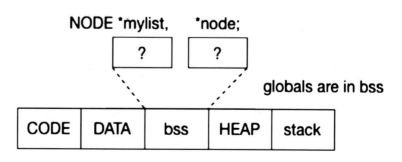

Example C2.3: The example program C2.3 builds a link list in the program's heap area but with individually allocated nodes.

```
/*************** C2.3.c file ****************/
#include "type.h"

NODE *mylist, *node;      // pointers, no NODE area yet

int printlist(NODE *p){ // same as in L1.c }

int main()
{
  int i;
  NODE *p, *q;
  for (i=0; i < N; i++){
      p = (NODE *)malloc(sizeof(NODE));   // allocate a node in heap
      sprintf(p->name, "%s%d", "node",i);
      p->id = i;
      p->next = 0;         // node[i].next = 0;
      if (i==0){
          mylist = q = p; // mylist -> node0; q->current node
      }
      q->next = p;
      q = p;
  }
  printlist(mylist);
}
```

2.10.4 Link List Traversal

Link list traversal is to step through the list elements in sequential order. The simplest link list traversal is to print the list elements. To do this, we may implement a generic printlist() function as follows.

```
int printlist(char *listname, NODE *list)
{
   printf("%s = ", name);
   while(list){
     printf("[%s %d]->", list->name, list->id);
     list = list->next;
   }
   printf("NULL\n");
}
```

Alternatively, the printlist() function can be implemented by recursion.

```
void rplist(NODE *p)
{
   if (p == 0){
```

```
       printf("NULL\n");
       return;
   }
   printf("[%s %d]->", p->name, p->id);
   rplist(p->next);           // recursive call to rplist(p->next)
}


int printlist(char *listname, NODE *list)
{
   printf("%s = ", name);    // print list name
   rplist(list);             // recursively print each element
}
```

In addition to printing a link list, there are many other list operations that are essentially variations of the list traversal problem. Here we cite such a problem, which is a favorite question during interviews for Computer Science jobs.

This example implements a function which computes the SUM of the node values in a link list.

```
int sum(NODE *list) // return SUM of node values in a link list
{
    int sum = 0;
    while(list){
       sum += list->value;   // add value of current node
       list = list->next;    // step to next node
    }
    return sum;
}
```

Alternatively, the sum() function can be implemented recursively, as in

```
int sum(NODE *list) // return SUM of node values in a link list
{
    if (list == 0)
       return 0;
    return list->value + sum(list->next);
}
```

Using the **? operator** of C, this can be simplified further as

```
int sum(NODE *list)
{ return (list==0)? 0: list->value + sum(list->next); }
```

When traversing a singly link list using a single node pointer, we can only access the current node but not the previous node. A simple way to remedy this problem is to use two pointers while traversing a link list. We illustrate this technique by an example.

Traversing a (singly) link list with two pointers.

```
NODE *p, *q;
p = q = list;          // both p and q start form list
while(p){
    // access current node by p AND previous node by q
    q = p;             // let q point at current node
    p = p->next;       // advance p to next node
}
```

In the above code segment, p points at the current node and q points at the previous node, if any. This allows us to access both the current and previous nodes. This technique can be used in such operations as to delete the current node, insert before the current node, etc.

2.10.5 Search Link List

The search operation searches a link list for an element with a given key, which can be either an integer value or a string. It returns a pointer to the element if it exists, or NULL if not. Assuming that the key is an integer value, we can implement a search() function as follows.

```
NODE *search(NODE *list, int key)
{
    NODE *p = list;
    while(p){
      if (p->key == key)  // found element with key
          return p;       // return node pointer
      p = p->next;        // advance p to next node
    }
    return 0;             // not found, return 0
}
```

2.10.6 Insert Operation

The insert operation inserts a new element into a link list by a specified criterion. For singly link lists, the simplest insertion is to insert to the end of a list. This amounts to traversing the list to the last element and then adding a new element to the end. We illustrate this by an example.

Example C2.4: The example program C2.4 builds a link list by inserting new nodes to the end of list.

(1) **The insertion function:** The insert() function enters a new node pointer p into a list. Since the insert operation may modify the list itself, we must pass the list parameter by reference, i.e. passing the address of the list. Normally, all elements in a link list should have unique keys. To ensure no two elements with the same key, the insert function may check this first. It should reject the insertion request if the node key already exists. We leave this as an exercise for the reader.

```
int insert(NODE **list, NODE *p) // insert p to end of *list
{
    NODE *q = *list;
    if (q == 0)            // if list is empty:
        *list = p;         //     insert p as first element
    else{                  // otherwise, insert p to end of list
        while(q->next)     // step to LAST element
            q = q->next;
        q->next = p;       // let LAST element point to p
    }
    p->next = 0;           // p is the new last element.
}
```

(2) The C2.4.c file:

```
/**************** C2.4.c file *************/
#include "type.h"
NODE *mylist;
int main()
{
  char line[128], name[64];
  int id;
  NODE *p;
  mylist = 0;   // initialize mylist to empty list
  while(1){
     printf("enter node name and id value : ");
     fgets(line, 128, stdin);    // get an input line
     line[strlen(line)-1] = 0;   // kill \n at end
     if (line[0] == 0)           // break out on empty input line
         break;
     sscanf("%s %d", name, &id); // extract name string and id value
     p = (NODE *)malloc(sizeof(NODE));
     if (p==0) exit(-1);         // out of HEAP memory
     strcpy(p->name, name);
     p->id = id;
     insert(&mylist, p);         // insert p to list end
     printlist(mylist);
  }
}
```

2.10.7   Priority Queue

A **priority queue** is a (singly) link list ordered by priority, with high priority values in front. In a priority queue, nodes with the same priority are ordered First-In-First-Out (FIFO). We can modify the insert() function to an enqueue() function, which inserts nodes into a priority queue by priority. Assume that each node has a priority field. The following shows the enqueue() function.

```
int enqueue(NODE **queue, NODE *p) // insert p into queue by priority
{
   NODE *q = *queue;
   if (q==0 || p->priority > q->priority){
      *queue = p;
      p->next = q;
   }
   else{
      while(q->next && p->priority <= q->next->priority)
         q = q->next;
      p->next = q->next;
      q->next = p;
   }
}
```

2.10.8 Delete Operation

Given a link list and a list element key, delete the element from the list if it exists. Since the delete operation may modify the list, the list parameter must be passed by reference. Here we assume the element key is an integer. The delete() function returns the deleted node pointer, which can be used to free the node if it was dynamically allocated earlier.

```
NODE *delete(NODE **list, int key)
{
  NODE *p, *q;
  if (*list == 0)            // empty list
      return 0;              // return 0 if deletion failed
  p = *list;
  if (p->key == key){        // found element at list beginning
    *list = p->next;         // modify *list
    return p;
  }
  // element to be deleted is not the first one; try to find it
  q = p->next;
  while(q){
    if (q->key == key){
       p->next = q->next;  // delete q from list
       return q;
    }
    p = q;
    q = q->next;
  }
  return 0;                  // failed to find element
}
```

Fig. 2.22 Circular link list

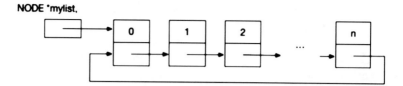

2.10.9   Circular Link List

A circular link list is one in which the last element points to the first element. As usual, an empty circular link list is a NULL pointer. Figure 2.22 shows a circular link list.

When traversing a circular list, we must detect the "end of list" condition properly to terminate the traversal. Assume that list is a non-empty circular list.

```
NODE *list, *p = list;
while(p->next != list){    // stop after last element
    // access current node p;
    p = p->next;
}
```

2.10.10 Open-Ended C Structures

In the original C language, all members of a structure must be fully specified so that the size of every structure is fixed at compile time. In practice, there are situations in which the size of a structure may vary. For convenience, the C language is extended to support **open-ended structures** containing an incompletely specified field. As an example, consider the following structure, in which the last member is an array of unspecified size.

```
struct node{
    struct node *next;
    int ID;
    char name[ ];   // unspecified array size
};
```

In the above open-ended structure, name[ ] denotes an incompletely specified field, which must be the last entry. The size of an open-ended structure is determined by the specified fields. For the above example, the structure size is 8 bytes. To use such a structure, the user must allocate the needed memory for the actual structure, as in

```
struct node *sp = malloc(sizeof(struct node) + 32);
strcpy(sp->name, "this is a test string");
```

The first line allocates a memory area of 8+32 bytes, with 32 bytes intended for the field name. The next line copies a string into the name field in the allocated memory area. What if the user does not allocate memory for an open-ended structure and use them directly? The following code lines illustrate the possible consequences.

```
    struct node x;                // define a variable x of size only 8 bytes
    strcpy(x.name, "test");       // copy "test" into x.name field
```

In this case, x has only 8 bytes but there is no memory area for the name field. The second statement would copy the string "test" into the memory area immediately following x at run-time, overwriting whatever was in it. This may corrupt other data objects of the program, causing it to crash later.

2.10.11 Doubly Link Lists

A doubly link list, or **dlist** for short, is one in which the list elements are linked together in two directions, both forward and backward. In a dlist, each element has two pointers, denoted by next and prev, as shown below.

```
    typedef struct node{
        struct node *next;    // pointer to next node
        struct node *prev;    // pointer to previous node
        // other fields, e.g. key, name, etc.
    }NODE;                    // list NODE type
```

In the node structure of dlist, the next pointer points to a next node, allowing forward traversal of the dlist from left to right. The prev pointer points to a previous node, allowing backward traversal of the dlist from right to left. Unlike a singly link list, which is represented by a single NODE pointer, doubly link lists may be represented in three different ways, each with its advantages and disadvantages. In this section, we shall use example programs to show doubly link list operations, which include

(1). Build dlist by inserting new elements to the end of list.
(2). Build dlist by inserting new elements to the front of list.
(4). Print dlist in both forward and backward directions.
(5). Search dlist for an element with a given key.
(6). Delete element from dlist.

2.10.12 Doubly Link Lists Example Programs

Example Program C2.5: Doubly Link List Version 1
In the first dlist example program, we shall assume that a dlist is represented by a single NODE pointer, which points to the first list element, if any. Figure 2.23 shows such a dlist.

Since the first element has no predecessor, its prev pointer must be NULL. Likewise, the last element has no successor, its next pointer must be NULL also. An empty dlist is just a NULL pointer. The following lists the C code of the example program C2.5.

```
/********** dlist Program C2.5.c **********/
#include <stdio.h>
#include <stdlib.h>
#include <string.h>
```

Fig. 2.23 Doubly link list
version 1

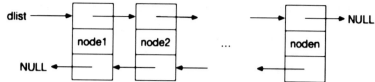

```
typedef struct node{
  struct node *next;
  struct node *prev;
  int key;
}NODE;
NODE *dlist;          // dlist is a NODE pointer

int insert2end(NODE **list, int key) // insert to list END
{
  NODE *p, *q;
  //printf("insert2end: key=%d ", key);
  p = (NODE *)malloc(sizeof(NODE));
  p->key = key;
  p->next = 0;
  q = *list;
  if (q==0){            // list empty
    *list = p;
    p->next = p->prev = 0;
  }
  else{
    while(q->next)      // step to LAST element
      q = q->next;
    q->next = p;        // add p as last element
    p->prev = q;
  }
}


int insert2front(NODE **list, int key) // insert to list FRONT
{
  NODE *p, *q;
  //printf("insert2front: key=%d ", key);
  p = (NODE *)malloc(sizeof(NODE));
  p->key = key;
  p->prev = 0;          // no previous node
  q = *list;
  if (q==0){            // list empty
    *list = p;
    p->next = 0;
  }
  else{
    p->next = *list;
    q->prev = p;
    *list = p;
  }
}
```

```
void printForward(NODE *list) // print list forward
{
  printf("list forward =");
  while(list){
    printf("[%d]->", list->key);
    list = list->next;
  }
  printf("NULL\n");
}


void printBackward(NODE *list) // print list backward
{
  printf("list backward=");
  NODE *p = list;
  if (p){
    while (p->next)     // step to last element
      p = p->next;
    while(p){
      printf("[%d]->", p->key);
      p = p->prev;
    }
  }
  printf("NULL\n");
}


NODE *search(NODE *list, int key) // search for an element with a key
{
  NODE *p = list;
  while(p){
    if (p->key==key){
      printf("found %d at %x\n", key, (unsigned int)p);
      return p;
    }
    p = p->next;
  }
  return 0;
}


int delete(NODE **list, NODE *p) // delete an element pointed by p
{
  NODE *q = *list;
  if (p->next==0 && p->prev==0){          // p is the only node
    *list = 0;
  }
  else if (p->next==0 && p->prev != 0){ // last but NOT first
    p->prev->next = 0;
  }
  else if (p->prev==0 && p->next != 0){ // first but NOT last
    *list = p->next;
    p->next->prev = 0;
```

```
  }
  else{                                  // p is an interior node
     p->prev->next = p->next;
     p->next->prev = p->prev;
  }
  free(p);
}


int main()
{
  int i, key;
  NODE *p;
  printf("dlist program #1\n");

  printf("insert to END\n");
  dlist = 0;                    // initialize dlist to empty
  for (i=0; i<8; i++){
     insert2end(&dlist, i);
  }
  printForward(dlist);
  printBackward(dlist);

  printf("insert to FRONT\n");
  dlist = 0;                    // initialize dlist to empty
  for (i=0; i<8; i++){
     insert2front(&dlist, i);
  }
  printForward(dlist);
  printBackward(dlist);

  printf("test delete\n");
   while(1){
    printf("enter a key to delete: ");
    scanf("%d", &key);
    if (key < 0) exit(0);     // exit if negative key
    p = search(dlist, key);
    if (p==0){
       printf("key %d not found\n", key);
       continue;
    }
    delete(&dlist, p);
    printForward(dlist);
    printBackward(dlist);
  }
}
```

Figure 2.24 show the outputs of running the Example program C2.5. First, it constructs a dlist by inserting new elements to the list end, and prints the resulting list in both forward and backward directions. Next, it constructs a dlist by inserting new elements to the list front, and prints the resulting

```
dlist program #1
insert to END
list forward =[0]->[1]->[2]->[3]->[4]->[5]->[6]->[7]->NULL
list backward=[7]->[6]->[5]->[4]->[3]->[2]->[1]->[0]->NULL
insert to FRONT
list forward =[7]->[6]->[5]->[4]->[3]->[2]->[1]->[0]->NULL
list backward=[0]->[1]->[2]->[3]->[4]->[5]->[6]->[7]->NULL
test delete
enter a key to delete: 0
found 0 at 9567088
list forward =[7]->[6]->[5]->[4]->[3]->[2]->[1]->NULL
list backward=[1]->[2]->[3]->[4]->[5]->[6]->[7]->NULL
enter a key to delete: 7
found 7 at 95670f8
list forward =[6]->[5]->[4]->[3]->[2]->[1]->NULL
list backward=[1]->[2]->[3]->[4]->[5]->[6]->NULL
enter a key to delete: 4
found 4 at 95670c8
list forward =[6]->[5]->[3]->[2]->[1]->NULL
list backward=[1]->[2]->[3]->[5]->[6]->NULL
enter a key to delete: █
```

Fig. 2.24 Outputs of example program C2.5

list in both directions. Then, it shows how to search for an element with a given key. Lastly, it shows how to delete elements from the list, and print the list after each delete operation to verify the results.

Discussions of Example C2.5: The primary advantage of the first version of dlist is that it only requires a single NODE pointer to represent a dlist. The disadvantages of this kind of dlist are:

(1). It is hard to access the last element of the list. In order to access the last element, as in the cases of inserting to the list end and print the list backward, we must use the next pointer to step to the last element first, which is time-consuming if the list has many elements.
(2). When inserting a new element, we must detect and handle the various cases of whether the list is empty or the new element is the first or last element, etc. These make the code non-uniform, which does not fully realize the capability of doubly link lists.
(3). Similarly, when deleting an element, we must detect and handle the different cases also.

As can be seen, the complexity of the insertion/deletion code stems mainly from two cases:

. the list is empty, in which case we must insert the first element.
. the inserted/deleted node is the first or last node, in which case we must modify the list pointer.

Alternatively, a doubly link list may be regarded as two singly link lists merged into one. Accordingly, we may represent doubly link lists by a listhead structure containing two pointers, as in

```
typedef struct listhead{
        struct node *next;          // head node pointer
        struct node *prev;          // tail node pointer
    }DLIST;                         // doubly link list type
    DLIST dlist;                    // dlsit is a structure
    dlist.next = dlist.prev = 0; // initialize dlist as empty
```

Figure 2.25 show the second version of doubly link lists.

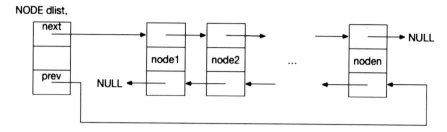

Fig. 2.25 Doubly link list version 2

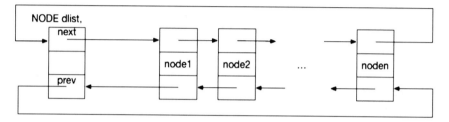

Fig. 2.26 Doubly link list version 3

The only advantage of using a list head structure is that it allows direct access to the last element via the list's prev pointer. The disadvantages are exactly the same as those in the first version of dlist. Specifically,

(1) Since dlist is a structure, it must be passed by reference to all list operation functions.
(2) In both the insertion and deletion functions, we must detect and handle the various cases of whether the list is empty, the element is the first or last element, etc. In these cases, doubly link lists are no better than singly link list in terms of processing time.

In order to realize the capability of doubly link lists, we need a better way to represent doubly link lists. In the next example, we shall define doubly lists as follows. A dlist is represented by a listhead, which is a NODE structure but a dlist is initialized with both pointers to the listhead, as in

```
NODE dlist;                        //  dlist is a NODE structure
dlist.next = dlist.prev = &dlist;  //  initialize both pointers to the NODE
                                   //  structure
```

Such a dlist may be regarded as two circular link lists merged into one, with the listhead as the initial dummy element. Figure 2.26 shows such a doubly link list.

Since there are no null pointers in the Version 3 dlist, every node can be treated as an interior node, which greatly simplifies the list operation code. We demonstrate this kind of dlist by an example.

Example Program C2.6: This example program assumes a dlist is represented by a NODE structure, which is initialized with both pointers to the NODE structure itself.

```
/************* C2.6.c Program Code ************/
#include <stdio.h>
#include <stdlib.h>
#include <string.h>
```

```
typedef struct node{
  struct node *next;
  struct node *prev;
  int key;
}NODE;
```

NODE dlist; // dlist is NODE struct using only next & prev pointers

int insert2end(NODE *list, int key)
```
{
  NODE *p, *q;
  //printf("insert2end: key=%d\n", key);
  p = (NODE *)malloc(sizeof(NODE));
  p->key = key;
  p->prev = 0;

  q = list->prev;        // to LAST element
  p->next = q->next;
  q->next->prev = p;
  q->next = p;
  p->prev = q;
}
```

int insert2front(NODE *list, int key)
```
{
  NODE *p, *q;
  //printf("insertFront key=%d\n", key);
  p = (NODE *)malloc(sizeof(NODE));
  p->key = key;
  p->prev = 0;

  q = list->next;      // to first element
  p->prev = q->prev;
  q->prev->next = p;
  q->prev = p;
  p->next = q;
}
```

void printForward(NODE *list)
```
{
  NODE *p = list->next;    // use dlist's next pointer
  printf("list forward =");
  while(p != list){          // detect end of list
    printf("[%d]->", p->key);
    p = p->next;
  }
  printf("NULL\n");
}
```

```
void printBackward(NODE *list)
{
  printf("list backward=");
  NODE *p = list->prev;      // use dlist's prev pointer
  while(p != list){          // detect end of list
    printf("[%d]->", p->key);
    p = p->prev;
  }
  printf("NULL\n");
}


NODE *search(NODE *list, int key)
{
  NODE *p = list->next;
  while(p != list){          // detect end of list
    if (p->key==key){
      printf("found %d at %x\n", key, (unsigned int)p);
      return p;
    }
    p = p->next;
  }
  return 0;
}


int delete(NODE *list, NODE *p)
{
  p->prev->next = p->next;
  p->next->prev = p->prev;
  free(p);
}


int main()
{
  int i, key;
  NODE *p;
  printf("dlist program #3\n");

  printf("insert to END\n");
  dlist.next = dlist.prev = &dlist; // empty dlist
  for (i=0; i<8; i++){
    insert2end(&dlist, i);
  }
  printForward(&dlist);
  printBackward(&dlist);

  printf("insert to front\n");
  dlist.next = dlist.prev = &dlist; // empty dlist to begin
  for (i=0; i<8; i++){
    insert2front(&dlist, i);
  }
```

```
printForward(&dlist);
printBackward(&dlist);

printf("do deletion\n");
while(1){
  printf("enter key to delete: ");
  scanf("%d", &key);
  if (key < 0) exit(0);     // exit if key negative
  p = search(&dlist, key);
  if (p==0){
    printf("key %d not found\n", key);
    continue;
  }
  delete(&dlist, p);
  printForward(&dlist);
  printBackward(&dlist);
}
}
```

Figure 2.27 shows the outputs of running the example program C2.6. Although the outputs are identical to those of Fig. 2.24, their processing codes are very different.

The primary advantages of the Example program C2.6 are as follows. Since every node can be treated as an interior node, it is no longer necessary to detect and handle the various cases of empty list, first and last elements, etc. As a result, both insertion and deletion operations are greatly simplified. The only modification needed is to detect the end of list condition during search or list traversal by the code segment

```
NODE *p = list.next;
while (p != &list){
  p = p->next;
}
```

```
dlist program #3
insert to END
list forward =[0]->[1]->[2]->[3]->[4]->[5]->[6]->[7]->NULL
list backward=[7]->[6]->[5]->[4]->[3]->[2]->[1]->[0]->NULL
insert to front
list forward =[7]->[6]->[5]->[4]->[3]->[2]->[1]->[0]->NULL
list backward=[0]->[1]->[2]->[3]->[4]->[5]->[6]->[7]->NULL
do deletion
enter key to delete: 0
found 0 at 8a71088
list forward =[7]->[6]->[5]->[4]->[3]->[2]->[1]->NULL
list backward=[1]->[2]->[3]->[4]->[5]->[6]->[7]->NULL
enter key to delete: 7
found 7 at 8a710f8
list forward =[6]->[5]->[4]->[3]->[2]->[1]->NULL
list backward=[1]->[2]->[3]->[4]->[5]->[6]->NULL
enter key to delete: 4
found 4 at 8a710c8
list forward =[6]->[5]->[3]->[2]->[1]->NULL
list backward=[1]->[2]->[3]->[5]->[6]->NULL
enter key to delete:
```

Fig. 2.27 Outputs of example program C2.6

Fig. 2.28 A general tree

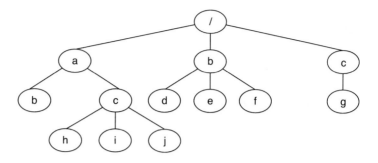

2.11   Trees

A **tree** is a dynamic data structure composed of multi-levels of linked lists. As a data structure, a tree is defined as a node, which itself consists of a value together with a list of references to other nodes. Symbolically, a tree is defined recursively as

```
node: value [&node[1], ..., &node[k]]
```

where each node[i] is itself a (possibly empty) tree. The very first node of a tree is called the **root** of the tree. Each node is called a **parent** node if it points to a list of other nodes, which are called the **children** nodes of the parent node. In a tree, each node has a unique parent, but each node may have a variable number of children nodes, including none. A tree can be represented by a diagram, which is usually drawn upside-down, with the root node at the top. Figure 2.28 shows a general tree.

2.12   Binary Tree

The simplest kind of tree is the **binary tree**, in which each node has two pointers, denoted by left and right. We may define the node type containing a single key value for binary trees as

```
typedef struct node{
        int    key;
        struct node *left;
        struct node *right;
}NODE;
```

Every general tree can be implemented as a binary tree. We shall demonstrate this in Sect. 2.13.

2.12.1   Binary Search Tree

A **Binary Search Tree (BST)** is a binary tree with the following properties:

. All node keys are distinct, i.e. the tree contains no nodes with duplicated keys.
. The left subtree of a node contains only nodes with keys less than the node's key.
. The right subtree of a node contains only nodes with keys greater than the node's key.
. Each of the left and right subtrees is also a binary search tree.

As an example, Fig. 2.29 shows a binary search tree.

Fig. 2.29 A binary
search tree

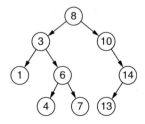

   Binary Search Tree provides an ordering among the node keys so that operations such as finding the
minimum, maximum keys and search for a given key can be done quickly. The search depth of a BST
depends on the shape of the tree. If a binary tree is balanced, i.e. every node has two children nodes, the
search depth is log2(n) for a tree with n nodes. For unbalanced BST, the worst search depth would be n,
if the nodes are all to the left or all to the right.

2.12.2 Build a Binary Search Tree (BST)

Example Program C2.7: Build a Binary Search Tree

```
/************ C2.7.c file ************/
#include <stdio.h>
#include <stdlib.h>
typedef struct node{
    int key;
    struct node *left, *right;
}NODE;
#define N 7
int nodeValue[N] = {50,30,20,40,70,60,80};
// create a new node
NODE *new_node(int key)
{
    NODE *node = (NODE *)malloc(sizeof(NODE));
    node->key = key;
    node->left = node->right = NULL;
    return node;
}
// insert a new node with given key into BST
NODE *insert(NODE *node, int key)
{
    if (node == NULL)
       return new_node(key);
    if (key < node->key)
       node->left  = insert(node->left, key);
    else if (key > node->key)
       node->right = insert(node->right, key);
    return node;
}
```

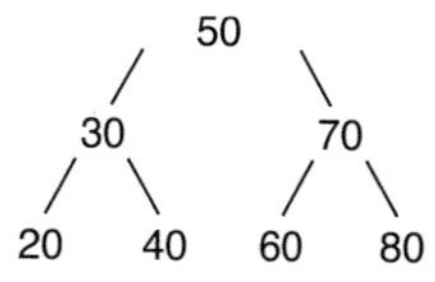

Fig. 2.30 A binary search tree

```
              50
            /    \
          30      70
         /  \    /  \
       20   40  60   80
```

```
int main()
{
  int i;
  NODE *root = NULL;
  root = insert(root, nodeValue[0]);
  for (i=1; i<N; i++){
      insert(root, nodeVlaue[i]);
  }
}
```

Figure 2.30 shows the BST generated by the Example Program C2.7.

2.12.3   Binary Tree Traversal Algorithms

From elementary data structure courses, the reader should have learned the following binary tree traversal algorithms.

. **Pre-order Traversal:** node; node.left; node.ight
. **In-order traversal:**   node.left; node; node.right
. **Post-order traversal:** node.left; node.right; node

2.12.4   Depth-First Traversal Algorithms

All the above algorithms belong to **Depth-First (DF)** search/traversal algorithms, which use a stack for back-tracking. As such, they can be implemented naturally by recursion. As an example, search a BST for a given key can be implemented by rercusion, which is basically an in-order traversal of the BST.

```
/******** Search BST for a give key ********/
NODE *search(NODE *t, int key)
{
    if (t == NULL || t->key == key)
       return t;
    if (key < t->key)                 // key is less than node key
       return search(t->left, key);
    else
       return search(t->right, key); // key is greater than node key
}
```

2.12.5 Breadth-First Traversal Algorithms

A tree can also be traversed by **Breadth-First (BF) algorithms**, which use a **queue** to store the yet to be traversal parts of the tree. When applying BF traversal algorithm to a tree, we may print the tree level by level, as shown by the next example program.

Example Program C2.8: Print Binary Tree by Levels

```c
/***** C2.8.c file: print binary tree by levels *****/
#include <stdio.h>
#include <stdlib.h>

typedef struct node{
    struct node *left;
    int key;
    struct node *right;
}NODE;

typedef struct qe{        // queue element structure
    struct qe    *next;  // queue pointer
    struct node  *node;  // queue contents
}QE;                      // queue element type

int enqueue(QE **queue, NODE *node)
{
  QE *q = *queue;
  QE *r = (QE *)malloc(sizeof(QE));
  r->node = node;
  if (q == 0)
     *queue = r;
  else{
    while (q->next)
       q = q->next;
    q->next = r;
  }
  r->next = 0;
}


NODE *dequeue(QE **queue)
{
  QE *q = *queue;
  if (q)
     *queue = q->next;
  return q->node;
}

int qlength(QE *queue)
{
  int n = 0;
```

```
    while (queue){
      n++;
      queue = queue->next;
    }
    return n;
}


// print a binary tree by levels, each level on a line
void printLevel(NODE *root)
{
    int nodeCount;
    if (root == NULL) return;
    QE queue = 0;              // create a FIFO queue
    enqueue(&queue, root);     // start with root
    while(1){
        nodeCount = qlength(queue);
        if (nodeCount == 0) break;
        // dequeue nodes of current level, enqueue nodes of next level
        while (nodeCount > 0){
            NODE *node = dequeue(&queue);
            printf("%d ", node->key);
            if (node->left != NULL)
                enqueue(&queue, node->left);
            if (node->right != NULL)
                enqueue(&queue, node->right);
            nodeCount--;
        }
        printf("\n");
    }
}
NODE *newNode(int key) // create a new node
{
    NODE *t = (NODE *)malloc(sizeof(NODE));
    t->key = key;
    t->left = NULL;
    t->right = NULL;
    return t;
}
int main()  // driver program to test printLevel()
{
    queue = 0;
    // create a simple binary tree
    NODE *root = newNode(1);
    root->left = newNode(2);
    root->right = newNode(3);
    root->left->left = newNode(4);
    root->left->right = newNode(5);
    root->right->leftt = newNode(6);
    root->right->right = 0; // right child = 0
    printLevel(root);
    return 0;
}
```

In the example program C2.8, each queue element has a next pointer and a NODE pointer to the node in the tree. The tree will be traversed but not altered in anyway; only its nodes (pointers) will be used in queue elements, which are entered into and removed from the queue. The printLevel() function starts with the root node in the queue. For each iteration, it dequeues a node of the current level, prints its key and enters the left child (if any), followed by the right child (if any), into the queue. The iteration ends when the queue becomes empty. For the simple binary tree constructed in main(), the program outputs are

```
            1
            2 3
            4 5 6
```

which print each level of the tree on a separate line.

2.13 Programming Project: Unix/Linux File System Tree Simulator

Summarizing the background information on C structures, link list processing and binary trees, we are ready to integrate these concepts and techniques into a programming project to solve a practical problem. The programming project is to design and implement a Unix/Linux file system tree simulator.

2.13.1 Unix/Linux File System Tree

The logical organization of a Unix file system is a general tree, as shown in the Fig. 2.28. Linux file systems are organized in the same way, so the discussions here apply to Linux files systems also. The file system tree is usually drawn upside down, with the root node / at the top. For simplicity, we shall assume that the file system contains only directories (DIRs) and regular FILEs, i.e. no special files, which are I/O devices. A DIR node may have a variable number of **children nodes**. Children nodes of the same parent are called **siblings**. In a Unix/Linux file system, each node is represented by a unique **pathname** of the form /a/b/c or a/b/c. A pathname is **absolute** if it begins with /, indicating that it starts from the root. Otherwise, it is relative to the **Current Working Directory** (CWD).

2.13.2 Implement General Tree by Binary Tree

A general tree can be implemented as a binary tree. For each node, let childPtr point to the oldest child, and siblingPtr point to the oldest sibling. For convenience, each node also has a parentPtr pointing to its parent node. For the **root node**, both parentPtr and siblingPtr point to itself. As an example, Fig. 2.31 shows a binary tree which is equivalent to the general tree of Fig. 2.28. In Fig. 2.31, thin lines represent childPtr pointers and thick lines represent siblingPtr. For clarify, NULL pointers are not shown.

2.13.3 Project Specification and Requirements

The project is to design and implement a C program to simulate the Unix/Linux file system tree. The program should work as follows.

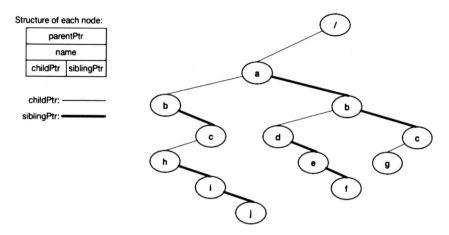

Fig. 2.31 Implementation of general tree by binary tree

(1). Start with a / node, which is also the Current Working Directory (CWD).
(2). Prompt the user for a command. Valid commands are:
   mkdir, rmdir, cd, ls, pwd, creat, rm, save, reload, menu, quit
(3). Execute the command, with appropriate tracing messages.
(4). Repeat (2) until the "quit" command, which terminates the program.

2.13.4   Commands Specification

mkdir pathname :make a new directory for a given pathname
rmdir pathname :remove the directory, if it is empty.
cd [pathname]   :change CWD to pathname, or to / if no pathname.
ls [pathname]   :list the directory contents of pathname or CWD
pwd   :print the (absolute) pathname of CWD
creat pathname :create a FILE node.
rm pathname   :remove the FILE node.
save filename   :save the current file system tree as a file
reload filename :construct a file system tree from a file
menu   :show a menu of valid commands
quit   :save the file system tree, then terminate the program.

2.13.5   Program Organization

There are many ways to design and implement such a simulator program. The following outlines the
suggested organization of the program.

(1) **NODE type:** Define a C structure for the NODE type containing

64 chars	: name string of the node;
char	: node type: 'D' for directory or 'F' for file
node pointers :	***childPtr, *siblingPtr, *parentPtr;**

(2) **Global Variables:**

```
NODE *root, *cwd;                   // root and CWD pointers
char line[128];                     // user input command line
char command[16], pathname[64];     // command and pathname strings
char dname[64], bname[64];          // dirname and basename string holders
(Others as needed)
```

(3) **The main() function:** The main function of the program can be sketched as follows.

```
int main()
{
  initialize();    //initialize root node of the file system tree
  while(1){
    get user input line = [command pathname];
    identify the command;
    execute the command;
    break if command="quit";
  }
}
```

(4) **Get user inputs:** Assume that each user input line contains a command with an optional pathname. The reader may use scanf() to read user inputs from stdin. A better technique is as follows

```
fgets(line, 128, stdin);   // get at most 128 chars from stdin
line[strlen(line)-1] = 0; // kill \n at end of line
sscanf(line, "%s %s", command, pathname);
```

The sscanf() function extracts items from the line[ ] area by format, which can be either chars, strings or integers. It is therefore more flexible than scanf().

(5) **Identify command:** Since each command is a string, most readers would probably try to identify the command by using strcmp() in a series of if-else-if statements, as in

```
if (!strcmp(command, "mkdir)
    mkdir(pathname);
else if (!strcmp(command, "rmdir"
    rmdir(pathname);
else if . . .
```

This requires many lines of string comparisons. A better technique is to use a command table containing command strings (pointers), which ends with a NULL pointer.

```
char *cmd[] = {"mkdir", "rmdir", "ls", "cd", "pwd", "creat", "rm",
            "reload", "save", "menu", "quit", NULL};
```

For a given command, search the command table for the command string and return its index, as shown by the following findCmd() function.

```
int findCmd(char *command)
{
    int i = 0;
    while(cmd[i]){
      if (!strcmp(command, cmd[i]))
          return i;   // found command: return index i
      i++;
    }
    return -1;        // not found: return -1
}
```

As an example, for the command = "creat",

```
int index = findCmd("creat");
```

returns the index 5, which can be used to invoke a corresponding creat() function.

(6) **The main() function:** Assume that, for each command, we have written a corresponding action function, e.g. mkdir(), rmdir(), ls(), cd(), etc. The main() function can be refined as shown below.

```
int main()
{
  int index;
  char line[128], command[16], pathname[64];
  initialize();   //initialize root node of the file system tree
  while(1){
    printf("input a commad line : ");
    fgets(line,128,stdin);
    line[strlen(line)-1] = 0;
    sscanf(line, "%s %s", command, pathname);
    index = fidnCmd(command);
    switch(index){
        case 0 : mkdir(pathname);      break;
        case 1 : rmdir(pathname);      break;
        case 2 : ls(pathname);         break;
        etc.
        default: printf("invalid command %s\n", command);
    }
  }
}
```

The program uses the command index as different cases in a switch table. This works fine if the number of commands is small. For large number of commands, it would be preferable to use a table of function pointers. Assume that we have implemented the command functions

```
    int mkdir(char *pathname){..........}
    int rmdir(char *pathname){..........}
    etc.
```

Define a **table of function pointers** containing function names in the same order as their indices, as in

```
                      0    1    2  3  4    5    6
int (*fptr[ ])(char *)={(int (*)())mkdir,rmdir,ls,cd,pwd,creat,rm,. .};
```

The linker will populate the table with the entry addresses of the functions. Given a command index, we may call the corresponding function directly, passing as parameter pathname to the function, as in

```
    int r  =  fptr[index](pathname);
```

2.13.6 Command Algorithms

Each user command invokes a corresponding action function, which implements the command. The following describes the algorithms of the action functions

mkdir pathname

(1). Break up pathname into dirname and basename, e.g.
     ABSOLUTE: pathname=/a/b/c/d. Then dirname=/a/b/c, basename=d
     RELATIVE: pathname= a/b/c/d. Then dirname=a/b/c, basename=d
(2). Search for the dirname node:
     ASSOLUTE pathname: start from /
     RELATIVE pathname: start from CWD.
         if nonexist : error messages and return FAIL
         if exist but not DIR: error message and return FAIL

(3). (dirname exists and is a DIR):
     Search for basename in (under) the dirname node:
     if already exists: error message and return FAIL;
     ADD a new DIR node under dirname;
     Return SUCCESS

rmdir pathname

(1). if pathname is absolute, start = /

     else   start = CWD, which points CWD node

(2). search for pathname node:
     tokenize pathname into components strings;
     begin from start, search for each component;
     return ERROR if fails
(3). pathname exists:
     check it's a DIR type;
     check DIR is empty; can't rmdir if NOT empty;
(4). delete node from parent's child list;

creat pathname
SAME AS mkdir except the node type is 'F'

rm pathname
SAME AS rmdir except check it's a file, no need to check for EMPTY.

cd pathname
(1). find pathname node;
(2). check it's a DIR;
(3). change CWD to point at DIR

ls pathname
(1). find pathname node
(2). list all children nodes in the form of [TYPE NAME] [TYPE NAME] . . .

pwd
Start from CWD, implement pwd by recursion:

(1). Save the name (string) of the current node
(2). Follow parentPtr to the parent node until the root node;
(3). Print the names by adding / to each name string

Save Tree to a FILE   The simulator program builds a file system tree in memory. When the program exits, all memory contents will be lost. Rather than building a new tree every time, we may save the current tree as a file, which can be used to restore the tree later. In order to save the current tree as a file, we need to open a file for write mode. The following code segment shows how to open a file stream for writing, and then write (text) lines to it.

```
FILE *fp = fopen("myfile", "w+");   // fopen a FILE stream for WRITE
fprintf(fp, "%c %s", 'D', "string\n"); // print a line to file
fclose(fp);                         // close FILE stream when done
```

save(filename)   This function save the absolute pathnames of the tree as (text) lines in a file opened for WRITE. Assume that the file system tree is as shown in Fig. 2.32.

```
type    pathname
----    -------
 D         /
 D        /A
 F        /A/x
 F        /A/y
 D        /B
 F        /B/z
 D        /C
 D       /C/E
```

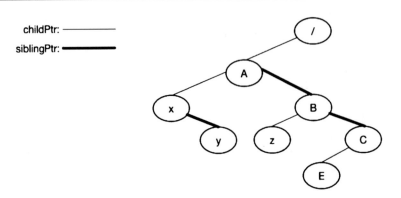

Fig. 2.32 A file system tree
where uppercase names A,
B, C, E are DIRs and
lowercase names x, y, z are
FILEs. The tree can be
represented by the (text)
lines

The pathnames are generated by **PRE-ORDER traversal** of a binary tree:

```
print node        name;     // current node
print node.left   name;     // left pointer = childPtr
print node.right  name;     // right pointer = siblingPtr
```

Each print function prints the absolute pathname of a node, which is essentially the same as pwd(). Since the root node always exists, it can be omitted from the save file.

reload(filename) The function reconstructs a tree from a file. First, initialize the tree as empty, i.e. with only the root node. Then read each line of the file. If the line contains "D pathname", call

mkdir(pathname) to make a directory.

If the line contains "F pathname", call

creat(pathname) to create a file.

These will reconstruct the tree saved earlier.

Quit Command save the current tree to a file. Then terminate the program execution.

On subsequent runs of the simulator program, the user may use the reload command to restore the tree saved earlier.

(8). Additional Programming HELP
(8).1. Tokenize pathname into components: Given a pathname, e.g. "/a/b/c/d", the following code segment shows how to tokenize pathname into component strings.

```
int tokenize(char *pathname)
{
  char *s;
  s = strtok(path, "/");  // first call to strtok()
  while(s){
    printf("%s ", s);
    s = strtok(0, "/");   // call strtok() until it returns NULL
  }
}
```

The strtok() function divides a string into substrings by the specified delimiter char "/". The substrings reside in the original string, thus destroying the original string. In order to preserve the original pathname, the user must pass a copy of pathname to the strtok() function. In order to access the tokenized substrings, the user must ensure that they are accessible by one of the following schemes.

. The copied pathname is a global variable, e.g. char path[128], which contains the tokenized substrings.
. If the copied pathname path[ ] is local in a function, access the substrings only in the function

(8).2. dir_name and base_name: For the simulator program, it is also often necessary to decompose a pathname into dir_name, and base_name, where dir_name is the directory part of pathname and base_name is the last component of pathname. As an example, if pathname="/a/b/c", then dir_name="/a/b" and base_name="c". This can be done by the library functions dirname() and basename(), both of which destroy the pathname also. The following code segments show how to decompose a pathname into dir_name and base_name.

```
#include <libgen.h>
char dname[64], bname[64]; // for decomposed dir_name and base_name

int dbname(char *pathname)
{
  char temp[128];   // dirname(), basename() destroy original pathname
  strcpy(temp, pathname);
  strcpy(dname, dirname(temp));
  strcpy(temp, pathname);
  strcpy(bname, basename(temp));
}
```

2.13.7   Sample Solution

Sample solution of the programming project is available online at the book's website for download. Source code of the project solution is available to instructors upon request from the author.

2.14   Summary

This chapter covers the background information needed for systems programming. It introduces several GUI based text editors, such as vim, gedit and EMACS, to allow readers to edit files. It shows how to use the EMACS editor in both command and GUI mode to edit, compile and execute C programs. It explains program development steps. These include the compile-link steps of GCC, static and dynamic linking, format and contents of binary executable files, program execution and termination. It explains function call conventions and run-time stack usage in detail. These include parameter passing, local variables and stack frames. It also shows how to link C programs with assembly code. It covers the GNU make facility and shows how to write makefiles by examples. It shows how to use the GDB debugger to debug C programs. It points out the common errors in C programs and suggests ways to prevent such errors during program development. Then it covers advanced programming techniques. It describes structures and pointer in C. It covers link lists and list processing by detailed examples. It covers binary trees and tree traversal algorithms. The chapter cumulates with a programming project, which is for the reader to implement a binary tree to simulate operations in the Unix/Linux file system tree. The project starts with a single root directory node. It supports mkdir, rmdir, creat, rm, cd, pwd, ls operations, saving the file system tree as a file and restoring the file system tree from saved file. The project allows the reader to apply and practice the programming techniques of tokenizing strings, parsing user commands and using function pointers to invoke functions for command processing.

Problems

1. Refer to the assembly code generated by GCC in Sect. 2.5.1. While in the function A(int x, int y), show how to access parameters x and y:
2. Refer to Example 1 in Sect. 2.5.2, Write assembly code functions to get CPU's ebx, ecx, edx, esi and edi registers.
3. Assume: The Intel x86 CPU registers CX=N, BX points to a memory area containing N integers. The following code segments implements a simple loop in assembly, which loads AX with each successive element of the integer array.

```
loop:   movl   (%ebx), %eax    # AX = *BX (consider BX as int * in C)
        addl   $4, %ebx         # ++BX
        subl   $1, %ecx         # CX--;
        jne                     # jump to loop if CX NON-zero
```

Implement a function int Asum(int *a, int N) in assembly, which computes and returns the sum of N integers in the array int a[N]. Test your Asum() function by

```
int a[100], N = 100;
int main()
{
    int i, sum;
    for (i=0; i<N; i++) // set a[] values to 1 to 100
        a[i] = i+1;
    sum = Asum(a, N);   // a[] is an int array, a is int *
    printf("sum = %d\n", sum);
}
```

The value of sum should be 5050.
4. Every C program must have a main() function.
   (1) Why?
   (2) The following program consists of a t.c file in C and a ts.s file in 32-bit assembly. The program's main() function is written in assssembly, which calls mymain() in C. The program is compile-linked by

```
gcc -m32 ts.s t.c
```

It is run as **a.out one two three.**

```
# ******* ts.s file *******
        .global main, mymain      # int mymain() is in C
main:   pushl %ebp
        movl  %esp, %ebp
(2).1:  WRITE assembly CODE TO call mymain(argc, argv, env)
        call mymain
        leave
        ret


/*********** t.c file of a C program ************/
int mymain(int argc, char *argv[], char *env[ ])
{
    int i;
    printf("argc=%d\n", argc);
    i = 0;
    while(argv[i]){
      printf("argv[%d] = %s\n", i, argv[i]);
      i++;
    }
(2).2: WRITE C code to print all env[ ] strings
 }
```

Complete the missing code at the labels (2).1 and (2).2 to make the program work.

5. In the Makefile Example 5 of Sect. 2.7.3, the suffix rule

```
.s.o: # build each .o file if its .s file has changed
        ${AS} -a $< -o $*.o > $*.map
```

$(AS) –a tells the assembler to generate an assembly listing, which is redirected to a map file. Assume that the PMTX Kernel directory contains the following assembly code files:

```
    entry.s, init.s, traps.s, ts.s
```

What are the file names of the resulting .o and .map files?

6. Refer to the Insertion function in Sect. 2.10.6. Rewrite the insert() function to ensure there are no duplicated keys in the link list.

7. Refer to the delete() function in Sect. 2.10.8. Rewrite the delete() function as

```
        NODE *delete(NODE **list, NODE *p)
```

which deletes a given node pointed by p from list..

8. The following diagram shows a Multilevel Priority Queue (MPQ).
   (1) Design a data structure for a MPQ.
   (2) Design and implement an algorithm to insert a queue element with a priority between 1 and n into a MPQ.

9. Assume that a Version 1 doubly link list is represented by a single NODE pointer, as in the Example Program C2.5 in Sect. 2.10.12.
   (1). Implement a insertAfter(NODE **dlist, NODE *p, int key) function, which inserts a new node with a given key into a dlist AFTER a given node p. If p does not exist, e.g. p=0, insert to the list end.

(2). Implement a insertBefore(NODE **dlist, NODE *p, int key) function, which inserts a new node with a given key BEFORE the node p. If p does not exist, e.g. p=0, insert to the list front.

(3). Write a complete C program, which builds a dlist by the insertAfter() and insertBefore() functions.

10. Assume that a Version 2 doubly link list is represented by a list head structure.

(1). Implement a insertAfter(NODE *dlist, NODE *p, int key) function, which inserts a new node with a given key into a dlist AFTER a given node p. If p does not exist, insert to the list end.

(2). Implement a insertBefore(NODE *dlist, NODE *p, int key) function, which inserts a new node with a given key BEFORE the node p. If p does not exist, insert to list front.

(3). Write a complete C program, which builds a dlist by the insertAfter() and insertBefore() functions.

11. Assume that a doubly link list is represented by an initialized listhead as in Example Program C2.6.

(1). Implement a insertBefore(NODE *dlist, NODE *p, NODE *new) function, which inserts a new node into a dlist BEFORE an existing node p.

(2). Implement a insertAfter(NODE *dlist, NODE *p, NODE *new) function, which inserts a new node into a dlist AFTER an existing node p.

(3). Write a complete C program to build a dlist by using the insertAfter() and insertBefore() functions.

12. Refer to the binary search tree (BST) program C2.7 in Sect. 2.9.2.

(1) Prove that the insert() function does not insert nodes with the same key twice.

(2) Rewrite the main() function, which builds a BST by keys generated by rand() % 100, so that the keys are in the range of [0-99]

13. A shortcoming of the print tree by level program in Sect. 2.10.1.is that it does not show whether any child node is NULL. Modify the program to print a '-' if any child node is NULL.

14. For the Programming Project, implement a rename command, which changes the name of a node in the file tree.

```
rename(char *pathname, char *newname)
```

15. For the Programming project, design and implement a mv command, which moves pathname1 to pathname2

```
mv(char *pathname1, char *pathname2);
```

16. For the Programming Project, discuss whether we can use IN-ORDER or POST-ORDER traversal to save and reconstruct a binary tree.

References

Debugging with GDB, https://ftp.gnu.org/Manuals/gdb/html_node/gdb_toc.html, 2002

Linux vi and vim editor, http://www.yolinux.com/TUTORIALS/LinuxTutorialAdvanced_vi.html, 2017

GDB: The GND Project Debugger, www.gnu.org/software/gdb/, 2017

GNU Emacs, https://www.gnu.org/s/emacs, 2015

GNU make, https://www.gnu.org/software/make/manual/make.html, 2008

Wang, K. C., Design and Implementation of the MTX Operating system, Springer A.G, 2015

Youngdale, E. The ELF Object File Format: Introduction, Linux Journal, April, 1995

Process Management in Unix/Linux

3

Abstract

This chapter covers process management in Unix/Linux. It explains the principle of multitasking and introduces the process concept. It uses a programming example to illustrate the principles and techniques of multitasking, context switching and processes. The multitasking system supports dynamic process creation, process termination, process synchronization by sleep and wakeup, process relations and implementation of process family tree as a binary tree, allowing parent process to wait for child process termination. It provides a concrete example of how process management functions work in an operating system kernel. Then it explains the origin of processes in Unix/Linux, from the initial process during booting to INIT process, daemon processes, login processes and sh process for user command execution. Next, it explains the execution modes of processes, transitions from User mode to Kernel mode by interrupts, exceptions and system calls. Then it describes Unix/Linux system calls for process management, which include fork, wait, exec and exit. It explains the relationship between parent and child processes, including a detailed description between process termination and the wait operation by parent process. It explains how to handle orphan processes by the INIT process, including subreaper processes in current Linux, and it demonstrates subreaper process by example. Then it explains changing process execution image by exec in detail, which includes the execve system call, command-line parameters and environment variables. It explains the principles and techniques of I/O redirections, pipes and shows pipe programming by examples. The programming project of this chapter is for the reader to integrate the concepts and techniques of process management to implement a sh simulator for command execution. The sh simulator works exactly the same as the standard sh. It supports executions of simple commands, commands with I/O redirections and multiple commands connected by pipes.

3.1 Multitasking

In general, multitasking refers to the ability of performing several independent activities at the same time. For example, we often see people talking on their cell phones while driving. In a sense, these people are doing multitasking, although a very bad kind. In computing, multitasking refers to the execution of several independent tasks at the same time. In a uniprocessor (single CPU) system, only

© Springer International Publishing AG, part of Springer Nature 2018

K. C. Wang, *Systems Programming in Unix/Linux*, https://doi.org/10.1007/978-3-319-92429-8_3

one task can execute at a time. Multitasking is achieved by multiplexing the CPU's execution time among different tasks, i.e. by switching the CPU's execution from one task to another. The mechanism of switching executions among different tasks is called context switching, which changes the execution environment of one task to that of another. If the switch is fast enough, it gives the illusion that all the tasks are executing simultaneously. This logical parallelism is called concurrency. In multiprocessor systems with many CPUs or processor cores, tasks can execute on different CPUs in parallel in real time. In addition, each processor may also do multitasking by executing different tasks concurrently. Multitasking is the basis of all operating systems. It is also the basis of concurrent programming in general.

3.2   The Process Concept

An operating system is a multitasking system. In an operating system, tasks are also called processes. For all practical purposes, the terms task and process can be used interchangeably. In Chap. 2, we defined an execution image as a memory area containing the execution's code, data and stack. Formally, we define process as

A process is the execution of an image.

It is a sequence of executions regarded by the OS kernel as a single entity for using system resources. System resources include memory space, I/O devices and, most importantly, CPU time. In an OS kernel, each process is represented by a unique data structure, called the Process Control Block (PCB) or Task Control Block (TCB), etc. In this book, we shall simply call it the PROC structure. Like a personal record, which contains all the information of a person, a PROC structure contains all the information of a process. In a real OS, the PROC structure may contain many fields and quite large. To begin with, we shall define a very simple PROC structure to represent processes.

```
typedef struct proc{
    struct proc *next;      // next proc pointer
    int   *ksp;             // saved sp: at byte offset 4
    int   pid;              // process ID
    int   ppid;            // parent process pid
    int   status;          // PROC status=FREE|READY, etc.
    int   priority;        // scheduling priority
    int   kstack[1024];    // process execution stack
}PROC;
```

In the PROC structure, **next** is a pointer to the next PROC structure. It is used to maintain the PROCs in various dynamic data structures, such as link lists and queues. The field **ksp** is the saved stack pointer. When a process gives up the CPU, it saves the execution context in stack and saves the stack pointer in PROC.ksp for resumption later. Among the other fields of the PROC structure, **pid** is the process ID number that identifies a process, **ppid** is the parent process ID number, status is the current status of the process, **priority** is the process scheduling priority and **kstack** is the process stack when it is executing. An OS kernel usually defines a finite number of PROC structures in its data area, denoted by

```
PROC proc[NPROC];           // NPROC a constant, e.g. 64
```

which are used to represent processes in the system. In a single CPU system, only one process can be executing at a time. The OS kernel usually uses a global PROC pointer, **running** or **current**, to point at the PROC that is currently executing. In a multiprocessor OS with multiple CPUs, many processes may be executing on different CPUs in parallel in real time. Accordingly, in a MP system **running [NCPU]** may be an array of pointers, each points at a PROC running on a specific CPU. For simplicity, we shall only consider single CPU systems.

3.3   A Multitasking System

In order for the reader to have a better understanding of multitasking and processes, we begin with a programming example, which is designed to illustrate the principles of multitasking, context switching and processes. The program implements a multitasking environment, which simulates the kernel mode operations of an operating system. The multitasking system, denoted by MT, consists of the following components.

3.3.1   type.h file

The type.h file defines system constants and a simple PROC structure to represent processes.

```
/*********** type.h file ************/
#define NPROC    9          // number of PROCs
#define SSIZE 1024          // stack size = 4KB

// PROC status
#define FREE      0
#define READY     1
#define SLEEP     2
#define ZOMBIE    3

typedef struct proc{
    struct proc *next;     // next proc pointer
    int   *ksp;            // saved stack pointer
    int    pid;            // pid = 0 to NPROC-1
    int    ppid;           // parent pid
    int    status;         // PROC status
    int    priority;       // scheduling priority
    int    kstack[SSIZE];  // process stack
}PROC;
```

As we expand the MT system, we shall add more fields to the PROC structure later.

3.3.2   The ts.s file

The ts.s file implements process context switching in 32-bit GCC assembly code, which will be explained in later sections.

```
#------------- ts.s file file -------------------
        .globl   running, scheduler, tswitch
tswitch:
SAVE:    pushl %eax
         pushl %ebx
         pushl %ecx
         pushl %edx
         pushl %ebp
         pushl %esi
         pushl %edi
         pushfl
         movl   running,%ebx    # ebx -> PROC
         movl   %esp,4(%ebx)    # PORC.save_sp = esp
FIND:    call   scheduler
RESUME:  movl   running,%ebx    # ebx -> PROC
         movl   4(%ebx),%esp    # esp = PROC.saved_sp
         popfl
         popl  %edi
         popl  %esi
         popl  %ebp
         popl  %edx
         popl  %ecx
         popl  %ebx
         popl  %eax
         ret
# stack contents = |retPC|eax|ebx|ecx|edx|ebp|esi|edi|eflag|
#                    -1   -2  -3  -4  -5  -6  -7  -8   -9
```

3.3.3   The queue.c file

The queue.c file implements queue and list operation functions. The function enqueue() enters a PROC into a queue by priority. In a priority queue, PROCs of the same priority are ordered by First-In-First-Out (FIFO). The function dequeue() returns the first element removed from a queue or a link list. The function printList() prints the elements of a link list.

```
/**************** queue.c file ****************/
int enqueue(PROC **queue, PROC *p)
{
  PROC *q = *queue;
  if (q == 0 || p->priority > q->priority){
     *queue = p;
     p->next = q;
  }
  else{
     while (q->next && p->priority <= q->next->priority)
            q = q->next;
     p->next = q->next;
     q->next = p;
```

```
   }
}
PROC *dequeue(PROC **queue)
{
     PROC *p = *queue;
     if (p)
         *queue = (*queue)->next;
     return p;
}
int printList(char *name, PROC *p)
{
  printf("%s = ", name);
  while(p){
     printf("[%d %d]->", p->pid, p->priority);
     p = p->next;
  }
  printf("NULL\n");
}
```

3.3.4   The t.c file

The t.c file defines the MT system data structures, system initialization code and process management functions.

```
/*********** t.c file of A Multitasking System *********/
#include <stdio.h>
#include "type.h"

PROC proc[NPROC];        // NPROC PROCs
PROC *freeList;          // freeList of PROCs
PROC *readyQueue;        // priority queue of READY procs
PROC *running;           // current running proc pointer

#include "queue.c"       // include queue.c file

/*******************************************************
   kfork() creates a child process; returns child pid.
   When scheduled to run, child PROC resumes to body();
*******************************************************/
int kfork()
{
  int  i;
  PROC *p = dequeue(&freeList);
  if (!p){
     printf("no more proc\n");
     return(-1);
  }
```

```
   /* initialize the new proc and its stack */
   p->status = READY;
   p->priority = 1;        // ALL PROCs priority=1,except P0
   p->ppid = running->pid;
   /************ new task initial stack contents ************
    kstack contains: |retPC|eax|ebx|ecx|edx|ebp|esi|edi|eflag|
                       -1   -2  -3  -4  -5  -6  -7  -8   -9
    *****************************************************/
   for (i=1; i<10; i++)                // zero out kstack cells
       p->kstack[SSIZE - i] = 0;
   p->kstack[SSIZE-1] = (int)body;     // retPC -> body()
   p->ksp = &(p->kstack[SSIZE - 9]);   // PROC.ksp -> saved eflag
   enqueue(&readyQueue, p);            // enter p into readyQueue
   return p->pid;
}


int kexit()
{
   running->status = FREE;
   running->priority = 0;
   enqueue(&freeList, running);
   printList("freeList", freeList);
   tswitch();
}


int do_kfork()
{
   int child = kfork();
   if (child < 0)
      printf("kfork failed\n");
   else{
      printf("proc %d kforked a child = %d\n", running->pid, child);
      printList("readyQueue", readyQueue);
   }
   return child;
}
int do_switch()
{
   tswitch();
}
int do_exit()
{
  kexit();
}


int body()    // process body function
{
  int c;
  printf("proc %d starts from body()\n", running->pid);
  while(1){
```

```
      printf("****************************************\n");
      printf("proc %d running: parent=%d\n", running->pid,running->ppid);
      printf("enter a key [f|s|q] : ");
      c = getchar(); getchar();    // kill the \r key
      switch(c){
        case 'f': do_kfork();      break;
        case 's': do_switch();     break;
        case 'q': do_exit();       break;
      }
  }
}
// initialize the MT system; create P0 as initial running process
int init()
{
  int i;
  PROC *p;
  for (i=0; i<NPROC; i++){ // initialize PROCs
    p = &proc[i];
    p->pid = i;                 // PID = 0 to NPROC-1
    p->status = FREE;
    p->priority = 0;
    p->next = p+1;
  }
  proc[NPROC-1].next = 0;
  freeList = &proc[0];       // all PROCs in freeList
  readyQueue = 0;            // readyQueue = empty

  // create P0 as the initial running process
  p = running = dequeue(&freeList); // use proc[0]
  p->status = READY;
  p->ppid = 0;               // P0 is its own parent
  printList("freeList", freeList);
  printf("init complete: P0 running\n");
}

/*************** main() function ***************/
int main()
{
   printf("Welcome to the MT Multitasking System\n");
   init();    // initialize system; create and run P0
   kfork();   // kfork P1 into readyQueue
   while(1){
     printf("P0: switch process\n");
     if (readyQueue)
         tswitch();
   }
}
```

```
/*********** scheduler *************/
int scheduler()
{
  printf("proc %d in scheduler()\n", running->pid);
  if (running->status == READY)
     enqueue(&readyQueue, running);
  printList("readyQueue", readyQueue);
  running = dequeue(&readyQueue);
  printf("next running = %d\n", running->pid);
}
```

3.3.5   Explanations of the Multitasking System Code

We explain the base code of the MT multitasking system by the following steps.

(1). The Virtual CPU: The MT system is compile-linked under Linux as

gcc –m32 t.c ts.s

Then run a.out. The entire MT system runs as Linux process in user mode. Within the Linux process, we create independent execution entities called tasks and schedule them to run inside the Linux process by our own scheduling algorithm. To the tasks in the MT system, the Linux process behaves as a virtual CPU. Barring any confusion, we shall refer to the execution entities in the MT system as either tasks or processes.

(2). init(): When the MT system starts, main() calls init() to initialize the system. Init() initializes the PROC structures and enters them into a freeList. It also initializes the readyQueue to empty. Then it uses proc[0] to create P0 as the initial running process. P0 has the lowest priority 0. All other tasks will have priority 1, so that they will take turn to run from the readyQueue.

(3). P0 calls kfork() to create a child process P1 with priority 1 and enter it into the ready queue. Then P0 calls tswitch(), which will switch task to run P1.

(4). tswitch(): The tswitch() function implements process context switching. It acts as a process switch box, where one process goes in and, in general, another process emerges. tswitch() consists of 3 separated steps, which are explained in more detail below.

(4).1. SAVE part of tswitch(): When an executing task calls tswitch(), it saves the return address on stack and enters tswitch() in assembly code. In tswitch(), the SAVE part saves CPU registers into the calling task's stack and saves the stack pointer into proc.ksp. The Intel x86 CPU in 32-bit mode has many registers, but only the registers eax, ebx, ecx, edx, ebp, esi, edi and eflag are visible to a Linux process in user mode, which is the virtual CPU of the MT system. So we only need to save and restore these registers of the virtual CPU. The following diagram shows the stack contents and the saved stack pointer of the calling task after executing the SAVE part of tswitch(), where xxx denote the stack contents before calling tswitch().

proc.ksp

|

|xxx|retPC|eax|ebx|ecx|edx|ebp|esi|edi|eflag|

In the Intel x86 based PCs in 32-bit mode, every CPU register is 4 bytes wide and stack operations are always in units of 4 bytes. Therefore, we may define each PROC stack as an integer array in the PROC structure.

(4).2. scheduler(): After executing the SAVE part of tswitch(), the task calls scheduler() to pick the next running task. In scheduler(), if the calling task is still READY to run, it calls enqueue() to put itself into the readyQueue by priority. Otherwise, it will not be in the readyQueue, which makes it non-runnable. Then it calls dequeue(), which returns the first PROC removed from readyQueue as the new running task.

(4).3. RESUME part of tswitch(): When execution returns from scheduler(), **running** may have changed to point at the PROC of a different task. Whichever PROC **running** points at, it is the current running task. The RESUME part of tswitch() sets the CPU's stack pointer to the saved stack pointer of the current running task. Then it pops saved registers, followed by RET, causing the current running task return to where it called tswitch() earlier.

(5). kfork(): The kfork() function creates a child task and enters it into the readyQueue. Every newly created task begins execution from the same body() function. Although the new task never existed before, we may pretend that it not only existed before but also ran before. The reason why it is not running now is because it called tswitch() to give up CPU earlier. If so, its stack must contain a frame saved by the SAVE part of tswitch(), and its saved ksp must point at the stack top. Since the new task never really ran before, we may assume that its stack was empty and all CPU register contents are 0 when it called tswitch(). Thus, in kfork(), we initialize the stack of the new task as follows.

```
                              proc.ksp
                                 |
            |< - all saved registers = 0 ->|
          |body|eax|ecx|edx|ebx|ebp|esi|edi|eflags|
           -1    -2  -3  -4  -5  -6  -7  -8    -9
```

where the index –i means SSIZE-i. These are done by the following code segment in kfork().

```
/************** task initial stack contents **************
  kstack contains: |retPC|eax|ebx|ecx|edx|ebp|esi|edi|eflag|
                     -1    -2  -3  -4  -5  -6  -7  -8   -9
******************************************************/
for (i=1; i<10; i++)              // zero out kstack cells
    p->kstack[SSIZE-i] = 0;
p->kstack[SSIZE-1] = (int)body;   // retPC -> body()
p->ksp = &(p->kstack[SSIZE-9]);   // PROC.ksp -> saved eflag
```

When the new task starts to run, it begins by executing the RESUME part of tswitch(), which causes it to return to the entry address of the body() function. When execution first enters body(), the task's stack is logically empty. As soon as execution starts, the task's stack will grow and shrink as described in Chap. 2 on stack usage and stack frames. In practice, the body() function never returns, so there is no need for a return address in the stack. For variations of the initial stack contents, the reader may consult Problem 3.2 in the Problem section.

(5). body(): For demonstration purpose, all tasks are created to execute the same body() function. This shows the difference between processes and programs. Many processes may execute the same program code, but each process executes in its own context. For instance, all (automatic) local variables in body() are private to the process since they are all allocated in the per process stack. If the body() function calls other functions, all the calling sequences are maintained in the per process stack, etc. While executing in body(), a process prompts for a command char = [f|s|q], where

　f : kfork a new child process to execute body();

　s : switch process;

　q : terminate and return the PROC as FREE to freeList

(6). The Idle Task P0: P0 is special in that it has the lowest priority among all the tasks. After system initialization, P0 creates P1 and switches to run P1. P0 will run again if and only if there are no runnable tasks. In that case, P0 simply loops. It will switch to another task whenever readyQueue becomes nonempty. In the base MT system, P0 runs again if all other processes have terminated. To end the MT system, the user may enter Control-C to kill the Linux process.

(7). Running the MT Multitasking System: Under Linux, enter

```
gcc -m32 t.c s.s
```

to compile-link the MT system and run the resulting a.out Figure 3.1 shows the sample outputs of running the MT multitasking system. The figures show the MT system initialization, the initial process P0, which creates P1 and switches task to run P1. P1 kforks a child process P2 and switches task to run P2. While a process is running, the reader may enter other commands to test the system.

```
Welcome to the MT Multitasking System
freeList = [1 0] -> [2 0] -> [3 0] -> [4 0] -> [5 0] -> [6 0] -> [7 0] -> [8 0] -> NULL
init complete: P0 running
P0: switch task
proc 0 in scheduler()
readyQueue = [1 1] -> [0 0] -> NULL
next running = 1
proc 1 starts from body()
****************************************
proc 1 running: Parent = 0
child = NULL
input a char [f|s|q] : f
proc 1 kforked a child = 2
readyQueue = [2 1] -> [0 0] -> NULL
****************************************
proc 1 running: Parent = 0
child = NULL
input a char [f|s|q] : s
proc 1 switching task
proc 1 in scheduler()
readyQueue = [2 1] -> [1 1] -> [0 0] -> NULL
next running = 2
proc 2 starts from body()
****************************************
proc 2 running: Parent = 1
child = NULL
input a char [f|s|q] : █
```

Fig. 3.1 Sample Outputs of the MT Multitasking System

3.4   Process Synchronization

An operating system comprises many concurrent processes, which may interact with one another. Process synchronization refers to the rules and mechanisms used to control and coordinate process interactions to ensure their proper executions. The simplest tools for process synchronization are sleep and wakeup operations.

3.4.1   Sleep Operation

Whenever a process needs something, e.g. a memory area for exclusive use, an input char from stdin, etc. that's currently not available, it goes to sleep on an event value, which represents the reason of the sleep. To implement the sleep operation, we can add an **event** field to the PROC structure and implement a ksleep(int event) function, which lets a process go to sleep. In the following, we shall assume that the PROC structure is modified to include the added fields shown in **bold face**.

```
typedef struct proc{
    struct proc *next;      // next proc pointer
    int  *ksp;              // saved sp: at byte offset 4
    int   pid;              // process ID
    int   ppid;             // parent process pid
    int   status;           // PROC status=FREE|READY, etc.
    int   priority;         // scheduling priority
    int   event;            // event value to sleep on
    int   exitCode;         // exit value
    struct proc *child;     // first child PROC pointer
    struct proc *sibling;   // sibling PROC pointer
    struct proc *parent;    // parent PROC pointer
    int   kstack[1024];     // process stack
 }PROC;
```

The algorithm of ksleep() is

```
/*********** Algorithm of ksleep(int event) *************/

1. record event value in PROC.event: running->event = event;
2. change status to SLEEP:            running->status = SLEEP;
3. for ease of maintenance, enter caller into a PROC *sleepList
                                      enqueue(&sleepList, running);
4. give up CPU:                       tswitch();
```

Since a sleeping process is not in the readyQueue, it's not runnable until it is woken up by another process. So after putting itself to sleep, the process calls tswitch() to give up the CPU.

3.4.2   Wakeup Operation

Many processes may sleep on the same event, which is natural since all of them may need the same resource, e.g. a printer, which is currently busy. In that case, all such processes would go to sleep on the same event value. When an awaited event occurs, another execution entity, which may be either a process or an interrupt handler, will call kwakeup(event), which wakes up ALL the processes sleeping on the event value. If no process is sleeping on the event, kwakeup() has no effect, i.e. it does nothing. The algorithm of kwakeup() is

```
/*********** Algorithm of kwakeup(int event) **********/
// Assume SLEEPing procs are in a global sleepList
   for each PROC *p in sleepList do{
           if (p->event == event){      // if p is sleeping for the event
               delete p from sleepList;
               p->status = READY;        // make p READY to run again
               enqueue(&readyQueue, p);  // enter p into readyQueue
           }
   }
```

It is noted that an awakened process may not run immediately. It is only put into the readyQueue, waiting for its turn to run. When an awakened process runs, it must try to get the resource again if it was trying to get a resource before the sleep. This is because the resource may no longer be available by the time it runs. The ksleep() and kwakeup() functions are intended for process synchronization in general, but they are also used in the special case to synchronize parent and child processes, which is our next topic.

3.5   Process Termination

In an operating system, a process may terminate or die, which is a common term of process termination. As mentioned in Chap. 2, a process may terminate in two possible ways:

Normal termination: The process calls exit(value), which issues _exit(value) system call to execute kexit(value) in the OS kernel, which is the case we are discussing here.

Abnormal termination: The process terminates abnormally due to a signal. Signals and signal handling will be covered later in Chap. 6.

In either case, when a process terminates, it eventually calls kexit() in the OS kernel. The general algorithm of kexit() is as follows.

3.5.1   Algorithm of kexit()

```
/*************** Algorithm of kexit(int exitValue) ***************/
1. Erase process user-mode context, e.g. close file descriptors,
     release resources, deallocate user-mode image memory, etc.
2. Dispose of children processes, if any
3. Record exitValue in PROC.exitCode for parent to get
```

4. Become a ZOMBIE (but do not free the PROC)
5. Wakeup parent and, if needed, also the INIT process P1

All processes in the MT system run in the simulated kernel mode of an OS. As such they do not have any user mode context. So we begin by discussing Step 2 of kexit(). In some OS, the execution environment of a process may depend on that of its parent. For example, the child's memory area may be within that of the parent, so that the parent process can not die unless all of its children have died. In Unix/Linux, processes only have the very loose parent-child relation but their execution environments are all independent. Thus, in Unix/Linux a process may die any time. If a process with children dies first, all the children processes would have no parent anymore, i.e. they become orphans. Then the question is: what to do with such orphans? In human society, they would be sent to grandma's house. But what if grandma already died? Following this reasoning, it immediately becomes clear that there must be a process which should not die if there are other processes still existing. Otherwise, the parent-child process relation would soon break down. In all Unix-like systems, the process P1, which is also known as the INIT process, is chosen to play this role. When a process dies, it sends all the orphaned children, dead or alive, to P1, i.e. become P1's children. Following suit, we shall also designate P1 in the MT system as such a process. Thus, P1 should not die if there are other processes still existing. The remaining problem is how to implement Step 2 of kexit() efficiently. In order for a dying process to dispose of orphan children, the process must be able to determine whether it has any child and, if it has children, find all the children quickly. If the number of processes is small, e.g. only a few as in the MT system, both questions can be answered effectively by searching all the PROC structures. For example, to determine whether a process has any child, simply search the PROCs for any one that is not FREE and its ppid matches the process pid. If the number of processes is large, e.g. in the order of hundreds or even thousands, this simple search scheme would be too slow to be acceptable. For this reason, most large OS kernels keep track of process relations by maintaining a process family tree.

3.5.2   Process Family Tree

Typically, the process family tree is implemented as a binary tree by a pair of child and sibling pointers in each PROC, as in

```
PROC *child, *sibling, *parent;
```

where child points to the first child of a process and sibling points to a list of other children of the same parent. For convenience, each PROC also uses a parent pointer to point at its parent. As an example, the process tree shown on the left-hand side of Fig. 3.2 can be implemented as the binary tree shown on the right-hand side, in which each vertical link is a child pointer and each horizontal link is a sibling pointer. For the sake of clarity, parent and null pointers are not shown.

With a process tree, it is much easier to find the children of a process. First, follow the child pointer to the first child PROC. Then follow the sibling pointers to traverse the sibling PROCs. To send all children to P1, simply detach the children list and append it to the children list of P1 (and change their ppid and parent pointer also).

Each PROC has an exitCode field, which is the process exitValue when it terminates. After recording exitValue in PROC.exitCode, the process changes its status to ZOMBIE but does not free the PROC structure. Then the process calls kwakeup(event) to wake up its parent, where event must be the same unique value used by both the parent and child processes, e.g. the address of the parent PROC structure or the parent pid. It also wakes up P1 if it has sent any orphans to P1. The final act of a dying

Fig. 3.2 Process Tree and
Binary Tree

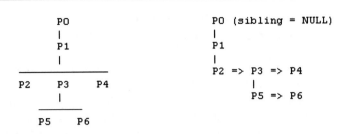

process is to call tswitch() for the last time. After these, the process is essentially dead but still has a
dead body in the form of a ZOMBIE PROC, which will be buried (set FREE) by the parent process
through the wait operation.

3.5.3   Wait for Child Process Termination

At any time, a process may call the kernel function

```
pid = kwait(int *status)
```

to wait for a ZOMBIE child process. If successful, the returned pid is the ZOMBIE child's pid and
status contains the exitCode of the ZOMBIE child. In addition, kwait() also releases the ZOMBIE child
PROC back to the freeList for reuse. The algorithm of kwait is

```
/******* Algorithm of kwait() *******/
  int kwait(int *status)
  {
     if (caller has no child) return -1 for error;
     while(1){    // caller has children
        search for a (any) ZOMBIE child;
        if (found a ZOMBIE child){
           get ZOMBIE child pid
           copy ZOMBIE child exitCode to *status;
           bury the ZOMBIE child (put its PROC back to freeList)
           return ZOMBIE child pid;
        }
        //**** has children but none dead yet ****
        ksleep(running);  // sleep on its PROC address
     }
  }
```

In the kwait algorithm, the process returns -1 for error if it has no child. Otherwise, it searches for a
ZOMBIE child. If it finds a ZOMBIE child, it collects the ZOMBIE child's pid and exitCode, releases
the ZOMBIE PROC to freeList and returns the ZOMBIE child's pid. Otherwise, it goes to sleep on its
own PROC address, waiting for a child to terminate. Since each PROC address is a unique value,
which is also known to all children processes, a waiting parent may sleep on its own PROC address for
child to wake it up later. Correspondingly, when a process terminates, it must issue

```
kwakeup(running->parent);
```

to wake up the parent. Instead of the parent PROC address, the reader may verify that using the parent pid should also work. In the kwait() algorithm, when the process wakes up, it will find a dead child when it executes the while loop again. Note that each kwait() call handles only one ZOMBIE child, if any. If a process has many children, it may have to call kwait() multiple times to dispose of all the dead children. Alternatively, a process may terminate first without waiting for any dead child. When a process dies, all of its children become children of P1. In a real system, P1 executes in an infinite loop, in which it repeatedly waits for dead children, including adopted orphans. Therefore, in a Unix-like system, the INIT process P1 wears many hats.

. It is the ancestor of all processes except P0. In particular, it is the grand daddy of all user processes since all login processes are children of P1.
. It is the head of an orphanage since all orphans are sent to his house and call him Papa.
. It is the manager of a morgue since it keeps looking for ZOMBIEs to bury their dead bodies.

So, in a Unix-like system if the INIT process P1 dies or gets stuck, the system would stop functioning because no user can login again and the system will soon be full of rotten corpses.

3.6   Process Management in the MT Multitasking System

This section presents a programming exercise for the reader to refine the base MT system to implement process management functions for the MT system. Specifically,

(1). Implement process family tree as a binary tree.
(2). Implement ksleep() and kwakeup() for process synchronization.
(3). Implement kexit() and kwait() for process management.
(4). Add a 'w' command to test and demonstrate the wait operation.

Sample solution to the programming exercise is available online for download. Figure 3.3 shows the sample outputs of running the modified MT system. As the figure shows, P1 forked a child P2, which forked its own children P3 and P4. Then P2 executes the 'q' command to terminate. The figure shows that P2 becomes a ZOMBIE and sends all the orphan children to P1, whose children list now includes all the orphans from P2. When P1 executes the 'w' command, it finds the ZOMBIE child P2 and returns it to the freeList. Alternatively, the reader may change the child-exit and parent-wait order to verify that the order does not matter.

3.7   Processes in Unix/Linux

With the above background information, we are now ready to describe processes in Unix/Linux (Bach 1990; Bovet and Cesati 2005; Silberschatz et al 2009; Love 2005). The reader may correlate the descriptions with processes in the MT system since all the terms and concepts apply equally well in both systems.

3.7.1   Process Origin

When an operating system starts, the OS kernel's startup code creates an initial process with PID=0 by brute force, i.e. by allocating a PROC structure, usually proc[0], initializes the PROC contents and lets

```
proc 2 running: Parent=1  child = NULL
input a char [f|s|q|w] : f
readyQ = [1 1] -> [3 1] -> [0 0] -> NULL
proc 2 kforked a child = 3
readyQueue = [1 1] -> [3 1] -> [0 0] -> NULL
*************************************
proc 2 running: Parent=1  child = [3 READY ]->NULL
input a char [f|s|q|w] : f
readyQ = [1 1] -> [3 1] -> [4 1] -> [0 0] -> NULL
proc 2 kforked a child = 4
readyQueue = [1 1] -> [3 1] -> [4 1] -> [0 0] -> NULL
*************************************
proc 2 running: Parent=1  child = [3 READY ]->[4 READY ]->NULL
input a char [f|s|q|w] : q
proc 2 in kexit()
P2 child = [3 READY ]->[4 READY ]->NULL
P1 child = [2 ZOMBIE]->[3 READY ]->[4 READY ]->null
proc 2 in scheduler()
readyQueue = [1 1] -> [3 1] -> [4 1] -> [0 0] -> NULL
next running = 1
proc 1 resuming
*************************************
proc 1 running: Parent=0  child = [2 ZOMBIE]->[3 READY ]->[4 READY ]->NULL
input a char [f|s|q|w] : w
freeList = [5 0] -> [6 0] -> [7 0] -> [8 0] -> [2 0] -> NULL
proc 1 waited for a ZOMBIE child 2 status=2
*************************************
proc 1 running: Parent=0  child = [3 READY ]->[4 READY ]->NULL
input a char [f|s|q|w] : █
```

Fig. 3.3 Sample Outputs of Modified MT System

running point at proc[0]. Henceforth, the system is executing the initial process P0. This is how most operating systems start to run the first process. P0 continues to initialize the system, which include both the system hardware and kernel data structures. Then it mounts a root file system to make files available to the system. After initializing the system, P0 forks a child process P1 and switches process to run P1 in user mode.

3.7.2 INIT and Daemon Processes

When the process P1 starts to run, it changes its execution image to the INIT program. Thus, P1 is commonly known as the **INIT process** because its execution image is the init program. P1 starts to fork many children processes. Most children processes of P1 are intended to provide system services. They run in the background and do not interact with any user. Such processes are called **daemon processes**. Examples of daemon processes are

```
syslogd: log daemon process
inetd  : Internet service daemon process
httpd  : HTTP server daemon process
etc.
```

3.7.3 Login Processes

In addition to daemon processes, P1 also forks many **LOGIN** processes, one on each terminal, for users to login. Each LOGIN process opens three **FILE streams** associated with its own terminal. The three file streams are **stdin** for standard input, **stdout** for standard output and **stderr** for standard error messages. Each file stream is a pointer to a **FILE structure** in the process HEAP area. Each FILE structure records a file descriptor (number), which is 0 for stdin, 1 for stdout and 2 for stderr. Then each LOGIN process displays a

```
login:
```

to its stdout, waiting for users to login. User accounts are maintained in the files **/etc/passwd** and **/etc/shadow**. Each user account has a line in the /etc/passwd file of the form

```
name:x:gid:uid:description:home:program
```

in which name is the user login name, x means check password during login, gid is the user's group ID, uid is the user ID, home is the user's home directory and program is the initial program to execute after the user login. Additional user account information are maintained in the **/etc/shadow** file. Each line of the **shadow** file contains the encrypted user password, followed by optional aging limit information, such as expiration date and time, etc. When a user tries to login with a login name and password, Linux will check both the /etc/passwd and /etc/shadow files to authenticate the user.

3.7.4 Sh Process

When a user login successfully, the LOGIN process acquires the user's gid and uid, thus becoming the user's process. It changes directory to the user's home directory and executes the listed program, which is usually the command interpreter **sh**. The user process now executes sh, so it is commonly known as the **sh process**. It prompts the user for commands to execute. Some special commands, such as cd (change directory), exit, logout, etc. are performed by sh itself directly. Most other commands are executable files in the various **bin** directories, such as /bin, /sbin, /usr/bin, /usr/local/bin, etc. For each (executable file) command, sh forks a child process and waits for the child to terminate. The child process changes its execution image to the command file and executes the command program. When the child process terminates, it wakes up the parent sh, which collects the child process termination status, frees the child PROC structure and prompts for another command, etc. In addition to simple commands, sh also supports **I/O redirections** and multiple commands connected by **pipes**.

3.7.5 Process Execution Modes

In Unix/Linux, a process may execute in two different modes; **Kernel mode** and **User mode**, denoted by **Kmode** and **Umode** for short. In each mode, a process has an execution image, as shown in Fig. 3.4.

In Fig.3.4, the index i indicates these are the images of process i. In general, the Umode images of processes are all different. However, while in Kmode they share the same Kcode, Kdata and Kheap, which are those of the OS Kernel, but each process has its own Kstack.

Images of Process i:

```
-----------------------------------------------------------
Kmode :   Kcode_i  Kdata_i  Kheapi  Kstack_i   (Kmode Space)
===========================================================
Umode :   Ucode_i  Udata_i  Uheapi  Ustack_i   (Umode Space)
-----------------------------------------------------------
```

Fig. 3.4 Process Execution Images

A process migrates between Kmode and Umode many times during its life time. Every process comes into existence and begins execution in Kmode. In fact, it does everything of interest in Kmode, including termination. While in Kmode, it can come to Umode very easily by changing CPU's status register from K to U mode. However, once in Umode it cannot change CPU's status arbitrarily for obvious reasons. A Umode process may enter Kmode only by one of three possible ways:

(1). **Interrupts:** Interrupts are signals from external devices to the CPU, requesting for CPU service. While executing in Umode, the CPU's interrupts are enabled so that it will respond to any interrupts. When an interrupt occurs, the CPU will enter Kmode to handle the interrupt, which causes the process to enter Kmode.

(2). **Traps:** Traps are error conditions, such as invalid address, illegal instruction, divide by 0, etc. which are recognized by the CPU as **exceptions**, causing it to enter Kmode to deal with the error. In Unix./Linux, the kernel trap handler converts the trap reason to a **signal** number and delivers the signal to the process. For most signals, the default action of a process is to terminate.

(3). **System Calls**: System call, or **syscall** for short, is a mechanism which allows a Umode process to enter Kmode to execute Kernel functions. When a process finishes executing Kernel functions, it returns to Umode with the desired results and a return value, which is normally 0 for success or -1 for error. In case of error, the external global variable **errno** (in errno.h) contains an ERROR code which identifies the error. The user may use the library function

```
perror("error message");
```

to print an error message, which is followed by a string describing the error.

Every time a process enters Kmode, it may not return to Umode immediately. In some cases, it may not return to Umode at all. For example, the _exit() syscall and most traps would cause the process to terminate in kernel, so that it never returns to Umode again. When a process is about to exit Kmode, the OS kernel may switch process to run another process of higher priority.

3.8   System Calls for Process Management

In this section, we shall discuss the following system calls in Linux, which are related to process management (Stallings 2011; Tanenbaum and Woodhull 2006).

```
fork(), wait(), exec(), exit()
```

Each is a library function which issues an actual syscall

```
int syscall(int a, int b, int c, int d);
```

where the first parameter a is the syscall number and b, c, d are parameters to the corresponding kernel function. In Intel x86 based Linux, syscall is implemented by the assembly instruction INT 0x80, which causes the CPU to enter the Linux kernel to execute the kernel function identified by the syscall number a.

3.8.1 fork()

```
Usage:   int pid = fork();
```

fork() creates a child process and returns the child's pid or -1 if fork() fails. In Linux, each user can only have a finite number of processes at the same time. User resource limits are set in the /etc/security/limits.conf file. A user may run the command **ulimit –a** to see the various resource limit values. Figure 3.5 shows the actions of fork(), which are explained below.

(1). The left-hand side of Fig. 3.5 shows the images of a process Pi, which issues the syscall pid=fork() in Umode.
(2). Pi goes to Kmode to execute the corresponding kfork() function in kernel, in which it creates a child process PROCj with its own Kmode stack and Umode image, as shown in the right-hand side of the figure. The Umode image of Pj is an IDENTICAL copy of Pi's Umode image. Therefore, Pj's code section also has the statement

```
pid=fork();
```

Furthermore, kfork() lets the child inherit all opened files of the parent. Thus, both the parent and child can get inputs from stdin and display to the same terminal of stdout and stderr.
(3). After creating a child, Pi returns to the statement

```
pid = fork();      // parent return child PID
```

in its own Umode image with the child's pid = j. It returns -1 if fork() failed, in which case no child is created.
(4). When the child process Pj runs, it exits Kmode and returns to the same statement

```
pid = fork();      // child returns 0
```

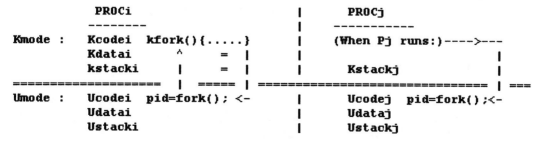

```
              PROCi                      |     PROCj
              --------                    |     -----------
Kmode :    Kcodei  kfork(){.....}         |     (When Pj runs:)---->---
           Kdatai       ^      =  |       |                            |
           kstacki      |      =  |       |     Kstackj                |
==================== |  ===== | =============================== | ===
Umode :    Ucodei  pid=fork(); <-         |     Ucodej  pid=fork();<-
           Udatai                         |     Udataj
           Ustacki                        |     Ustackj
```

Fig. 3.5 Actions of fork()

in its own Umode image with a 0 return value.

After a successful fork(), both the parent and child execute their own Umode images, which are identical immediately after fork(). From the program code point of view, the only way to tell which process is executing now is by the returned pid. Thus the program code should be written as

```
int pid = fork();
if (pid){
    // parent executes this part
}
else{
    // child executes this part
}
```

We illustrate fork() by an example.

Example 3.1: The example program C3.1 demonstrates fork().

```
/******************** C3.1.c: fork() **********************/
#include <stdio.h>
int main()
{
    int pid;
    printf("THIS IS %d  MY PARENT=%d\n", getpid(), getppid());
(1). pid = fork();   // fork syscall; parent returns child pid,
    if (pid){ // PARENT EXECUTES THIS PART
(2).    printf("THIS IS PROCESS %d  CHILD PID=d\n", getpid(), pid);
    }
    else{            // child executes this part
(3).    printf("this is process %d  parent=%d\n", getpid(), getppid());
    }
}
```

The program is run by a child process of sh. In the example code, getpid() and getppid() are system calls. getpid() returns the calling process PID and getppid() returns the parent process PID.

Line (1) forks a child process.
Line 2 prints (in uppercase for easier identification) the PID of the executing process and the newly forked child PID.
Line (3) prints (in lowercase) the child process PID, which should be the same child PID in Line (2), and its parent PID, which should be the same process PID in Line (2).

3.8.2   Process Execution Order

After fork(), the child process competes with the parent and all other processes in the system for CPU time to run. Which process will run next depends on their scheduling priorities, which change dynamically. The following example illustrates the possible different execution orders of processes.

Example 3.2: The example program C3.2 demonstrates process execution orders.

```
/***************** C3.2.c file *******************/
#include <stdio.h>
int main()
{
    int pid=fork();  // fork a child
    if (pid){        // PARENT
      printf("PARENT %d CHILD=%d\n", getpid(), pid);
(1).  // sleep(1);  // sleep 1 second ==> let child run next
      printf("PARENT %d EXIT\n", getpid());
    }
    else{            // child
      printf("child %d start my parent=%d\n", getpid(), getppid());
(2).  // sleep(2);  // sleep 2 seconds => let parent die first
      printf("child %d exit  my parent=%d\n", getpid(), getppid());
    }
}
```

In the Example 3.2 code, the parent process forks a child. After fork(), which process will run next depends on their priority. The child may run and terminate first, but it may also be the other way around. If the processes execute very lengthy code, they may take turn to run, so that their outputs may be interleaved on the screen. In order to see the different process execution orders, the reader may perform the following experiments.

(1). Uncomment line (1) to let the parent sleep for one second. Then the child should run to completion first.
(2). Uncomment Line (2) but not Line (1) to let the child sleep for 2 seconds. Then the parent will run to completion first. If the parent process terminates first, the child's ppid will change to 1 or to some other PID number. The reason for this will be explained later.
(3). Uncomment both Line (1) and Line (2). The results should be the same as in case (2).

In addition to sleep(seconds), which suspends a calling process for a number of seconds, Unix/Linux also provide the following syscalls, which may affect the execution order of processes.

. **nice(int inc):** nice() increases the process priority value by a specified value, which lowers the process scheduling priority (larger priority value means lower priority). If there are processes with higher priority, this will trigger a process switch to run the higher priority process first. In a non-preemptive kernel, process switch may not occur immediately. It occurs only when the executing process is about to exit Kmode to return to Umode.
. **sched_yield(void):** sched_yield() causes the calling process to relinquish the CPU, allowing other process of higher priority to run first. However, if the calling process still has the highest priority, it will continue to run.

3.8.3 Process Termination

As pointed in Chap. 2 (Sect. 2.3.8), a process executing a program image may terminate in two possible ways.

(1). **Normal Termination:** Recall that the main() function of every C program is called by the C startup code **crt0.o.** If the program executes successfully, main() eventually returns to crt0.o, which calls the library function exit(0) to terminate the process. The **exit(value)** function does some clean-up work first, such as flush stdout, close I/O streams, etc. Then it issues an **_exit (value)** system call, which causes the process to enter the OS kernel to terminate. A 0 exit value usually means normal termination. If desired, a process may call exit(value) directly from anywhere inside a program without going back to crt0.o. Even more drastically, a process may issue a _exit(value) system call to terminate immediately without doing the clean-up work first. When a process terminates in kernel, it records the value in the _exit(value) system call as the exit status in the process PROC structure, notifies its parent and becomes a ZOMBIE. The parent process can find the ZOMBIE child, get its pid and exit status by the

```
pid = wait(int *status);
```

system call, which also releases the ZMOBIE child PROC structure as FREE, allowing it to be reused for another process.

(2). **Abnormal Termination:** While executing a program, the process may encounter an error condition, such as illegal address, privilege violation, divide by zero, etc. which is recognized by the CPU as an **exception**. When a process encounters an exception, it is forced into the OS kernel by a trap. The kernel's **trap handler** converts the trap error type to a magic number, called **SIGNAL**, and delivers the signal to the process, causing it to terminate. In this case, the process terminates abnormally and the exit status of the ZOMBIE process is the signal number. In addition to trap errors, signals may also originate from hardware or from other processes. For example, pressing the Control_C key generates a hardware interrupt, which sends a number 2 signal (**SIGINT**) to all processes on the terminal, causing them to terminate. Alternatively, a user may use the command

```
kill -s signal_number pid          # signal_number=1 to 31
```

to send a signal to a target process identified by pid. For most signal numbers, the default action of a process is to terminate. Signals and signal handling will be covered later in Chap. 6.

In either case, when a process terminates, it eventually calls a kexit() function in the OS kernel. The general algorithm of kexit() was described in Sect. 3.5.1. The only difference is that the Unix/Linux kernel will erase the user mode image of the terminating process.

In Linux, each PROC has a 2-byte exitCode field, which records the process exit status. The high byte of exitCode is the exitValue in the _exit(exitValue) syscall, if the process terminated normally. The low byte is the signal number that caused it to terminate abnormally. Since a process can only die once, only one of the bytes has meaning.

3.8.4 Wait for Child Process Termination

At any time, a process may use the

```
int pid = wait(int *status);
```

system call, to wait for a ZOMBIE child process. If successful, wait() returns the ZOMBIE child PID and status contains the exitCode of the ZOMBIE child. In addition, wait() also releases the ZOMBIE child PROC as FREE for reuse. The wait() syscall invokes the kwait() function in kernel. The algorithm of kwait() is exactly the same as that described in Sect. 3.5.3

Example 3.3: The example program C3.3 demonstrates wait and exit system calls

```
/************* C3.3.c: wait() and exit() *************/
#include <stdio.h>
#include <stdlib.h>

int main()
{
    int pid, status;
    pid = fork();
    if (pid){ // PARENT:
        printf("PARENT %d WAITS FOR CHILD %d TO DIE\n", getpid(),pid);
        pid=wait(&status);  // wait for ZOMBIE child process
        printf("DEAD CHILD=%d, status=0x%04x\n", pid, status);
    }
    else{// child:
        printf("child %d dies by exit(VALUE)\n", getpid());
(1).    exit(100);
    }
}
```

When running the Example 3.3 program, the child termination status will be 0x6400, in which the high byte is the child's exit value 100.

The reason why wait() waits for any ZOMBIE child can be justified as follows. After forking several login processes, P1 waits for any ZOMBIE children. As soon as a user logout from a terminal, P1 must respond immediately to fork another login process on that terminal. Since P1 does not know which login process will terminate first, it must wait for any ZOMBIE login child, rather than waiting for a specific one. Alternatively, a process may use the syscall

```
int pid = waitpid(int pid, int *status, int options);
```

to wait for a specific ZOMBIE child specified by the pid parameter with several options. For instance, wait(&status) is equivalent to waitpid(-1, &status, 0). The reader may consult the Linux man pages of wait for more details.

3.8.5   Subreaper Process in Linux

Since kernel version 3.4, Linux handles orphan processes in a slightly different way. A process may define itself as a **subreaper** by the syscall

```
prctl(PR_SET_CHILD_SUBREAPER);
```

If so, the init process P1 will no longer be the parent of orphan processes. Instead, the nearest living ancestor process that is marked as a subreaper will become the new parent. If there is no living subreaper process, orphans still go to the INIT process as usual. The reason to implement this mechanism is as follows. Many user space service managers, such as upstart, systemd, etc. need to track their started services. Such services usually create daemons by forking twice but let the intermediate child exit immediately, which elevates the grandchild to be a child of P1. The drawback of this scheme is that the service manager can no longer receive the SIGCHLD (death_of_child) signals from the service daemons, nor can it wait for any ZOMBIE children. All information about the children will be lost when P1 cleans up the re-parented processes. With the subreaper mechanism, a service manager can mark itself as a "sub-init", and is now able to stay as the parent for all orphaned processes created by the started services. This also reduces the workload of P1, which does not have to handle all orphaned processes in the system. A good analogy is the following. Whenever a corporation gets too big, it's time to break it up to prevent monopoly, as what happened to AT&T in the early 80's. In the original Linux, P1 is the only process that is authorized to operate an orphanage. The subreaper mechanism essentially breaks the monopoly of P1, allowing any process to operate a local orphanage by declaring itself as a subreaper (even without a license!). As an example, in Ubuntu-15.10 and later, the per user init process is marked as a subreaper. It runs in Umode and belongs to the user. The reader may use the sh command

ps fxau | grep USERNAME | grep "/sbin/upstart"

to display the PID and information of the subreaper process. Instead of P1, it will be the parent of all orphaned processes of the user. We demonstrate the subreaper process capability of Linux by an example.

Example 3.4: The example program C3.4 demonstrates subreaper processes in Linux

```
/************** C3.4.c: Subreaper Process ***************/
#include <stdio.h>
#include <unistd.h>
#include <wait.h>
#include <sys/prctl.h>
int main()
{
  int pid, r, status;
  printf("mark process %d as a subreaper\n", getpid());
  r = prctl(PR_SET_CHILD_SUBREAPER);
  pid = fork();
  if (pid){          // parent
    printf("subreaper %d child=%d\n", getpid(), pid);
    while(1){
        pid = wait(&status); // wait for ZOMBIE children
        if (pid>0)
           printf("subreaper %d waited a ZOMBIE=%d\n", getpid(), pid);
        else                // no more children
           break;
    }
  }
```

Fig. 3.6 Sample Outputs
of Example 3.4

```
mark process 9620 as a subreaper
subreaper 9620 child=9621
child 9621 parent=9620
child=9621 grandchild=9622
child=9621 EXIT: grandchild=9622
grandchild=9622 start: myparent=9621
subreaper 9620 waited a ZOMBIE=9621
grandchild=9622 EXIT : myparent=9620
subreaper 9620_waited a ZOMBIE=9622
```

```
  else{             // child
    printf("child %d parent=%d\n", getpid(), (pid_t)getppid());
    pid = fork();  // child fork a grandchild
    if (pid){        // child
       printf("child=%d start: grandchild=%d\n", getpid(), pid);
       printf("child=%d EXIT : grandchild=%d\n", getpid(), pid);
    }
    else{            // grandchild
       printf("grandchild=%d start: myparent=%d\n", getpid(),
              getppid());
       printf("grandchild=%d EXIT : myparent=%d\n", getpid(),
              getppid());
    }
  }
}
```

Figure 3.6 shows the sample outputs of running the Example 3.4 program.

In the Example 3.4 program, the process (9620) first marks itself as a subreaper. Then it forks a child (9621) and uses a while loop to wait for ZOBMIE children until there is none. The child process forks a child of its own, which is the grandchild (9622) of the first process. When the program runs, either the child (9621) or the grandchild (9622) may terminate first. If the grandchild terminates first, its parent would still be the same (9621). However, if the child terminates first, the grandchild would become a child of P1 if there is no living ancestor marked as a subreaper. Since the first process (9620) is a subreaper, it will adopt the grandchild as an orphan if its parent died first. The outputs show that the parent of the grandchild was 9621 when it starts to run, but changed to 9620 when it exits since its original parent has already died. The outputs also show that the subreaper process 9620 has reaped both 9621 and 9622 as ZOMBIE children. If the user kills the per user init process, it would amounts to a user logout. In that case, P1 would fork another user init process, asking the user to login again.

3.8.6   exec(): Change Process Execution Image

A process may use exec() to change its Umode image to a different (executable) file. The exec() library functions have several members:

```
int execl( const char *path, const char *arg, ...);
int execlp(const char *file, const char *arg, ...);
int execle(const char *path, const char *arg,..,char *const envp[]);
```

```
int execv( const char *path, char *const argv[]);
int execvp(const char *file, char *const argv[]);
```

All of these are wrapper functions, which prepare the parameters and eventually issue the syscall

```
int execve(const char *filename, char *const argv[ ], char *const envp[ ]);
```

In the execve() syscall, the first parameter filename is either relative to the Current Working Directory (**CWD**) or an absolute pathname. The parameter argv[ ] is a NULL terminated array of string pointers, each points to a command line parameter string. By convention, argv[0] is the program name and other argv[ ] entries are command line parameters to the program. As an example, for the command line

```
a.out one two three
```

the following diagram shows the layout of argv [ ].

```
            0       1     2     3       4
argv[ ] = [ .   |   .   | . | .     | NULL ]
            |       |     |     |
          "a.out"  "one" "two" "three"
```

3.8.7   Environment Variables

Environment variables are variables that are defined for the current sh, which are inherited by children sh or processes. Environment variables are set in the login profiles and .bashrc script files when sh starts. They define the execution environment of subsequent programs. Each Environment variable is defined as

```
KEYWORD=string
```

Within a sh session the user can view the environment variables by using the env or printenv command. The following lists some of the important environment variables

```
SHELL=/bin/bash
TERM=xterm
USER=kcw
PATH=/usr/local/bin:/usr/bin:/bin:/usr/local/games:/usr/games:./
HOME=/home/kcw
```

SHELL: This specifies the sh that will be interpreting any user commands.
TERM : his specifies the type of terminal to emulate when running the sh.
USER : The current logged in user.
PATH : A list of directories that the system will check when looking for commands.
HOME: home directory of the user. In Linux, all user home directories are in /home

While in a sh session, environment variables can be set to new (string) values, as in

HOME=/home/newhome

which can be passed to descendant sh by the **EXPORT** command, as in

```
export HOME
```

They can also be unset by setting them to null strings. Within a process, environment variables are passed to C programs via the env[ ] parameter, which is a NULL terminated array of string pointers, each points to an environment variable.

Environment variables define the execution environment of subsequent programs. For example, when sh sees a command, it searches for the executable command (file) in the directories of the PATH environment variable. Most full screen text editors must know the terminal type they are running on, which is set in the TERM environment variable. Without the TERM information, a text editor may misbehave. Therefore, both command line parameters and environment variables must be passed to an executing program. This is the basis of the main() function in all C programs, which can be written as

int main(int argc, char *argv[ ], char *env[ ])

Exercise 3.1. Inside the main() function of a C program, write C code to print all the command line parameters and environment variables.

Exercise 3.2. Inside the main() function of a C program, find the PATH environment variable, which is of the form

PATH=/usr/local/bin:/usr/bin:/bin:/usr/local/games:/usr/games:./

Then write C code to tokenize the PATH variable string into individual directories.

If successful, exec("filename",....) replaces the process Umode image with a new image from the executable filename. It's still the same process but with a new Umode image. The old Umode image is abandoned and therefore never returned to, unless exec() fails, e.g. filename does not exist or is non-executable.

In general, after exec(), all opened files of the process remain open. Opened file descriptors that are marked as close-on-exec are closed. Most signals of the process are reset to default. If the executable file has the **setuid** bit turned on, the process effective uid/gid are changed to the owner of the executable file, which will be reset back to the saved process uid/gid when the execution finishes.

Example 3.5: The example program C3.5 demonstrates change process image by **execl()**, which is of the form

```
execl("a.out", "a.out", arg1, arg2, ..., 0);
```

The library function execl() assembles the parameters into argv[ ] form first before calling execve ("a.out", argv[ ], env[ ]).

```
/********** C3.5 program files **************/
// (1). --------- b.c file: gcc to b.out ----------
#include <stdio.h>
int main(int argc, char *argv[])
{
  printf("this is %d in %s\n", getpid(), argv[0]);
}
// (2). --------- a.c file: gcc to a.out ----------
#include <stdio.h>
int main(int argc, char *argv[])
{
  printf("THIS IS %d IN %s\n", getpid(), argv[0]);
  int r = execl("b.out", "b.out", "hi", 0);
  printf("SEE THIS LINE ONLY IF execl() FAILED\n");
}
```

The reader may compile b.c into b.out first. Then compile a.c and run a.out, which will change the execution image from a.out to b.out, but the process PID does not change, indicating that it's still the same process.

Example 3.6: The example program C3.6 demonstrates change process image by **execve()**.

In this example program, we shall demonstrate how to run Linux commands in the /bin directory by execve(). The program should be run as

a.out command [options]

where command is any Linux command in the /bin directory and [options] are optional parameters to the command program, e.g.

a.out ls -l;   a.out cat filename; etc.

The program assembles command and [options] into myargv[ ] and issues the syscall

execve("/bin/command", myargv, env);

to execute the /bin/command file. The process returns to the old image if execve() fails.

```
/********** C3.6.c file: compile and run a.out **********/
#include <stdio.h>
#include <stdlib.h>
#include <string.h>

char *dir[64], *myargv[64]; // assume at most 64 parameters
char cmd[128];

int main(int argc, char *argv[], char *env[])
{
  int i, r;
```

```
printf("THIS IS PROCESS %d IN %s\n", getpid(), argv[0]);
if (argc < 2){
    printf("Usage: a.out command [options]\n");
    exit(0);
}
printf("argc = %d\n", argc);
for (i=0; i<argc; i++)      // print argv[ ] strings
    printf("argv[%d] = %s\n", i, argv[i]);

for (i=0; i<argc-1; i++)    // create myargv[ ]
    myargv[i] = argv[i+1];
myargv[i] = 0;              // NULL terminated array

strcpy(cmd, "/bin/");       // create /bin/command
strcat(cmd, myargv[0]);
printf(cmd = %s\n", cmd);   // show filename to be executed
int r = execve(cmd, myargv, env);
// come to here only if execve() failed
printf("execve() failed: r = %d\n", r);
}
```

3.9   I/O Redirection

3.9.1   FILE Streams and File Descriptors

Recall that the sh process has three FILE streams for terminal I/O: stdin, stdout and stderr. Each is a pointer to a FILE structure in the execution image's HEAP area, as shown below.

```
FILE *stdin -------> FILE structure
            ----------------------------------
            char fbuf[SIZE]
            int counter, index, etc.
            int fd = 0;  // fd[0] in PROC <== from KEYBOARD
            ----------------------------------

FILE *stdout ------>  FILE structure
            ----------------------------------
            char fbuf[SIZE]
            int counter, index, etc.
            int fd = 1;  // fd[1] in PROC ==> to SCREEN
            ----------------------------------

FILE *stderr ------>  FILE structure
            ----------------------------------
            char fbuf[SIZE]
            int counter, index, etc.
            int fd = 2;  // fd[2] in PROC ==> to SCREEN also
            ----------------------------------
```

Each FILE stream corresponds to an opened file in the Linux kernel. Each opened file is represented by a **file descriptor** (number). The file descriptors of stdin, stdout, stderr are 0, 1, 2, respectively. When a process forks a child, the child inherits all the opened files of the parent. Therefore, the child also has the same FILE streams and file descriptors as the parent.

3.9.2 FILE Stream I/O and System Call

When a process executes the library function

```
scanf("%s", &item);
```

it tries to input a (string) item from stdin, which points to a FILE structure. If the FILE structure's fbuf[ ] is empty, it issues a READ system call to the Linux kernel to read data from the file descriptor 0, which is mapped to the keyboard of a terminal (/dev/ttyX) or a pseudo-terminal (/dev/pts/#).

3.9.3 Redirect stdin

If we replace the file descriptor 0 with a newly opened file, inputs would come from that file rather than the original input device. Thus, if we do

```
#include <fcntl.h>   // contains O_RDONLY, O_WRONLY,O_APPEND, etc
close(0);            // syscall to close file descriptor 0
int fd=open("filename", O_RDONLY);  // open filename for READ,
                                    // fd replace 0
```

The syscall close(0) closes the file descriptor 0, making 0 an unused file descriptor. The open() syscall opens a file and uses the lowest unused descriptor number as the file descriptor. In this case, the file descriptor of the opened file would be 0. Thus the original fd 0 is replaced by the newly opened file. Alternatively, we may also use

```
int fd = open("filename", O_RDOMLY);  // get a fd first
close(0);                             // zero out fd[0]
dup(fd);                              // duplicate fd to 0
```

The syscall dup(fd) duplicates fd into the lowest numbered and unused file descriptor, allowing both fd and 0 to access the same opened file. In addition, the syscall

```
dup2(fd1, fd2)
```

duplicates fd1 into fd2, closing fd2 first if it was already open. Thus, Unix/Linux provides several ways to replace/duplicate file descriptors. After any one of the above operations, the file descriptor 0 is either replaced or duplicated with the opened file, so that every scanf() call will get inputs from the opened file.

3.9.4   Redirect stdout

When a process executes the library function

```
printf("format=%s\n", items);
```

it tries to write to the fbuf[ ] in the stdout FILE structure, which is line buffered. If fbuf[ ] has a complete line, it issues a WRITE syscall to write data from fbuf[ ] to file descriptor 1, which is mapped to the terminal screen. To redirect the standard outputs to a file, do as follows.

```
close(1);
open("filename", O_WRONLY|O_CREAT, 0644);
```

These change file descriptor 1 to point to the opened filename. Then the outputs to stdout will go to that file instead of the screen. Likewise, we may also redirect stderr to a file. When a process terminates (in Kernel), it closes all opened files.

3.10   Pipes

Pipes are unidirectional inter-process communication channels for processes to exchange data. A pipe has a read end and a write end. Data written to the write end of a pipe can be read from the read end of the pipe. Since their debut in the original Unix, pipes have been incorporated into almost all OS, with many variations. Some systems allow pipes to be bidirectional, in which data can be transmitted in both directions. Ordinary pipes are for related processes. **Named pipes** are FIFO communication channels between unrelated processes. Reading and writing pipes are usually synchronous and blocking. Some systems support non-blocking and asynchronous read/write operations on pipes. For the sake of simplicity, we shall consider a pipe as a finite-sized FIFO communication channel between a set of related processes. Reader and writer processes of a pipe are synchronized in the following manner. When a reader reads from a pipe, if the pipe has data, the reader reads as much as it needs (up to the pipe size) and returns the number of bytes read. If the pipe has no data but still has writers, the reader waits for data. When a writer writes data to a pipe, it wakes up the waiting readers, allowing them to continue. If the pipe has no data and also no writer, the reader returns 0. Since readers wait for data if the pipe still has writers, a 0 return value means only one thing, namely the pipe has no data and also no writer. In that case, the reader can stop reading from the pipe. When a writer writes to a pipe, if the pipe has room, it writes as much as it needs to or until the pipe is full, i.e. no more room. If the pipe has no room but still has readers, the writer waits for room. When a reader reads data from the pipe to create more room, it wakes up the waiting writers, allowing them to continue. However, if a pipe has no more readers, the writer must detect this as a **broken pipe** error and aborts.

3.10.1   Pipe Programming in Unix/Linux

In Unix/Linux, pipes are supported by a set of pipe related syscalls. The syscall

```
int pd[2];              // array of 2 integers
int r = pipe(pd);       // return value r=0 if OK, -1 if failed
```

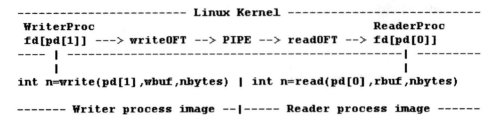

Fig. 3.7 Pipe Operation Model

creates a pipe in kernel and returns two file descriptors in pd[2], where pd[0] is for reading from the pipe and pd[1] is for writing to the pipe. However, a pipe is not intended for a single process. For example, after creating a pipe, if the process tries to read even 1 byte from the pipe, it would never return from the read syscall. This is because when the process tries to read from the pipe, there is no data yet but the pipe has a writer, so it waits for data. But who is the writer? It's the process itself. So the process waits for itself, thereby locking itself up so to speak. Conversely, if the process tries to write more than the pipe size (4KB in most cases), the process would again wait for itself when the pipe becomes full. Therefore, a process can only be either a reader or a writer on a pipe, but not both. The correct way of using pipes is as follows. After creating a pipe, the process forks a child process to share the pipe. During fork, the child inherits all the opened file descriptors of the parent. Thus the child also has pd[0] for read from the pipe and pd[1] for write to the pipe. The user must designate one of the processes as a writer and the other one as a reader of the pipe. The order does not matter as long as each process is designated to play only a single role. Assume that the parent is chosen as the writer and the child as the reader. Each process must close its unwanted pipe descriptor, i.e. writer must close its pd [0] and reader must close its pd[1]. Then the parent can write to the pipe and the child can read from the pipe. Figure 3.7 shows the system model of pipe operations.

On the left-hand side of Fig. 3.7, a writer process issues a

```
write(pd[1], wbuf, nbytes)
```

syscall to enter the OS kernel. It uses the file descriptor pd[1] to access the PIPE through the writeOFT. It executes write_pipe() to write data into the PIPE's buffer, waiting for room if necessary.

On the right-hand side of Fig. 3.7, a reader process issues a

```
read(pd[0],rbuf,nbytes)
```

syscall to enter the OS kernel. It uses the file descriptor pd[0] to access the PIPE through the readOFT. Then it executes read_pipe() to read data from the PIPE's buffer, waiting for data if necessary.

The writer process may terminate first when it has no more data to write, in which case the reader may continue to read as long as the PIPE still has data. However, if the reader terminates first, the writer should see a **broken pipe** error and also terminate.

Note that the broken pipe condition is not symmetrical. It is a condition of a communication channel in which there are writers but no reader. The converse is not a broken pipe since readers can still read as long as the pipe has data. The following program demonstrates pipes in Unix/Linux.

Example 3.7: The example program C3.7 demonstrates pipe operations.

```
/*************** C3.7: Pipe Operations ************/
#include <stdio.h>
#include <stdlib.h>
#include <string.h>

int  pd[2], n, i;
char line[256];

int main()
{
    pipe(pd);                // create a pipe
    printf("pd=[%d, %d]\n", pd[0], pd[1]);
    if (fork()){             // fork a child to share the pipe
       printf("parent %d close pd[0]\n", getpid());
       close(pd[0]);     // parent as pipe WRITER
       while(i++ < 10){ // parent writes to pipe 10 times
           printf("parent %d writing to pipe\n", getpid());
           n = write(pd[1], "I AM YOUR PAPA", 16);
           printf("parent %d wrote %d bytes to pipe\n", getpid(), n);
       }
       printf("parent %d exit\n", getpid());
    }
    else{
       printf("child  %d close pd[1]\n", getpid());
       close(pd[1]);    // child as pipe READER
       while(1){         // child read from pipe
           printf("child  %d reading from pipe\n", getpid());
           if ((n = read(pd[0], line, 128))){ // try to read 128 bytes
              line[n]=0;
              printf("child read %d bytes from pipe: %s\n", n, line);
           }
           else // pipe has no data and no writer
              exit(0);
       }
    }
}
```

The reader may compile and run the program under Linux to observe its behavior. Figure 3.8 shows the sample outputs of running the Example 3.7 program.

In the above pipe program, both the parent and child will terminate normally. The reader may modify the program to do the following experiments and observe the results.

1. Let the parent be the reader and child be the writer.
2. Let the writer write continuously and the reader only read a few times.

In the second case, the writer should terminate by a BROKEN_PIPE error.

```
pd=[3, 4]
child  5101 close pd[1]
child  5101 reading from pipe
parent 5100 close pd[0]
parent 5100 writing to pipe
child read 16 bytes from pipe: I AM YOUR PAPA
child  5101 reading from pipe
parent 5100 wrote 16 bytes to pipe
parent 5100 writing to pipe
child read 16 bytes from pipe: I AM YOUR PAPA
child  5101 reading from pipe
parent 5100 wrote 16 bytes to pipe
parent 5100 writing to pipe
child read 16 bytes from pipe: I AM YOUR PAPA
```

Fig. 3.8 Sample Outputs of Pipe Program

3.10.2   Pipe Command Processing

In Unix/Linux, the command line

$$cmd1 \ | \ cmd2$$

contains a pipe symbol 'l'. Sh will run cmd1 by a process and cmd2 by another process, which are connected by a PIPE, so that the outputs of cmd1 become the inputs of cmd2. The following shows typical usages of pipe commands.

```
ps x | grep "httpd"      # show lines of ps x containing httpd
cat filename | more      # display one screen of text at a time
```

3.10.3   Connect PIPE writer to PIPE reader

(1). When sh gets the command line cmd1 l cmd2, it forks a child sh and waits for the child sh to terminate as usual.

(2). Child sh: scan the command line for l symbol. In this case,

$$cmd1 \ | \ cmd2$$

has a pipe symbol l. Divide the command line into head=cmd1, tail=cmd2

(3). Then the child sh executes the following code segment

```
int pd[2];
pipe(pd);          // creates a PIPE
pid = fork();      // fork a child (to share the PIPE)
if (pid){          // parent as pipe WRITER
   close(pd[0]); // WRITER MUST close pd[0]
   close(1);     // close 1
```

```
        dup(pd[1]);     // replace 1 with pd[1]
        close(pd[1]);   // close pd[1]
        exec(head);     // change image to cmd1
    }
    else{               // child as pipe READER
        close(pd[1]);   // READER MUST close pd[1]
        close(0);
        dup(pd[0]);     // replace 0 with pd[0]
        close(pd[0]);   // close pd[0]
        exec(tail);     // change image to cmd2
    }
```

The pipe writer redirects its fd=1 to pd[1], and the pipe reader redirects its fd=0 to pd[0]. Thus, the two processes are connected through the pipe.

3.10.4   Named pipes

Named pipes are also called FIFOs. They have "names" and exist as special files within the file system. They exist until they are removed with rm or unlink. They can be used with unrelated process, not just descendants of the pipe creator.

Examples of named pipe

(1). From the sh, create a named pipe by the mknod command

```
mknod mypipe p
```

(2). OR from C program, issue the mknod() syscall

```
int r = mknod("mypipe", S_IFIFO, 0);
```

Either (1) or (2) creates a special file named mypipe in the current directory. Enter

```
ls -l mypipe
```

will show it as

```
prw-r—r— 1 root root   0   time   mypipe
```

where the file type p means it's a pipe, link count =1 and size=0

(3). Processes may access named pipe as if they are ordinary files. However, write to and read from named pipes are synchronized by the Linux kernel

The following diagram shows the interactions of writer and reader processes on a named pipe via sh commands. It shows that the writer stops if no one is reading from the pipe. The reader stops if the pipe has no data.

```
      Writer commands                   |    Reader commands
   ----------------------------------------------------------------
   echo test > mypipe (writer stops)  |
                                      |  cat mypipe
   (writer continues)                 |  test        (data read from pipe)
                                      |  cat mypipe (reader stops)
   echo test again > mypipe           |  test again (data read from pipe)
   (writer continues)                 |  (reader continues)
   ----------------------------------------------------------------
```

Instead of sh commands, processes created in C programs may also use named pipes.

Example 3.8: The example program C3.8 demonstrates named pipe operations. It shows how to open a named pipe for read/write by different processes.

```
/******* C3.8: Create and read/write named pipe *******/
```

(3).1 Writer process program:

```
#include <stdio.h>
#include <sys/stat.h>
#include <fcntl.h>
char *line = "tesing named pipe";

int main()
{
  int fd;
  mknod("mypipe", I_SFIFO, 0);      // create a named pipe
  fd = open("mypipe), O_WRONLY);   // open named pipe for write
  write (fd, line, strlen(line)); // write to pipe
  close (fd);
}
```

(3).2. Reader process program:

```
#include <stdio.h>
#include <sys/stat.h>
#include <fcntl.h>

int main()
{
  char buf[128];
  int fd = open("mypipe", O_RDONLY);
  read(fd, buf, 128);
  printf ("%s\n", buf);
  close (fd);
}
```

3.11   Programming Project: sh Simulator

The programming project is to write a C program which simulates the Linux sh for commands executions. The object is for the reader to understand how Linux sh works. The tools used are fork (), exec(), close(), exit(), pipe() system calls and string operations. It is suggested that the reader should try to implement the project in successive steps.

3.11.1   Single Command with I/O Redirection

1. Prompt the user for an input line, which is of the form

   cmd arg1 arg2 arg3 .... argn

   where cmd is a command, and arg1 to argn are command line parameters to the cmd program. Valid commands include "cd", "exit" and ANY Linux executable files, e.g. echo, ls, date, pwd, cat, cp, mv, cc, emacs, etc. In short, the sh simulator can run the same set of commands as Linux sh.
2. Handle simple commands:

   ```
   cmd = "cd"   :  chdir(arg1) OR chdir(HOME) if no arg1;
   cmd = "exit" :  exit(0) to terminate;
   ```

3. For all other commands:

   ```
   fork a child process;
   wait for the child to terminate;
   print child's exit status code
   continue step 1;
   ```

4. **Child process:** First, assume NO pipe in command line:

4-1. Handle I/O redirection:

   ```
   cmd  arg1 arg2 ...  <  infile    // take inputs from infile
   cmd  arg1 arg2 ...  >  outfile   // send outputs to outfile
   cmd  arg1 arg2 ...  >> outfile   // APPEND outputs to outfile
   ```

4-2. Execute cmd by execve(), passing parameters

   ```
   char *myargv[ ], char *env[ ]
   ```

   to the cmd file, where myargv[ ] is an array of char * with

   ```
   myargv[0]->cmd,
   myargv[1]->arg1, .....,
   End with a NULL pointer
   ```

Sh searches for executable commands in the directories of the PATH environment variable. The sh simulator must do the same. Thus, the simulator program must tokenize the PATH variable into individual directories for locating the command files.

3.11.2 Commands with Pipes

5. After verifying mysh works for simple commands, extend it to handle pipes. If the command line has a | symbol, divide it into head and tail: e.g.

```
        cmd1 < infile | cmd 2 > outfile
  head = "cmd < infile";   tail = "cmd 2 > outfile"
```

Then implement the pipe by the following steps.

   create a pipe
   fork a child process to share the pipe
   arrange one process as the pipe writer, and the other one as the pipe reader.
   Then let each process execve() its command (possibly with I/O redirection).

6. **Multiple pipes:** If the command line contains multiple pipe symbols, implement the pipes by recursion. The reader may consult Chap. 13 of (Wang 2015) for the recursive algorithm.

3.11.3 ELF executable vs. sh script files

In Linux, binary executables are in the ELF file format. The first 4 bytes of an ELF file are the ELF identifier '0x7F'ELF. Sh scripts are text files. The first line of most sh script files contains

```
        #!  /bin/sh
```

With these hints, the reader should be able to devise ways to test whether a command is an ELF executable or a sh script. For sh script files, run the Linux command /bin/bash on the files.

3.11.4 Sample Solution

Sample solution of the programming project is available online for download. The reader may download the binary executable file kcsh.bin and run it under Linux. Source code of the project for instructors is also available on request. Figure 3.9 shows the sample outputs of running the sh simulator program.

```
root@wang:~/abc/360/F17/sh.simulator# kcsh.bin
************ Welcome to kcsh **************
show PATH: PATH=PATH=/usr/local/sbin:/usr/sbin:/sbin:/usr/local/bin:/usr/bin:/b
in:/usr/games:.:/usr/lib/java/bin:/usr/lib/java/jre/bin:/usr/lib/qt/bin
decompose PATH into dir strings:
/usr/local/sbin  /usr/sbin  /sbin  /usr/local/bin  /usr/bin  /bin  /usr/games
.  /usr/lib/java/bin  /usr/lib/java/jre/bin  /usr/lib/qt/bin
show HOME directory: HOME = /root
********** kcsh processing loop **********
kcsh % : ls
32431 line=ls
32431 scan: head=ls  tail=(null)
32431 do_command: line=ls
32431 tries ls in each PATH dir
i=0    cmd=/usr/local/sbin/ls
i=1    cmd=/usr/sbin/ls
i=2    cmd=/sbin/ls
i=3    cmd=/usr/local/bin/ls
i=4    cmd=/usr/bin/ls
kcsh.bin  shve.c
parent kcsh 32430 forks a child process 32431
parent sh 32430 waits
child sh 32431 died : exit status = 0000
kcsh % : ▉
```

Fig. 3.9 Sample Outputs of sh Simulator Program

3.12 Summary

This chapter covers process management in Unix/Linux. It explains the principle of multitasking and introduces the process concept. It uses a programming example to illustrate the principles and techniques of multitasking, context switching and processes. The multitasking system supports dynamic process creation, process termination, process synchronization by sleep and wakeup, process relations and implementation of process family tree as a binary tree, allowing parent process to wait for child process termination. It provides a concrete example of how process management functions work in an operating system kernel. Then it explains the origin of processes in Unix/Linux, from the initial process during booting to INIT process, daemon processes, login processes and sh process for user command execution. Next, it explains the execution modes of processes, transitions from User mode to Kernel mode by interrupts, exceptions and system calls. Then it describes Unix/Linux system calls for process management, which include fork, wait, exec and exit. It explains the relationship between parent and child processes, including a detailed description between process termination and the wait operation by parent process. It explains how to handle orphan processes by the INIT process, including subreaper processes in current Linux, and it demonstrates subreaper process by example. Then it explains changing process execution image by exec in detail, which includes the execve system call, command-line parameters and environment variables. It explains the principles and techniques of I/O redirections, pipes and shows pipe programming by examples. The programming project of this chapter is for the reader to integrate the concepts and techniques of process management to implement a sh simulator for command execution. The sh simulator works exactly the same as the standard sh. It supports executions of simple commands, commands with I/O redirections and multiple commands connected by pipes.

Problems

1. On the Intel 32-bit x86 CPU, the assembly instruction pushal pushes CPU registers eax, ecx, ebx, old_esp, ebp, esi, edi in that order. Correspondingly, the instruction popal pops the registers in reverse order. Assume that the tswitch() function in the MT system is written as

```
tswitch:
SAVE:    pushal # save all CPU registers on stack
         pushfl
         movl    running,%ebx    # ebx -> PROC
         movl    %esp,4(%ebx)    # PORC.save_sp = esp
FIND:    call    scheduler
RESUME:  movl    running,%ebx    # ebx -> PROC
         movl    4(%ebx),%esp    # esp = PROC>saved_sp
         popfl
         popal  # restore all saved CPU registers from stack
         ret
```

Show how to initialize new processes in kfork() for them to execute the body() function. Recompile and run the modified MT system and demonstrate it works.

2. Assume that in the MT system the body() function is written as

```
int body(int pid){ // use pid inside the body function }
```

where pid is the PID of the new task. Show how to initialize the new task stack in kfork(). HINT: parameter passing in function calls as described in Chap. 2.

3. Refer to the Example Program C3.3. What is the child exit status value if Line (1) is replaced with
   (1). exit(123); Ans: 0x7B00 // normal termination
   (2). { int *p=0; *p = 123; } Ans: 0x000B // died by signal 11
   (3). { int a,b=0; a = a/b; } Ans: 0x0008 // died by signal 8

4. Refer to the Example Program C3.5. Explain what would happen if
   (1). In the a.c file, replace the execl() line with execl("a.out", "a.out", "hi", 0);
   (2). In the b.c file, add a line execl("a.out", "a.out", "again", 0);
   Verify your answers by running the modified programs.

5. Linux has a vfork() system call, which creates a child process just like fork() but is more efficient than fork().
   (1). Read the Linux man pages of vfork() to find out why it is more efficient than fork().
   (2). Replace all fork() system calls with vfork() in the programming project. Verify that the project program still works.

References

Bach, M. J., "The Design of the Unix operating system", Prentice Hall, 1990
Bovet, D. P., Cesati, M., Understanding the Linux Kernel, O'Reilly, 2005
Silberschatz, A., P.A. Galvin, P.A., Gagne, G, "Operating system concepts, 8th Edition", John Wiley & Sons, Inc. 2009
Love, R. Linux Kernel Development, 2nd Edition, Novell Press, 2005
Stallings, W. "Operating Systems: Internals and Design Principles (7th Edition)", Prentice Hall, 2011
Tanenbaum, A.S., Woodhull, A.S., "Operating Systems, Design and Implementation, third Edition", Prentice Hall, 2006
Wang, K.C., "Design and Implementation of the MTX Operating System", Springer A.G. 2015

Concurrent Programming

4

Abstract

This chapter covers concurrent programming. It introduces the concept of parallel computing and points out its importance. It compares sequential algorithms with parallel algorithms, and parallelism vs. concurrency. It explains the principles of threads and their advantages over processes. It covers threads operations in Pthreads by examples. These include threads management functions, threads synchronization tools of mutex, join, condition variables and barriers. It demonstrates concurrent programming using threads by detailed examples. These include matrix computation, quicksort and solving systems of linear equations by concurrent threads. It explains the deadlock problem and shows how to prevent deadlocks in concurrent programs. It covers semaphores and demonstrates their advantages over condition variables. It also explains the unique way of supporting threads in Linux. The programming project is to implement user-level threads. It presents a base system to help the reader get started. The base system supports dynamic creation, execution and termination of concurrent tasks, which are equivalent to threads executing in the same address space of a process. The project is for the reader to implement threads join, mutex and semaphores for threads synchronization and demonstrate their usage in concurrent programs. The programming project should allow the reader to have a deeper understanding of the principles and techniques of multitasking, threads synchronization and concurrent programming.

4.1 Introduction to Parallel Computing

In the early days, most computers have only one processing element, known as the processor or Central Processing Unit (CPU). Due to this hardware limitation, computer programs are traditionally written for serial computation. To solve a problem, a person would first design an algorithm, which describes how to solve the problem step by step, and then implement the algorithm by a computer program as a serial stream of instructions. With only a single CPU, both the individual instructions and the steps of an algorithm can only be executed sequentially one at a time. However, algorithms based on the principle of divide and conquer, e.g. binary search and quicksort, etc. often exhibit a high degree of parallelism, which can be exploited by using parallel or concurrent executions to speed up the computation. Parallel computing is a computing scheme which tries to use multiple processors executing parallel algorithms to solve problems faster. In the past, parallel computing is rarely

© Springer International Publishing AG, part of Springer Nature 2018

K. C. Wang, *Systems Programming in Unix/Linux*, https://doi.org/10.1007/978-3-319-92429-8_4

accessible to average programmers due to its extensive requirements of computing resources. With the advent of multicore processors in recent years, most operating systems, such as Linux, support Symmetrical Multiprocessing (SMP). Parallel computing has become a reality even for average programmers. The future of computing is clearly in the direction of parallel computing. It is imperative to introduce parallel computing to Computer Science and Computer Engineering students in an early stage. In this chapter, we shall cover the basic concepts and techniques of parallel computing through concurrent programming.

4.1.1   Sequential Algorithms vs. Parallel Algorithms

When describing sequential algorithms, a common way is to express the algorithm in a **begin-end** block, as show in the left-hand side of the following diagram.

```
--- Sequential Algorithm---|--- Parallel Algorithm ---
        begin              |        cobegin
         step_1            |         task_1
         step_2            |         task_2
         . . .             |         . . .
         step_n            |         task_n
        end                |        coend
        // next step       |        // next step
    -------------------------------------------------
```

The sequential algorithm inside the begin-end block may consist of many steps. All the steps are to be performed by a single task serially one step at a time. The algorithm ends when all the steps have completed. In contrast, the right-hand side of the diagram shows the description of a parallel algorithm, which uses a **cobegin-coend** block to specify separate tasks of a parallel algorithm. Within the cobegin-coend block, all tasks are to be performed in parallel. The next step following the cobegin-coend block will be performed only after all such tasks have completed.

4.1.2   Parallelism vs. Concurrency

In general, a parallel algorithm only identifies tasks that can be executed in parallel, but it does not specify how to map the tasks to processing elements. Ideally, all the tasks in a parallel algorithm should be executed simultaneously in real time. However, true parallel executions can only be achieved in systems with multiple processing elements, such as multiprocessor or multicore systems. On single CPU systems, only one task can execute at a time. In this case, different tasks can only execute concurrently, i.e. logically in parallel. In single CPU systems, concurrency is achieved through multitasking, which was covered in Chap. 3. We shall explain and demonstrate the principle and techniques of multitasking again in a programming project at the end of this chapter.

4.2   Threads

4.2.1   Principle of Threads

An operating system (OS) comprises many concurrent processes. In the process model, processes are independent execution units. Each process executes in either kernel mode or user mode. While in user mode, each process executes in a unique address space, which is separated from other processes. Although each process is an independent unit, it has only one execution path. Whenever a process must wait for something, e.g. an I/O completion event, it becomes suspended and the entire process execution stops. Threads are independent execution units in the same address space of a process. When creating a process, it is created in a unique address space with a main thread. When a process begins, it executes the main thread of the process. With only a main thread, there is virtually no difference between a process and a thread. However, the main thread may create other threads. Each thread may create yet more threads, etc. All threads in a process execute in the same address space of the process but each thread is an independent execution unit. In the threads model, if a thread becomes suspended, other threads may continue to execute. In addition to sharing a common address space, threads also share many other resources of a process, such as user id, opened file descriptors and signals, etc. A simple analogy is that a process is a house with a house master (the main thread). Threads are people living in the same house of a process. Each person in a house can carry on his/her activities independently, but they share some common facilities, such as the same mailbox, kitchen and bathroom, etc. Historically, most computer vendors used to support threads in their own proprietary operating systems. The implementations vary considerably from system to system. Currently, almost all OS support Pthreads, which is the threads standard of IEEE POSIX 1003.1c (POSIX 1995). For more information, the reader may consult numerous books (Buttlar et al. 1996) and online articles on Pthreads programming (Pthreads 2017).

4.2.2   Advantages of Threads

Threads have many advantages over processes.

(1). **Thread creation and switching are faster:** The context of a process is complex and large. The complexity stems mainly from the need for managing the process image. For example, in a system with virtual memory, a process image may be composed of many units of memory called **pages.** During execution some of the pages are in memory while others may not. The OS kernel must use several page tables and many levels of hardware assistances to keep track of the pages of each process. To create a new process, the OS must allocate memory and build the page tables for the process. To create a thread within a process, the OS does not have to allocate memory and build page tables for the new thread since it shares the same address space of the process. So, creating a thread is faster than creating a process. Also, thread switching is faster than process switching for the following reasons. Process switching involves replacing the complex paging environment of one process with that of another, which requires a lot of operations and time. In contrast, switching among threads in the same process is much simpler and faster because the OS kernel only needs to switch the execution points without changing the process image.

(2). **Threads are more responsive:** A process has only a single execution path. When a process becomes suspended, the entire process execution stops. In contrast, when a thread becomes suspended, other threads in the same process can continue to execute. This allows a program with threads to be more responsive. For example, in a process with multiple threads, while one thread becomes blocked to wait for I/O, other threads can still do computations in the background. In a server with threads, the server can serve multiple clients concurrently.

(3). **Threads are better suited to parallel computing:** The goal of parallel computing is to use multiple execution paths to solve problems faster. Algorithms based on the principle of divide and conquer, e.g. binary search and quicksort, etc. often exhibit a high degree of parallelism, which can be exploited by using parallel or concurrent executions to speed up the computation. Such algorithms often require the execution entities to share common data. In the process model, processes cannot share data efficiently because their address spaces are all distinct. To remedy this problem, processes must use **Interprocess Communication (IPC)** to exchange data or some other means to include a common data area in their address spaces. In contrast, threads in the same process share all the (global) data in the same address space. Thus, writing programs for parallel executions using threads is simpler and more natural than using processes.

4.2.3   Disadvantages of Threads

On the other hand, threads also have some disadvantages, which include

(1). Because of shared address space, threads needs explicit synchronization from the user.
(2). Many library functions may not be threads safe, e.g. the traditional strtok() function, which divides a string into tokens in-line. In general, any function which uses global variables or relies on contents of static memory is not threads safe. Considerable efforts are needed to adapt library functions to the threads environment.
(3). On single CPU systems, using threads to solve problems is actually slower than using a sequential program due to the overhead in threads creation and context switching at run-time.

4.3   Threads Operations

The execution locus of a thread is similar to that a process. A thread can execute in either kernel mode or user mode. While in user mode, threads executes in the same address space of a process but each has its own execution stack. As an independent execution unit, a thread can make system calls to the OS kernel, subject to the kernel's scheduling policy, becomes suspended, activated to resume execution, etc. To take advantage of the shared address space of threads, the OS kernel's scheduling policy may favor threads of the same process over those in different processes. As of now, almost all operating systems support POSIX Pthreads, which defines a standard set of Application Programming Interfaces (**APIs**) to support threads programming. In the following, we shall discuss and demonstrate concurrent programming by Pthreads in Linux (Goldt et al 1995; IBM; Love 2005; Linux Man Page Project 2017).

4.4   Threads Management Functions

The Pthreads library offers the following APIs for threads management.

```
pthread_create(thread, attr, function, arg): create thread
pthread_exit(status)        : terminate thread
```

```
pthread_cancel(thread)      : cancel thread
pthread_attr_init(attr)     : initialize thread attributes
pthread_attr_destroy(attr): destroy thread attribute
```

4.4.1   Create Thread

threads are created by the pthread_create() function.

```
int pthread_create (pthread_t *pthread_id, pthread_attr_t *attr,
                    void *(*func)(void *),  void *arg);
```

which returns 0 on success or an error number on failure. Parameters to the pthread_create() function are

.pthread_id is a pointer to a variable of the pthread_t type. It will be filled with the unique thread ID assigned by the OS kernel. In POSIX, pthread_t is an opaque type. The programmer should not know the contents of an opaque object because it may depend on implementation. A thread may get its own ID by the pthread_self() function. In Linux, pthread_t type is defined as **unsigned long**, so thread ID can be printed as %lu.

.attr is a pointer to another opaque data type, which specifies the thread attributes, which are explained in more detail below.

.func is the entry address of a function for the new thread to execute.

.arg is a pointer to a parameter for the thread function, which can be written as

```
void *func(void *arg)
```

Among these, the attr parameter is the most complex one. The steps of using an attr parameter are as follows.

(1). Define a pthread attribute variable `pthread_attr_t` **attr**
(2). Initialize the attribute variable with `pthread_attr_init`**(&attr)**
(3). Set the attribute variable and use it in pthread_create() call
(4). If desired, free the attr resource by `pthread_attr_destroy`**(&attr)**

The following shows some examples of using the attribute parameter. By default, every thread is created to be joinable with other threads. If desired, a thread can be created with the detached attribute, which makes it non-joinable with other threads. The following code segment shows how to create a detached thread.

```
pthread_attr_t attr;              // define an attr variable
pthread_attr_init(&attr);         // initialize attr
pthread_attr_setdetachstate(&attr, PTHREAD_CREATE_DETACHED); // set attr
pthread_create(&thread_id, &attr, func, NULL);  // create thread with attr
pthread_attr_destroy(&attr);      // optional: destroy attr
```

Every thread is created with a default stack size. During execution, a thread may find out its stack size by the function

```
                    size_t pthread_attr_getstacksize()
```

which returns the default stack size. The following code segment shows how to create a thread with a specific stack size.

```
pthread_attr_t attr;            // attr variable
size_t stacksize;               // stack size
pthread_attr_init(&attr);       // initialize attr
stacksize = 0x10000;            // stacksize=16KB;
pthread_attr_setstacksize (&attr, stacksize);   // set stack size in attr
pthread_create(&threads[t], &attr, func, NULL); // create thread with stack
                                                               size
```

If the attr parameter is NULL, threads will be created with default attributes. In fact, this is the recommended way of creating threads, which should be followed unless there is a compelling reason to alter the thread attributes. In the following, we shall always use the default attributes by setting attr to NULL.

4.4.2   Thread ID

Thread ID is an opaque data type, which depends on implementation. Therefore, thread IDs should not be compared directly. If needed, they can be compared by the pthread_equal() function.

```
            int pthread_equal (pthread_t t1, pthread_t t2);
```

which returns zero if the threads are different threads, non-zero otherwise.

4.4.3   Thread Termination

A thread terminates when the thread function finishes. Alternatively, a thread may call the function

```
            int pthread_exit (void *status);
```

to terminate explicitly, where status is the exit status of the thread. As usual, a 0 exit value means normal termination, and non-zero values mean abnormal termination.

4.4.4   Thread Join

A thread can wait for the termination of another thread by

```
            int pthread_join (pthread_t thread, void **status_ptr);
```

The exit status of the terminated thread is returned in status_ptr.

4.5   Threads Example Programs

4.5.1   Sum of Matrix by Threads

Example 4.1: Assume that we want to compute the sum of all the elements in an N × N matrix of integers. The problem can be solved by a concurrent algorithm using threads. In this example, the main thread first generates an N × N matrix of integers. Then it creates N working threads, passing as parameter a unique row number to each working thread, and waits for all the working threads to terminate. Each working thread computes the partial sum of a distinct row, and deposits the partial sum in a corresponding row of a global array int sum[N]. When all the working threads have finished, the main thread resumes. It computes the total sum by adding the partial sums generated by the working threads. The following shows the complete C code of the example program C4.1. Under Linux, the program must be compiled as

```
gcc   C4.1.c   -pthread
```

```c
/**** C4.1.c file: compute matrix sum by threads ***/
#include <stdio.h>
#include <stdlib.h>
#include <pthread.h>
#define N    4
int A[N][N], sum[N];

void *func(void *arg)              // threads function
{
   int j, row;
   pthread_t tid = pthread_self(); // get thread ID number
   row = (int)arg;                 // get row number from arg
   printf("Thread %d [%lu] computes sum of row %d\n", row, tid, row);
   for (j=0; j<N; j++)     // compute sum of A[row]in global sum[row]
       sum[row] += A[row][j];
   printf("Thread %d [%lu] done: sum[%d] = %d\n",
                 row, tid, row, sum[row]);
   pthread_exit((void*)0); // thread exit: 0=normal termination
}

int main (int argc, char *argv[])
{
   pthread_t thread[N];        // thread IDs
   int i, j, r, total = 0;
   void *status;
   printf("Main: initialize A matrix\n");
   for (i=0; i<N; i++){
     sum[i] = 0;
     for (j=0; j<N; j++){
       A[i][j] = i*N + j + 1;
       printf("%4d ", A[i][j]);
     }
     printf("\n");
```

```
    }
    printf("Main: create %d threads\n", N);
    for(i=0; i<N; i++) {
        pthread_create(&thread[i], NULL, func, (void *)i);
    }
    printf("Main: try to join with threads\n");
    for(i=0; i<N; i++) {
        pthread_join(thread[i], &status);
        printf("Main: joined with %d [%lu]: status=%d\n",
                            i, thread[i], (int)status);
    }
    printf("Main: compute and print total sum: ");
    for (i=0; i<N; i++)
        total += sum[i];
    printf("tatal = %d\n", total);
    pthread_exit(NULL);
}
```

Figure 4.1 shows the outputs of running the Example Program C4.1. It shows the executions of individual threads and their computed partial sums. It also demonstrates the thread join operation.

4.5.2 Quicksort by Threads

Example 4.2: Quicksort by Concurrent Threads

In this example, we shall implement a parallel quicksort program by threads. When the program starts, it runs as the main thread of a process. The main thread calls qsort(&arg), with arg =[lowerbound=0, upperbound=N-1]. The qsort() function implements quicksort of an array of N integers. In qsort(), the thread picks a pivot element to divide the array into two parts such that all elements in the left part are less than the pivot and all elements in the right part are greater than the

```
Main: initialize A matrix
    1    2    3    4
    5    6    7    8
    9   10   11   12
   13   14   15   16
Main: create 4 threads
Thread 0 [3075390272] computes sum of row 0
Thread 0 [3075390272] done: sum[0] = 10
Thread 3 [3050212160] computes sum of row 3
Thread 3 [3050212160] done: sum[3] = 58
Thread 2 [3058604864] computes sum of row 2
Thread 2 [3058604864] done: sum[2] = 42
Thread 1 [3066997568] computes sum of row 1
Main: try to join with threads
Thread 1 [3066997568] done: sum[1] = 26
Main: joined with 0 [3075390272]: status=0
Main: joined with 1 [3066997568]: status=0
Main: joined with 2 [3058604864]: status=0
Main: joined with 3 [3050212160]: status=0
Main: compute and print total sum: tatal = 136
```

Fig. 4.1 Sample Outputs of Example 4.1

pivot. Then it creates two subthreads to sort each of the two parts, and waits for the subthreads to finish. Each subthread sorts its own range by the same algorithm recursively. When all the subthreads have finished, the main thread resumes. It prints the sorted array and terminates. As is well known, the number of sorting steps of quicksort depends on the order of the unsorted data, which affects the number of threads needed in the qsort program.

```c
/****** C4.2.c: quicksort by threads *****/
#include <stdio.h>
#include <stdlib.h>
#include <pthread.h>

typedef struct{
  int upperbound;
  int lowerbound;
}PARM;

#define N 10
int A[N] = {5,1,6,4,7,2,9,8,0,3};  // unsorted data

int print()   // print current a[] contents
{
  int i;
  printf("[ ");
  for (i=0; i<N; i++)
    printf("%d ", a[i]);
  printf("]\n");
}


void *qsort(void *aptr)
{
  PARM *ap, aleft, aright;
  int pivot, pivotIndex, left, right, temp;
  int upperbound, lowerbound;

  pthread_t me, leftThread, rightThread;
  me = pthread_self();
  ap = (PARM *)aptr;
  upperbound = ap->upperbound;
  lowerbound = ap->lowerbound;
  pivot = a[upperbound];        // pick low pivot value
  left = lowerbound - 1;        // scan index from left side
  right = upperbound;           // scan index from right side
  if (lowerbound >= upperbound)
    pthread_exit(NULL);

  while (left < right) {         // partition loop
    do { left++;} while (a[left] < pivot);
      do { right--;} while (a[right] > pivot);
      if (left < right ) {
```

```
            temp = a[left];
            a[left] = a[right];
            a[right] = temp;
        }
    }
    print();
    pivotIndex = left;              // put pivot back
    temp = a[pivotIndex];
    a[pivotIndex] = pivot;
    a[upperbound] = temp;
    // start the "recursive threads"
    aleft.upperbound = pivotIndex - 1;
    aleft.lowerbound = lowerbound;
    aright.upperbound = upperbound;
    aright.lowerbound = pivotIndex + 1;
    printf("%lu: create left and right threads\n", me);
    pthread_create(&leftThread,  NULL, qsort, (void *)&aleft);
    pthread_create(&rightThread, NULL, qsort, (void *)&aright);
    // wait for left and right threads to finish
    pthread_join(leftThread, NULL);
    pthread_join(rightThread, NULL);
    printf("%lu: joined with left & right threads\n", me);
}

int main(int argc, char *argv[])
{
    PARM arg;
    int i, *array;
    pthread_t me, thread;
    me = pthread_self();
    printf("main %lu: unsorted array = ", me);
    print();
    arg.upperbound = N-1;
    arg.lowerbound = 0;
    printf("main %lu create a thread to do QS\n", me);
    pthread_create(&thread, NULL, qsort, (void *)&arg);
    // wait for QS thread to finish
    pthread_join(thread, NULL);
    printf("main %lu sorted array = ", me);
    print();
}
```

Figure 4.2 shows the outputs of running the Example Program C4.2, which demonstrates parallel quicksort by concurrent threads.

```
main 3075553024: unsorted array = [ 5 1 6 4 7 2 9 8 0 3 ]
main 3075553024 create a thread to do QS
[ 0 1 2 4 7 6 9 8 5 3 ]
3075550016: create left and right threads
[ 0 1 2 3 7 6 9 8 5 4 ]
3067157312: create left and right threads
[ 0 1 2 3 7 6 9 8 5 4 ]
3057646400: create left and right threads
[ 0 1 2 3 4 6 9 8 5 7 ]
3049253696: create left and right threads
[ 0 1 2 3 4 6 5 8 9 7 ]
3003116352: create left and right threads
[ 0 1 2 3 4 6 5 7 9 8 ]
2986330944: create left and right threads
[ 0 1 2 3 4 6 5 7 8 9 ]
2994723648: create left and right threads
3049253696: joined with left & right threads
3067157312: joined with left & right threads
2986330944: joined with left & right threads
2994723648: joined with left & right threads
3003116352: joined with left & right threads
3057646400: joined with left & right threads
3075550016: joined with left & right threads
main 3075553024 sorted array = [ 0 1 2 3 4 5 6 7 8 9 ]
```

Fig. 4.2 Outputs of Parallel Quicksort Program

4.6   Threads Synchronization

Since threads execute in the same address space of a process, they share all the global variables and data structures in the same address space. When several threads try to modify the same shared variable or data structure, if the outcome depends on the execution order of the threads, it is called a **race condition**. In concurrent programs, race conditions must not exist. Otherwise, the results may be inconsistent. In addition to the join operation, concurrently executing threads often need to cooperate with one another. In order to prevent race conditions, as well as to support threads cooperation, threads need synchronization. In general, synchronization refers to the mechanisms and rules used to ensure the integrity of shared data objects and coordination of concurrently executing entities. It can be applied to either processes in kernel mode or threads in user mode. In the following, we shall discuss the specific problem of threads synchronization in Pthreads.

4.6.1   Mutex Locks

The simplest kind of synchronizing tool is a lock, which allows an execution entity to proceed only if it possesses the lock. In Pthreads, locks are called **mutex,** which stands for **Mutual Exclusion**. Mutex variables are declared with the type pthread_mutex_t, and they must be initialized before using. There are two ways to initialize a mutex variable.

(1) Statically, as in

```
pthread_mutex_t m =  PTHREAD_MUTEX_INITIALIZER;
```

which defines a mutex variable m and initializes it with default attributes.

(2) Dynamically with the **pthread_mutex_init**() function, which allows setting the mutex attributes by an attr parameter, as in

```
pthread_mutex_init (pthread_mutex_t *m, pthread_mutexattr_t,*attr);
```

As usual, the attr parameter can be set to NULL for default attributes.

After initialization, mutex variables can be used by threads via the following functions.

```
int pthread_mutex_lock (pthread_mutex_t *m);     // lock mutex
int pthread_mutex_unlock (pthread_mutex_t *m);   // unlock mutex
int pthread_mutex_trylock (pthread_mutex_t *m);  // try to lock mutex
int pthread_mutex_destroy (pthread_mutex_t *m);  // destroy mutex
```

Threads use mutexes as locks to protect shared data objects. A typical usage of mutex is as follows. A thread first creates a mutex and initializes it once. A newly created mutex is in the unlocked state and without an owner. Each thread tries to access a shared data object by

```
pthread_mutex_lock(&m);     // lock mutex
 access shared data object; // access shared data in a critical region
pthread_mutex_unlock(&m);   // unlock mutex
```

When a thread executes pthread_mutex_lock(&m), if the mutex is unlocked, it locks the mutex, becomes the mutex owner and continues. Otherwise, it becomes blocked and waits in the mutex waiting queue. Only the thread which has acquired the mutex lock can access the shared data object. A sequence of executions which can only be performed by one execution entity at a time is commonly known as a **Critical Region** (CR). In Pthreads, mutexes are used as locks to protect Critical Regions to ensure at most one thread can be inside a CR at any time. When the thread finishes with the shared data object, it exits the CR by calling pthread_mutex_unlock(&m) to unlock the mutex. A locked mutex can only be unlocked by the current owner. When unlocking a mutex, if there are no blocked threads in the mutex waiting queue, it unlocks the mutex and the mutex has no owner. Otherwise, it unblocks a waiting thread from the mutex waiting queue, which becomes the new owner, and the mutex remains locked. When all the threads are finished, the mutex may be destroyed if it was dynamically allocated. We demonstrate threads synchronization using mutex lock by an example.

Example 4.3: This example is a modified version of Example 4.1. As before, we shall use N working threads to compute the sum of all the elements of an N × N matrix of integers. Each working thread computes the partial sum of a row. Instead of depositing the partial sums in a global sum[ ] array, each working thread tries to update a global variable, total, by adding its partial sum to it. Since all the working threads try to update the same global variable, they must be synchronized to prevent race conditions. This can be achieved by a mutex lock, which ensures that only one working thread can update the total variable at a time in a Critical Region. The following shows the Example Program C4.3.

```
/** C4.3.c: matrix sum by threads with mutex lock **/
#include <stdio.h>
#include <stdlib.h>
#include <pthread.h>
```

```
#define  N    4
int A[N][N];

int total = 0;               // global total
pthread_mutex_t *m;          // mutex pointer
void *func(void *arg)        // working thread function
{
   int i, row, sum = 0;
   pthread_t tid = pthread_self(); // get thread ID number
   row = (int)arg;                 // get row number from arg
   printf("Thread %d [%lu] computes sum of row %d\n", row, tid, row);
   for (i=0; i<N; i++)        // compute partial sum of A[row]in
       sum += A[row][i];
   printf("Thread %d [%lu] update total with %d : ", row, tid, sum);
   pthread_mutx_lock(m);
     total += sum;           // update global total inside a CR
   pthread_mutex_unlock(m);
   printf("total = %d\n", total);
}


int main (int argc, char *argv[])
{
   pthread_t thread[N];
   int i, j, r;
   void *status;
   printf("Main: initialize A matrix\n");
   for (i=0; i<N; i++){
     sum[i] = 0;
     for (j=0; j<N; j++){
       A[i][j] = i*N + j + 1;
       printf("%4d ", A[i][j]);
     }
     printf("\n");
   }
   // create a mutex m
   m = (pthread_mutex_t *)malloc(sizeof(pthread_mutex_t));
   pthread_mutex_init(m, NULL); // initialize mutex m
   printf("Main: create %d threads\n", N);
   for(i=0; i<N; i++) {
     pthread_create(&thread[i], NULL, func, (void *)i);
   }
   printf("Main: try to join with threads\n");
   for(i=0; i<N; i++) {
     pthread_join(thread[i], &status);
     printf("Main: joined with %d [%lu]: status=%d\n",
             i, thread[i], (int)status);
   }
   printf("Main: tatal = %d\n", total);
   pthread_mutex_destroy(m); // destroy mutex m
   pthread_exit(NULL);
}
```

```
Main: initialize A matrix
    1    2    3    4
    5    6    7    8
    9   10   11   12
   13   14   15   16
Main: create thread 0
Main: create thread 1
Main: create thread 2
Thread 0 [3076299584] computes sum of row 0
thread 0 [3076299584] update total with 10 : Thread 0: total = 10
Main: create thread 3
Thread 1 [3067906880] computes sum of row 1
thread 1 [3067906880] update total with 26 : Thread 1: total = 36
Thread 2 [3059514176] computes sum of row 2
thread 2 [3059514176] update total with 42 : Thread 2: total = 78
Thread 3 [3051019072] computes sum of row 3
thread 3 [3051019072] update total with 58 : Thread 3: total = 136
Main: joined with 0 [3076299584]: status=0
Main: joined with 1 [3067906880]: status=0
Main: joined with 2 [3059514176]: status=0
Main: joined with 3 [3051019072]: status=0
Main: tatal = 136
```

Fig. 4.3 Outputs of Example 4.3 Program

Figure 4.3 show the sample outputs of running the Example 4.3 program, which demonstrates mutex lock in Pthreads.

4.6.2   Deadlock Prevention

Mutexes use the locking protocol. If a thread can not acquire a mutex lock, it becomes blocked, waiting for the mutex to be unlocked before continuing. In any locking protocol, misuse of locks may lead to problems. The most well-known and prominent problem is deadlock. **Deadlock** is a condition, in which many execution entities mutually wait for one another so that none of them can proceed. To illustrate this, assume that a thread T1 has acquired a mutex lock m1 and tries to lock another mutex m2. Another thread T2 has acquired the mutex lock m2 and tries to lock the mutex m1, as shown in the following diagram.

```
    Thread T1:            |      Thread T2:
-------------------|---------------
    lock(m1);            |      lock(m2);
    . . . .             |      . . . .
    lock(m2);            |      lock(m1);
------------------------------------
```

In this case, T1 and T2 would mutually wait for each other forever, so they are in a deadlock due to crossed locking requests. Similar to no race conditions, deadlocks must not exist in concurrent programs. There are many ways to deal with possible deadlocks, which include **deadlock prevention**, deadlock avoidance, deadlock detection and recovery, etc. In real systems, the only practical way is deadlock prevention, which tries to prevent deadlocks from occurring when designing parallel algorithms. A simple way to prevent deadlock is to order the mutexes and ensure that every thread requests mutex locks only in a single direction, so that there are no loops in the request sequences.

However, it may not be possible to design every parallel algorithm with only uni-directional locking requests. In such cases, the conditional locking function, **pthread_mutex_trylock()**, may be used to prevent deadlocks. The trylock() function returns immediately with an error if the mutex is already locked. In that case, the calling thread may back-off by releasing some of the locks it already holds, allowing other threads to continue. In the above crossed locking example, we may redesign one of the threads, e.g. T1, as follows, which uses conditional locking and back-off to prevent the deadlock.

```
                        Thread T1:
------------------------------------------
while(1){
   lock(m1);
   if (!trylock(m2)) // if trylock m2 fails
      unlock(m1);    // back-off and retry
   else
      break;
   // delay some random time before retry
}
------------------------------------------
```

4.6.3   Condition Variables

Mutexes are used only as locks, which ensure threads to access shared data objects exclusively in Critical Regions. Condition variables provide a means for threads cooperation. Condition variables are always used in conjunction with mutex locks. This is no surprise because mutual exclusion is the basis of all synchronizing mechanisms. In Pthreads, condition variables are declared with the type **pthread_cond_t**, and must be initialized before using. Like mutexes, condition variables can also be initialized in two ways.

(1) Statically, when it is declared, as in

```
    pthread_cond_t con = PTHREAD_COND_INITIALIZER;
```

which defines a condition variable, con, and initializes it with default attributes.

(2) Dynamically with the **pthread_cond_init()** function, which allows setting a condition variable with an attr parameter. For simplicity, we shall always use a NULL attr parameter for default attributes.

The following code segments show how to define a condition variable with an associated mutex lock.

```
pthread_mutex_t con_mutex; // mutex for a condition variable
pthread_cond_t  con;       // a condition variable that relies on con_mutex
pthread_mutex_init(&con_mutex, NULL);  // initialize mutex
pthread_cond_init(&con, NULL);         // initialize con
```

When using a condition variable, a thread must acquire the associated mutex lock first. Then it performs operations within the Critical Region of the mutex lock and releases the mutex lock, as in

```
pthread_mutex_lock(&con_mutex);
    modify or test shared data objects
    use condition variable con to wait or signal conditions
pthread_mutex_unlock(&con_mutex);
```

Within the CR of the mutex lock, threads may use condition variables to cooperate with one another via the following functions.

pthread_cond_wait(condition, mutex): This function blocks the calling thread until the specified condition is signaled. This routine should be called while mutex is locked. It will automatically release the mutex lock while the thread waits. After signal is received and a blocked thread is awakened, mutex will be automatically locked.

pthread_cond_signal(condition): This function is used to signal, i.e. to wake up or unblock, a thread which is waiting on the condition variable. It should be called after mutex is locked, and must unlock mutex in order for **pthread_cond_wait()** to complete.

pthread_cond_broadcast(condition): This function unblocks all threads that are blocked on the condition variable. All unblocked threads will compete for the same mutex to access the condition variable. Their order of execution depends on threads scheduling.

We demonstrate thread cooperation using condition variables by an example.

4.6.4   Producer-Consumer Problem

Example 4.4: In this example, we shall implement a simplified version of the **producer-consumer problem,** which is also known as the **bounded buffer** problem, using threads and condition variables. The producer-consumer problem is usually defined with processes as executing entities, which can be regarded as threads in the current context. The problem is defined as follows.

A set of producer and consumer processes share a finite number of buffers. Each buffer contains a unique item at a time. Initially, all the buffers are empty. When a producer puts an item into an empty buffer, the buffer becomes full. When a consumer gets an item from a full buffer, the buffer becomes empty, etc. A producer must wait if there are no empty buffers. Similarly, a consumer must wait if there are no full buffers. Furthermore, waiting processes must be allowed to continue when their awaited events occur.

In the example program, we shall assume that each buffer holds an integer value. The shared global variables are defined as

```
// shared global variables
int buf[NBUF];      // circular buffers
int head, tail;     // indices
int data;           // number of full buffers
```

The buffers are used as a set of circular buffers. The index variables **head** is for putting an item into an empty buffer, and **tail** is for taking an item out of a full buffer. The variable data is the number of full buffers. To support cooperation between producer and consumer, we define a mutex and two condition variables.

```
pthread_mutex_t mutex;        // mutex lock
pthread_cond_t empty, full;  // condition variables
```

where **empty** represents the condition of any empty buffers, and **full** represents the condition of any full buffers. When a producer finds there are no empty buffers, it waits on the **empty** condition variable, which is signaled whenever a consumer has consumed a full buffer. Likewise, when a consumer finds there are no full buffers, it waits on the **full** condition variable, which is signaled whenever a producer puts an item into an empty buffer.

The program starts with the main thread, which initializes the buffer control variables and the condition variables. After initialization, it creates a producer and a consumer thread and waits for the threads to join. The buffer size is set to NBUF=5 but the producer tries to put N=10 items into the buffer area, which would cause it to wait when all the buffers are full. Similarly, the consumer tries to get N=10 items from the buffers, which would cause it to wait when all the buffers are empty. In either case, a waiting thread is signaled up by another thread when the awaited conditions are met. Thus, the two threads cooperate with each other through the condition variables. The following shows the program code of Example Program C4.4, which implements a simplified version of the producer-consumer problem with only one producer and one consumer.

```
/* C4.4.c: producer-consumer by threads with condition variables */
#include <stdio.h>
#include <stdlib.h>
#include <pthread.h>

#define NBUF     5
#define N        10

// shared global variables
int buf[NBUF];        // circular buffers
int head, tail;       // indices
int data;             // number of full buffers
pthread_mutex_t mutex;        // mutex lock
pthread_cond_t empty, full;  // condition variables

int init()
{
  head = tail = data = 0;
  pthread_mutex_init(&mutex, NULL);
  pthread_cond_init(&fullBuf, NULL);
  pthread_cond_init(&emptyBuf, NULL);
}

void *producer()
{
  int i;
  pthread_t me = pthread_self();
  for (i=0; i<N; i++){ // try to put N items into buf[ ]
      pthread_mutex_lock(&mutex);     // lock mutex
      if (data == NBUF){
          printf ("producer %lu: all bufs FULL: wait\n", me);
```

```
          pthread_cond_wait(&empty, &mutex); // wait
      }
      buf[head++] = i+1;                    // item = 1,2,..,N
      head %= NBUF;                         // circular bufs
      data++;                               // inc data by 1
      printf("producer %lu: data=%d value=%d\n", me, bp->data, i+1);
      pthread_mutex_unlock(&mutex);   // unlock mutex
      pthread_cond_signal(&full);     // unblock a consumer, if any
  }
  printf("producer %lu: exit\n", me);
}

void *consumer()
{
  int i, c;
  pthread_t me = pthread_self();
  for (i=0; i<N; i++) {
      pthread_mutex_lock(&mutex);       // lock mutex
      if (data == 0) {
         printf ("consumer %lu: all bufs EMPTY: wait\n", me);
         pthread_cond_wait(&full, &mutex); // wait
      }
      c = buf[tail++];                    // get an item
      tail %= NBUF;
      data--;                             // dec data by 1
      printf("consumer %lu: value=%d\n", me, c);
      pthread_mutex_unlock(&mutex);   // unlock mutex
      pthread_cond_signal(&empty);    // unblock a producer, if any
  }
  printf("consumer %lu: exit\n", me);
}

int main ()
{
  pthread_t pro, con;
  init();
  printf("main: create producer and consumer threads\n");
  pthread_create(&pro, NULL, producer, NULL);
  pthread_create(&con, NULL, consumer, NULL);
  printf("main: join with threads\n");
  pthread_join(pro, NULL);
  pthread_join(con, NULL);
  printf("main: exit\n");
}
```

Figure 4.4 shows the output of running the producer-consumer example program.

```
main: create producer and consumer threads
main: join with threads
producer 3076275008: data=1 value=1
producer 3076275008: data=2 value=2
producer 3076275008: data=3 value=3
producer 3076275008: data=4 value=4
producer 3076275008: data=5 value=5
producer 3076275008: all bufs FULL: wait
consumer 3067882304: value=1
consumer 3067882304: value=2
consumer 3067882304: value=3
consumer 3067882304: value=4
consumer 3067882304: value=5
consumer 3067882304: all bufs EMPTY: wait
producer 3076275008: data=1 value=6
producer 3076275008: data=2 value=7
producer 3076275008: data=3 value=8
producer 3076275008: data=4 value=9
consumer 3067882304: value=6
consumer 3067882304: value=7
consumer 3067882304: value=8
consumer 3067882304: value=9
consumer 3067882304: all bufs EMPTY: wait
producer 3076275008: data=1 value=10
producer 3076275008: exit
consumer 3067882304: value=10
consumer 3067882304: exit
main: exit
```

Fig. 4.4 Outputs of Producer-Consumer Program

4.6.5   Semaphores

Semaphores are general mechanisms for process synchronization. A (counting) semaphore is a data structure

```
struct sem{
    int value;              // semaphore (counter) value;
    struct process *queue   // a queue of blocked processes
}s;
```

Before using, a semaphore must be initialized with an initial value and an empty waiting queue. Regardless of the hardware platform, i.e. whether on single CPU systems or multiprocessing systems, the low level implementation of semaphores guarantees that each semaphore can only be operated by one executing entity at a time and operations on semaphores are **atomic** (indivisible) or **primitive** from the viewpoint of executing entities. The reader may ignore such details here and focus on the high level operations on semaphores and their usage as a mechanism for process synchronization. The most well-known operations on semaphores are P and V (Dijkstra 1965), which are defined as follows.

```
--------------------------------------------------------
P(struct sempahore *s)    |   V(struct sempahore *s)
{                         |   {
  s->value--;             |     s->value++;
  if (s->value < 0)       |     if (s->value <= 0)
    BLOCK(s);             |       SIGNAL(s);
}                         |   }
--------------------------------------------------------
```

where BLOCK(s) blocks the calling process in the semaphore's waiting queue, and SIGNAL (s) unblocks a process from the semaphore's waiting queue.

Semaphores are not part of the original Pthreads standard. However, most Pthreads now support semaphores of POSIX 1003.1b. POSIX semaphores include the following functions

```
int sem_init(sem, value)  : initialize sem with an initial value
int sem_wait(sem)         : similar to P(sem)
int sem_post(sem)         : similar to V(sem)
```

The major difference between semaphores and condition variables is that the former includes a counter, manipulate the counter, test the counter value to make decisions, etc. all in the Critical Region of atomic or primitive operations, whereas the latter requires a specific mutex lock to enforce the Critical Region. In Pthreads, mutexes are strictly for locking and condition variables are for threads cooperation. In contrast, counting semaphores with initial value 1 can be used as locks. Semaphores with other initial values can be used for cooperation. Therefore, semaphores are more general and flexible than condition variables. The following example illustrates the advantages of semaphores over condition variables.

Example 4.5: The producer-consumer problem can be solved more efficiently by using semaphores. In this example, **empty=N and full=0** are semaphores for producers and consumers to cooperate with one another, and **mutex =1** is a lock semaphore for processes to access shared buffers one at a time in a Critical Region. The following shows the pseudo code of the producer-consumer problem using semaphores.

```
ITEM buf[N];           // N buffers of ITEM type
int head=0, tail=0;    // buffer indices
struct semaphore empty=N, full=0, mutex=1; // semaphores

--------- Producer ------------- Consumer------------
    while(1){               |    while(1){
      produce an item;      |       ITEM item;
      P(&empty);            |       P(&full);
      P(&mutex);            |       P(&mutex)
        buf[head++]=item;   |         item=buf[tail++];
        head %= N;          |         tail %= N;
      V(&mutex);            |       V(&mutex);
      V(&full);             |       V(&empty);
    }                       |    }
-----------------------------------------------------
```

4.6.6 Barriers

The threads join operation allows a thread (usually the main thread) to wait for the termination of other threads. After all awaited threads have terminated, the main thread may create new threads to continue executing the next parts of a parallel program. This requires the overhead of creating new threads. There are situations in which it would be better to keep the threads alive but require them not to go on until all of them have reached a prescribed point of synchronization. In Pthreads, the mechanism is the **barrier**, along with a set of barrier functions. First, the main thread creates a barrier object

```
                    pthread_barrier_t barrier;
```

and calls

```
          pthread_barrier_init(&barrier NULL, nthreads);
```

to initialize it with the number of threads that are to be synchronized at the barrier. Then the main thread creates working threads to perform tasks. The working threads use

```
          pthread_barrier_wait( &barrier)
```

to wait at the barrier until the specified number of threads have reached the barrier. When the last thread arrives at the barrier, all the threads resume execution again. In this case, a barrier acts as a rendezvous point, rather than as a graveyard, of threads. We illustrate the use of barriers by an example.

4.6.7   Solve System of Linear Equations by Concurrent Threads

We demonstrate applications of concurrent threads and threads join and barrier operations by an example.

Example 4.6: The example is to solve a system of linear equations by concurrent threads. Assume $AX = B$ is a system of linear equations, where A is an $N \times N$ matrix of real numbers, X is a column vector of N unknowns and B is column vector of constants. The problem is to compute the solution vector X. The most well known algorithm for solving systems of linear equations is **Gauss elimination**. The algorithm consists of 2 major steps; **row reduction**, which reduces the combined matrix [A|B] to an upper-triangular form, followed by **back substitution**, which computes the solution vector X. In the row-reduction steps, **partial pivoting** is a scheme which ensures the leading element of the row used to reduce other rows has the maximum absolute value. Partial pivoting helps improve the accuracy of the numerical computations. The following shows a Gauss elimination algorithm with partial pivoting.

/******** **Gauss Elimination Algorithm with Partial Pivoting** *******/
Step 1: Row reduction: reduce [A|B] to upper triangular form

```
       for (i=0; i<N ; i++){       // for rows i = 0 to N-1
         do partial pivoting;      // exchange rows if needed
(1).     // barrier
         for (j=i+1; j<=N; j++){    // for rows j = i+1 to N
           for (k=i+1; k<=N; k++){ // for columns k = i+1 to N
             f = A[j,i]/A[i,i];    // reduction factor
             A[j,k] -= A[j,k]*f;   // reduce row j
           }
           A[j][i] = 0;            // A[j,i] = 0
         }
(2).     // barrier
       }
(3).  // join
```

Step 2: Back Substitution: compute xN-1, xN-2, ... , x0 in that order

The Gauss elimination algorithm can be parallelized as follows. The algorithm starts with a main thread, which creates N working threads to execute the **ge(thread_id)** function and waits for all the working threads to join. The threads function ge() implements the row reduction step of the Gauss elimination algorithm. In the ge() function, for each iteration of row = 0 to N-2, the thread with thread_ID=i does the partial pivoting on a corresponding row i. All other threads wait at a barrier (1) until partial pivoting is complete. Then each working thread does row reduction on a unique row equal to its ID number. Since all working threads must have finished the current row reductions before iteration on the next row can start, so they wait at another barrier (2). After reducing the matrix [A|B] to upper triangular form, the final step is to compute the solutions x[N-i], for i=1 to N in that order, which is inherently sequential. The main thread must wait until all the working threads have ended before starting the back substitution. This is achieved by join operations by the main thread. The following shows the complete code of the Example Program C4.5.

```
/** C4.5.c: Gauss Elimination with Partial Pivoting **/
#include <stdio.h>
#include <stdlib.h>
#include <math.h>
#include <pthread.h>

#define N 4
double A[N][N+1];
pthread_barrier_t barrier;

int print_matrix()
{
    int i, j;
    printf("-------------------------------------\n");
    for(i=0; i<N; i++){
        for(j=0;j<N+1;j++)
            printf("%6.2f  ", A[i][j]);
        printf("\n");
    }
}

void *ge(void *arg) // threads function: Gauss elimination
{
    int i, j, prow;
    int myid = (int)arg;
    double temp, factor;
    for(i=0; i<N-1; i++){
        if (i == myid){
            printf("partial pivoting by thread %d on row %d: ", myid, i);
            temp = 0.0; prow = i;
            for (j=i; j<=N; j++){
                if (fabs(A[j][i]) > temp){
                    temp = fabs(A[j][i]);
                    prow = j;
                }
```

```
        }
        printf("pivot_row=%d  pivot=%6.2f\n", prow, A[prow][i]);
        if (prow != i){  // swap rows
            for (j=i; j<N+1; j++){
                temp = A[i][j];
                A[i][j] = A[prow][j];
                A[prow][j] = temp;
            }
        }
    }
    // wait for partial pivoting done
    pthread_barrier_wait(&barrier);
    for(j=i+1; j<N; j++){
        if (j == myid){
            printf("thread %d do row %d\n", myid, j);
            factor = A[j][i]/A[i][i];
            for (k=i+1; k<=N; k++)
                A[j][k] -= A[i][k]*factor;
            A[j][i] = 0.0;
        }
    }
    // wait for current row reductions to finish
    pthread_barrier_wait(&barrier);
    if (i == myid)
        print_matrix();
    }
}


int main(int argc, char *argv[])
{
    int i, j;
    double sum;
    pthread_t threads[N];

    printf("main: initialize matrix A[N][N+1] as [A|B]\n");
    for (i=0; i<N; i++)
      for (j=0; j<N; j++)
          A[i][j] = 1.0;
    for (i=0; i<N; i++)
        A[i][N-i-1] = 1.0*N;
    for (i=0; i<N; i++){
        A[i][N] = 2.0*N - 1;
    }
    print_matrix();  // show initial matrix [A|B]

    pthread_barrier_init(&barrier, NULL, N); // set up barrier

    printf("main: create N=%d working threads\n", N);
    for (i=0; i<N; i++){
        pthread_create(&threads[i], NULL, ge, (void *)i);
    }
```

```
printf("main: wait for all %d working threads to join\n", N);
for (i=0; i<N; i++){
    pthread_join(threads[i], NULL);
}
printf("main: back substitution : ");
for (i=N-1; i>=0; i--){
    sum = 0.0;
    for (j=i+1; j<N; j++)
        sum += A[i][j]*A[j][N];
        A[i][N] = (A[i][N]- sum)/A[i][i];
}
// print solution
printf("The solution is :\n");
for(i=0; i<N; i++){
    printf("%6.2f  ", A[i][N]);
}
printf("\n");
}
```

Figure 4.5 shows the sample outputs of running the Example 4.6 program, which solves a system of equations with N=4 unknowns by Gauss elimination with partial pivoting.

```
main: initialize matrix A[N][N+1] as [A|B]
-------------------------------------
   1.00    1.00    1.00    4.00    7.00
   1.00    1.00    4.00    1.00    7.00
   1.00    4.00    1.00    1.00    7.00
   4.00    1.00    1.00    1.00    7.00
main: create N=4 working threads
partial pivoting by thread 0 on row 0: pivot_row=3  pivot= 4.00
main: wait for all 4 working threads to join
thread 1 do row 1
thread 2 do row 2
thread 3 do row 3
-------------------------------------
   4.00    1.00    1.00    1.00    7.00
   0.00    0.75    3.75    0.75    5.25
   0.00    3.75    0.75    0.75    5.25
   0.00    0.75    0.75    3.75    5.25
partial pivoting by thread 1 on row 1: pivot_row=2  pivot= 3.75
thread 3 do row 3
thread 2 do row 2
partial pivoting by thread 2 on row 2: pivot_row=2  pivot= 3.60
-------------------------------------
   4.00    1.00    1.00    1.00    7.00
   0.00    3.75    0.75    0.75    5.25
   0.00    0.00    3.60    0.60    4.20
   0.00    0.00    0.60    3.60    4.20
thread 3 do row 3
-------------------------------------
   4.00    1.00    1.00    1.00    7.00
   0.00    3.75    0.75    0.75    5.25
   0.00    0.00    3.60    0.60    4.20
   0.00    0.00    0.00    3.50    3.50
main: back substition : The solution is :
   1.00    1.00    1.00    1.00
```

Fig. 4.5 Sample Outputs of Example 4.6 Program

4.6.8 Threads in Linux

Unlike many other operating systems, Linux does not distinguish processes from threads. To the Linux kernel, a thread is merely a process that shares certain resources with other processes. In Linux both processes and threads are created by the clone() system call, which has the prototype

```
int clone(int (*fn)(void *), void *child_stack, int flags, void *arg)
```

As can be seen, clone() is more like a thread creation function. It creates a child process to execute a function fn(arg) with a child_stack. The flags field specifies the resources to be shared by the parent and child, which includes

CLONE_VM: parent and child share address space
CLONE_FS: parent and child share file system information, e.g. root. CWD
CLONE_FILES: parent and child share opened files
CLONE_SIGHAND: parent and child share signal handlers and blocked signals

If any of the flags is specified, both processes share exactly the SAME resource, not a separate copy of the resource. If a flag is not specified, the child process usually gets a separate copy of the resource. In this case, changes made to a resource by one process do not affect the resource of the other process. The Linux kernel retains fork() as a system call but it may be implemented as a library wrapper that calls clone() with appropriate flags. An average user does not have to worry about such details. It suffices to say that Linux has an efficient way of supporting threads. Moreover, most current Linux kernels support Symmetric Multiprocessing (SMP). In such Linux systems, processes (threads) are scheduled to run on multiprocessors in parallel.

4.7 Programming Project: User-Level Threads

The programming project is to implement **user-level threads** to simulate threads operations in Linux. The project consists of 4 parts. Part 1 presents the base code of the project to help the reader get started. The base code implements a multitasking system, which supports independent executions of tasks within a Linux process. It is the same MT multitasking system presented in Chap. 3, but adapted to the user-level threads environment. Part 2 is to extend the base code to implement support for task join operation. Part 3 is to extend the base code to support mutex operations. Part 4 is to implement counting semaphores to support task cooperation, and demonstrate semaphores in the multitasking system.

4.7.1 Project Base Code: A Multitasking System

Programming Project PART 1: Base Code: The following shows the base code of the programming project, which will be explained in latter sections.

(1). **ts.s file** in 32-bit GCC assembly code:

```
#------------ ts.s file ------------
.global tswitch, running, scheduler
tswitch:
SAVE:        pushal
             pushfl
             movl   running,%ebx
             movl   %esp, 4(%ebx)   # integers in GCC are 4 bytes
FIND:        call   scheduler
RESUME:      movl   running, %ebx
             movl   4(%ebx), %esp
             popfl
             popal
             ret
```

(2). **type.h file:** This file defines the system constants and the PROC structure

```
/*********** type.h file *************/
#define NPROC    9
#define SSIZE 1024
// PROC status
#define FREE      0
#define READY     1
#define SLEEP     2
#define BLOCK     3
#define ZOMBIE    4

typedef struct proc{
  struct proc *next;     // next proc pointer
  int ksp;               // saved stack pointer
  int pid;               // proc PID
  int priority;          // proc scheduling priority
  int status;            // current status: FREE|READY, etc.
  int event;             // for sleep/wakeup
  int exitStatus;        // exit status
  int joinPid;           // join target pid
  struct proc *joinPtr;  // join target PROC pointer
  int stack[SSIZE];      // proc 4KB stack area
}PROC;
```

(3). **queue.c file**, which implements queue operation functions

```
// same as in MT system of Chapter 3
```

(4). **t.c file,** which is the main file of the program

```
#include <stdio.h>
#include "type.h"
```

```
PROC proc[NPROC];        // NPROC proc structures
PROC *freeList;          // free PROC list
PROC *readyQueue;        // ready proc priority queue
PROC *sleepList;         // sleep PROC list
PROC *running;           // running proc pointer
#include "queue.c"       // enqueue(), dequeue(), printList()

int init()
{
  int i, j;
  PROC *p;
  for (i=0; i<NPROC; i++){
    p = &proc[i];
    p->pid = i;
    p->priority = 0;
    p->status = FREE;
    p->event = 0;
    p->joinPid = 0;
    p->joinPtr = 0;
    p->next = p+1;
  }
  proc[NPROC-1].next = 0;
  freeList = &proc[0];     // all PROCs in freeList
  readyQueue = 0;
  sleepList  = 0;
  // create P0 as initial running task
  running = p = dequeue(&freeList);
  p->status = READY;
  p->priority = 0;
  printList("freeList", freeList);
  printf("init complete: P0 running\n");
}

int texit(int value)
{
  printf("task %d in texit value=%d\n", running->pid, running->pid);
  running->status = FREE;
  running->priority = 0;
  enqueue(&freeList, running);
  printList("freeList", freeList);
  tswitch();
}

int do_create()
{
  int pid = create(func, running->pid); // parm = pid
}
```

```
int do_switch()
{
  tswitch();
}

int do_exit()
{
  texit(running->pid); // for simplicity: exit with pid value
}

void func(void *parm)
{
  int c;
  printf("task %d start: parm = %d\n", running->pid, (int)parm);
  while(1){
    printf("task %d running\n", running->pid);
    printList("readyQueue", readyQueue);
    printf("enter a key [c|s|q] : ");
    c = getchar(); getchar();
    switch (c){
        case 'c' : do_create(); break;
        case 's' : do_switch(); break;
        case 'q' : do_exit(); break;
    }
  }
}

int create(void (*f)(), void *parm)
{
  int i;
  PROC *p = dequeue(&freeList);
  if (!p){
    printf("create failed\n");
    return -1;
  }
  p->status = READY;
  p->priority = 1;
  p->joinPid = 0;
  p->joinPtr = 0;

  // initialize new task stack for it to resume to f(parm)
  for (i=1; i<13; i++)                # zero out stack cells
      p->stack[SSIZE-i] = 0;
  p->stack[SSIZE-1] = (int)parm;     # function parameter
  p->stack[SSIZE-2] = (int)do_exit;  # function return address
  p->stack[SSIZE-3] = (int)f;        # function entry
  p->ksp = (int)&p->stack[SSIZE-12]; # ksp -> stack top
  enqueue(&readyQueue, p);
  printList("readyQueue", readyQueue);
  printf("task %d created a new task %d\n", running->pid, p->pid);
  return p->pid;
```

```
  }

int main()
{
  printf("Welcome to the MT User-Level Threads System\n");
  init();
  create((void *)func, 0);
  printf("P0 switch to P1\n");
  while(1){
    if (readyQueue)
      tswitch();
  }
}

int scheduler()
{
  if (running->status == READY)
    enqueue(&readyQueue, running);
  running = dequeue(&readyQueue);
  printf("next running = %d\n", running->pid);
}
```

To compile and run the base code under Linux, enter

gcc −m32 t.c ts.s

Then run a.out. While running the program, the reader may enter the commands

'c': create a new task

's': switch to run the next task from readyQueue

'q': let the running task terminate

to test and observe task executions in the system. Figure 4.6 shows the sample outputs of running the base code program.

4.7.2 User-Level Threads

The entire base code program runs as a Linux process in user mode. Inside the Linux process are independent execution entities, which are equivalent to conventional threads. In order not to be confused with either Linux process or threads, we shall refer to the execution entities as tasks. In the system, tasks run concurrently by multitasking. Figure 4.7 shows the model of concurrent tasks inside a Linux process.

Since all the tasks execute inside a Linux process, the Linux kernel does not know their existence. To the Linux kernel, the entire MT system is a single Linux process, but we subdivide the CPU's execution time to run different tasks inside the Linux process. For this reason, the tasks are known as **user-level threads.** The purpose of this programming project is to create a multitasking environment in a Linux process to support user-level threads. The same technique can also be used to create user-level threads under any operating system. Next, we explain the base code in more detail by the following steps.

```
Welcome to the MT User-Level Threads System
freeList = [1 0]->[2 0]->[3 0]->[4 0]->[5 0]->[6 0]->[7 0]->[8 0]->NULL
init complete
readyQueue = [1 1]->NULL
task 0 created a new task 1
P0 switch to P1
next running = 1
task 1 start: parm = 0
task 1 running
readyQueue = [0 0]->NULL
enter a key [c|s|q] : c
readyQueue = [2 1]->[0 0]->NULL
task 1 created a new task 2
task 1 running
readyQueue = [2 1]->[0 0]->NULL
enter a key [c|s|q] : s
next running = 2
task 2 start: parm = 1
task 2 running
readyQueue = [1 1]->[0 0]->NULL
enter a key [c|s|q] : q
task 2 in texit value=2
freeList = [3 0]->[4 0]->[5 0]->[6 0]->[7 0]->[8 0]->[2 0]->NULL
next running = 1
task 1 running
readyQueue = [0 0]->NULL
enter a key [c|s|q] : █
```

Fig. 4.6 Sample Outputs of the Base Code Program

Fig. 4.7 Concurrent Tasks
in a Linux Process

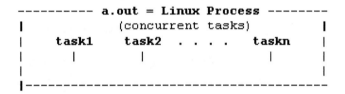

(1). **Task PROC structure:** A major difference between processes and threads is that the former obey
a parent-child relation but the latter do not. In the threads model, all threads are equal. Relations
between threads are peer-to-peer, rather than parent to child. So there is no need for parent task PID
and the task family tree. Therefore, these fields are deleted from the PROC structure. The new
fields joinPid and joinPtr are for implementing the threads join operation, which will be discussed
later.

(2). **init():** When the system starts, main() calls init() to initialize the system. Init() initializes the PROC
structures and enter them into a freeList. It also initializes the readyQueue to empty. Then it uses
proc[0] to creates P0 as the initial running task. P0 has the lowest priority 0. All other tasks have a
priority 1, so that they will take turn to run from the readyQueue.

(3). P0 calls create() to create a task P1 to execute the func(parm) function with a parameter parm=0,
and enters it into the readyQueue. Then P0 calls tswitch() to switch task to run P1.

(4). **tswitch():** The tswitch() function implements task context switching. Instead of pushl/popl
individual CPU registers, it uses the PUSHAL and POPAL instructions. tswitch() acts as a task
switch box, where one task goes in and, in general, another tasks emerges. It consists of 3 separated
steps, which are explained in more detail below.

(4).1. **SAVE part of tswitch():** When a task calls tswitch(), it saves the return address on its own stack
and enters tswitch() in assembly code. In tswitch(), the SAVE part saves CPU registers into the
calling task's stack, save the stack pointer into proc.ksp. The Intel x86 CPU in 32-bit mode has
many registers, but only the registers eax, ebx, ecx, edx, esp, ebp, esi, edi and eflags are visible to

user mode processes. So we only need to save and restore these registers while a (Linux) process is executing. The following diagram shows the stack contents and the saved stack pointer of the calling task after executing the SAVE part of tswitch(), where xxx denote the stack contents before calling tswitch().

```
                                                     proc.ksp
                                                        |
     |xxx|retPC|eax|ecx|edx|ebx|old_esp|ebp|esi|edi|eflags|
```

In the Intel x86 based PCs in 32-bit mode, every CPU register is 4 bytes wide and stack operations are always in units of 4 bytes. Thus, we may define the PROC stack as an integer array.

(4).2. **scheduler():** After executing the SAVE part of tswitch(), the task calls scheduler() to pick the next running task. In scheduler(), if the calling task is still READY to run, it calls enqueue() to put itself into the readyQueue by priority. Otherwise, the task will not be in readyQueue, which makes it non-runnable. Then it calls dequeue(), which returns the first ready PROC removed from readyQueue as the next running task.

(4).3. **RESUME part of tswitch():** When execution returns from scheduler(), running may have changed to point at the PROC of a different task. The RESUME part of tswitch() sets the CPU's stack pointer to the saved stack pointer of the current running task. Then it pops saved registers, followed by RET, causing the current running task return to where it called tswitch() earlier.

(5). **create():** The **create(func, parm)** function creates a new task and enters it into the readyQueue. The new task will begin execution from the named **func()** function with **parm** as parameter. Although the new task never existed before, we may pretend it not only existed before but also ran before. The reason why it is not running now is because it called tswitch() to give up CPU earlier. If so, its stack must contain a frame saved by the SAVE part of tswitch(), and its saved ksp must point at the stack top. Furthermore, when a new task begins execution from func(), which is written as func(void *parm), it must have a return address and a parameter parm on the stack. When func() finishes, the task shall "return to where func() was called earlier". Thus, in create(), we initialize the stack of the new task as follows.

```
                                                    proc.ksp
                    |< ------- all saved registers = 0- -----> |
     |parm|do_exit|func|eax|ecx|edx|ebx|oldesp|ebp|esi|edi|eflags|
      -1     -2     -3  -4  -5  -6  -7   -8    -9 -10 -11    -12
```

where the index –i means SSIZE-i. These are done by the following code segment in create().

```
for (i=1; i<13; i++)              # zero out stack cells
    p->stack[SSIZE-i] = 0;
p->stack[SSIZE-1] = (int)parm;    # function parameter
p->stack[SSIZE-2] = (int)do_exit; # function return address
p->stack[SSIZE-3] = (int)func;    # function entry
p->ksp = (int)&p->stack[SSIZE-12]; # ksp -> stack top
```

When the new task begins to run, it executes the RESUME part of tswitch(), causing it to return to the entry address of func(). When execution enters func(), the stack top contains a pointer to do_exit() and a parameter parm, as if it was called as func(parm) from the entry address of do_exit(). In practice, the task function rarely returns. If it does, it would return to do_texit(), which causes the task to terminate.

(5). **func():** For demonstration purpose, all tasks are created to execute the same function, func(parm). For simplicity, the function parameter is set to the pid of the creator task, but the reader may pass any parameter, e.g. a structure pointer, to the function. While executing in func(), a task prompts for a command char = [c | s | q], where

'c' : create a new task to execute func(parm), with parm=caller pid
's' : switch task;
'q' : terminate and return the PROC as FREE to freeList

(6). **The Idle Task P0:** P0 is special in that it has the lowest priority among all the tasks. After system initialization, P0 creates P1 and switches to run P1. P0 will run again if and only if there are no runnable tasks. In that case, P0 simply loops. The reader may enter Control-C to terminate the (Linux) process. It is noted that the stack of P0 is actually the user mode stack of the Linux process.

4.7.3 Implementation of Thread Join Operation

PART 2: Extend Base Code to support task join operation. The extensions are listed in order below.

(1). **tsleep(int event):** Whenever a task must wait for something that's not available, it calls tsleep() to go to sleep on an event value, which represents the reason of the sleep. The algorithm of tsleep() is

```
/*********** Algorithm of tsleep(int event) **************/
  1. record event value in proc.event:  running->event = event;
  2. change status to SLEEP:             running->status = SLEEP;
  3. for ease of maintenance, enter caller into a (global) PROC *sleepList:
                                         enqueue(&sleepList, running);
  4. give up CPU:                        tswitch();
```

A sleeping task is not runnable until it is woken up by another task. So in tsleep(), the task calls tswitch() to give up the CPU.

(2). **int twakeup(int event):** twakeup() wakes up ALL tasks that are sleeping on the specified event value. If no task is sleeping on the event, it does nothing. The algorithm of twakeup() is

```
/*********** Algorithm of twakeup(int event) *********/
for each PROC *p in sleepList do{ // assume sleepers are in a global sleepList
    if (p->event == event){
        delete p from sleepList;
        p->status = READY;          // make p READY to run again
        enqueue(&readyQueue, p);    // enter p into readyQueue by priority
    }
}
```

(3). **texit(int status):** Modified texit() in the base code for tasks to terminate. In the process model, every process has a unique parent (which may be the INIT process P1), which always waits for the process to terminate. So a terminating process can become a ZOMBIE and wakes up its parent, which will dispose of the ZOMBIE child. If a terminating process has children, it must give away the children to either the INIT process or a subreaper process before becoming a ZOMBIE. In the threads model, threads are all equal. A thread does not have a parent or children. When a thread terminates, if there is no other threads waiting for it to terminate, it must exit as FREE. If there is any thread waiting for it to terminate, it should become a ZOMBIE, wake up all such threads, allowing one of them to find and dispose of the ZOMBIE. In the threads model, the thread termination algorithm is

```
/************ Algorithm of texit(int status) ************/
1.    try to find a (any) task which wants to join with this task;
2.    if no task wants to join with this task: exit as FREE
      //  some task is waiting for this task to terminate
3.    record status value in proc.exitStatus: running->exitStatus = status;
4.    become a ZOMBIE:                         running->status = ZOMBIE;
5.    wake up joining  tasks:                  twakeup(running->pid)
6.    give up CPU:                             tswitch();
```

(4). **join(int targetPid, int *status)**: The join operation waits for a thread with targetPid to terminate. In the process model, every process can only be waited by a unique parent, and a process never waits for its own parent to terminate. So the waiting sequence is always a unidirectional chain. In the threads model, a thread is allowed to join with any other thread. This may cause two problems. First, when a thread tries to join with a target thread, the target thread may no longer exist. In this case, the joining thread must return with an error. If the target thread exists but has not terminated yet, the joining thread must go to sleep on the target thread PID, waiting for the target thread to terminate. Second, since threads do not obey the parent-child relation, a sequence of joining threads may lead to a deadlock waiting loop. In order to prevent such deadlocks, every joining thread must record the identity of the target thread in its PROC structure to allow other joining threads to check whether the join request would lead to a deadlock. When the targeted thread terminates, it can check whether there are any threads waiting for it to terminate. If so, it would become a ZOMBIE and wake up all such joining threads. Upon waking up, the joining threads must execute the join operation again since the ZOMBIE may already be freed by another joining thread. Thus, the algorithm of the thread join operation is as follows.

```
/********* Algorithm of join(int targetPid, int *status) *********/
while(1)
{
  1.  if (no task with targetPid) return NOPID error;
  2.  if (targetPid's joinPtr list leads to this task) return DEADLOCK error;
  3.  set running->joinPid = targetPid, running->joinPtr ->targetPid's PROC;
  4.  if (found targetPid's ZOMBIE proc *p){
         *status = p->exitStatus;  // extract ZOMBIE exit status
         p->status =  FREE; p->priority = 0;
         enqueue(&freeList, p); // release p to freeList
         return p->pid;
      }
  5.  tsleep(targetPid); // sleep on targetPID until woken up by target task
}
```

Steps 2 of the join() algorithm prevents deadlock due to either crossed or circular joining requests, which can be checked by traversing the targetPid's joinPtr pointer list. Each joining task's joinPtr points to a target PROC it intends to join with. If the list points back to the current running task, it would be a circular waiting list, which must be rejected due to a potential deadlock.

Programming Project PART 2: Part 2 of the programming project is for the reader to implement the tsleep(), twakeup() and join() functions. Then test the resulting system by the following program code, which uses task creation and join operations of the programming project.

```c
/************ PART 2 of Programming Project ***********/
#include <stdio.h>
#include <stdlib.h>
#include "type.h"

PROC proc[NPROC];
PROC *freeList;
PROC *sleepList;
PROC *readyQueue;
PROC *running;

/****** implement these functions ******/
int tsleep(int event){ }
int twakeup(int event){ }
int texit(int status){ }
int join(int pid, int *status){ }
/****** end of implementations *********/

int init(){ }   // SAME AS in PART 1

int do_exit()
{
  // for simplicity: exit with pid value as status
  texit(running->pid);
}

void task1(void *parm) // task1: demonstrate create-join operations
{
  int pid[2];
  int i, status;
  //printf("task %d create subtasks\n", running->pid);
  for (i=0; i<2; i++){    // P1 creates P2, P3
     pid[i] = create(func, running->pid);
  }
  join(5, &status);      // try to join with targetPid=5
  for (i=0; i<2; i++){   // try to join with P2, P3
     pid[i] = join(pid[i], &status);
     printf("task%d joined with task%d: status = %d\n",
            running->pid, pid[i], status);
  }
}

void func(void *parm)   // subtasks: enter q to exit
{
  char c;
  printf("task %d start: parm = %d\n", running->pid, parm);
  while(1){
```

```
        printList("readyQueue", readyQueue);
        printf("task %d running\n", running->pid);
        printf("enter a key [c|s|q|j]: ");
        c = getchar(); getchar(); // kill \r
        switch (c){
            case 'c' : do_create(); break;
            case 's' : do_switch(); break;
            case 'q' : do_exit();   break;
            case 'j' : do_join();   break;
        }
    }
}

int create(void (*f)(), void *parm)
{
    int i;
    PROC *p = dequeue(&freeList);
    if (!p){
        printf("create failed\n");
        return -1;
    }
    p->status = READY;
    p->priority = 1;
    p->joinPid = 0;
    p->joinPtr = 0;
    for (i=1; i<13; i++)
        p->stack[SSIZE-i] = 0;
    p->stack[SSIZE-1] = (int)parm;
    p->stack[SSIZE-2] = (int)do_exit;
    p->stack[SSIZE-3] = (int)f;
    p->ksp = &p->stack[SSIZE-12];

    enqueue(&readyQueue, p);
    printList("readyQueue", readyQueue);
    printf("task%d created a new task%d\n", running->pid, p->pid);
    return p->pid;
}

int main()
{
    int i, pid, status;
    printf("Welcome to the MT User-Threads System\n");
    init();
    create((void *)task1, 0);
    printf("P0 switch to P1\n");
    tswitch();
    printf("All tasks ended: P0 loops\n");
    while(1);
}
```

```
Welcome to the MT User-Level Threads System
freeList = 1 --> 2 --> 3 --> 4 --> 5 --> 6 --> 7 --> 8 --> NULL
init complete
task0 create a new task 1
P0 switch to P1
task 1 running
task1 create a new task 2
task1 create a new task 3
task1 try to join with task5: join error: no such pid 5
task1 try to join with task2: sleepList = 1 --> NULL
readyQueue = 3 --> 0 --> NULL
task 2 running: enter a key [c|s|q|j]: j
enter a pid to join with : 1
task2 try to join with task1: join error: DEADLOCK
readyQueue = 3 --> 0 --> NULL
task 2 running: enter a key [c|s|q|j]: q
readyQueue = 3 --> 1 --> 0 --> NULL
task 2 exited with status = 2
readyQueue = 1 --> 0 --> NULL
task 3 running: enter a key [c|s|q|j]: q
task 3: no joiner=>exit as FREE: task 3 exited with status = 3
task1 joined with task2 status = 2
task1 try to join with task3: join error: no such pid 3
task 1: no joiner=>exit as FREE: task 1 exited with status = 1
All tasks ended: P0 loops
```

Fig. 4.8 Sample Outputs of Task Join Program

```
int scheduler()
{
   if (running->status == READY)
       enqueue(&readyQueue, running);
   running = dequeue(&readyQueue);
}
```

In the test program, P0 creates a new task P1, which executes the function task1(). When P1 runs, it creates two new tasks P2 and P3 to execute the function func(). P1 first tries to join the targetPid =5. Then it tries to join with both P2 and P3. Figure 4.8 shows the sample outputs of running Part 2 of the Project Program, which demonstrates task join operations. As the figure shows, when P1 tries to join with P5, it results in a join error due to invalid targetPid. Then P1 tries to join with task 2, which causes it to wait. When P2 runs, it tries to join with P1, which is rejected because this would lead to a deadlock. Then P2 exits, which switches task to run P3. When P3 exits, P1 is still waiting to join with P2, so P3 exits as FREE, allowing P1 to complete its join operation with P2. When P1 tries to join with P3, it gets an invalid targetPid error since P3 no longer exists. Instead of letting P3 exit first, the reader may let P3 switch to P1, which will dispose of the ZOMBIE P2 and then tries to join with P3. In that case, when P3 exits, P1 will complete its join operation with P3 successfully. The reader may modify the test program to create more tasks and enter different command sequences to test the system.

4.7.4   Implementation of Mutex Operations

Programming Project PART 3: Extend Part 2 of the project to support mutex operations. The extensions are described below.

(1). **Mutex Structure**

```
typedef struct mutex{
  int   lock;     // mutex lock state: 0 for unlocked, 1 for locked
  PROC *owner;    // pointer to owner of mutex; may also use PID
  PROC *queue;    // FIFO queue of BLOCKED waiting PROCs
}MUTEX;

MUTEX *mutex_create() // create a mutex and initialize it
{
  MUTEX *mp = (MUTEX *)malloc(sizeof(MUTEX));
  mp->lock = mp->owner = mp->queue = 0;
  return mp;
}


void mutex_destroy(MUTEX *mp){ free(mp); }
int mutex_lock(MUTEX *mp){  // implement mutex locking operation }
int mutex_unlock(MUTEX *mp){// implement mutex unlocking operation }

/******** Algorithm of mutex_lock() ************/
(1). if (mutex is in unlocked state){
        change mutex to locked state;
        record caller as mutex owner;
     }
(2). else{
        BLOCK caller in mutex waiting queue;
        switch task;
     }


/******* Algorithm of mutex_unlock() *********/
(1). if (mutex is unlocked ||(mutex is locked && caller NOT owner))
        return error;
(2). // mutex is locked && caller is owner
     if (no waiter in mutex waiting queue){
        change mutex to unlocked state;
        clear mutex owner field to 0;
     }
(3). else{ // mutex has waiters
        PROC *p = dequeue a waiter from mutex waiting queue;
        change mutex owner to p; // mutex remains locked
        enter p into readyQueue;
     }
```

4.7.5   Test Project with Mutex by Concurrent Programs

Part 3: Implement mutex_lock() and mutex_unlock() functions for the MT system. Test mutex operations by the following program. The test program is a modified version of the Example 4.3 program using Pthreads. It computes the sum of the elements of a matrix by concurrent tasks and mutex of the MT system. In the test program, P0 initializes a 4×4 matrix, creates P1 to execute task1(). P1 creates 4 working tasks to execute the function func(parm). Each working task computes the partial sum of a row and updates the global variable total using mutex for synchronization. The outputs should look like Fig. 4.9.

```c
/*********** test program for mutex operations ***********/
#include <stdio.h>
#include <stdlib.h>
#include "type.h"

PROC proc[NPROC], *freeList, *sleepList, *readyQueue, *running;

#include "queue.c"   // queue operation functions
#include "wait.c"    // tsleep/twakeup/texit/join functions
#include "mutex.c"   // mutex operation functions

#define N 4
int A[N][N];         // matrix A
MUTEX *mp;           // mutex for task synchronization
int total;           // global total

int init()
{
  int i, j;
  PROC *p;
  for (i=0; i<NPROC; i++){
    p = &proc[i];
    p->pid = i;
    p->ppid = 1;
    p->priority = 0;
    p->status = FREE;
    p->event = 0;
    p->next = p+1;
  }
  proc[NPROC-1].next = 0;
  freeList = &proc[0];
  readyQueue = 0;
  sleepList  = 0;
  p = running = dequeue(&freeList);
  p->status = READY;
  p->priority = 0;
  printList("freeList", freeList);

  printf("P0: initialize A matrix\n");
  for (i=0; i<N; i++){
    for (j=0; j<N; j++){
      A[i][j] = i*N + j + 1;
    }
  }
```

```
  for (i=0; i<N; i++){    // show the matrix
     for (j=0; j<N; j++){
        printf("%4d ", A[i][j]);
     }
     printf("\n");
  }
  mp = mutex_create();    // create a mutex
  total = 0;
  printf("init complete\n");
}


int myexit()                  // for task exit
{
  texit(0);
}


void func(void *arg)
{
  int i, row, s;
  int me = running->pid;
  row = (int)arg;
  printf("task %d computes sum of row %d\n", me, row);
  s = 0;
  for (i=0; i < N; i++){
     s += A[row][i];
  }
  printf("task %d update total with %d\n", me, s);
  mutex_lock(mp);
   total += s;
   printf("[total = %d] ", total);
  mutex_unlock(mp);
}


void task1(void *parm)
{
  int pid[N];
  int i, status;
  int me = running->pid;
  printf("task %d: create working tasks : ", me);
  for(i=0; i < N; i++) {
     pid[i] = create(func, (void *)i);
     printf("%d ", pid[i]);

  }
  printf(" to compute matrix row sums\n");
  for(i=0; i<N; i++) {
    printf("task %d tries to join with task %d\n",
               running->pid, pid[i]);
    join(pid[i], &status);
  }
```

```
  printf("task %d : total = %d\n", me, total);
}

int create(void (*f)(), void *parm)
{
  int i;
  PROC *p = dequeue(&freeList);
  if (!p){
    printf("fork failed\n");
    return -1;
  }
  p->ppid = running->pid;
  p->status = READY;
  p->priority = 1;
  p->joinPid = 0;
  p->joinPtr = 0;
  for (i=1; i<12; i++){
    p->stack[SSIZE-i] = 0;
    p->stack[SSIZE-1] = (int)parm;
    p->stack[SSIZE-2] = (int)myexit;
    p->stack[SSIZE-3] = (int)f;
    p->ksp = &p->stack[SSIZE-12];
  }
  enqueue(&readyQueue, p);
  return p->pid;
}

int main()
{
  printf("Welcome to the MT User-Level Threads System\n");
  init();
  create((void *)task1, 0);
  //printf("P0 switch to P1\n");
  tswitch();
  printf("all task ended: P0 loops\n");
  while(1);
}

int scheduler()
{
  if (running->status == READY)
     enqueue(&readyQueue, running);
  running = dequeue(&readyQueue);
}
```

Figure 4.9 shows the sample outputs of running the test program of mutex.

```
Welcome to the MT User-Level Threads System
freeList = 1 --> 2 --> 3 --> 4 --> 5 --> 6 --> 7 --> 8 --> NULL
P0: initialize A matrix
     1    2    3    4
     5    6    7    8
     9   10   11   12
    13   14   15   16
init complete
task 1: create working tasks : 2 3 4 5  to compute matrix row sums
task 1 tries to join with task 2
sleepList = 1 --> NULL
task 2 computes sum of row 0
task 2 update total with 10
task 2 mutex_lock() [total = 10] task 2 mutex_unlock()
task 3 computes sum of row 1
task 3 update total with 26
task 3 mutex_lock() [total = 36] task 3 mutex_unlock()
task 4 computes sum of row 2
task 4 update total with 42
task 4 mutex_lock() [total = 78] task 4 mutex_unlock()
task 5 computes sum of row 3
task 5 update total with 58
task 5 mutex_lock() [total = 136] task 5 mutex_unlock()
task 1 tries to join with task 3
task 1 tries to join with task 4
task 1 tries to join with task 5
task 1 : tatal = 136
all task ended: P0 loops
■
```

Fig. 4.9 Matrix Sum by Concurrent Tasks and Mutex

4.7.6   Implementation of Semaphores

Programming Project PART 4: Implement counting semaphores as described in Sect. 4.6.5. Demonstrate semaphores by the following test program, which is the producer-consumer problem of Example 4.5 adapted to the MT system.

4.7.7   Producer-Consumer Problem using Semaphores

```
/********** test program for semaphore operations ********/
#include <stdio.h>
#include "type.h"
PROC proc[NPROC], *freeList, *sleepList, *readyQueue, *running;
#include "queue.c"    // queue operation function
#include "wait.c"     // tsleep/twakeup/texit/join functions

#define NBUF   4
#define N      8
int buf[NBUF], head, tail;    // buffers for producer-consumer

typedef struct{
   int value;
   PROC *queue;
}SEMAPHORE;
SEMAPHORE full, empty, mutex; // semaphores
```

```c
int P(SEMAPHORE *s)
{  // implement P function }

int V(SEMAPHORE *s)
{  // implement V function }

void producer()              // produce task code
{
  int i;
  printf("producer %d start\n", running->pid);
  for (i=0; i<N; i++){
    P(&empty);
    P(&mutex);
     buf[head++] = i+1;
     printf("producer %d: item = %d\n", running->pid, i+1);
     head %= NBUF;
    V(&mutex);
    V(&full);
  }
  printf("producer %d exit\n", running->pid);
}

void consumer()              // consumer task code
{
  int i, c;
  printf("consumer %d start\n", running->pid);
  for (i=0; i<N; i++) {
    P(&full);
    P(&mutex);
     c = buf[tail++];
     tail %= NBUF;
     printf("consumer %d: got item = %d\n", running->pid, c);
    V(&mutex);
    V(&empty);
  }
  printf("consumer %d exit\n", running->pid);
}

int init()
{
  int i, j;
  PROC *p;
  for (i=0; i<NPROC; i++){
    p = &proc[i];
    p->pid = i;
    p->ppid = 1;
    p->priority = 0;
    p->status = FREE;
    p->event = 0;
    p->next = p+1;
  }
```

```
  proc[NPROC-1].next = 0;
  freeList = &proc[0];
  readyQueue = 0;
  sleepList  = 0;
  p = running = dequeue(&freeList);
  p->status = READY;
  p->priority = 0;
  printList("freeList", freeList);

  // initialize semaphores full, empty, mutex
  head = tail = 0;
  full.value = 0;  full.queue = 0;
  empty.value=NBUF; empty.queue = 0;
  mutex.value = 1; mutex.queue = 0;
  printf("init complete\n");
}
int myexit(){  texit(0); }

int task1()
{
  int status;
  printf("task %d creates producer-consumer tasks\n", running->pid);
  create((void *)producer, 0);
  create((void *)consumer, 0);
  join(2, &status);
  join(3, &status);
  printf("task %d exit\n", running->pid);
}

int create(void (*f)(), void *parm)
{
  int i;
  PROC *p = dequeue(&freeList);
  if (!p){
    printf("fork failed\n");
    return -1;
  }
  p->ppid = running->pid;
  p->status = READY;
  p->priority = 1;
  p->joinPid = 0;
  p->joinPtr = 0;
  for (i=1; i<12; i++){
    p->stack[SSIZE-i] = 0;
    p->stack[SSIZE-1] = (int)parm;
    p->stack[SSIZE-2] = (int)myexit;
    p->stack[SSIZE-3] = (int)f;
    p->ksp = &p->stack[SSIZE-12];
  }
  enqueue(&readyQueue, p);
  return p->pid;
}
```

```
int main()
{
  printf("Welcome to the MT User-Level Threads System\n");
  init();
  create((void *)task1, 0);
  printf("P0 switch to P1\n");
  tswitch();
  printf("all task ended: P0 loops\n");
  while(1);
}


int scheduler()
{
  if (running->status == READY)
     enqueue(&readyQueue, running);
  running = dequeue(&readyQueue);
}
```

Figure 4.10 shows the sample outputs of the producer-consumer problem using semaphores.

Solutions to the programming project are available online for download. Source code of the programming project is available for instructors upon request.

```
Welcome to the MT User-Level Threads System
freeList = 1 --> 2 --> 3 --> 4 --> 5 --> 6 --> 7 --> 8 --> NULL
init complete
P0 switch to P1
task 1 creates producer-consumer tasks
sleepList = 1 --> NULL
producer 2 start
producer 2: item = 1
producer 2: item = 2
producer 2: item = 3
producer 2: item = 4
task 2 block  on sem=0x80541e8
consumer 3 start
consumer 3: got item = 1
task 3 V up 2 on sem=0x80541e8
consumer 3: got item = 2
consumer 3: got item = 3
consumer 3: got item = 4
task 3 block  on sem=0x805420c
producer 2: item = 5
task 2 V up 3 on sem=0x805420c
producer 2: item = 6
producer 2: item = 7
producer 2: item = 8
producer 2 exit
consumer 3: got item = 5
consumer 3: got item = 6
consumer 3: got item = 7
consumer 3: got item = 8
consumer 3 exit
task 1 exit
all task ended: P0 loops
■
```

Fig. 4.10 Producer-Consumer Problem using Semaphores

4.8 Summary

This chapter covers concurrent programming. It introduces the concept of parallel computing and points out its importance. It compares sequential algorithms with parallel algorithms, and parallelism vs. concurrency. It explains the principles of threads and their advantages over processes. It covers threads operations in Pthreads by examples. These include threads management functions, threads synchronization tools of mutex, join, condition variables and barriers. It demonstrates concurrent programming using threads by detailed examples. These include matrix computation, quicksort and solving systems of linear equations by concurrent threads. It explains the deadlock problem and shows how to prevent deadlocks in concurrent programs. It covers semaphores and demonstrates their advantages over condition variables. It also explains the unique way of supporting threads in Linux. The programming project is to implement user-level threads. It presents a base system to help the reader get started. The base system supports dynamic creation, execution and termination of concurrent tasks, which are equivalent to threads executing in the same address space of a process. The project is for the reader to implement threads join, mutex and semaphores for threads synchronization and demonstrate their usage in concurrent programs. The programming project should allow the reader to have a deeper understanding of the principles and techniques of multitasking, threads synchronization and concurrent programming.

Problems
1. Modify the Example Program C4.1 to find the maximum element value of an $N \times N$ matrix by concurrent threads.
2. In the qsort() function of the Example Program C4.2, it picks the rightmost element of an unsorted interval as the pivot. Modify it to use the leftmost element as the pivot, and compare the number of sorting steps needed in both cases.
3. Modify the Example Program C4.4 to create multiple producer and consumer threads.
4. Implement the producer-consumer problem using semaphores, as suggested in Example 4.5.
5. In the Example Program C4.5, the number of working threads, N, is equal to the dimension of the A matrix. This may be undesirable if N is large. Modify the program to use NTHREADS working threads, where NTHREADS <= N. For example, with N=8, NTHREADS may be 2, 4 or any number <=N.
6. Modify the Example Program C4.1 to compute the sum of all the elements in a matrix by concurrent tasks in the MT system. The results should be the same as in Example 4.1.
7. Assume that in the user-level threads MT system every task will be joined by some task. When the system ends, there should be no ZOMBIE tasks left behind. Implement texit() and join() to meet these requirements.

References

Buttlar, D, Farrell, J, Nichols, B., "PThreads Programming, A POSIX Standard for Better Multiprocessing", O'Reilly Media, 1996
Dijkstra, E.W., Co-operating Sequential Processes, Programming Languages, Academic Press, 1965
Goldt, S,. van der Meer, S. Burkett, S. Welsh, M. The Linux Programmer's Guide, Version 0.4. March 1995.
IBM MVS Programming Assembler Services Guide, Oz/OS V1R11.0, IBM
Love, R. Linux Kernel Development, 2nd Edition, Novell Press, 2005
POSIX.1C, Threads extensions, IEEE Std 1003.1c, 1995
Pthreads: https://computing.llnl.gov/tutorials/pthreads, 2017
The Linux Man page Project: https://www.kernel.org/doc/man-pages, 2017

Timers and Time Service

5

Abstract

This chapter covers timers and timer services. It explains the principle of hardware timers and the hardware timers in Intel x86 based PCs. it covers CPU operations and interrupts processing. It describes timer related system calls, library functions and commands for timer services in Linux. It discusses process interval timers, timer generated signals and demonstrates process interval timers by examples. The programming project is to implement timer, timer interrupts and interval timers in a multitasking system. The multitasking system runs as a Linux process, which acts as a virtual CPU for concurrent tasks inside the Linux process. The real-time mode interval timer of the Linux process is programmed to generate SIGALRM signals periodically, which acts as timer interrupts to the virtual CPU, which uses a SIGALRM signal catcher as the timer interrupt handler. The project is for the reader to implement interval timers for tasks by a timer queue. It also lets the reader use Linux signal masks to implement critical regions to prevent race conditions between tasks and interrupt handlers.

5.1   Hardware Timer

A timer is a hardware device comprising a clock source and a programmable counter. The clock source is usually a crystal oscillator, which generates periodic electrical signals to drive the counter at a precise frequency. The counter is programmed with a count-down value, which decrements by 1 on each clock signal. When the count decrements to 0, the counter generates a **timer interrupt** to the CPU, reloads the count value into the counter and repeats the count-down again. The period of the counter is known as a timer tick, which is the basic timing unit of the system.

5.2   PC Timers

The Intel x86 based PC has several timers (Bovet and Cesati 2005).

(1). Real-Time Clock (RTC): The RTC is powered by a small backup battery. It runs continually even when the PC's power is turned off. It is used to keep real time to provide time and date information. When Linux boots up, it uses the RTC to update a system time variable to keep track of the current

© Springer International Publishing AG, part of Springer Nature 2018
K. C. Wang, *Systems Programming in Unix/Linux*, https://doi.org/10.1007/978-3-319-92429-8_5

time. In all Unix-like systems, the time variable is a long integer containing the number of seconds elapsed since the beginning of January 1 of 1970.

(2). Programmable Interval Timer (PIT) (Wang 2015]: The PIT is a hardware timer separated from the CPU. It can be programmed to provide timer ticks in resolutions of milliseconds. Among all I/O devices, the PIT interrupts at the highest priority IRQ0. PIT timer interrupts are handled by the timer interrupt handler of the Linux kernel to provide basic timing units for system operation, such as process scheduling, process interval timers and a host of other timing events.

(3). Local Timers in Multicore CPUs (Intel 1997; Wang 2015): In a multicore CPU, each core is an independent processor, which has its own local timer driven by the CPU clock.

(4). High Resolution Timers: Most PCs have a Time Stamp Counter (TSC), which is driven by the system clock. Its contents can be read via a 64-bit TSC register. Since the clock rates of different system boards may vary, the TSC is unsuited as a real-time device but it can provide timer resolutions in nanoseconds. Some high-end PCs may also be equipped with a special high speed timer to provide timer resolutions in nanoseconds range.

5.3   CPU Operations

Every CPU has a Program Counter (PC), also known as the Instruction Pointer (IP), a flag or status register (SR), a Stack Pointer (SP) and several general registers, where PC points to the next instruction to be executed in memory, SR contains current status of the CPU, e.g. operating mode, interrupt mask and condition code, and SP points to the top of the current stack. The stack is a memory area used by the CPU for special operations, such as push, pop call and return, etc. The operations of a CPU can be modeled by an infinite loop.

```
while(power-on){
    (1). fetch instruction: load *PC as instruction, increment PC to point to the
         next instruction in memory;
    (2). decode instruction: interpret the instruction's operation code and
         generate operands;
    (3). execute instruction: perform operation on operands, write results to
         memory if needed; execution may use the stack, implicitly change PC,
         etc.
    (4). check for pending interrupts; may handle interrupts;
}
```

In each of the above steps, an error condition, called an **exception** or trap, may occur due to invalid address, illegal instruction, privilege violation, etc. When the CPU encounters an exception, it follows a pre-installed pointer in memory to execute an exception handler in software. At the end each instruction execution, the CPU checks for pending interrupts. **Interrupts** are external signals from I/O devices or coprocessors to the CPU, requesting for CPU service. If there is a pending interrupt request but the CPU is not in the state of accepting interrupts, i.e. its status register has interrupts masked out, the CPU will ignore the interrupt request and continue to execute the next instruction. Otherwise, it will direct its execution to do interrupt processing. At the end of interrupt processing, it will resume the normal execution of instructions. Interrupts handling and exceptions processing are handled in the operating system kernel. For the most part they are inaccessible from user level programs but they are keys to understanding timer services and signals in operating systems, such as Linux.

5.4   Interrupt Processing

Interrupts from external devices, such as the timer, are fed to predefined input lines of an **Interrupt Controller** (Intel 1990; Wang 2015) which prioritizes the interrupt inputs and routes the interrupt with the highest priority as an interrupt request (IRQ) to the CPU. At the end of each instruction execution, if the CPU is not in the state of accepting interrupts, i.e. it has interrupts masked out in the CPU's status register, it will ignore the interrupt request, keeping it pending, and continue to execute the next instruction. If the CPU is in the state of accepting interrupts, i.e. interrupts are not masked out, the CPU will divert its normal execution sequence to do interrupt processing. For each interrupt, the Interrupt Controller can be programmed to generate a unique number, called an **interrupt vector,** which identifies the interrupt source. After acquiring an interrupt vector number, the CPU uses it as an index to an entry in an **Interrupt Vector Table** (AMD64 2011) in memory, which contains a pointer to the entry address of an **Interrupt handler,** which actually handles the interrupt. When interrupt processing finishes, the CPU resumes normal execution of instructions.

5.5   Time Service Functions

In almost every operating system (OS), the OS kernel provides a variety of time related services. Time services can be invoked by system calls, library functions and user level commands. In this section, we shall cover some of the basic time service functions of Linux.

5.5.1   Gettimeofday-Settimeofday

```
#include <sys/time.h>
int gettimeofday(struct timeval *tv, struct timezone *tz);
int settimeofday(const struct timeval *tv, const struct timezone *tz);
```

These are system calls to the Linux kernel. The first parameter, tv, points to a timeval structure.

```
struct timeval {
        time_t          tv_sec;         /* seconds */
        suseconds_t     tv_usec;        /* microseconds */
};
```

The second parameter, timezone, is obsolete and should be set to NULL. The gettimeofday() function returns the current time in seconds and microseconds of the current second. The settimeofday() function sets the current time. In Unix/Linux, time is represented by the number of seconds elapsed since 00:00:00 of January 1, 1970. It can be converted to calendar form by the library function ctime (&time). The following examples demonstrate gettimeofday() and settimeofday().

(1). Gettimeofday system call

Example 5.1 Get system time by gettimeofday()

```
/********* gettimeofday.c file *********/
#include <stdio.h>
```

```
#include <stdlib.h>
#include <sys/time.h>

struct timeval t;

int main()
{
  gettimeofday(&t, NULL);
  printf("sec=%ld usec=%d\n", t.tv_sec, t.tv_usec);
  printf((char *)ctime(&t.tv_sec));
}
```

The program should display the current time in seconds, microseconds and also the current date and time in calendar form, as in

```
sec=1515624303 usec=860772
Wed Jan 10 14:45:03 2018
```

(2). Settimeofday system call

Example 5.2 Set system time by settimeofday()

```
/********* settimeofday.c file *********/
#include <stdio.h>
#include <stdlib.h>
#include <sys/time.h>
#include <time.h>

struct timeval t;

int main()
{
  int r;
  t.tv_sec = 123456789;
  t.tv_usec= 0;
  r = settimeofday(&t, NULL);
  if (!r){
     printf("settimeofday() failed\n");
     exit(1);
  }
  gettimeofday(&t, NULL);
  printf("sec=%ld usec=%ld\n", t.tv_sec, t.tv_usec);
  printf("%s", ctime(&t.tv_sec)); // show time in calendar form
}
```

The output of the program should show something like

```
sec=123456789 usec=862
Thu Nov 29 13:33:09 1973
```

Based on the printed date and year (1973), it seems that the settimeofday() operation has succeeded. However, in some Linux systems, e.g. Ubuntu 15.10, the effect may only be temporary. If the reader runs the gettimeofday program again, it will show that Linux has changed the system time back to the correct real time. This shows that the Linux kernel has the ability to use the real-time clock (and other time synchronization protocols) to correct any deviations of system time from real time.

5.5.2 The Time System Call

Example 5.3 The **time** system call

time_t time(time_t *t)

returns the current time in seconds. If the parameter t is not NULL, it also stores the time in the memory pointed by t. The limitation of the time system call is that it only provides resolutions in seconds, not in microseconds. This example shows how to get system time in seconds.

```
/*********** time.c file **********/
#include <stdio.h>
#include <time.h>

time_t start, end;

int main()
{
  int i;
  start = time(NULL);
  printf("start=%ld\n", start);
  for (i=0; i<123456789; i++); // delay to simulate computation
  end = time(NULL);
  printf("end  =%ld time=%ld\n", end, end-start);
}
```

The output should print the start time, end time and the number of seconds from start to end.

5.5.3 The Times System Call

The times system call

clock_t times(struct tms *buf);

can be used to get detailed execution time of a process. It stores the process time in a struct tms buf, which is

```
struct tms{
        clock_t tms_utime;   // user mode time
        clock_t tms_stime;   // system mode time
        clock_t tms_cutime;  // user time of children
        clock_t tms_cstime;  // system time of children
};
```

All times reported are in clock ticks. This provides information for profiling an executing process, including the time of its children processes, if any.

5.5.4   Time and Date Commands

date: print or set the system date and time
time: report process execution time in user mode, system mode and total time
hwclock: query and set the hardware clock (RTC), can also be done through BIOS.

5.6   Interval Timers

Linux provides each process with three different kinds of interval timers, which can be used as virtual clocks for process timing. Interval timers are created by the **setitimer()** system call. The **getitimer()** system call returns the status of an interval timer.

```
int getitimer(int which, struct itimerval *curr_value);
int setitimer(int which, const struct itimerval *new_value,
              struct itimerval *old_value);
```

Each interval timer operates in a distinct time domain specified by the parameter **which**. When an interval timer expires, a signal is sent to the process, and the timer is reset to the specified interval value (if nonzero). A **signal** is a number (1 to 31) sent to a process for the process to handle. Signals and signal processing will be covered in Chap. 6. For the time being, the reader may regard timer related signals as interrupts to a process, just like physical timer interrupts to a CPU. The 3 kinds of interval timers are

(1). ITIMER_REAL: decrement in real time, generate a **SIGALRM (14)** signal upon expiration.

(2). ITIMER_VIRTUAL: decrement only when the process is executing in user mode, generate a **SIGVTALRM (26)** signal upon expiration.

(3). ITIMER_PROF: decrement when the process is executing in user mode and also in system (kernel) mode. Coupled with ITIMER_VIRTUAL, this interval timer is usually used to profile the time spent by the application in user and kernel modes. It generates a **SIGPROF (27)** signal upon expiration.

Interval timer values are defined by the following structures (in <sys/time.h>):

```
struct itimerval {
   struct timeval it_interval;   /* interval for periodic timer */
   struct timeval it_value;      /* time until next expiration */
};
struct timeval {
   time_t      tv_sec;           /* seconds */
   suseconds_t tv_usec;          /* microseconds */
};
```

The function getitimer() fills the structure pointed to by curr_value with the current value i.e., the time remaining until the next expiration, of the timer specified by which (one of ITIMER_REAL, ITIMER_VIRTUAL, or ITIMER_PROF). The subfields of the field it_value are set to the amount of time remaining on the timer, or zero if the timer is disabled. The it_interval field is set to the timer interval (period); a value of zero returned in (both subfields of) this field indicates that this is a single-shot timer.

The function setitimer() sets the specified timer to the value in new_value. If old_value is non-NULL, the old value of the timer,i.e. the same information as returned by getitimer(), is stored there.

Periodic timers decrement from it_value to zero, generate a signal, and reset to it_interval. A timer which is set to zero (it_value is zero or the timer expires and it_interval is zero) stops the timer. Both tv_sec and tv_usec are significant in determining the duration of a timer. We demonstrate process interval timers by examples.

Example 5.4 This example shows how to set a VIRTUAL mode interval timer, which decrements its count only when the process is executing in user mode. The timer is set to start after an initial count of 100 msec has expired. Then it runs with a period of 1 second. When the timer count decrements to zero, it generates a SIGVTALRM(26) signal to the process. If the process did not install a catcher for the signal, it will handle the signal by default, which is to terminate. In that case, the process will terminate with a signal number 26. If the process has installed a signal catcher, the Linux kernel will let the process execute the signal catcher to handle the signal in user mode. Before starting the interval time, the program installs a signal catcher for the SIGVTALRM signal by

```
void timer_handler(int sig){ . . . .}
signal(SIGALRM, timer_handler)
```

After installing the signal catcher, the program starts the timer and then executes in a while(1) loop. While executing in the loop, every hardware interrupt, e.g. interrupts from hardware timers, causes the CPU, hence the process executing on the CPU, to enter the Linux kernel to handle the interrupt. Whenever a process is in kernel mode, it checks for pending signals. If there is a pending signal, it tries to handle the signal before returning to user mode. In this case, a SIGVTALRM signal would cause the process to execute the signal catcher in user mode. Since the interval timer is programmed to generate a signal every second, the process would execute timer_handler() once every second, making the printed message to appear once per second like a pulsar. The signal catcher function, timer_handler(), counts the number of times the interval timer has expired. When the count reaches a prescribed value, e.g. 8, it cancels the interval timer by setitimer() with a timer value 0. Although the timer has stopped, the process is still executing in an infinite while(1) loop. In this case, entering a Control-C key from the keyboard would cause the process to terminate with a SIGINT(2) signal. Details of signals and signal handling will be covered in Chap. 6. The following shows the setitimer.c program code of Example 5.5.

```
/*********** setitimer.c file ********/
#include <signal.h>
#include <stdio.h>
#include <sys/time.h>
int count = 0;
struct itimerval t;

void timer_handler(int sig)
{
  printf("timer_handler: signal=%d count=%d\n", sig, ++count);
  if (count>=8){
    printf("cancel timer\n");
    t.it_value.tv_sec = 0;
    t.it_value.tv_usec = 0;
    setitimer(ITIMER_VIRTUAL, &t, NULL);
  }
}

int main()
{
  struct itimerval timer;
  // Install timer_handler as SIGVTALRM signal handler
  signal(SIGVTALRM, timer_handler);
  // Configure the timer to expire after 100 msec
  timer.it_value.tv_sec = 0;
  timer.it_value.tv_usec = 100000; // 100000 nsec
  // and every 1 sec afterward
  timer.it_interval.tv_sec = 1;
  timer.it_interval.tv_usec = 0;
  // Start a VIRTUAL itimer
  setitimer(ITIMER_VIRTUAL, &timer, NULL);
  printf("looping: enter Control-C to terminate\n");
  while(1);
}
```

Figure 5.1 show the outputs of running the setitimer program.

```
looping: enter Control-C to terminate
timer_handler: signal=26 count=1
timer_handler: signal=26 count=2
timer_handler: signal=26 count=3
timer_handler: signal=26 count=4
timer_handler: signal=26 count=5
timer_handler: signal=26 count=6
timer_handler: signal=26 count=7
timer_handler: signal=26 count=8
cancel timer
^C
```

Fig. 5.1 Outputs of setitimer program

5.7   REAL Mode Interval Timer

Interval timers in both VIRTUAL and PROF modes take effect only when a process is executing. Information of such timers can be maintained in the PROC structure of each process. The (hardware) timer interrupt handler only needs to access the PROC structure of the current running process to decrement the timer count, reload the timer count when it expires and generate a signal to the process. The OS kernel does not have to use additional data structures to handle VIRTUAL and PROF timers of processes. However, REAL mode interval timers are different, because they must be updated by the timer interrupt handler whether the process is executing or not. Therefore, the OS kernel must use additional data structures for REAL mode timers of processes and take actions when their timers expire or are cancelled. In most OS kernels, the data structure used is a timer queue. We shall explain the timer queue in the programming project at the end of this chapter.

5.8   Programming Project

The programming project is to implement timer, timer interrupts and interval timers in a multitasking system with concurrent executing tasks. The programming project consists of four steps. Step 1 provides the base code of a multitasking system for the reader to get started. Step 2 is to add timer and timer interrupts to the base system. Step 3 is to implement interval timers for tasks. Step 4 is to implement Critical Regions in the system and task scheduling by time-slice. The object of the project is for the reader to learn not only how to use timers but also how they are implemented in an OS kernel.

5.8.1   System Base Code

The base code of the multitasking system is essentially the same as the programming project on user-level threads of Chap. 4. For ease of reference and completeness, we repeat the same code here. The following lists the base code of a multitasking system. It consists of a ts.s file in 32-bit assembly and a t.c file in C.

```
#------------ ts.s file -------------
.global tswitch, scheduler, running
tswitch:
SAVE:     pushal
          pushfl
          movl running, %ebx
          movl %esp, 4(%ebx)
FIND:     call scheduler
RESUME:   movl running, %ebx
          movl 4(%ebx), %esp
          popfl
          popal
          ret
```

```
/********* t.c file *********/
#include <stdio.h>
#include <stdlib.h>
```

```c
#include <signal.h>
#include <string.h>
#include <sys/time.h>

#define NPROC     9
#define SSIZE 1024
// PROC status
#define FREE      0
#define READY     1
#define SLEEP     2
#define BLOCK     3
#define PAUSE     4
#define ZOMBIE    5

typedef struct proc{
  struct proc *next;
  int ksp;            // saved sp when NOT running
  int pid;            // task PID
  int priority;       // task priority
  int status;         // status=FREE|READY, etc.
  int event;          // sleep event
  int exitStatus;
  int joinPid;
  struct proc joinPtr;
  int time;           // time slice in ticks
  int pause;          // pause time in seconds
  int stack[SSIZE];   // per task stack
}PROC;

PROC proc[NPROC];        // task PROCs
PROC *freeList, *readyQueue, *running;
PROC *sleepList;         // list of SLEEP tasks
PROC *pauseList;         // list of PAUSE tasks

#include "queue.c"     // same queue.c file as before
#include "wait.c"      // tsleep, twakeup, texit, join functions
int menu() // command menu: to be expanded later
{
  printf("********** menu **********\n");
  printf("* create  switch  exit  ps *\n");
  printf("**************************\n");
}

int init()
{
  int i, j;
  PROC *p;
  for (i=0; i<NPROC; i++){
    p = &proc[i];
    p->pid = i;
    p->priority = 1;
```

```
     p->status = FREE;
     p->event = 0;
     p->next = p+1;
  }
  proc[NPROC-1].next = 0;
  freeList = &proc[0];      // all PROCs in freeList
  readyQueue = 0;
  sleepList  = 0;
  pauseList  = 0;
  // create P0 as initial running task
  running = dequeue(&freeList);
  running->status = READY;
  running->priority = 0;  // P0 has lowest priority 0
  printList("freeList", freeList);
  printf("init complete: P0 running\n");
}


int do_exit()  // task exit as FREE
{
  printf("task %d exit: ", running->pid);
  running->status = FREE;
  running->priority = 0;
  enqueue(&freeList, running);
  printList("freeList", freeList);
  tswitch();
}


int do_ps()     // print task status
{
  printf("--------- ps ----------\n");
  printList("readyQueue", readyQueue);
  printList("sleepList ", sleepList);
  printf("---------------------\n");
}


int create(void (f)(), void *parm) // create a new task
{
  int i;
  PROC *p = dequeue(&freeList);
  if (!p){
     printf("create failed\n");
     return -1;
  }
  p->ppid = running->pid;
  p->status = READY;
  p->priority = 1;
  for (i=1; i<12; i++)
      p->stack[SSIZE-i] = 0;
  p->stack[SSIZE-1] = (int)parm;
  p->stack[SSIZE-2] = (int)do_exit;
```

```
  p->stack[SSIZE-3] = (int)f;
  p->ksp = &p->stack[SSIZE-12];
  enqueue(&readyQueue, p);
  printf("%d created a new task %d\n", running->pid, p->pid);
  return p->pid;
}

void func(void *parm) // task function
{
  char line[64], cmd[16];
  printf("task %d start: parm = %d\n", running->pid, parm);
  while(1){
    printf("task %d running\n", running->pid);
    menu();
    printf("enter a command line: ");
    fgets(line, 64, stdin);
    line[strlen(line)-1] = 0; // kill \n at end of line
    sscanf(line, "%s", cmd);
    if (strcmp(cmd, "create")==0)
      create((void *)func, 0);
    else if (strcmp(cmd, "switch")==0)
      tswitch();
    else if (strcmp(cmd, "exit")==0)
      do_exit();
    else if (strcmp(cmd, "ps")==0)
      do_ps();
  }
}

int main()
{
  int i;
  printf("Welcome to the MT multitasking system\n");
  init();
  for (i=1; i<5; i++)     // create tasks
      create(func, 0);
  printf("P0 switch to P1\n");
  while(1){
    if (readyQueue)
      tswitch();
  }
}

int scheduler()
{
  if (running->status == READY)
      enqueue(&readyQueue, running);
  running = dequeue(&readyQueue);
  printf("next running = %d\n", running->pid);
}
```

```
Welcome to the MT multitasking system
freeList = 1 -> 2 -> 3 -> 4 -> 5 -> 6 -> 7 -> 8 -> NULL
init complete
task 0 created new task 1
task 0 created new task 2
task 0 created new task 3
task 0 created new task 4
P0 switch to P1
task 1 start: parm = 0
task 1 running
*********** menu ***********
* create  switch  exit  ps *
***************************
enter a command line: switch
task 2 start: parm = 0
task 2 running
*********** menu ***********
* create  switch  exit  ps *
***************************
enter a command line: █
```

Fig. 5.2 Sample outputs of the base MT system

The reader may consult Chap. 4 for the create() function, which creates a new task to execute a specified function. To compile and run the base system under Linux, enter

gcc –m32 t.c ts.s # assembly code ts.s is for 32-bit Linux

Then run a.out. When a task runs, it displays a command menu, where the commands are

create: create a new task
switch: switch task
exit   : task exit
ps   : show status of tasks

Figure 5.2 shows the sample outputs of running the base code of the multitasking system.

5.8.2   Timer Interrupts

Step 2 The entire base system runs on a virtual CPU, which is a Linux process. Timer generated signals to the Linux process can be regarded as interrupts to the virtual CPU of the base system. Create a REAL mode interval timer for the Linux process. Program the interval timer to generate a SIGALRM signal every 10 msec. Install a SIGALRM signal catcher as the timer interrupt handler of the virtual CPU. In the timer interrupt handler, keep track of the number of seconds, minutes and hours elapsed. The needed extension code segments are shown below.

```
void thandler(int sig)
{
  // count the number of timer ticks; update ss, mm, hh
  // print a message every second
}
```

```
signal(SIGALRM, thandler);        // install SIGALRM catcher
struct itimerval t;               // configure timer
t.it_value.tv_sec = 0;
t.it_value.tv_usec = 10000;       // start in 10 msec
t.it_interval.tv_sec = 0;
t.it_interval.tv_usec = 10000;    // period = 10 msec
setitimer(ITIMER_REAL, &t, NULL); // start REAL mode timer
```

The outputs of Step 2 should be similar to Fig. 5.2, except it displays a message on each second.

5.8.3   Timer Queue

Step 3 Add interval timer support for tasks in the base system. Add the commands

> **pause t :** task pauses for t seconds
> **timer t :** task sets an (REAL mode) interval timer of t seconds

The pause command causes a task to go to sleep for the specified number of seconds, which will be woken up when the pause time expires. After setting an interval timer, the task may continue, which will be notified by a signal when its timer expires. Since the MT system can not generate and send signals yet, we shall assume that the task will go to sleep after executing the timer command, which will be woken up when its timer expires.

As pointed out in Sect. 5.7, the system must use a timer queue to keep track of the status of REAL mode timers of tasks. The timer queue consists of TQE (Timer Queue Element) entries of the form

```
typedef struct tqe{
   struct tqe *next;
   PROC *proc;        // pointer to requesting process
   int   time;        // expiration time count
   void (action)()    // action function = twakeup
}TQE;
TQE *timerQueue = 0; // initialized to NULL
```

The TQEs may be allocated and deallocated from a pool of TQEs. Since each process can have only one REAL mode timer, the number of TQEs is at most equal to the number of PROCs. If desired, they can be included in the PROC structure. Here we assume that the TQEs are allocated/deallocated dynamically from a pool of free TQEs. When a process requests a REAL mode interval timer, a TQE is allocated to record the requesting process, the expiration time, and the action to take when the timer expires. Then it enters the TQE into the timerQueue. The simplest timerQueue is a link list ordered by non-decreasing expiration time. If there are many requests for REAL mode timers, such a timerQueue may look like the following diagram, in which the numbers represents the expiration time of the TQEs.

```
timerQueue = TQE1 ->TQE2 ->TQE3
               2      7      15
```

At each second, the (hardware) timer interrupt handler decrements each and every TQE by 1. When a TQE's time decrements to 0, it is removed from the timerQueue and the action function invoked. The default action is to generate a SIGALRM(14) signal to the process, but it may also be other kinds of actions. In general, a (hardware) interrupt handler should run to completion as quickly as possible. The drawback of the above timerQueue organization is that the timer interrupt handler must decrement each and every TQE by 1, which is time-consuming. A better way is to maintain the TQEs in a **cumulative** queue, in which the expiration time of each TQE is relative to the cumulative sum of all the expiration time of preceding TQEs. The following shows a cumulative timerQueue, which is equivalent to the original timerQueue.

```
timerQueue = TQE1 ->TQE2 ->TQE3
              2      5      8
```

With this organization of the tiemrQueue, the timer interrupt handler only needs to decrement the first TQE and handle any TQE whose time has expired, which greatly speeds up the timer interrupt processing.

Step 3 of the project is to add a REAL mode interval timer for the Linux process and implement interval timers for tasks in the MT system.

Figure 5.3 shows the sample outputs of running such a system. As the figure shows, task1 requested a timer of 6 seconds. Task 2 requested a timer of 2 seconds, 4 seconds after that of task 1. At this moment, the cumulative timerQueue contents are shown as

timerQueue = [2, 2] =>[1, 2]

In each TQE, the first number is the task PID and the second number is the expiration time. At each second, the timer interrupt handler only decrements the first TQE of task 2. When the TQE of task

```
Welcome to the multitasking system
freeList = 1 -> 2 -> 3 -> 4 -> 5 -> 6 -> 7 -> 8 -> NULL
P0 creates tasks
readyQueue = 1 -> 2 -> 3 -> 4 -> NULL
task 1 running
**************** menu *******************
* create  switch  exit  pause  ps  timer *
*******************************************
enter a command line: timer 6
timerQueue = [1, 6] =>
task 2 running
**************** menu *******************
* create  switch  exit  pause  ps  timer *
*******************************************
enter a command line: timerQueue = [1, 5] =>
timer timerQueue = [1, 4] =>
2
timerQueue = [2, 2] => [1, 2] =>
task 3 running
**************** menu *******************
* create  switch  exit  pause  ps  timer *
*******************************************
enter a command line: timerQueue = [2, 1] => [1, 2] =>
timerQueue = [2, 0] => [1, 2] =>
timer wakeup task 2
timerQueue = [1, 1] =>
timerQueue = [1, 0] =>
timer wakeup task 1
■
```

Fig. 5.3 Sample outputs of task interval timers

2 expires, it deletes the TQE from the timerQueue and wakes up task 2. After these, the TQE of task 1 will be the first one in the timerQueue. On the next second, it will decrement the TQE of task 1. Similarly, the pause command allows a task to pause for t seconds, which will be woken up when its pause time expires.

5.8.4   Critical Regions

In the base code system, there is only one kind of execution entities, namely tasks, which execute one at a time. A task keeps executing until is gets a switch command, goes to sleep or exits. Furthermore, task switch occurs only at the end of an operation, but never in the middle of any operation. Therefore, there are no competitions among tasks, hence no **Critical Regions** in the base code system. However, the situation changes once we introduce interrupts to the system. With interrupts, there are two kinds of execution entities, tasks and interrupt handler, which may compete for the same (shared) data objects in the system. For example, when a task requests an interval timer, it must enter the request as a TQE into the timerQueue. While a task is modifying the timerQueue, if a timer interrupt occurs, it would divert the task to execute the interrupt handler, which may modify the same timerQueue, resulting in a race condition. Thus, the timerQueue forms a Critical Region, which must be protected to ensure it can only be accessed by one execution entity at a time. Likewise, while a process is executing in the middle of the sleep() function, it may be diverted to execute the interrupt handler, which may execute wakeup(), trying to wake up the process before it has completed the sleep operation, resulting in yet another race condition. So the problem is how to prevent task and interrupt handler from interfering with each other.

Step 4: Implementation of Critical Regions
When an interrupt handler executes, the task is logically not executing, so tasks can not interfere with interrupt handler, but the reverse is not true. While a task executes, timer interrupts may occur, which divert the task to execute the interrupt handler, which may interfere with the task. In order to prevent this, it suffices for the executing task to mask out interrupts in Critical Regions. As pointed out before, the MT multitasking system runs on a virtual CPU, which is a Linux process. To the MT system, timer interrupts are SIGALRM signals to the Linux process. In Linux, signals other than SIGKILL(9) and SIGSTOP(19) can be blocked/unblocked by the following means.

(1). sigset_t sigmask, oldmask;   // define signal mask sets
(2). sigemptyset(&sigmask);   // initialize signal mask set to empty
(3). **sigaddset(&sigmask, SIGALRM); // add signal numbers to the set**
(4). To block signals specified in the mask set, issue the system call
     sigprocmask(SIG_BLOCK, &sigmask, &oldmask);
(5). To unblock signals specified in the mask set, issue the system call
     sigprocmask(SIG_UNBLOCK, &sigmask, &oldmask);
(6). For convenience, the reader may use the following functions to block/unblock
     signals
     int_off(){ sigprocmask(SIG_BLOCK, &sigmask, &oldmask); }
     int_on(){ sigprocmask(SIG_UNBLOCK, &oldmask, &sigmask); }

Step 4 of the programming project is to use sigprocmask() of Linux to block/unblock timer interrupts in Critical Regions in the MT system to ensure no race conditions between tasks and the timer interrupt handler.

5.8.5   Advanced Topics

As a topic for advanced study, the reader may try to implement task scheduling by time-slice and discuss its implications. In time-slice based task scheduling, each task is given a fixed number of timer ticks, known as the time-slice, to run. While a task runs, its time-slice is decremented by the timer interrupt handler. When the time-slice of the running task decrements to 0, the system switches task to run another task. These sounds simple and easy but there are serious implications. The reader is encouraged to think of the problems and possible solutions.

5.9   Summary

This chapter covers timers and timer services. It explains the principle of hardware timers and the hardware timers in Intel x86 based PCs. it covers CPU operations and interrupts processing. It describes timer related system calls, library functions and commands for timer services in Linux. It discusses process interval timers, timer generated signals and demonstrates process interval timers by examples. The programming project is to implement timer, timer interrupts and interval timers in a multitasking system. The multitasking system runs as a Linux process, which acts as a virtual CPU for concurrent tasks inside the Linux process. The real-time mode interval timer of the Linux process is programmed to generate SIGALRM signals periodically, which acts as timer interrupts to the virtual CPU, which uses a SIGALRM signal catcher as the timer interrupt handler. The project is for the reader to implement interval timers for tasks by a timer queue. It also lets the reader use Linux signal masks to implement critical regions to prevent race conditions between tasks and interrupt handlers.

Problems
1. The library function **ctime(&seconds)** converts time in seconds to calendar form, which is a string. Modify the Example 5.1 program to print the current date and time in calendar form.
2. Modify the Example 5.1 program to include a delay loop to simulate a lengthy computation of the program. Use gettimeofday() to get the current time both before and after the loop. Then print the difference between the two times. Can we measure the total execution time of a program this way? Justify your answer.
3. Modify the program in Example 5.1 as follows.

   (1). Install a signal catcher for the SIGPROF(27) signal.
   (2). Start another interval timer in the PROF mode with the same period as the VIRTUAL mode timer.
   (3). Let pcount=number signals generated by the PROF timer, and
        vcount=number signals generated by the VIRTUAL timer.
        In the signal handlers, print both pcount and vcount. When either count reaches 100, stop the timers and print the counts.
   (4). In the while(1) loop of the main program, add the system calls getpid() and getppid(), so that the process will spend some time in system mode.

   Compile and run the program, and answer the following questions.

   (5). Which timer will generate signals faster and WHY?
   (6). How to determine the process execution time in user mode and system mode?

(7). Run the program as time a.out. It will print the execution time of a.out in real mode, user mode and system mode. Explain how is the time command implemented?

4. Modify the program in Example 5.1 to set a REAL mode interval timer.
5. In a cumulative timer queue, the expiration time of each TQE is relative to the cumulative sum of the expiration time of all preceding TQEs. Design an algorithm to insert a TQE with an expiration time t into the timerQueue. Design an algorithm to delete a TQE when a timer request is cancelled before expiration.

References

AMD64 Architecture Programmer's manual Volume 2: System Programming, 2011
Bovet, D.P., Cesati, M., "Understanding the Linux Kernel, Third Edition", O'Reilly, 2005
Intel i486 Processor Programmer's Reference Manual, 1990
Intel MultiProcessor Specification, v1.4, 1997
Wang, K. C., "Design and Implementation of the MTX Operating System", Springer A.G., 2015

Signals and Signal Processing

6

Abstract

This chapter covers signals and signal processing. It presents a unified treatment of signals and interrupts, which helps put signals into a proper perspective. It treats signals as interrupts to processes, which diverts a process from its normal executions to do signal processing. It explains sources of signals, which include signals from hardware, exceptions and other processes. Then it uses examples to illustrate common usage of signals in Unix/Linux. It explains signal processing in Unix/Linux in detail. These include signal types, signal vector bits, signal mask bits, signal handlers in the process PROC structure and signal processing steps. It uses examples to show how to install signal catchers to handle program exceptions, such as segmentation faults, in user mode. It also discusses the suitability of using signals as a mechanism for Interprocess Communication (IPC). The programming project is for the reader to use signals and pipes to implement an IPC mechanism for processes to exchange message.

6.1   Signals and Interrupts

Interrupts are external requests from I/O devices or coprocessors sent to a CPU, which divert the CPU from its normal executions to do interrupt processing. Like interrupts to a CPU, signals are requests sent to a process, which divert the process from its normal executions to do signal processing. Before discussing signals and signal processing, we shall review the concepts and mechanism of interrupts, which help put signals into a proper perspective.

(1). First, we generalize the notion of process to mean: a "process" (in quotes) is a sequence of activities. Examples of generalized "processes" include
   . a person, who carries on his/her daily routine chores.
   . a Unix/Linux process, which runs in either user mode or kernel mode.
   . a CPU, which executes machine instructions.

© Springer International Publishing AG, part of Springer Nature 2018   205
K. C. Wang, *Systems Programming in Unix/Linux*, https://doi.org/10.1007/978-3-319-92429-8_6

(2). An "interrupt" is an event sent to a "process", which diverts the "process" from its normal activities to do something else, called "interrupt processing". The "process" may resume its normal activities after it finishes processing the "interrupt".

(3). The term "interrupt" can be applied to any "process", not just to a CPU in a computer. For example, we may speak of the following kinds of "interrupts".

(3).1. PERSON interrupts

While I am reading, grading, day-dreaming, etc. in my office, some real events may occur, such as

Real Events	ID	Action Function
----------------	----	---
Building on fire	1	Get out immediately!
Telephone rings	2	Pick up phone to chat with the caller.
Knock on door	3	Yell come in (or pretend not there).
Cut own finger	4	Apply band-aid.
. . . .		

All these may be called PERSON interrupts because they divert a person from his/her normal activities to "handle or process the interrupt". After processing an interrupt, a person may resume whatever he/she was doing before (if the person survives and still remembers what he/she was doing before). Each interrupt is assigned a unique ID number for identification, and has a pre-installed action function, which a person can "execute" upon receiving an interrupt. Depending on their origin, interrupts may be classified into 3 categories:

From hardware   : building on fire, alarm clock goes off, etc.
From other person: phone call, knocking on door, etc.
Self-inflicted   : cut own finger, eat too much, etc.

Depending on their urgency, interrupts can be classified as

Non-maskable (NMI): Building on fire!
Maskable   : Knocking on door, etc.

Each of the action functions of a PERSON is installed either by instincts or by experience. It is impossible to complete the above table since there are too many different kinds of PERSON interrupts, but the idea should be clear.

(3).2. PROCESS interrupts

These are interrupts sent to a process. While a process is executing, it may receive interrupts from 3 different sources:

From hardware   : Control_C key from terminal, interval timer, etc.
From other process: kill(pid, SIG#), death_of_child, etc.
Self-inflicted   : divide by zero, invalid address, etc.

Each process interrupt is converted to a unique ID number, which is sent to the process. Unlike PERSON interrupts, which has too many kinds, we can always limit the number of interrupts to a process. In Unix/Linux, process interrupts are called SIGNALS, which are numbered 1 to 31. For each signal, a process has an action function in its PROC structure, which the process can execute upon receiving a signal. Similar to a person, a process may mask out certain kinds of signals to defer their processing. If needed, a process may also change its signal action functions.

(3).3. HARDWARE Interrupts:

These are signals sent to a processor or CPU. They also originate from 3 possible sources:

From hardware   : Timer, I/O devices, etc.
From other processors: FFP, DMA, other CPUs in a multiprocessor system.
Self-inflicted   : divide by 0, protection error, INT instruction.

Each interrupt has a unique interrupt vector number. The action function is an interrupt handler in the interrupt vector table. Recall that a CPU is always executing a process. The CPU does not cause any self-inflicted interrupts (unless faulty). Such interrupts are due to the process that is using or, in most cases, misusing the CPU. The former includes the INT n or equivalent instructions, which cause the CPU to switch from user mode to kernel mode. The latter includes all trap errors recognized by the CPU as exceptions. Therefore, we may rule out the self-inflicted interrupts from a CPU, leaving only those external to the CPU.

(3).4. Trap Errors of Process

A process may cause self-inflicted interrupts to itself. Such interrupts are due to errors, e.g. divide by 0, invalid address, illegal instruction, privilege violation, etc. which are recognized by the CPU as exceptions. When a process encounters an exception, it traps to the OS kernel, converts the trap reason to a signal number and sends the signal to itself. If the exception occurs in user mode, the default action of a process is to terminate, with an optional memory dump for debugging. As we shall see later, a process may replace the default action function with a signal catcher, allowing it to handle signal in user mode. If the trap occurs in kernel mode, which must be due to hardware error or, most likely, bugs in the kernel code, there is nothing the kernel can do. In Unix/Linux, the kernel simply prints a PANIC error message and stops. Hopefully the problem can be traced and fixed in the next kernel release.

6.2   Examples of Unix/Linux Signals

(1). Pressing the Control_C key usually causes a running process to terminate. Here is why. The Control_C key generates a keyboard hardware interrupt. The keyboard interrupt handler converts the Control_C key to a SIGINT(2) signal to all processes on the terminal and wake up such processes if they are waiting for keyboard inputs. While in kernel mode, every process is required to check and handle outstanding signals. For most signals, the default action of a process is to call the kernel's kexit(exitValue) function to terminate. In Linux, the low byte of exitValue is the signal number that caused the process to terminate.

(2). The user may use the **nohup a.out &** command to run a process in the background. The process will continue to run even after the user logout. The nohup command causes the sh to fork a child to execute the program as usual, but the child ignores the SIGHUP(1) signal. When the user logout, the sh sends a SIGHUP signal to all processes associated with the terminal. Upon receiving such a signal, the background process simply ignores it and continues to run. To prevent the background process from using the terminal for I/O, the background process usually disconnects itself from the terminal (by redirecting its file descriptors 0,1,2 to /dev/null), making it totally immune to any terminal oriented signals.

(3). Perhaps a few days later the user login again and finds (by ps -u UID) that the background process is still running. The user may use the sh command

```
kill pid    (or  kill -s 9 pid)
```

to kill it. Here is how. The process executing kill sends a SIGTERM(15) signal to the target process identified by pid, requesting it to die. The targeted process will comply with the request and terminate. If the process has chosen to ignore the SIGTERM signal, it may refuse to die. In that case, we may use kill -s 9 pid, which will kill it for sure. This is because processes cannot change their actions for the number 9 signal. The reader may wonder, why number 9? In the original Unix, there were only 9 signals. The number 9 signal was reserved as the last resort to kill a process. Although later Unix/Linux systems expand the signal numbers to 31, the meaning of signal number 9 is still retained.

6.3   Signal Processing in Unix/Linux

6.3.1   Signal Types

Unix/Linux supports 31 different signals, which are defined in the signal.h file.

```
#define SIGHUP            1
#define SIGINT            2
#define SIGQUIT           3
#define SIGILL            4
#define SIGTRAP           5
#define SIGABRT           6
#define SIGIOT            6
#define SIGBUS            7
#define SIGFPE            8
#define SIGKILL           9
#define SIGUSR1          10
#define SIGSEGV          11
#define SIGUSR2          12
#define SIGPIPE          13
#define SIGALRM          14
#define SIGTERM          15
#define SIGSTKFLT        16
#define SIGCHLD          17
#define SIGCONT          18
#define SIGSTOP          19
#define SIGTSTP          20
#define SIGTTIN          21
#define SIGTTOU          22
#define SIGURG           23
#define SIGXCPU          24
#define SIGXFSZ          25
#define SIGVTALRM        26
#define SIGPROF          27
#define SIGWINCH         28
#define SIGPOLL          29
#define SIGPWR           30
#define SIGSYS           31
```

Each signal has a symbolic name, such as SIGHUP(1), SIGINT(2), SIGKILL(9), SIGSEGV(11), etc.

6.3.2   Origin of Signals

. **Signals from Hardware Interrupts:** While a process executes, some hardware interrupts are converted to signals sent to the process. Examples of hardware signals are
Interrupt key (Control-C), which results in a SIGINT(2) signal.
Interval timers, which generate a SIGALRM(14) or SIGVTALRM(26) or
SIGPROF(27) signal when their time expires.
Other hardware errors, such as bus-error, IO trap, etc.

. **Signals from Exceptions:** When a process in user mode encounters an exception, it traps to kernel mode to generate a signal to itself. Examples of familiar trap signals are SIGFPE(8) for floating point exception (divide by 0) and the most common and dreadful SIGSEGV(11) for segmentation fault, etc.

. **Signals from Other Processes:** Processes may use the kill(pid, sig) system call to send a signal to a target process identified by pid. The reader may try the following experiment. Under Linux, run the trivial C program

```
main(){ while(1); }
```

which causes the process to loop forever. From another (X-window) terminal, use ps -u to find the looping process pid. Then enter the sh command

```
kill -s 11 pid
```

The looping process will die with segmentation fault. The reader may wonder: how can that be? All the process does is executing in a while(1) loop, how can it generate a segmentation fault? The answer is: it does not matter. Whenever a process dies by a signal, its exitValue contains the signal number. The parent sh simply converts the signal number of the dead child process to an error string, whatever that is.

6.3.3   Signals in Process PROC Structure:

Each process PROC has a 32-bit vector, which records signals sent to the process. In the bit vector, each bit (except bit 0) represents a signal number. In addition, it also has a signal MASK bit-vector for masking out the corresponding signals. A set of system calls, such as sigmask, sigsetmask, siggetmask, sigblock, etc. can be used to set, clear and examine the MASK bit-vector. A pending signal becomes effective only if it is not masked out. This allows a process to defer processing masked out signals, similar to CPU masking out certain interrupts.

6.3.4   Signal Handlers

Each process PROC has a signal handler array, int sig[32]. Each entry of the sig[32] array specifies how to handle a corresponding signal, where 0 means DEFault, 1 means IGNore, other nonzero value means by a preinstalled signal catcher (handler) function in user mode. Figure 6.1 shows the signal bit-vector, masking bit-vector and signal handlers
A signal I is **generated** or sent to the process if bit-I in the signal-bit vector is 1. The signal is **blocked** or masked out if bit-I of the mask bit-vector is 1. Otherwise, it is **unblocked.** A signal will take effect or **delivered** to the process only if the signal is present and unblocked. When the process in

```
                    31 30            I            1   0
                    -----------------------------------
signal bits         |  |  |  . . |1 | . .  |  |  |  0=no signal,1=signal
                    -----------------------------------


                    -----------------------------------
signal masks        |  |  |  . . |0 | . .  |  |  |  0=no BLOCK, 1=BLOCK
                    -----------------------------------


                    -----------------------------------
signal handler  |  |  |  . . |0 | . .  |  |  |  0=DEFault, 1=IGNore
                    ----------------------------------- other=catcher address
```

Fig. 6.1 Signal Handling Diagram

kernel mode finds an unblocked signal, it clears the signal bit to 0 and tries to handle the signal by the handler function in the signal handler array. A 0 entry means DEFault, a 1 means IGNore and other values means a preinstalled catcher function in user space.

6.3.5   Install Signal Catchers

A process may use the system call

```
int r = signal(int signal_number, void *handler);
```

to change the handler function of a selected signal number, except SIGKILL(9) and SIGSTOP(19), which can not be changed. The installed handler, if not 0 or 1, must be the entry address of a signal catcher function in user space of the form

```
void catcher(int signal_number){.............}
```

The signal() system call is available in all Unix-like systems but it has some undesirable features.

(1). Before executing the installed signal catcher, the signal handler is usually reset to DEFault. In order to catch the next occurrence of the same signal, the catcher must be installed again. This may lead to a race condition between the next signal and reinstalling the signal handler. In contrast, sigaction() automatically blocks the next signal while executing the current catcher, so there is no race condition.

(2). Signal() can not block other signals. If needed, the user must use sigprocmask() to explicitly block/ unblock other signals. In contrast, sigaction() can specify other signals to be blocked.

(3). Signal() can only transmit a signal number to the catcher function. Sigaction() can transmit addition information about the signal.

(4). Signal() may not work for threads in a multi-threaded program. Sigaction() works for threads.

(5). Signal() may vary across different versions of Unix. Sigaction() is the POISX standard, which is more portable.

For these reasons, signal() has been replaced by the POSIX **sigaction()** function. In Linux (Bovet and Cesati 2005), sigaction() is a system call. It has the prototype

```
int sigaction (int signum, const struct sigaction *act, struct sigaction
*oldact);
```

The sigaction structure is defined as

```
struct sigaction{
   void      (*sa_handler)(int);
   void      (*sa_sigaction)(int, siginfo_t *, void *);
   sigset_t sa_mask;
   int       sa_flags;
   void      (*sa_restorer)(void);
};
```

The most important fields are:

. **sa_handler:** This is the pointer to a handler function that has the same prototype as a handler for signal().
. **sa_sigaction:** This is an alternative way to run the signal handler. It has two additional arguments beside the signal number where the siginfo_t * provides more information about the received signal.
. **sa_mask:** allows to set signals to be blocked during execution of the handler.
. **sa_flags:** allows to modify the behavior of the signal handling process. To use the sa_sigaction handler, sa_flags must be set to SA_SIGINFO.

For a detailed description of the sigaction structure fields, see the sigaction manual page. The following shows a simple example of using the sigaction() system call.

Example 6.6 Example use of sigaction()

```
/****** sigaction.c file *******/
#include <stdio.h>
#include <unistd.h>
#include <signal.h>

void handler(int sig, siginfo_t *siginfo, void *context)
{
  printf("handler: sig=%d from PID=%d UID=%d\n",
                  sig, siginfo->si_pid, siginfo->si_uid);
}

int main(int argc, char *argv[])
{
  struct sigaction act;
  memset(&act, 0, sizeof(act));
  act.sa_sigaction = &handler;
  act.sa_flags = SA_SIGINFO;
  sigaction(SIGTERM, &act, NULL);
  printf("proc PID=%d looping\n");
  printf("enter kill PID to send SIGTERM signal to it\n", getpid());
  while(1){
    sleep(10);
  }
}
```

While the program is running, the reader may enter **kill PID** from another X-terminal, which sends a SIGTERM(15) signal to the process. Any signal would wake up the process even if it is in the sleep state, allowing it to handle the signal. In the signal handler we read two fields from the siginfo parameter to show the signal sender's PID and UID, which are unavailable if the signal handler was installed by the signal() system call.

(6). A process may use the system call

```
int r = kill(pid, signal_number);
```

to send a signal to another process identified by pid. The sh command

```
kill -s signal_number pid
```

uses the kill system call. In general, only related processes, e.g. those with the same uid, may send signals to each other. However, a superuser process (uid=0) may send signals to any process. The kill system call uses an invalid pid, to mean different ways of delivering the signal. For example, pid=0 sends the signal to all processes in the same process group, pid=-1 for all processes with pid>1, etc. The reader may consult Linux man pages on signal/kill for more details.

6.4   Signal Processing Steps

(7). A process checks signals and handles outstanding signals when it is in kernel mode. If a signal has a user installed catcher function, the process first clears the signal, fetches the catcher's address and, for most trap related signals, resets the installed catcher to DEFault. Then it manipulates the return path in such a way that it returns to execute the catcher function in user mode. When the catcher function finishes, it returns to the original point of interruption, i.e. from where it lastly entered kernel mode. Thus, the process takes a detour to execute the catcher function first. Then it resumes normal execution.

(8). Reset user installed signal catchers: User installed catcher functions for trap related signals are intended to deal with trap errors in user code. Since the catcher function is also executed in user mode, it may commit the same kind of errors again. If so, the process would end up in an infinite loop, jumping between user mode and kernel mode forever. To prevent this, the Unix kernel typically resets the handler to DEFault before letting the process execute the catcher function. This implies that a user installed catcher function is good for only one occurrence of the signal. To catch another occurrence of the same signal, the catcher must be installed again. However, the treatment of user installed signal catchers is not uniform as it varies across different versions of Unix. For instance, in BSD Unix the signal handler is not reset but the same signal is blocked while executing the signal catcher. Interested readers may consult the man pages of signal and sigaction of Linux for more details.

(9). Signal and Wakeup: There are two kinds of SLEEP processes in the Unix/Linux kernel; sound sleepers and light sleepers. The former are non-interruptible, but the latter are interruptible by signals. If a process is in the non-interruptible SLEEP state, arriving signals (which must originate from hardware interrupts or another process) do not wake up the process. If it is in the interruptible SLEEP state, arriving signals will wake it up. For example, when a process waits for terminal inputs, it sleeps with a low priority, which is interruptible, a signal such as SIGINT will wake it up.

6.5   Signals and Exceptions

(10). Proper use of signals: Unix signals are originally designed for these purposes.

. As a unified treatment of process exceptions: When a process encounters an exception, it traps to kernel mode, converts the trap reason to a signal number and sends the signal to itself. If the exception occurred in kernel mode, the kernel prints a PANIC message and stops. If the exception occurred in user mode, the process typically terminates with a memory dump for debugging.

. To allow processes to handle program errors in user mode by preinstalled signal catchers. This is similar to the ESPIE macro in MVS [IBM MVS].

. Under unusual conditions, it allows a process to kill another process by a signal. Note that kill does not kill a process outright; it is only a "please die" plea to the target process. Why can't we kill a process outright? The reader is encouraged to think of the reasons. (Hint: the large number of unclaimed anonymous accounts in Swiss banks).

6.6   Signals as IPC

(11). Misuse of Signals: In many OS books, signals are classified as a mechanism for inter-process communication. The rationale is that a process may send a signal to another process, causing it to execute a preinstalled signal handler function. The classification is highly debatable, if not inappropriate, for the following reasons.

. The mechanism is unreliable due to possible missing signals. Each signal is represented by a single bit in a bit-vector, which can only record one occurrence of a signal. If a process sends two or more identical signals to another process, they may show up only once in the recipient PROC. Real-time signals are queued and guaranteed to be delivered in the same order as they are sent, but an OS kernel may not support real-time signals.

. Race condition: Before processing a signal, a process usually resets the signal handler to DEFault. In order to catch another occurrence of the same signal, the process must reinstall the catcher function BEFORE the next signal arrives. Otherwise, the next signal may cause the process to terminate. Although the race condition could be prevented by blocking the same signal while executing the signal catcher, there is no way to prevent missing signals.

. Most signals have predefined meaning. Indiscriminate use of signals may not achieve communication but confusion. For example, sending a SIGSEGV(11) segmentation fault signal to a looping process is like yelling to a swimmer in the water: "Your pants are on fire!".

Therefore, trying to use signals as a means of interprocess communication is over stretching the intended purpose of signals, which should be avoided.

Example 6.7. Catcher for Segmentation Faults   As pointed out Chap. 2, the most common causes of segmentation faults in C programs are due to dereferencing null or invalid pointers, array out of bounds, etc. When a process encounters a invalid memory exception, it traps to the OS kernel to generate a SIGSEGV(11) signal to itself. The default handler of the SIGSEGV signal is 0, which causes the process to terminate. If the process has ignored the signal, it would return to the same bad instruction again, resulting in an infinite loop. If the user has installed a catcher for the SIGSEGV signal, it would execute the signal catcher but still return to the same bad instruction when the catcher finishes. It seems that the only option is for the process to terminate abnormally in case of any segmentation fault. This example shows how to use signal catcher and long jump to bypass the program code that caused the segmentation fault, allowing the program to continue or terminate gracefully.

```c
/********** t7.c file **********/
#include <stdio.h>
#include <stdlib.h>
#include <unistd.h>
#include <signal.h>
#include <setjmp.h>  // for long jump

jmp_buf env; // for saving longjmp environment
int count = 0;

void handler(int sig, siginfo_t *siginfo, void *context)
{
  printf ("handler: sig=%d from PID=%d UID=%d count=%d\n",
          sig, siginfo->si_pid, siginfo->si_uid, ++count);
  if (count >= 4) // let it occur up to 4 times
     longjmp(env, 1234);
}


int BAD()
{
  int *ip = 0;
  printf("in BAD(): try to dereference NULL pointer\n");
  *ip = 123;          // dereference a NULL pointer
  printf("should not see this line\n");
}


int main (int argc, char *argv[])
{
  int r;
  struct sigaction act;
  memset (&act, 0, sizeof(act));
  act.sa_sigaction = &handler;
  act.sa_flags = SA_SIGINFO;
  sigaction(SIGSEGV, &act, NULL); // install SIGSEGV catcher
  if ((r = setjmp(env)) == 0)     // call setjmp(env)
     BAD();                       // call BAD()
  else
     printf("proc %d survived SEGMENTATION FAULT: r=%d\n",getpid(), r);

  printf("proc %d looping\n");
  while(1);
}
```

Figure 6.2 show the outputs of the segfault.c program.

Fig. 6.2 Demonstration of
segmentation fault catcher

```
in BAD(): try to dereference NULL pointer
handler: sig=11 from PID=0 UID=4 count=1
handler: sig=11 from PID=0 UID=4 count=2
handler: sig=11 from PID=0 UID=4 count=3
handler: sig=11 from PID=0 UID=4 count=4
proc 2855 survived SEGMENTATION FAULT: r=1234
proc 2855 looping
```

Exercise 6.7 Modify the Example 6 program to catch divide by zero exceptions.

6.7   IPC in Linux

IPC refers to the mechanisms used for Interprocess Communication. In Linux, IPC comprises the following components.

6.7.1   Pipes and FIFOs

Pipes and pipe programming are covered in section 3.10.1 of Chap. 3. A pipe has a read end and a write end. A typical usage of pipe is to connect a pair of pipe writer and read processes. A pipe writer process writes data to a pipe and a reader process reads data form the pipe. Pipe write and read operations are synchronized by the pipe's control mechanism. Unnamed pipes are for related processes. Named pipes are FIFOs, which can be used by unrelated processes. In Linux, pipe read operation is synchronous and blocking. The reader process waits if the pipe still has writer but no data.

If desired, pipe operations can be changed to nonblocking by the fcntl system call on pipe descriptors.

6.7.2   Signals

Processes may use the kill system call to send signals to other processes, which use signal catchers to handle the signals. A major weakness of using signals as IPC is that they can only be used as notifications, which do not contain any information contents.

6.7.3   System V IPC

Linux supports System V IPC, which include shared memory, semaphores and message queues. In Linux, System V IPC functions, such as shmat/shmdt for attaching/detaching shared memory, semget/semop for getting/ operating on semaphores and msgsnd/msgrcv for sending/receiving messages are library wrapper functions, all of which issue the single ipc() system call to the Linux kernel. The implementation of ipc() is Linux specific, which may not be portable.

6.7.4   POSIX Message Queues

The POSIX standard (IEEE 1003.1-2001) defines an IPC mechanism based on message queues. They are similar to the System V IPC's message queues but more general and portable.

6.7.5   Threads Synchronization Mechanisms

Linux dose not distinguish between processes and threads. In Linux, processes are threads sharing some common resources. If processes are created with the clone() system call with shared address space, they can communicate by shared memory using mutex and condition variables for synchronization. Alternatively, regular processes can attach to a shared memory, allowing them to be synchronized as threads.

6.7.6   Sockets

Sockets are IPC mechanisms for process communication over networks. Sockets and network programming will be covered in Chap. 13.

6.8   Programming Project: Implement an IPC for Messages

As pointed out before, pipes can be used for processes to exchange information, but processes must either wait for pipe contents if using blocking protocol, or repeatedly check for the availability of pipe contents if using nonblocking protocol. Signals can be used as notifications when certain events occur but they do not convey other information. The programming project is for the reader to combine signals and pipes to implement an IPC mechanism for processes to exchange messages. In the project, messages may be defined as fixed length text strings, e.g. a string of 64 chars. Processes do not have to wait for messages. When a process sends a message by writing to a pipe, it sends a signal to the target process to notify it of the arriving message. Responding to the signal, the receiving process can read the message from the pipe without checking or being blocked. The project consists of two parts. Part 1 presents a base code for the reader to get started, which is shown below.

Part 1: Project Base Code

```
/******* Base Code of Programming Project *******/
#include <stdio.h>
#include <signal.h>
#include <fcntl.h>
#include <string.h>

#define LEN 64
int ppipe[2];                    // pipe descriptors
int pid;                         // child pid
char line[LEN];
```

```
int parent()
{
  printf("parent %d running\n", getpid());
  close(ppipe[0]);                 // parent = pipe writer
  while(1){
    printf("parent %d: input a line : \n", getpid());
    fgets(line, LEN, stdin);
    line[strlen(line)-1] = 0; // kill \n at end
    printf("parent %d write to pipe\n", getpid());
    write(ppipe[1], line, LEN); // write to pipe
    printf("parent %d send signal 10 to %d\n", getpid(), pid);
    kill(pid, SIGUSR1);          // send signal to child process
  }
}


void chandler(int sig)
{
  printf("\nchild %d got an interrupt sig=%d\n", getpid(), sig);
  read(ppipe[0], line, LEN);    // read pipe
  printf("child %d get a message = %s\n", getpid(), line);
}


int child()
{
  char msg[LEN];
  int parent = getppid();
  printf("child %d running\n", getpid());
  close(ppipe[1]);               // child is pipe reader
  signal(SIGUSR1, chandler);     // install signal catcher
  while(1);
}


int main()
{
  pipe(ppipe);                   // create a pipe
  pid = fork();                  // fork a child process
  if (pid) // parent
    parent();
  else
    child();
}
```

In the base code, the parent process creates a pipe, forks a child and behaves as a writer to the pipe. The child is the pipe reader. It installs a SIGUSR1 signal catcher and then loops. When the parent runs, it gets an input string, writes the string to the pipe as a message and sends a SIGUSR1 signal to the child, which receives and displays the message in the signal catcher. Then it repeats the loop. Figure 6.3 shows the sample outputs of running the base code program.

Fig. 6.3 Sample outputs of
project base code

```
parent 28931 running
parent 28931: input a line :
child  28932 running
message one
parent 28931 write to pipe
parent 28931 send signal 10 to 28932
parent 28931: input a line :
child  28932 got an interrupt sig=10
child  28932 got a message = message one
message two
parent 28931 write to pipe
parent 28931 send signal 10 to 28932
parent 28931: input a line :
child  28932 got an interrupt sig=10
child  28932 got a message = message two
■
```

Programming Project Part 2 Modify the project base code to implement the following.

(1). Send Reply: After sending a message the sender waits for a reply before sending the next message. Correspondingly, after receiving a message the receiver sends a reply back to the sender. For example, the reply may be the original message converted to uppercase.

(2). Time Stamp: When sending a message or reply, add a time stamp to the message by the current time. After receiving a reply, compute and show the message round trip time.

(3). Timeout and Resend: Assume that the parent process is unreliable. After receiving a message, it may decide randomly not to send a reply, which would cause the sender to wait indefinitely. Add timeout and resend as follows. After sending a message, set a real-time mode interval timer of 10 msec. If received a reply before the timer expires, cancel the timer. Otherwise, resend the message again (with a new time stamp) until a reply is received.

HINT: Chap. 5 on interval timer signals.

6.9   Summary

This chapter covers signals and signal processing. It presents a unified treatment of signals and interrupts, which helps put signals into a proper perspective. It treats signals as interrupts to processes, which diverts a process from its normal executions to do signal processing. It explains sources of signals, which include signals from hardware, exceptions and other processes. Then it uses examples to illustrate common usage of signals in Unix/Linux. It explains signal processing in Unix/Linux in detail. These include signal types, signal vector bits, signal mask bits, signal handlers in the process PROC structure and signal processing steps. It uses examples to show how to install signal catchers to handle program exceptions, such as segmentation faults, in user mode. It also discusses the suitability of using signals as a mechanism for Interprocess Communication (IPC). The programming project is for the reader to use signals and pipes to implement an IPC mechanism for processes to exchange message.

Problems

1. Review Questions:
   (1). Define "interrupts" in your own words.
   (2). What are Hardware interrupts, Process interrupts?

(3). INT n instructions are usually called software interrupts. What's the difference between INT n and PROCESS interrupt?

(4). How does a process get PROCESS interrupts?

(5). How does a process handle PROCESS interrupts?

2. What is the role of signal 9? Why is it needed?

3. A CPU usually checks for pending interrupts at the end of current instruction. What are the time and places for a process to check for pending signals?

4. Before handling a signal, the kernel usually resets the signal's handler to DEFault. Why is this necessary?

5. In Linux, pressing the Control_C key will cause a process to terminate. However, when a main sh is running on a pseudo terminal, pressing the Control_C key does not cause the main sh to terminate. How does the main sh do it?

6. In C programming, a callback function (pointer) is passed as a parameter to a called function, which may execute the callback function. What's the difference between callback functions and signal catchers?

7. Assume that a process has installed a signal catcher for SIGALRM(14). What if the process exec to a different image? How to deal with this kind of problem?

References

Bovet, D.P., Cesati, M., "Understanding the Linux Kernel, Third Edition", O'Reilly, 2005

IBM MVS Programming Assembler Services Guide, Oz/OS V1R11.0, IBM

Linux: http://www.linux.org signal(7), Linux Programmer's Manual: descriptions of Posix/Linux signals, including real-time signals.

File Operations

7

Abstract

This chapter covers file systems. It explains the various levels of file operations in operating systems. These include preparing storage devices for file storage, file system support functions in kernel, system calls, library I/O functions on file streams, user commands and sh scripts for file operations. It presents a systematic overview of file operations, from read/write file streams in user space to system calls to kernel space down to the device I/O driver level. It describes low level file operations, which include disk partitions, example programs to display partition tables, format partitions for file systems and mount disk partitions. It presents an introduction to the EXT2 file system of Linux, which include the EXT2 file system data structures, example programs to display superblock, group descriptor, blocks and inodes bitmaps and directory contents. The programming project is to integrate the knowledge about EXT2/3 file systems and programming techniques presented in the chapter into a program which converts file pathnames into inodes and print their information.

7.1   File Operation Levels

File operations consist of five levels, from low to high, as shown in the following hierarchy.

(1). **Hardware Level:** File operations at hardware level include

> fdisk : divide a hard disk, USB or SDC drive into partitions.
> mkfs : format disk partitions to make them ready for file systems.
> fsck : check and repair file system.
> defragmentation: compact files in a file system.

Most of these are system-oriented utility programs. An average user may never need them, but they are indispensable tools for creating and maintaining file systems.

© Springer International Publishing AG, part of Springer Nature 2018
K. C. Wang, *Systems Programming in Unix/Linux*, https://doi.org/10.1007/978-3-319-92429-8_7

(2). **File System Functions in OS Kernel:** Every operating system kernel provides support for basic file operations. The following lists some of these functions in a Unix-like system kernel, where the prefix k denotes kernel functions.

```
kmount(), kumount()                (mount/umount file systems)
kmkdir(), krmdir()                 (make/remove directory)
kchdir(), kgetcwd()                (change directory, get CWD pathname)
klink(),  kunlink()                (hard link/unlink files)
kchmod(), kchown(), kutime()       (change r|w|x permissions,owner,time)
kcreat(), kopen()                  (create/open file for R,W,RW,APPEND)
kread(),  kwrite()                 (read/write opened files)
klseek(); kclose()                 (lseek/close file descriptors)
ksymlink(), kreadlink()            (create/read symbolic link files)
kstat(),  kfstat(), klstat()       (get file status/information)
kopendir(), kreaddir()             (open/read directories)
```

(3). **System Calls:** User mode programs use system calls to access kernel functions. As an example, the following program reads the second 1024 bytes of a file.

```c
#include <fcntl.h>
int main(int argc, char *argv[ ]) // run as a.out filename
{
    int fd, n;
    char buf[1024];
    if ((fd = open(argv[1], O_RDONLY)) < 0) // if open() fails
        exit(1);
    lseek(fd, 1024, SEEK_SET);      // lseek to byte 1024
    n = read(fd, buf, 1024);        // try to read 1024 bytes
    close(fd);
}
```

The functions **open()**, **read()**, **lseek()** and **close()** are C library functions. Each of these library functions issues a system call, which causes the process to enter kernel mode to execute a corresponding kernel function, e.g. open goes to kopen(), read goes to kread(), etc. When the process finishes executing the kernel function, it returns to user mode with the desired results. Switch between user mode and kernel mode requires a lot of actions (and time). Data transfer between kernel and user spaces is therefore quite expensive. Although it is permissible to issue a read(fd, buf, 1) system call to read only one byte of data, it is not very wise to do so since that one byte would come with a terrific cost. Every time we have to enter kernel, we should do as much as we can to make the journey worthwhile. In the case of read/write files, the best way is to match what the kernel does. The kernel reads/writes files by block size, which ranges from 1KB to 8KB. For instance, in Linux, the default block size is 4KB for hard disks and 1KB for floppy disks. So each read/write system call should also try to transfer one block of data at a time.

(4). **Library I/O Functions:** System calls allow the user to read/write chunks of data, which are just a sequence of bytes. They do not know, nor care, about the meaning of the data. A user often needs to read/write individual chars, lines or data structure records, etc. With only system calls, a user mode program must do these operations from/to a buffer area by itself. Most users would consider this too inconvenient. The C library provides a set of standard I/O functions for convenience, as well as for run-time efficiency. Library I/O functions include:

```
FILE mode I/O: fopen(),fread();  fwrite(),fseek(),fclose(),fflush()
char mode I/O: getc(), getchar() ugetc(); putc(),putchar()
line mode I/O: gets(), fgets();  puts(), fputs()
formatted I/O: scanf(),fscanf(),sscanf(); printf(),fprintf(),sprintf()
```

With the exceptions of sscanf()/sprintf(), which read/write memory locations, all other library I/O functions are built on top of system calls, i.e. they ultimately issue system calls for actual data transfer through the system kernel.

(5). **User Commands:** Instead of writing programs, users may use Unix/Linux commands to do file operations. Examples of user commands are

```
mkdir, rmdir, cd, pwd, ls, link, unlink, rm, cat, cp, mv, chmod, etc.
```

Each user command is in fact an executable program (except cd), which typically calls library I/O functions, which in turn issue system calls to invoke the corresponding kernel functions. The processing sequence of a user command is either

```
Command => Library I/O function => System call => Kernel Function
OR Command ========================= > System call => Kernel Function
```

(6). **Sh Scripts:** Although much more convenient than system calls, commands must be entered manually, or in the case of using GUI, by dragging file icons and clicking the pointing device, which is tedious and time-consuming. Sh scripts are programs written in the sh programming language, which can be executed by the command interpreter sh. The sh language include all valid Unix/Linux commands. It also supports variables and control statements, such as if, do, for, while, case, etc. In practice, sh scripts are used extensively in Unix/Linux systems programming. In addition to sh, many other script languages, such as Perl and Tcl, are also in wide use.

7.2   File I/O Operations

Figure 7.1 shows the diagram of file I/O operations.

In Fig. 7.1, the upper part above the double line represents kernel space and the lower part represents user space of a process. The diagram shows the sequence of actions when a process read/ write a file stream. Control flows are identified by the labels (1) to (10), which are explained below.

```
---------------------- User Mode Operations ---------------------------
```

(1). A process in User mode executes

```
FILE *fp = fopen("file", "r"); or FILE *fp = fopen("file", "w");
```

which opens a file stream for READ or WRITE.

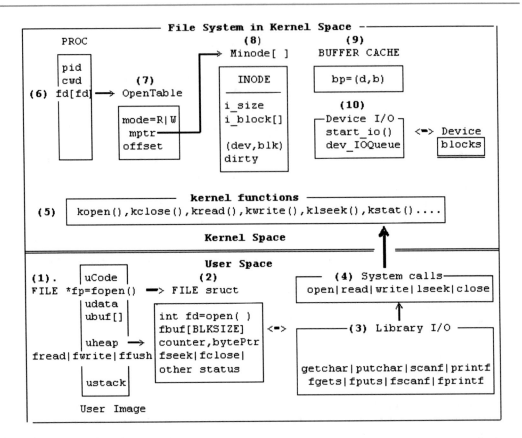

Fig. 7.1 File Operation Diagram

(2). fopen() creates a FILE structure in user (heap) space containing a file descriptor, fd, a fbuf
[BLKSIZE] and some control variables. It issues a fd = open("file", flags=READ or WRITE)
syscall to kopen() in kernel, which constructs an OpenTable to represent an instance of the opened
file. The OpenTable's mptr points to the file's INODE in memory. For non-special files, the
INODE's i_block array points to data blocks on the storage device. On success, fp points to the
FILE structure, in which fd is the file descriptor returned by the open() syscall.

(3). fread(ubuf, size, nitem, fp): READ nitem of size each to ubuf by

```
. copy data from FILE structure's fbuf to ubuf, if enough, return;
. if fbuf has no more data, then execute (4a).
```

(4a). issue read(fd, fbuf, BLKSIZE) system call to read a file block from kernel to fbuf, then copy data
to ubuf until enough or file has no more data.

(4b). fwrite(ubuf, size, nitem, fp): copy data from ubuf to fbuf;

```
. if (fbuf has room): copy data to fbuf, return;
. if (fbuf is full) : issue write(fd, fbuf, BLKSIZE) system call to write a
                      block to kernel, then write to fbuf again.
```

Thus, fread()/fwrite() issue read()/write() syscalls to kernel, but they do so only if necessary and
they transfer data in chunks of block size for better efficiency. Similarly, other Library I/O Functions,

such as fgetc/fputc, fgets/fputs, fscanf/fprintf, etc. also operate on fbuf in the FILE structure, which is in user space.

======================   **Kernel Mode Operations**   ======================

(5).   File system functions in kernel:

```
Assume read(fd, fbuf[ ], BLKSIZE) system call of non-special file.
```

(6).   In a read() system call, fd is an opened file descriptor, which is an index in the running PROC's fd array, which points to an OpenTable representing the opened file.

(7).   The OpenTable contains the files's open mode, a pointer to the file's INODE in memory and the current byte offset into the file for read/write. From the OpenTable's offset,

```
. Compute logical block number, lbk;
. Convert logical block number to physical block number, blk, via INODE.i_block
[ ] array.
```

(8).   Minode contains the in-memory INODE of the file. The INODE.i_block[ ] array contains pointers to physical disk blocks. A file system may use the physical block numbers to read/ write data from/to the disk blocks directly, but these would incur too much physical disk I/O.

(9).   In order to improve disk I/O efficiency, the OS kernel usually uses a set of I/O buffers as a cache memory to reduce the number of physical I/O. Disk I/O buffer management will be covered in Chap. 12.

(9a). For a read(fd, buf, BLKSIZE) system call, determine the needed (dev, blk) number, then consult the I/O buffer cache to

```
.get a buffer = (dev, blk);
.if (buffer's data are invalid){
    start_io on buffer;
    wait for I/O completion;
 }
.copy data from buffer to fbuf;
.release buffer to buffer cache;
```

(9b). For a write(fd, fbuf, BLKSIZE) system call, determine the needed (dev, blk) number, then consult the I/O buffer cache to

```
.get a buffer = (dev, blk);
.write data to the I/O buffer;
.mark buffer as dataValid and DIRTY (for delay-write to disk);
.release the buffer to buffer cache;
```

(10). Device I/O: Physical I/O on the I/O buffers ultimately go through the device driver, which consists of start_io() in the upper-half and disk interrupt handler in the lower-half of the driver.

```
------------------ Upper-half of disk driver --------------------
start_io(bp): //bp=a locked buffer in dev_list, opcode=R|W(ASYNC)
{
    enter bp into dev's I/O_queue;
    if (bp is FIRST in I/O_queue)
        issue I/O command to device;
}


------------------ Lower-half of disk driver --------------------
Device_Interrupt_Handler:
{
    bp = dequeue(first buffer from dev.I/O_queue);
    if (bp was READ){
        mark bp data VALID;
        wakeup/unblock waiting process on bp;
    }
    else       // bp was for delay write
        release bp into buffer cache;

    if (dev.I/O_queue NOT empty)
        issue I/O command for first buffer in dev.I/O_queue;
}
```

7.3   Low Level File Operations

7.3.1   Partitions

A block storage device, e.g. hard disk, USB drive, SD card, etc. can be divided into several logical
units, called partitions. Each partition can be formatted as a specific file system and may be installed
with a different operating system. Most booting programs, e.g. GRUB, LILO, etc. can be configured to
boot up different operating systems from the various partitions. The partition table is at the byte offset
446 (0x1BE) in the very first sector, which is called the **Master Boot Record (MBR)** of the device.
The table has 4 entries, each defined by a 16-byte partition structure, which is

```
stuct partition {
        u8   drive;        // 0x80 - active
        u8   head;         // starting head
        u8   sector;       // starting sector
        u8   cylinder;     // starting cylinder
        u8   sys_type;     // partition type
        u8   end_head;     // end head
        u8   end_sector;   // end sector
        u8   end_cylinder; // end cylinder
        u32  start_sector; // starting sector counting from 0
        u32  nr_sectors;   // number of sectors in partition
};
```

Fig. 7.2 Link List of Extend Partitions

If a partition is EXTEND type (type number =5), it can be divided into more partitions. Assume that partition P4 is EXTEND type and it is divided into extend partitions P5, P6, P7. The extend partitions form a link list in the extend partition area, as shown in Fig. 7.2.

The first sector of each extend partition is a **local MBR**. Each local MBR also has a partition table at the byte offset 0x1BE, which contains only two entries. The first entry defines the start sector and size of the extend partition. The second entry points to the next local MBR. All the local MBR's sector numbers are relative to P4's start sector. As usual, the link list ends with a 0 in the last local MBR. In a partition table, the CHS values are valid only for disks smaller than 8GB. For disks larger than 8GB but fewer than 4G sectors, only the last 2 entries, **start_sector** and **nr_sectors**, are meaningful. In the following, we demonstrate fdisk and partitions by examples. Since working with real disks of a computer is very risky, we shall use a virtual disk image, which is just an ordinary file but looks like a real disk.

(1). Under Linux, e.g. Ubuntu, create a virtual disk image file named mydisk.

```
dd if=/dev/zero of=mydisk bs=1024 count=1440
```

dd is a program which writes 1440 (1KB) blocks of zeros to the target file mydisk. We choose count=1440 because it is the number of 1KB blocks of old floppy disks. If desired, the reader may specify a larger block number.

(2). Run fdisk on the disk image file:

```
fdisk mydisk
```

fdisk is an interactive program. It has a help menu showing all the commands. It collects inputs from the user to create a partition table in memory, which is written to the MBR of the disk image only if the user enters the w command. While in memory, it allows the user to create, examine and modify the partitions. After writing the partition to disk, exit fdisk by the q command. The following figure shows the result of a fdisk session, which partitions the disk image into 3 primary partitions (P1 to P3) and an extend partition P4. The extend partition P4 is further divided into more partitions (P5 to P7), all within the extend partition area. The partition types are all default to Linux when first created. They can be changed to different file system types by the t command. Each file system type has a unique value in HEX, e.g. 0x07 for HPFS/NTFS, 0x83 for Linux, etc. which can be displayed by the t command (Fig. 7.3).

Exercise 7.1: Write a C program to display the partitions, including extend partitions, if any, of a virtual disk image in the same format as does fdisk.

Helps: For readers with less programming experiences, the following may be of help.

```
Device      Boot Start    End Sectors    Size Id Type
mydisk1            1    719      719  359.5K  7 HPFS/NTFS/exFAT
mydisk2          720   1439      720    360K 83 Linux
mydisk3         1440   1799      360    180K 81 Minix / old Linux
mydisk4         1800   2879     1080    540K  5 Extended
mydisk5         1801   2159      359  179.5K  6 FAT16
mydisk6         2161   2519      359  179.5K 83 Linux
mydisk7         2521   2879      359  179.5K 82 Linux swap / Solaris

Command (m for help): q
```

Fig. 7.3. Partition Table

(1). Access partition tables in MBR:

```
#include <stdio.h>
#include <fcntl.h>
char buf[512];

int fd = open("mydisk", O_RDONLY);  // open mydisk for READ
read(fd, buf, 512);                 // read MBR into buf[512]
struct partition *p = (struct partition *)&buf[0x1BE];
printf("p->start_sector = %d\n", p->start_sector); // access p->start_sector
p++;        // advance p to point to the next partition table in MBR, etc.
```

(2). Assume that P4 is extend type (type=5) with start_sector = n.

```
lseek(fd, (long)(n*512), SEEK_SET);    // lseek to P4 begin
read(fd, char buf[ ], 512);            // read local MBR
p = (struct partition *)&buf[0x1BE]);  // access local ptable
```

(3). Extend partitions form a "link list", which ends with a NULL "pointer".

Conversely, we can also write a simple mkfs program to partition a virtual disk by the following steps.

(1). Open a virtual disk for read/write (O_RDWR).
(2). Read MBR into a char buf[512]; In a real disk, the MBR may contain the beginning part of a boot program, which must not be disturbed.
(3). Modify the partition table entries in buf[ ]: In each partition table entry, only the fields type, start_sector and nr_sectors are important. All other fields do not matter, so they can all be left as they are or set to zeros.
(4). Write buf[ ] back to the MBR.

Exercise 7.2: Write a C program myfdisk to divide a virtual disk into 4 primary partitions. After running the program, run Linux fdisk on the virtual disk to verify the results.

7.3.2   Format Partitions

fdisk merely divides a storage device into partitions. Each partition has an intended file system type, but the partition is not yet ready for use. In order to store files, a partition must be made ready for a specific file system first. The operation is traditionally called **format** a disk or disk partition. In Linux, it is called **mkfs**, which stands for Make File System. Linux supports many different kinds of file systems. Each file system expects a specific format on the storage device. In Linux, the command

> `mkfs -t TYPE [-b bsize] device nblocks`

makes a file system of TYPE on a device of nblocks, each block of bsize bytes. If bsize is not specified, the default block size is 1KB. To be more specific, we shall assume the EXT2/3 file system, which used to be the default file systems of Linux. Thus,

> `mkfs -t ext2 vdisk 1440`   OR   `mke2fs vdisk 1440`

formats vdisk to an EXT2 file system with 1440 (1KB) blocks. A formatted disk should be an empty file system containing only the root directory. However, mkfs of Linux always creates a default lost +found directory under the root directory. After mkfs, the device is ready for use. In Linux, a new file system is not yet accessible. It must be mounted to an existing directory in the root file system. The / mnt directory is usually used to mount other file systems. Since virtual file systems are not real devices, they must be mounted as loop devices, as in

> `sudo mount -o loop vdisk /mnt`

which mounts vdisk onto the /mnt directory. The mount command without any parameter shows all the mounted devices of the Linux system. After mounting, the mounting point /mnt becomes equivalent to the root directory of the mounted device. The user may change directory (cd) into /mnt, do file manipulations on the device as usual. After using the mounted device, cd out of /mnt, then enter

> `sudo umount /mnt`   OR   `sudo umount vdisk`

to un-mount the device, detaching it from the root file system. Files saved on the device should be retained in that device.

It is noted that most current Linux systems, e.g. Slackware 14.1 and Ubuntu 15.10, can detect portable devices containing file systems and mount them directly. For example, when a Ubuntu user inserts a USB drive into a USB port, Ubuntu can detect the device, mount it automatically and display the files in a pop up window, allowing the user to access files directly. The user may enter the **mount** command to see where the device (usually /dev/sdb1) is mounted on, as well as the mounted file system type. If the user pulls out the USB drive, Ubuntu will detect it also and **umount** the device automatically. However, pulling out a portable device arbitrarily may corrupt data on the device. This is because the Linux kernel typically uses delayed writes of data to devices. To ensure data consistency, the user should umount the device first before detaching it.

The Linux mount command can mount partitions of real devices or an entire virtual disk, but it can not mount partitions of a virtual disk. If a virtual disk contains partitions, the partitions must be associated with **loop devices** first. The following example demonstrates how to mount partitions of virtual disks.

7.3.3   Mount Partitions

Man 8 losetup: display losetup utility command for system administration

(1). Create a virtual disk image by the dd command:

```
dd if=/dev/zero of=vdisk bs=1024 count=32768    #32K (1KB) blocks
```

(2). Run fdisk on vdisk to create a partition P1

```
fdisk vdisk
```

Enter the n (new) command to create a partition P1 by using default start and last sector numbers. Then, enter the w command to write the partition table to vdisk and exit fdisk. vdisk should contain a partition P1=[start=2048, end=65535]. The partition is 63488 sectors.

(3). Create a loop device on partition 1 of vdisk using sector numbers

```
losetup -o $(expr 2048 \* 512) --sizelimit $(expr 65535 \* 512) /dev/loop1
vdisk
```

losetup needs the start byte (start_sector*512) and end byte (end_sector*512) of the partition. The reader may compute these values by hand and use them in the losetup command. Loop devices for other partitions can be set up in a similar way. After creating a loop device, the reader may use the command

```
losetup -a
```

which displays all loop devices as /dev/loopN.

(4). Format /dev/loop1 an EXT2 file system

```
mke2fs -b 4096 /dev/loop1 7936           # mke2fs with 7936 4KB blocks
```

The size of the partition is 63488 sectors. The number of 4KB blocks is 63488 / 8 = 7936

(5). Mount the loop device

```
mount /dev/loop1 /mnt                     # mount as loop device
```

(6). Access mounted device as part of the file system

```
(cd /mnt; mkdir bin boot dev etc user)   # populate with DIRs
```

(7). When finished with the device, umount it.

```
umount /mnt
```

(8). When finished with a loop device, detach it by the command

```
losetup -d /dev/loop1                     # detach a loop device.
```

Exercise 7.3: Partition a vdisk into 4 partitions. Create 4 loop devices for the partitions. Format the partitions as EXT2 file systems, mount the partitions and copy files into them. Then umount the loop devices and detach the loop devices. If the reader knows how to write sh scripts, all the above steps can be done by a simple sh script.

7.4   Introduction to EXT2 File System

For many years, Linux used EXT2 (Card et al. 1995; EXT2 2001) as the default file system. EXT3 (EXT3 2015) is an extension of EXT2. The main addition in EXT3 is a journal file, which records changes made to the file system in a journal log. The log allows for quicker recovery from errors in case of a file system crash. An EXT3 file system with no error is identical to an EXT2 file system. The newest extension of EXT3 is EXT4 (Cao et al. 2007). The major change in EXT4 is in the allocation of disk blocks. In EXT4, block numbers are 48 bits. Instead of discrete disk blocks, EXT4 allocates contiguous ranges of disk blocks, called extents.

7.4.1   EXT2 File System Data Structures

Under Linux, we can create a virtual disk containing a simple EXT2 file system as follows.

```
(1). dd if=/dev/zero of=mydisk bs=1024 count=1440
(2). mke2fs -b 1024 mydisk 1440
```

The resulting EXT2 file system has 1440 blocks, each of block size 1KB bytes. We choose 1440 blocks because it is the number of blocks of (old) floppy disks. The resulting disk image can be used directly as a virtual (floppy) disk on most virtual machines that emulate the Intel x86 based PCs, e.g. QUEM, VirtualBox and Vmware, etc. The layout of such an EXT2 file system is shown in Figure 7.4.

For ease of discussion, we shall assume this basic file system layout first. Whenever appropriate, we point out the variations, including those in large EXT2/3 FS on hard disks. The following briefly explains the contents of the disk blocks.

Block#0: Boot Block: B0 is the boot block, which is not used by the file system. It is used to contain a booter program for booting up an OS from the disk.

7.4.2   Superblock

Block#1: Superblock: (at byte offset 1024 in hard disk partitions): B1 is the superblock, which contains information about the entire file system. Some of the important fields of the superblock structure are shown below.

```
| 0  |  1  |  2 |  3-7  |  8  |  9  | 10 | . . . 32|33              1439|
---------------------------------------------------------------------
|boot|super| GD |reserved|bmap|imap|inodes blocks |   data blocks  |
---------------------------------------------------------------------
```

Fig. 7.4 Simple EXT2 File System Layout

```
struct ext2_super_block {
    u32   s_inodes_count;            /* Inodes count */
    u32   s_blocks_count;            /* Blocks count */
    u32   s_r_blocks_count;          /* Reserved blocks count */
    u32   s_free_blocks_count;       /* Free blocks count */
    u32   s_free_inodes_count;       /* Free inodes count */
    u32   s_first_data_block;        /* First Data Block */
    u32   s_log_block_size;          /* Block size */
    u32   s_log_cluster_size;        /* Allocation cluster size */
    u32   s_blocks_per_group;        /* # Blocks per group */
    u32   s_clusters_per_group;      /* # Fragments per group */
    u32   s_inodes_per_group;        /* # Inodes per group */
    u32   s_mtime;                   /* Mount time */
    u32   s_wtime;                   /* Write time */
    u16   s_mnt_count;               /* Mount count */
    s16   s_max_mnt_count;           /* Maximal mount count */
    u16   s_magic;                   /* Magic signature */
    // more non-essential fields
    u16   s_inode_size;              /* size of inode structure */
}
```

The meanings of most superblock fields are obvious. Only a few deserve more explanation.

s_first_data_block = 0 for 4KB block size and 1 for 1KB block size. It is used to determine the start block of group descriptors, which is s_first_data_block + 1.

s_log_block_size determines the file block size, which is 1KB*(2**s_log_block_size), e.g.. 0 for 1KB block size, 1 for 2KB block size and 2 for 4KB block size, etc. The most often used block size is 1KB for small file systems and 4KB for large file systems.

s_mnt_count= number of times the file system has been mounted. When the mount count reaches the **max_mount_count**, a fsck session is forced to check the file system for consistency.

s_magic is the magic number which identifies the file system type. For EXT2/3/4 files systems, the magic number is **0xEF53**.

7.4.3   Group Descriptor

Block#2: Group Descriptor Block (s_first_data_block+1 on hard disk): EXT2 divides disk blocks into groups. Each group contains 8192 (32K on HD) blocks. Each group is described by a group descriptor structure.

```
struct ext2_group_desc {
    u32   bg_block_bitmap;          // Bmap block number
    u32   bg_inode_bitmap;          // Imap block number
    u32   bg_inode_table;           // Inodes begin block number
    u16   bg_free_blocks_count;     // THESE are OBVIOUS
    u16   bg_free_inodes_count;
```

```
  u16   bg_used_dirs_count;
  u16   bg_pad;                    // ignore these
  u32   bg_reserved[3];
};
```

Since a FD has only 1440 blocks, B2 contains only 1 group descriptor. The rest are 0's. On hard disks with a large number of groups, group descriptors may span many blocks. The most important fields in a group descriptor are bg_block_bitmap, bg_inode_bitmap and bg_inode_table, which point to the group's blocks bitmap, inodes bitmap and inodes start block, respectively. For the Linux formatted EXT2 file system, blocks 3 to 7 are reserved. So bmap=8, imap=9 and inode_table= 10.

7.4.4   Bitmaps

Block#8: Block Bitmap (Bmap): (bg_block_bitmap): A bitmap is a sequence of bits used to represent some kind of items, e.g. disk blocks or inodes. A bitmap is used to allocate and deallocate items. In a bitmap, a 0 bit means the corresponding item is FREE, and a 1 bit means the corresponding item is IN_USE. A FD has 1440 blocks but block#0 is not used by the file system. So the Bmap has only 1439 valid bits. Invalid bits are treated as IN_USE and set to 1's.

Block#9: Inode Bitmap (Imap): (bg_inode_bitmap): An **inode** is a data structure used to represent a file. An EXT2 file system is created with a finite number of inodes. The status of each inode is represented by a bit in the Imap in B9. In an EXT2 FS, the first 10 inodes are reserved. So the Imap of an empty EXT2 FS starts with ten 1's, followed by 0's. Invalid bits are again set to 1's.

7.4.5   Inodes

Block#10: Inodes (begin) Block: (bg_inode_table): Every file is represented by a unique inode structure of 128 (256 in EXT4) bytes. The essential inode fields are listed below.

```
struct ext2_inode {
  u16   i_mode;          // 16 bits = |tttt|ugs|rwx|rwx|rwx|
  u16   i_uid;           // owner uid
  u32   i_size;          // file size in bytes
  u32   i_atime;         // time fields in seconds
  u32   i_ctime;         // since 00:00:00,1-1-1970
  u32   i_mtime;
  u32   i_dtime;
  u16   i_gid;           // group ID
  u16   i_links_count;   // hard-link count
  u32   i_blocks;        // number of 512-byte sectors
  u32   i_flags;         // IGNORE
  u32   i_reserved1;     // IGNORE
  u32   i_block[15];     // See details below
  u32   i_pad[7];        // for inode size = 128 bytes
}
```

In the inode structure, i_mode is a u16 or 2-byte unsigned integer.

```
                 |  4  | 3 |    9    |
    i_mode =  |tttt|ugs|rwxrwxrwx|
```

In the i_mode field, the leading 4 bits specify the file type. For example, tttt=1000 for REG file, 0100 for DIR, etc. The next 3 bits ugs indicate the file's special usage. The last 9 bits are the rwx permission bits for file protection.

The i_size field is the file size in bytes. The various time fields are number of seconds elapsed since 0 hour, 0 minute, 0 second of January 1, 1970. So each time filed is a very large unsigned integer. They can be converted to calendar form by the library function

```
              char *ctime(&time_field)
```

which takes a pointer to a time field and returns a string in calendar form. For example,

```
              printf("%s", ctime(&inode.i_atime);      // note: pass & of time field
```

prints i_atime in calendar form.

The i_block[15] array contains pointers to disk blocks of a file, which are

Direct blocks: i_block[0] to i_block[11], which point to direct disk blocks.
Indirect blocks: i_block[12] points to a disk block, which contains 256 (for 1KB BLKSIZE) block numbers, each points to a disk block.
Double Indirect blocks: i_block[13] points to a block, which points to 256 blocks, each of which points to 256 disk blocks.
Triple Indirect blocks: i_block[14] is the triple-indirect block. We may ignore this for "small" EXT2 file systems.

The inode size (128 or 256) is designed to divides block size (1KB or 4KB) evenly, so that every inode block contains an integral number of inodes. In the simple EXT2 file system, the number of inodes is (a Linux default) 184. The number of inodes blocks is equal to 184/8=23. So the inodes blocks include B10 to B32. Each inode has a unique **inode number**, which is the inode's position in the inode blocks plus 1. Note that inode positions count from 0, but inode numbers count from 1. A 0 inode number means no inode. The root directory's inode number is 2. Similarly, disk block numbers also count from 1 since block 0 is never used by a file system. A zero block number means no disk block.

Data Blocks: Immediately after the inodes blocks are data blocks for file storage. Assuming 184 inodes, the first real data block is B33, which is i_block[0] of the root directory /.

7.4.6   Directory Entries

EXT2 Directory Entries: A directory contains dir_entry structures, which is

```
struct ext2_dir_entry_2{
    u32 inode;                    // inode number; count from 1, NOT 0
    u16 rec_len;                  // this entry's length in bytes
```

```
    u8   name_len;            // name length in bytes
    u8   file_type;           // not used
    char name[EXT2_NAME_LEN]; // name: 1-255 chars, no ending NULL
  };
```

The dir_entry is an open-ended structure. The name field contains 1 to 255 chars without a terminating NULL byte. So the dir_entry's rec_len also varies.

7.5   Programming Examples

In this section, we shall show how to access and display the contents of EXT2 file systems by example programs. In order to compile and run these programs, the system must have the **ext2fs.h** header file installed, which defines the data structures of EXT2/3/4 file systems. Ubuntu Linux user may get and install the ext2fs development package by

sudo apt-get install ext2fs-dev

7.5.1   Display Superblock

The following C program in Example 7.1 displays the superblock of an EXT2 file system. The basic technique is to read the superblock (block #1 or 1KB at offset 1024) into a char buf[1024]. Let a struct ext2_super_block *p point to buf[ ]. Then use p->field to access the various fields of the superblock structure. The technique is similar to that of accessing partition tables in the MBR.

Example 7.1: superblock.c program: display superblock information of an EXT2 file system.

```
/*********** superblock.c program ************/
#include <stdio.h>
#include <stdlib.h>
#include <fcntl.h>
#include <ext2fs/ext2_fs.h>
// typedef u8, u16, u32 SUPER for convenience
typedef unsigned char   u8;
typedef unsigned short u16;
typedef unsigned int    u32;
typedef struct ext2_super_block SUPER;

SUPER *sp;
char buf[1024];
int fd, blksize, inodesize;

int print(char *s, u32 x)
{
  printf("%-30s = %8d\n", s, x);
}
```

```
int super(char *device)
{
  fd = open(device, O_RDONLY);
  if (fd < 0){
    printf("open %sfailed\n", device); exit(1);
  }
  lseek(fd, (long)1024*1, 0);   // block 1 or offset 1024
  read(fd, buf, 1024);
  sp = (SUPER *)buf;            // as a super block structure
  // check for EXT2 FS magic number:
  printf("%-30s = %8x ", "s_magic", sp->s_magic);
  if (sp->s_magic != 0xEF53){
    printf("NOT an EXT2 FS\n"); exit(2);
  }
  printf("EXT2 FS OK\n");
  print("s_inodes_count",       sp->s_inodes_count);
  print("s_blocks_count",       sp->s_blocks_count);
  print("s__r_blocks_count",    sp->s_r_blocks_count);
  print("s_free_inodes_count",  sp->s_free_inodes_count);
  print("s_free_blocks_count",  sp->s_free_blocks_count);
  print("s_first_data_blcok",   sp->s_first_data_block);
  print("s_log_block_size",     sp->s_log_block_size);
  print("s_blocks_per_group",   sp->s_blocks_per_group);
  print("s_inodes_per_group",   sp->s_inodes_per_group);
  print("s_mnt_count",          sp->s_mnt_count);
  print("s_max_mnt_count",      sp->s_max_mnt_count);
  printf("%-30s = %8x\n", "s_magic", sp->s_magic);
  printf("s_mtime = %s", ctime(&sp->s_mtime));
  printf("s_wtime = %s", ctime(&sp->s_wtime));
  blksize = 1024 * (1 << sp->s_log_block_size);
  printf("block size = %d\n", blksize);
  printf("inode size = %d\n",  sp->s_inode_size);
}

char *device = "mydisk";        // default device name
int main(int argc, char *argv[])
{
  if (argc>1)
    device = argv[1];
  super(device);
}
```

Figure 7.5 shows the outputs of running the super.c example program.

Exercise 7.4: Write a C program to display the group descriptor of an EXT2 file system on a device.

```
s_magic                    =    ef53   EXT2 FS OK
s_inodes_count             =     184
s_blocks_count             =    1440
s__r_blocks_count          =      72
s_free_inodes_count        =     173
s_free_blocks_count        =    1393
s_first_data_blcok         =       1
s_log_block_size           =       0
s_blocks_per_group         =    8192
s_inodes_per_group         =     184
s_mnt_count                =       1
s_max_mnt_count            =      -1
s_magic                    =    ef53
s_mtime = Sun Oct  8 14:22:03 2017
s_wtime = Sun Oct  8 14:22:07 2017
block size = 1024
inode size = 128         _
```

Fig. 7.5 Superblock of Ext2 File System

7.5.2   Display Bitmaps

The C program in Example 7.2 display the inodes bitmap (imap) in HEX form.

Example 7.2: imap.c program: display inodes bitmap of an EXT2 file system.

```
/************** imap.c program *************/
#include <stdio.h>
#include <stdlib.h>
#include <fcntl.h>
#include <ext2fs/ext2_fs.h>
typedef struct ext2_super_block SUPER;
typedef struct ext2_group_desc  GD;

#define BLKSIZE 1024
SUPER *sp;
GD    *gp;
char buf[BLKSIZE];
int fd;

// get_block() reads a disk block into a buf[ ]
int get_block(int fd, int blk, char *buf)
{
  lseek(fd, (long)blk*BLKSIZE, 0);
  read(fd, buf, BLKSIZE);
}

int imap(char *device)
{
  int i, ninodes, blksize, imapblk;
  fd = open(dev, O_RDONLY);
  if (fd < 0){printf("open %s failed\n", device); exit(1);}
```

```
get_block(fd, 1, buf);           // get superblock
sp = (SUPER *)buf;
ninodes = sp->s_inodes_count;    // get inodes_count
printf("ninodes = %d\n", ninodes);
get_block(fd, 2, buf);           // get group descriptor
gp = (GD *)buf;
imapblk = gp->bg_inode_bitmap;   // get imap block number
printf("imapblk = %d\n", imapblk);
get_block(fd, imapblk, buf);     // get imap block into buf[ ]
for (i=0; i<=nidoes/8; i++){     // print each byte in HEX
    printf("%02x ", (unsigned char)buf[i]);
}
printf("\n");
}

char * dev="mydisk";             // default device
int main(int argc, char *argv[ ] )
{
  if (argc>1) dev = argv[1];
  imap(dev);
}
```

The program prints each byte of the inodes bitmap as 2 HEX digits. The outputs look like the following.

```
|--------------- niodes = 184 bits (23 bytes)--------------------|
ff 07 00 00 00 00 00 00 00 00 00 00 00 00 00 00 00 00 00 00 00 00 ff
```

In the imap, bits are stored linearly from low to high address. The first 16 bits (from low to high) are b'11111111 11100000', but they are printed as ff 07 in HEX, which is not very informative since the bits are printed in reverse order, i.e. from high to low address.

Exercise 7.5: Modify the imap.c program to print the inodes bitmap in char map form, i.e. for each bit, print a '0' if the bit is 0, print a '1' if the bit is 1.

Hints:
(1). Examine the bit patterns of $(1 << j)$ for j=0 to 7.
(2). If char c is a byte, the C statement

```
            if ( c & (1<<j) )     (j=0 to 7)
```

tests whether bit j of c is 1 or 0.

The outputs of the modified program should look like Fig. 7.6, in which each char represents a bit in the imap.

```
ninodes = 184  imapblk = 9
11111111 11100000 00000000 00000000 00000000 00000000 00000000 00000000
00000000 00000000 00000000 00000000 00000000 00000000 00000000 00000000
00000000 00000000 00000000 00000000 00000000 00000000 00000000 11111111
```

Fig. 7.6. Inodes Bitmap of an EXT2 File System

Exercise 7.6: Write a C program to display the blocks bitmap of an Ext2 file system, also in char map form.

7.5.3 Display root Inode

In an EXT2 file system, the number 2 (count from 1) inode is the inode of the root directory /. If we read the root inode into memory, we should be able to display its various fields such as mode, uid, gid, file size, creation time, hard link count and data block numbers, etc. The program in Example 7.3 displays the INODE information of the root directory of an EXT2 file system.

Example 7.3: inode.c program: display root inode information of an EXT2 file system

```
/*********** inode.c file **********/
#include <stdio.h>
#include <stdlib.h>
#include <fcntl.h>
#include <ext2fs/ext2_fs.h>

#define BLKSIZE 1024
typedef struct ext2_group_desc  GD;
typedef struct ext2_super_block SUPER;
typedef struct ext2_inode       INODE;
typedef struct ext2_dir_entry_2 DIR;
SUPER *sp;
GD    *gp;
INODE *ip;
DIR   *dp;
char buf[BLKSIZE];
int fd, firstdata, inodesize, blksize, iblock;
char *dev = "mydisk"; // default to mydisk

int get_block(int fd, int blk, char *buf)
{
  lseek(fd, blk*BLKSIZE, SEEK_SET);
  return read(fd, buf, BLKSIZE);
}
int inode(char *dev)
{
  int i;
  fd = open(dev, O_RDONLY) < 0);
  if (fd < 0){
    printf("open failed\n"); exit(1);
  }
  get_block(fd, 1, buf);                 // get superblock
  sp = (SUPER *)buf;
  firstdata = sp->s_first_data_block;
  inodesize = sp->s_inode_size;
  blksize = 1024*(1<<sp->s_log_block_size);
```

```
    printf("first_data_block=%d block_size=%d inodesize=%d\n",
            firstdata, blksize, inodesize);
    get_block(fd, (firstdata+1), buf);   // get group descriptor
    gp = (GD *)buf;
    printf("bmap_block=%d imap_block=%d inodes_table=%d ",
            gp->bg_block_bitmap,
            gp->bg_inode_bitmap,
            gp->bg_inode_table,
            gp->bg_free_blocks_count);
    printf("free_blocks=%d free_inodes=%d\n",
            gp->bg_free_inodes_count,
            gp->bg_used_dirs_count);
    iblock = gp->bg_inode_table;
    printf("root inode information:\n", iblock);
    printf("---------------------\n");
    get_block(fd, iblock, buf);
    ip = (INODE *)buf + 1;                    // ip point at #2 INODE
    printf("mode=%4x ", ip->i_mode);
    printf("uid=%d  gid=%d\n", ip->i_uid, ip->i_gid);
    printf("size=%d\n", ip->i_size);
    printf("ctime=%s", ctime(&ip->i_ctime));
    printf("links=%d\n", ip->i_links_count);
    for (i=0; i<15; i++){                 // print disk block numbers
      if (ip->i_block[i])                 // print non-zero blocks only
          printf("i_block[%d]=%d\n", i, ip->i_block[i]);
    }
}
int main(int argc, char *argv[ ])
{
    if (argc>1) dev = argv[1];
    inode(dev);
}
```

Figure 7.7 shows the root inode of an EXT2 file system.

In Fig. 7.7, the i_mode =0x41ed or b'0100 0001 1110 1101' in binary. The first 4 bits 0100 is the file type (DIRectory). The next 3 bits 000=ugs are all 0's, meaning the file has no special usage, e.g. it is not a setuid program. The last 9 bits can be divided into 3 groups 111,101,101, which are the rwx permission bits of the file's owner, same group and others. For regular files, x bit = 1 means the file is executable. For directories, x bit = 1 means access to (i.e. cd into) the directory is allowed; a 0 x bit means no access to the directory.

```
        first_data_block=1 block_size=1024  inodesize=128
        bmap_block=8 imap_block=9 inodes_table=10
        free_blocks=1393 free_inodes=173 used_dirs=2
        root inode information:
        -------------------------
        mode=41ed uid=0  gid=0
        size=1024
        links=3
        ctime=Mon Oct  9 16:11:44 2017
        i_block[0]=33
```

Fig. 7.7 root Inode of EXT2 file system

7.5.4   Display Directory Entries

Each data block of a directory INODE contains dir_entries, which are

```
struct ext2_dir_entry_2 {
    u32 inode;                  // inode number; count from 1, NOT 0
    u16 rec_len;                // this entry's length in bytes
    u8  name_len;               // name length in bytes
    u8  file_type;              // not used
    char name[EXT2_NAME_LEN];   // name: 1-255 chars, no ending NULL
};
```

Thus, the contents of each data block of a directory has the form

```
[inode rec_len name_len NAME] [inode rec_len name_len NAME] ......
```

where NAME is a sequence of name_len chars (without a terminating NULL). The following
algorithm shows how to step through the dir_entries in a directory data block.

```
/**** Algorithm to step through entries in a DIR data block ****/
struct ext2_dir_entry_2 *dp;            // dir_entry pointer
char *cp;                               // char pointer
int blk = a data block (number) of a DIR (e.g. i_block[0]);
char buf[BLKSIZE], temp[256];
get_block(fd, blk, buf);                // get data block into buf[ ]

dp = (struct ext2_dir_entry_2 *)buf;    // as dir_entry
cp = buf;
while(cp < buf + BLKSIZE){
  strncpy(temp, dp->name, dp->name_len); // make name a string
  temp[dp->name_len] = 0;                // in temp[ ]
  printf("%d %d %d %s\n", dp->inode, dp->rec_len, dp->name_len, temp);
  cp += dp->rec_len;                     // advance cp by rec_len
  dp = (struct ext2_dir_entry_2 *)cp;    // pull dp to next entry
}
```

Exercise 7.7: Write a C program to print the dir_entries of a directory. For simplicity, we may assume
a directory INODE has at most 12 direct blocks, i_block[0] to i_block[11]. This assumption is
reasonable. With 1KB block size and an average file name length of 16 chars, a single disk block
can contain up to 1024/(8+16)=42 dir_entries. With 12 disk blocks, a directory can contain more than
500 entries. We may safely assume that no user would put that many files in any directory. So we only
need to go through at most 12 direct blocks. For an empty EXT2 file system, the program's output
should look like Fig. 7.8.

Exercise 7.8: Mount mydisk under Linux. Create new directories and copy files to it. Umount it. Then
run the dir.c program on mydisk again to see the outputs, which should look like Fig. 7.9. The reader
should have noticed that the name_len of each entry is the exact number of chars in the name field, and

```
check ext2 FS : OK
GD info: 8 9 10 1393 173 2
inodes begin block=10
****** root inode info ********
mode=41ed  uid=0  gid=0
size=1024
ctime=Sun Oct  8 14:04:52 2017
links=3
i_block[0]=33
*******************************
inode# rec_len name_len name
   2      12        1    .
   2      12        2    ..
  11    1000       10  _ lost+found
```

Fig. 7.8 Entries of a Directory

```
****** root inode info ********
mode=41ed  uid=0  gid=0
size=1024
ctime=Sun Oct  8 17:19:15 2017
links=7
i_block[0]=33
*******************************
inode# rec_len name_len name
   2      12        1    .
   2      12        2    ..
  11      20       10    lost+found
  12      12        1    a
  13      16        8    shortDir
  14      20       12    longNamedDir
  15      28       17    aVeryLongNamedDir
  16      16        7    super.c
  17      16        6    bmap.c
  18      16        6    imap.c
  19     856        5    dir.c
```

Fig. 7.9 List Entries of a Directory

every rec_len is a multiple of 4 (for memory alignment), which is (8+name_len) raised to the next multiple of 4, except the last entry, whose rec_len covers the remaining block length.

Exercise 7.9: Assume INODE is the struct ext2_inode type. Given an inode number, ino, write C statements to return a pointer to its INODE structure.

Hints:
(1). int fd = Open vidsk for READ;
(2). int offset = inodes_start_block * BLKSIZE + (ino-1)*inode_szie;
(3). lseek fd to offset;
(4). read inode_size bytes into an INODE inode;
(5). return (INODE *ip = &inode);

Exercise 7.10: Given an INODE pointer to a DIRectory inode. Write a

```
int  search(INODE *dir, char *name)
```

function which searches for a name string in the directory; return its inode number if found, return 0 if not.

7.6 Programming Project: Convert File Pathname to Inode

In every file system, almost every operation starts with a filename, e.g.

```
cat filename
open filename for R|W
copy file1 to file2
etc.
```

The fundamental problem of every file system is to convert a filename into the file's representation data structure in the file system. In the case of EXT2/3/4 file systems, it amounts to converting a pathname to the file's INODE. The programming project is to integrate the knowledge and programming techniques in the above examples and exercises into a program which finds a file in an EXT2 file system and prints its information. Assume vdisk is a virtual disk containing many levels of directories and files. Given the pathname of a file, e.g. /a/b/c/d, write a C program to find the file and prints its information, such as the file type, owner id, size, date of creation and data block numbers, including indirect and double indirect blocks.

HINTS and helps:
(1). Tokenize pathname into component strings. Denote them as char *name[0],
   *name[1], .. ,*name[n-1], where n is the number of component strings.
(2). Start from INODE *ip -> root inode (ino=2)
(3). for (int i=0; i<n; i++){

```
    int ino = search(ip, name[i]);
    if (!ino) exit(1);              // can't find name[i]
    ip ->inode of name[i];         // ip point at INODE of name[i]
    if (*ip is not a DIR) exit(2);  // name[i] is not a DIR
}
```

(4). If reach here: ip must point at file's inode. Use ip-> to access the fields of inode
(5). To print indirect block numbers:

```
    read i_block[12] into a char buf[BLKSIZE];
    u32 *up = (u32 *)buf;
    *up is an indirect block number; up++ points to the next number, etc.
```

Similar technique can be used to print double indirect block numbers.

7.7   Summary

This chapter covers file systems. It explains the various levels of file operations in operating systems. These include preparing storage devices for file storage, file system support functions in kernel, system calls, library I/O functions on file streams, user commands and sh scripts for file operations. It presents a systematic overview of file operations, from read/write file streams in user space to system calls to kernel space down to the device I/O driver level. It describes low level file operations, which include disk partitions, example programs to display partition tables, format partitions for file systems and mount disk partitions. It presents an introduction to the EXT2 file system of Linux, which include the EXT2 file system data structures, program code to display superblock, group descriptor, blocks and inodes bitmaps and directory contents. The programming project is to integrate the knowledge and programming techniques presented in the chapter into a program which finds a file in an EXT2 file system and prints its information. The purpose of the project is to let the reader understand how to convert a file's pathname into its inode, which is the fundamental problem of any file system.

Problems
1. Modify the program of Exercise 7.2 to support extend partitions.
2. Large EXT2/3 file system comprise more than 32K blocks of 4KB block sizes. Extend the Project program to large EXT2/3 file systems.

References

Card, R., Theodore Ts'o, T., Stephen Tweedie, S., "Design and Implementation of the Second Extended Filesystem", web.mit.edu/tytso/www/linux/ext2intro.html, 1995
Cao, M., Bhattacharya, S, Tso, T., "Ext4: The Next Generation of Ext2/3 File system", IBM Linux Technology Center, 2007.
EXT2: www.nongnu.org/ext2-doc/ext2.html, 2001
EXT3: jamesthornton.com/hotlist/linux-filesystems/ext3-journal, 2015

System Calls for File Operations

8

Abstract

This chapter covers system calls for file operations. It explains the role of system calls and the online manual pages of Linux. It shows how to use system calls for file operations. It lists and explains the most commonly used system calls for file operations. It explains hard link and symbolic link files. It explains the stat system call in detail. Based on the stat information, it develops a ls-like program to display directory contents and file information. Next, it explains the open-close-lseek system calls and file descriptors. Then it shows how to use read-write system calls to read-write file contents. Based on these, it shows how to use system calls to display and copy files. It shows how to develop a selective file copying program which behaves like a simplified dd utility program of Linux. The programming project is to use Linux system calls to implement a C program, which recursively copies a directory to a destination. The purpose of the project is for the reader to practice the design of hierarchical program structures and use stat(), open(), read(), write() system calls for file operations.

8.1 Systems Calls

In an operating system, a process runs in two different modes; kernel mode and user mode, denoted by Kmode and Umode for short. While in Umode, a process has very limited privileges. It can not do anything that requires special privileges. Privileged operations must be done in Kmode. System call, or syscall for short, is a mechanism which allows a process to enter Kmode to perform operations not allowed in Umode. Operations such as fork child process, exec to change execution image, even termination must all be done in Kernel. In this chapter, we shall discuss syscalls for file operations in Unix/Linux.

8.2 System Call Man Pages

In Unix and most versions of Linux, the online manual (man) pages are maintained in the /usr/man/ directory (Goldt et al. 1995; Kerrisk 2010, 2017). In Ubuntu Linux, they are in the /usr/share/man

© Springer International Publishing AG, part of Springer Nature 2018
K. C. Wang, *Systems Programming in Unix/Linux*, https://doi.org/10.1007/978-3-319-92429-8_8

directory. All the syscall man pages are listed in the man2 subdirectory. The sh command **man 2 NAME** displays the man pages of the syscall NAME. For example,

```
man 2 stat  : display man pages of stat(), fstat() and lstat() syscalls
man 2 open: display man pages of open() syscall
man 2 read: display man pages of read() syscall, etc.
```

Many syscalls require specific included header files, which are listed in the **SYNOPSIS** part of the man pages. Without proper header files, the C compiler may generate many warnings due to mismatches in syscall function name types. Some syscalls may also require specific data structures as parameters, which must be present as described in the man pages.

8.3   System Calls for File Operations

Syscalls must be issued from a program. Their usage is just like ordinary function calls. Each syscall is a library function, which assembles the syscall parameters and ultimately issues a syscall to the OS kernel.

```
int syscall(int a, int b, int c, int d);
```

where the first parameter a is the syscall number, and b, c, d are parameters to the corresponding kernel function. In Intel x86 based Linux, syscalls are implemented by the INT 0x80 assembly instruction, which causes the CPU to switch from User mode to Kernel mode. The kernel's syscall handler routes the call to a corresponding kernel function based on the syscall number. When the process finishes executing the kernel function, it returns to User mode with the desired results. A return value $>=0$ means SUCCESS, -1 means FAILED. In case of failure, an errno variable (in errno.h) records the error number, which can be mapped to a string describing the error reason. The following example shows how to use some of simple syscalls.

Example C8.1. mkdir, chdir, getcwd, syscalls.

```
/*********** C8.1.c file ***********/
#include <stdio.h>
#include <errno.h>
int main()
{
    char buf[256], *s;
    int r;
    r = mkdir("newdir", 0766); // mkdir syscall
    if (r < 0)
       printf("errno=%d : %s\n", errno, strerror(errno));
    r = chdir("newdir");       // cd into newdir
    s = getcwd(buf, 256);      // get CWD string into buf[ ]
    printf("CWD = %s\n", s);
}
```

The program issues a **mkdir()** syscall to make a new directory. The mkdir() syscall requires a pathname and a permission (0766 in octal). If newdir does not exist, the syscall would succeed with a 0 return value. If we run the program more than once, it should fail on the second or any successive runs with a return value -1 since the directory already exists. In that case, the program would print the message

```
errno=17 : File exists
```

In addition to mkdir(), the program also illustrates the usage of chdir() and getcwd() syscalls.

EXERCISE: Modify the C8.1 program to make many directories in one run, e.g.

```
mymkdir dir1 dir2 dir3, ... dirn
```

Hint: write main() as main(int argc, char *argv[ ])

Simple System Calls: The following lists some of the simple syscalls for file operations. The reader is encouraged to write C programs to use and test them.

access : check user permissions for a file.

```
int access(char *pathname, int mode);
```

chdir : change directory

```
int chdir(const char *path);
```

chmod : change permissions of a file

```
int chmod(char *path, mode_t mode);
```

chown : change owner of file

```
int chown(char *name, int uid, int gid);
```

chroot : change (logical) root directory to pathname

```
int chroot(char *pathname);
```

getcwd : get absolute pathname of CWD

```
char *getcwd(char *buf,  int size);
```

mkdir : create a directory

```
int mkdir(char *pathname, mode_t mode);
```

rmdir : remove a directory (must be empty)

```
int rmdir(char *pathname);
```

link   : hard link new filename to old filename

```
int link(char *oldpath, char *newpath);
```

unlink : decrement file's link count; delete file if link count reaches 0

```
int unlink(char *pathname);
```

symlink : create a symbolic link for a file

```
int symlink(char *oldpath, char *newpath);
```

rename : change the name of a file

```
int rename(char *oldpath, char *newpath);
```

utime   : change access and modification times of file

```
int utime(char *pathname,  struct utimebuf *time)
```

The following syscalls require superuser privilege.

mount   : attach a file system to a mounting point directory

```
int  mount(char *specialfile, char *mountDir);
```

umount : detach a mounted file system

```
int umount(char *dir);
```

mknod : make special files

```
int mknod(char *path, int mode, int device);
```

8.4   Commonly used system Calls

In this section, we shall discuss some of the most commonly used syscalls for file operations. These include

stat :   get file status information

```
int stat(char *filename, struct stat *buf)
int fstat(int filedes, struct stat *buf)
int lstat(char *filename, struct stat *buf)
```

open : open a file for READ, WRITE, APPEND

```
int open(char *file, int flags, int mode)
```

close : close an opened file descriptor

```
int close(int fd)
```

read : read from an opened file descriptor

```
int read(int fd, char buf[ ], int count)
```

write : write to an opened file descriptor

```
int write(int fd, char buf[ ], int count)
```

lseek : reposition R|W offset of a file descriptor

```
int lseek(int fd, int offset, int whence)
```

dup : duplicate file descriptor into the lowest available descriptor number

```
int dup(int oldfd);
```

dup2 : duplicate oldfd into newfd; close newfd first if it was open

```
int  dup2(int oldfd, int newfd)
```

link : hard link newfile to oldfile

```
int link(char *oldPath, char *newPath)
```

unlink : unlink a file; delete file if file's link count reaches 0

```
int unlink(char *pathname);
```

symlink : create a symbolic link

```
int symlink(char *target, char *newpath)
```

readlink: read contents of a symbolic link file

```
int readlink(char *path, char *buf, int bufsize)
```

umask : set file creation mask; file permissions will be (mask & ~umask)

```
int umask(int umask);
```

8.5   Link Files

In Unix/Linux, every file has a pathname. However, Unix/Linux allows different pathnames to represent the same file. These are called LINK files. There are two kinds of links, HARD link and SOFT or symbolic link.

8.5.1   Hard Link Files

HARD Links: The command

```
ln  oldpath  newpath
```

creates a HARD link from newpath to oldpath. The corresponding syscall is

```
link(char *oldpath, char *newpath)
```

Hard linked files share the same file representation data structure (inode) in the file system. The file's links count records the number of hard links to the same inode. Hard links can only be applied to non-directory files. Otherwise, it may create loops in the file system name space, which is not allowed. Conversely, the syscall

```
unlink(char *pathname)
```

decrements the links count of a file. The file is truly removed if the links count becomes 0. This is what the rm (file) command does. If a file contains very important information, it would be a good idea to create many hard links to the file to prevent it from being deleted accidentally.

8.5.2   Symbolic Link Files

SOFT Links: The command

```
ln -s  oldpath newpath     # ln command with the -s flag
```

creates a SOFT or **Symbolic link** from newpath to oldpath. The corresponding syscall is

```
symlink(char *oldpath, char *newpath)
```

The newpath is a regular file of the LNK type containing the oldpath string. It acts as a detour sign, directing access to the linked target file. Unlike hard links, soft links can be applied to any file, including directories. Soft links are useful in the following situations.

(1). To access to a very long and often used pathname by a shorter name, e.g.

```
x -> aVeryLongPathnameFile
```

(2). Link standard dynamic library names to actual versions of dynamic libraries, e.g.

```
libc.so.6 -> libc.2.7.so
```

When changing the actual dynamic library to a different version, the library installing program only needs to change the (soft) link to point to the newly installed library.

One drawback of soft link is that the target file may no longer exist. If so, the detour sign might direct the poor driver to fall off a cliff. In Linux, such dangers are displayed in the appropriate color of dark RED by the ls command, alerting the user that the link is broken. Also, if foo -> /a/b/c is a soft link, the open("foo", 0) syscall will open the linked file /a/b/c, not the link file itself. So the open()/read() syscalls can not read soft link files. Instead, the **readlink** syscall must be used to read the contents of soft link files.

8.6   The stat Systen Call

The syscalls, **stat/lstat/fstat**, return the information of a file. The command **man 2 stat** displays the man pages of the stat system call, which are shown below for discussions.

8.6.1   Stat File Status

8.6.1.1   STAT(2) Linux Programmer's Manual STAT(2)

NAME

```
stat, fstat, lstat - get file status
```

SYNOPSIS

```
#include <sys/types.h>
#include <sys/stat.h>
#include <unistd.h>
int stat(const char *file_name, struct stat *buf);
int fstat(int filedes, struct stat *buf);
int lstat(const char *file_name, struct stat *buf);
```

DESCRIPTION

These functions return information about the specified file. You do not need any access rights to the file to get this information but you need search rights to all directories named in the path leading to the file.

stat stats the file pointed to by filename and fills in buf with stat information.
lstat is identical to stat, except in the case of a symbolic link, where the link itself is stated, not the file that it refers to. So the difference between stat and lstat is: stat follows link but lstat does not.
fstat is identical to stat, only the open file pointed to by filedes (as returned by open(2)) is stated in place of filename.

8.6.2   The stat Structure

All the stat syscalls return information in a stat structure, which contains the following fields:

```
struct stat{
    dev_t      st_dev;      /* device */
    ino_t      st_ino;      /* inode */
    mode_t     st_mode;     /* protection */
    nlink_t    st_nlink;    /* number of hard links */
    uid_t      st_uid;      /* user ID of owner */
    gid_t      st_gid;      /* group ID of owner */
    dev_t      st_rdev;     /* device type (if inode device) */
    off_t      st_size;     /* total size, in bytes */
    u32        st_blksize;  /* blocksize for filesystem I/O */
    u32        st_blocks;   /* number of blocks allocated */
    time_t     st_atime;    /* time of last access */
    time_t     st_mtime;    /* time of last modification */
    time_t     st_ctime;    /* time of last change */
};
```

The st_size field is the size of the file in bytes. The size of a symlink is the length of the pathname it contains, without a trailing NULL.

The value st_blocks gives the size of the file in 512-byte blocks. (This may be smaller than st_size/ 512, e.g. when the file has holes.) The value st_blksize gives the "preferred" blocksize for efficient file system I/O. (Writing to a file in smaller chunks may cause an inefficient read-modify-rewrite.)

Not all of the Linux file systems implement all of the time fields. Some file system types allow mounting in such a way that file accesses do not cause an update of the st_atime field. (See 'noatime' in mount(8).)

The field st_atime is changed by file accesses, e.g. by exec(2), mknod(2), pipe(2), utime(2) and read (2) (of more than zero bytes). Other routines, like mmap(2), may or may not update st_atime.

The field st_mtime is changed by file modifications, e.g. by mknod(2), truncate(2), utime(2) and write(2) (of more than zero bytes). Moreover, st_mtime of a directory is changed by the creation or deletion of files in that directory. The st_mtime field is not changed for changes in owner, group, hard link count, or mode.

The field st_ctime is changed by writing or by setting inode information (i.e., owner, group, link count, mode, etc.).

The following POSIX macros are defined to check the file type:

```
S_ISREG(m)   is it a regular file?
S_ISDIR(m)   directory?
S_ISCHR(m)   character device?
S_ISBLK(m)   block device?
S_ISFIFO(m)  fifo?
S_ISLNK(m)   symbolic link? (Not in POSIX.1-1996.)
S_ISSOCK(m)  socket? (Not in POSIX.1-1996.)
```

The following flags are defined for the st_mode field:

```
S_IFMT      0170000   bitmask for the file type bitfields
S_IFSOCK    0140000   socket
S_IFLNK     0120000   symbolic link
S_IFREG     0100000   regular file
S_IFBLK     0060000   block device
S_IFDIR     0040000   directory
S_IFCHR     0020000   character device
S_IFIFO     0010000   fifo

S_ISUID     0004000   set UID bit
S_ISGID     0002000   set GID bit (see below)
S_ISVTX     0001000   sticky bit (see below)

S_IRWXU     00700     mask for file owner permissions
S_IRUSR     00400     owner has read permission
S_IWUSR     00200     owner has write permission
S_IXUSR     00100     owner has execute permission
S_IRWXG     00070     mask for group permissions
S_IRGRP     00040     group has read permission
S_IWGRP     00020     group has write permission
S_IXGRP     00010     group has execute permission
S_IRWXO     00007     mask for permissions for others (not in group)
S_IROTH     00004     others have read permission
S_IWOTH     00002     others have write permission
S_IXOTH     00001     others have execute permission
```

RETURN VALUE: On success, zero is returned. On error, -1 is returned, and errno is set appropriately.

SEE ALSO chmod(2), chown(2), readlink(2), utime(2)

8.6.3 Stat and File Inode

Stat and file inode: First, we clarify how stat works. Every file has a unique **inode** data structure, which contains all the information of the file. The following shows the inode structure of EXT2 file systems in Linux.

```
struct ext2_inode{
    u16  i_mode;
    u16  i_uid;
    u32  i_size;
    u32  i_atime;
    u32  i_ctime;
    u32  i_mtime;
    u32  i_dtime;
    u16  i_gid;
    u16  i_links_count;
```

```
    u32   i_blocks;
    u32   i_flags;
    u32   i_reserved1;
    u32   i_block[15];
    u32   pad[7];
};  // inode=128 bytes in ext2/3 FS; 256 bytes in ext4
```

Each inode has a unique inode number (ino) on a storage device. Each device is identified by a pair of (major, minor) device numbers, e.g. 0x0302 means /dev/hda2, 0x0803 means /dev/sda3, etc. The stat syscall simply finds the file's inode and copies information from inode into the stat structure, except st_dev and st_ino, which are the file's device and inode numbers, respectively. In Unix/Linux, all time fields are the number of seconds elapsed since 0 hour, 0 minute, 0 second of January 1, 1970. They can be converted to calendar form by the library function ctime(&time).

8.6.4   File Type and Permissions

In the stat structure, most fields are self-explanatory. Only the st_mode field needs some explanation:

```
    mode_t   st_mode;              /* copied from i_mode of INODE */
```

The TYPE of st_mode is a u16 (16 bits).The 16 bits have the following meaning:

```
|Type|   |permissions|
---------------------
|tttt|fff|uuu|ggg|ooo|
---------------------
```

The leading 4 bits are file types, which can be interpreted as (in octal)

```
    S_IFMT      0170000    bitmask for the file type bitfields
    S_IFSOCK    0140000    socket
    S_IFLNK     0120000    symbolic link
    S_IFREG     0100000    regular file
    S_IFBLK     0060000    block device
    S_IFDIR     0040000    directory
    S_IFCHR     0020000    character device
    S_IFIFO     0010000    fifo
```

As of now, the man pages of all Unix-like systems still use octal numbers, which has its roots dated back to the old PDP-11 era in the 1970's. For convenience, we shall redefine them in HEX, which are much more readable, e.g.

```
    S_IFDIR     0x4000     directory
    S_IFREG     0x8000     regular file
    S_IFLNK     0xA000     symbolic link
```

The next 3 bits of st_mode are flags, which indicate special usage of the file

```
S_ISUID     0004000    set UID bit
S_ISGID     0002000    set GID bit
S_ISVTX     0001000    sticky bit
```

We shall show the meaning and usage of setuid programs later. The remaining 9 bits are permission bits for file protection. They are divided into 3 categories by the (effective) uid and gid of the process:

```
   owner    group    other
    rwx      rwx      rwx
```

By interpreting these bits, we may display the st_mode field as

```
-rwxr-xr-x          (REG file with r,x but w by owner only)
drwxr-xr-x          (DIR with r,x, but w by owner only)
lrw-r--r--          (LNK file with permissions)
```

where the first letter (**-ldll**) shows the file type and the next 9 chars are based on the permission bits. Each char is printed as r|w|x if the bit is 1 or – if the bit is 0. For directory files, the x bit means whether access (cd into) to the directory is allowed or not.

8.6.5   Opendir-Readdir Functions

A directory is also a file. We should be able to open a directory for READ, then read and display its contents just like any other ordinary file. However, depending on the file system, the contents of a directory file may vary. As a result, the user may not be able to read and interpret the contents of directory files properly. For this reason, POSIX specifies the following interface functions to directory files.

```
#include <dirent.h>
DIR *open(dirPath); // open a directory named dirPath for READ
struct dirent *readdir(DIR *dp); // return a dirent pointer
```

In Linux, the dirent structure is

```
struct dirent{
    u32 d_ino; // inode number
    u16 d_reclen;
    char d_name[ ]
}
```

In the dirent structure, only the d_name field is mandated by POSIX. The other fields are system dependent. opendir() returns a DIR pointer dirp. Each readdir(dirp) call return a dirent pointer to an dirent structure of the next entry in the directory. It returns a NULL pointer when there are no more entries in the directory. We illustrate their usage by an example. The following code segment prints all the file names in a directory.

```
#include <dirent.h>
struct dirent *ep;
DIR *dp = opendir("dirname");
while (ep = readdir(dp)){
    printf("name=%s ", ep->d_name);
}
```

The reader may consult the **man 3** pages of **opendir and readddir** for more details.

8.6.6   Readlink Function

Linux's open() syscall follow symlinks. It is therefore not possible to open a symlink file and read its contents. In order to read the contents of symlink files, we must use the readlink syscal, which is

```
int readlink(char *pathname, char buf[ ], int bufsize);
```

It copies the contents of a symlink file into buf[ ] of bufsize, and returns the actual number of bytes copied.

8.6.7   The ls Program

The following shows a simple ls program which behaves like the **ls –l** command of Linux. The purpose here is not to re-invent the wheel by writing yet another ls program. Rather, it is intended to show how to use the various syscalls to display information of files under a directory. By studying the example program code, the reader should also be able to figure out how Linux's ls command is implemented.

```
/************* myls.c file **********/
#include <stdio.h>
#include <stdlib.h>
#include <string.h>
#include <sys/stat.h>
#include <time.h>
#include <sys/types.h>
#include <dirent.h>

struct stat mystat, *sp;
char *t1 = "xwrxwrxwr-------";
char *t2 = "----------------";

int ls_file(char *fname)
{
  struct stat fstat, *sp;
  int r, i;
  char ftime[64];
  sp = &fstat;
  if ( (r = lstat(fname, &fstat)) < 0){
     printf("can't stat %s\n", fname);
     exit(1);
```

```
  }
  if ((sp->st_mode & 0xF000) == 0x8000) // if (S_ISREG())
     printf("%c",'-');
  if ((sp->st_mode & 0xF000) == 0x4000) // if (S_ISDIR())
     printf("%c",'d');
  if ((sp->st_mode & 0xF000) == 0xA000) // if (S_ISLNK())
     printf("%c",'l');
  for (i=8; i >= 0; i--){
    if (sp->st_mode & (1 << i)) // print r|w|x
      printf("%c", t1[i]);
    else
      printf("%c", t2[i]);        // or print -
  }
  printf("%4d ",sp->st_nlink);   // link count
  printf("%4d ",sp->st_gid);     // gid
  printf("%4d ",sp->st_uid);     // uid
  printf("%8d ",sp->st_size);    // file size
  // print time
  strcpy(ftime, ctime(&sp->st_ctime)); // print time in calendar form
  ftime[strlen(ftime)-1] = 0;    // kill \n at end
  printf("%s  ",ftime);
  // print name
  printf("%s", basename(fname)); // print file basename
  // print -> linkname if symbolic file
  if ((sp->st_mode & 0xF000)== 0xA000){
     // use readlink() to read linkname
     printf(" -> %s", linkname); // print linked name
  }
  printf("\n");
}


int ls_dir(char *dname)
{
  // use opendir(), readdir(); then call ls_file(name)
}


int main(int argc, char *argv[])
{
  struct stat mystat, *sp = &mystat;
  int r;
  char *filename, path[1024], cwd[256];
  filename = "./";        // default to CWD
  if (argc > 1)
     filename = argv[1];  // if specified a filename
  if (r = lstat(filename, sp) < 0){
     printf("no such file %s\n", filename);
     exit(1);
  }
  strcpy(path, filename);
  if (path[0] != '/'){ // filename is relative : get CWD path
```

```
      getcwd(cwd, 256);
      strcpy(path, cwd); strcat(path, "/"); strcat(path,filename);
   }
   if (S_ISDIR(sp->st_mode))
      ls_dir(path);
   else
      ls_file(path);
}
```

Exercise 1: fill in the missing code in the above example program, i.e. the ls_dir() and readlink() functions, to make it work for any directory.

8.7   open-close-lseek System Calls

open : open a file for READ, WRITE, APPEND

        int open(char *file, int flags, int mode);

close : close an opened file descriptor

        int close(int fd);

read : read from an opened file descriptor

        int read(int fd, char buf[ ], int count);

write : write to an opened file descriptor

        int write(int fd, char buf[ ], int count);

lseek : reposition the byte offset of a file descriptor to offset from whence

        int lseek(int fd, int offset, int whence);

umask: set file creation mask; file permissions will be (mask & ~umask)

8.7.1   Open File and File Descriptor

```
#include <sys/type.h>
#include <sys/stat.h>
#include <fcntl.h>
int open(char *pathname, int flags, mode_t mode)
```

Open() opens a file for READ, WRITE or APPEND. It returns a **file descriptor**, which is the lowest available file descriptor number of the process, for use in subsequent read(), write(), lseek() and close() syscalls. The flags field must include one of the following access mode O_RDONLY, O_WRONLY, or O_RDWR. In addition, flags may be bit-wise ORed with other flags O_CREAT, O_APPEND, O_TRUNC, O_CLOEXEC, etc. All these symbolic constants are defined in the **fcntl.h** header file. The optional mode field specifies the permissions of the file in Octal. The permissions of a newly created file or directory are the specified permissions bit-wise ANDed with ~umask, where **umask** is set in the login profile as (octal) 022, which amounts to deleting the w (write) permission bits for non-owners. The umask can be changed by the **umask()** syscall. **Creat()** is equivalent to open() with flags equal to O_CREAT|O_WRONLY|O_TRUNC, which creates a file if it does not exist, opens it for write and truncates the file size to zero.

8.7.2 Close File Descriptor

```
#include <unistd.h>
int close(inf fd);
```

Close() closes the specified file descriptor fd, which can be reused to open another file.

8.7.3 lseek File Descriptor

```
#include <sys/type.h>
#include <unistd.h>
off_t lseek(int fd, off_t offset, int whence);
```

In Linux, **off_t** is defined as u64. When a file is opened for read or write, its RW-pointer is initialized to 0, so that read|write starts from the beginning of the file. After each read |write of n bytes, the RW-pointer is advanced by n bytes for the next read|write. lssek() repositions the RW-pointer to the specified offset, allowing the next read|write from the specified byte position. The whence parameter specifies SEEK_SET (from file beginning), SEEK_CUR (current RW-pointer plus offset) SEEK_END (file size plus offset).

8.8 Read() System Call

```
#include <unistd.h>
int read(int fd, void *buf, int nbytes);
```

read() reads nbytes from an opened file descriptor into buf[ ] in user space. The return value is the actual number of bytes read or -1 if read() failed, e.g. due to invalid fd. Note that the buf[ ] area must have enough space to receive nbytes, and the return value may be less than nbytes, e.g. if the file size is less than nbytes or when the file has no more data to read. Note also that the return value is an integer, not any End-Of-File (EOF) symbol since there is no EOF symbol in a file. EOF is a special integer value (-1) returned by I/O library functions when a FILE stream has no more data.

8.9   Write() System Call

```
#include <unistd.h>
int write(int fd, void *buf, int nbytes);
```

write() writes nbytes from buf[ ] in user space to the file descriptor, which must be opened for write, read-write or append mode. The return value is the actual number of bytes written, which usually equal to nbytes, or -1 if write() failed, e.g. due to invalid fd or fd is opened for read-only, etc.

Example: The following code segment uses open(), read(), lseek(), write() and close() syscalls. It copies the first 1KB bytes of a file to byte 2048.

```
char buf[1024];
int fd=open("file", O_RDWR);    // open file for READ-WRITE
read(fd, buf[ ], 1024);         // read first 1KB into buf[ ]
lseek(fd, 2048, SEEK_SET);      // lseek to byte 2048
write(fd, buf, 1024);           // write 1024 bytes
close(fd);                      // close fd
```

8.10   File Operation Example Programs

Syscalls are suitable for file I/O operations on large blocks of data, i.e. operations that do not need lines, chars or structured records, etc. The following sections show some example programs that use syscalls for file operations.

8.10.1   Display File Contents

Example 8.2: Display File Contents. This program behaves somewhat like the Linux cat command, which displays the contents of a file to stdout. If no filename is specified, it gets inputs from the default stdin.

```
/********* C8.2 file ********/
#include <stdio.h>
#include <stdlib.h>
#include <fcntl.h>
#include <unistd.h>

#define BLKSIZE 4096
int main(int argc, char *argv[ ])
{
  int fd, i, m, n;
  char buf[BLKSIZE], dummy;
  fd = 0; // default to stdin
  if (argc > 1){
    fd = open(argv[1], O_RDONLY);
```

```
        if (fd < 0) exit(1);
    }
    while (n = read(fd, buf, BLKSIZE)){
        m = write(1, buf, n);
    }
}
```

When running the program with no file name, it collects inputs from fd=0, which is the standard input stream stdin. To terminate the program, enter Control-D (0x04), which is the default EOF on stdin. When running the program with a filename, it first opens the file for read. Then it uses a while loop to read and display the file contents until read() returns 0, indicating the file has no more data. In each iteration, it reads up to 4KB chars into a buf[ ] and writes the n chars to the file descriptor 1. In Unix/Linux files, lines are terminated by the LF=\n char. If a file descriptor refers to a terminal special file, the pseudo terminal emulation program automatically adds a \r for each \n char in order to produce the right visual effect. If the file descriptor refers to an ordinary file, no extra \r chars will be added to the outputs.

8.10.2   Copy Files

Example 8.3: Copy Files. This example program behaves like the Linux **cp src dest** command, which copies a src file to a dest file.

```
/******** c8.3.c file *******/
#include <stdio.h>
#include <stdlib.h>
#include <fcntl.h>
#include <unistd.h>

#define BLKSIZE 4096
int main(int argc, char *argv[ ])
{
    int fd, gd, n, total=0;
    char buf[BLKSIZE];
    if (argc < 3) exit(1);   // usage a.out src dest
    if ((fd = (open(argv[1], O_RDONLY)) < 0)
        exit(2);
    if ((gd = open(argv[2],O_WRONLY|O_CREAT)) < 0)
        exit(3);
    while (n = read(fd, buf, BLKSIZE)){
        write(gd, buf, n);
        total += n;
    }
    printf("total bytes copied=%d\n", total);
    close(fd); close(gd);
}
```

Exercise 1. The Example program c8.3 has a serious flaw in that we should never copy a file to itself. Besides wasting time, the reader may also find out the reason by looking at the program code. If the src and dest files are the same file, rather than copying, it would just truncate the file size to 0. Modify the program to ensure that src and dest are not the same file. Note that different filenames may refer to the same file due to hard links.

HINT: stat both pathnames and compare their (st_dev, st_ino).

8.10.3 Selective File Copy

Example 8.4: Selective File Copy: This example program is a refinement of the simple file copying program in Example 8.3. It behaves like the Linux **dd** command, which copies selected parts of files. The reader may consult the man pages of dd to find out its full capabilities. Since our objective here is to show how to use syscalls for file operations, the example program is a simplified version of dd. The program runs as follows.

```
a.out if=in of=out bs=size count=k [skip=m] [seek=n] [conv=notrunc]
```

where [ ] denote optional entries. If these entries are specified, skip=m means skip m blocks of the input file, seek=n means step forward n blocks of the output file before writing and conv=notrunc means do not truncate the output file if it already exits. The default values of skip and seek are 0, i.e. no skip or seek. For simplicity, we assume the command line parameters contain no white spaces, which simplifies command-line parsing. The only new feature of this program is to parse the command line parameters to set file names, counting variables and flags. For example, if conv=notrunc is specified, the target file must be opened without truncating the file. Second, if skip and seek are specified, opened files must use lseek() to set the RW offsets accordingly.

```c
/************ c8.4.c file *********/
#include <stdio.h>
#include <stdlib.h>
#include <fcntl.h>
#include <unistd.h>
#include <string.h>

char in[128], out[128], buf[4096];
int bsize, count, skip, seek, trnc;
int records, bytes;
// parse command line parameters and set variables
int parse(char *s)
{
  char cmd[128], parm[128];
  char *p = index(s, '=');
  s[p-s] = 0; // tokenize cmd=parm by '='
  strcpy(cmd, s);
  strcpy(parm, p+1);
  if (!strcmp(cmd, "if"))
    strcpy(in, parm);
```

```
   if (!strcmp(cmd, "of"))
      strcpy(out, parm);
   if (!strcmp(cmd, "bs")
      bsize = atoi(parm);
   if (!strcmp(cmd, "count"))
      count = atoi(parm);
   if (!strcmp(cmd, "skip"))
      skip = atoi(parm);
   if (!strcmp(cmd, "seek"))
      seek = atoi(parm);
   if (!strcmp(cmd, "conv")){
      if (!strcmp(parm, "notrunc"))
         trnc = 0;
   }
}


int main(int argc, char *argv[])
{
   int fd, gd, n, i;
   if (argc < 3){
      printf("Usage: a.out if of ....\n"); exit(1);
   }
   in[0] = out[0] = 0;             // null file names
   bsize = count = skip = seek = 0; // all 0 to start
   trnc = 1;                       // default = trunc
   for (i=1; i<argc; i++){
       parse(argv[i]);
   }
   // error checkings
   if (in[0]==0) || out[0]==0{
      printf("need in/out files\n"); exit(2);
   }
   if (bsize==0 || count==0){
      printf("need bsize and count\n"); exit(3);
   }
   // ADD: exit if in and out are the same file
   if ((fd = open(in, O_RDONLY)) < 0){
      printf("open %s error\n", in); exit(4);
   }
   if (skip) lseek(fd, skip*bsize, SEEK_SET);
   if (trnc) // truncate out file
      gd = open(out, O_WRONLY|O_CREAT|O_TRUNC);
   else
      gd = open(out, O_WRONLY|O_CREAT); // no truncate
   if (gd < 0){
      printf("open %s error\n", out); exit(5);
   }
   if (seek) lseek(gd, seek*bsize, SEEK_SET);

   records = bytes = 0;
```

```
  while (n = read(fd, buf, bsize)){
    write(gd, buf, n);
    records++; bytes += n;
    count--;                      // dec count by 1
    if (count==0) break;
  }
  printf("records=%d bytes=%d copied\n", records, bytes);
}
```

8.11   Programming Project: Recursive Copy Files using System Calls

The programming project is to use Linux system calls to write a C program, mycp, which recursively copies src to dest. It should work exactly the same as the Linux command

       cp -r src dest

which recursively copies src to dest.

8.11.1   Hints and Helps

1. Analyze the various conditions whether copy is allowed. The following are some example cases, but they are incomplete. The reader should complete the case analyses before attempting to develop any code.
   (1). src must exist but dest may or may not exist.
   (2). If src is a file, dest may not exist, is a file or a directory.
   (3). If src is a directory, dest must be an existing or non-existing directory.
   (4). If src is a DIR and dest does not exist, create dest DIR and copy src to dest.
   (5). If src is a DIR and dest is an existing DIR: do not copy if dest is a descendant of src.
   Otherwise, copy src into dest/, i.e. as dest/(basename(src))
   (6). Never copy a file or directory to itself.
   Whenever in doubt, run the Linux **cp -r src dest** command and compare the results.

2. Organize the project program into 3 layers:
   Base case: cpf2f(file 1, filef2): copy file 1 to file 2; handle REG and LNK files
   Middle case: cpf2d(file, dir): copy file into an existing dir
   Top case: cpd2d(dir1,dir2): copy (recursively) dir1 to dir2

8.11.2   Sample Solution

Sample solution of the programming project can be downloaded from the book's website. Source code for instructors is also available upon request from the author.

8.12 Summary

This chapter covers system calls for file operations. It explains the role of system calls and the online manual pages of Linux. It shows how to use system calls for file operations. It lists and explains the most commonly used system calls for file operations. It explains hard link and symbolic link files. It explains the stat system call in detail. Based on the stat information, it develops a ls-like program to display directory contents and file information. Next, it explains the open-close-lseek system calls and file descriptors. Then it shows how to use read-write system calls to read-write file contents. Based on these, it shows how to use system calls to display and copy files. It shows how to develop a selective file copying program which behaves like a simplified dd utility program of Linux. The programming project is to use Linux system calls to implement a C program, which recursively copies a directory to a destination. The purpose of the project is for the reader to practice on the design of hierarchical program structures and use stat(), open(), read(), write() system calls for file operations.

References

Goldt, S. Van Der Meer, S., Burkett, S., Welsh, M., The Linux Programmer's Guide-The Linux Documentation Project, 1995

Kerrisk, M., The Linux Programming Interface, No Starch Press, Inc., 2010

Kerrisk, M. The Linux man-pages project, https://www.kernel.org/doc/man-pages/, 2017

Library I/O Functions

9

Abstract

This chapter covers library I/O functions. It explains the roles of library I/O functions and their advantages over system calls. It uses sample programs to show the relationship between library I/O functions and system calls, and it explains their similarities and fundamental differences. It describes the algorithms of library I/O functions in detail. These include the algorithms of fread, fwrite and fclose, with an emphasis on their interactions with read, write and close system calls. It describes the different modes of library I/O functions, which include char mode, line mode, structured records mode and formatted I/O operations. It explains the buffering schemes of file streams and shows the effects of different buffering schemes by example programs. It explains functions with varying parameters and how to access parameters using stdarg macros.

The programming project is to integrate the principles and programming techniques of the chapter to implement a printf-like function for formatted printing of chars, strings and numbers in different number bases in accordance with a format string. The basis of the printf-like function is putchar() of Linux, but it works exactly the same as the library function printf(). The purpose of the project is to let the reader understand how library I/O functions are implemented.

9.1   Library I/O Functions

System calls are the basis of file operations, but they only support read/write of chunks of data. In practice, a user program may want to read/write files in logical units most suited to the application, e.g. as lines, chars, structured records, etc. which are not supported by system calls. Library I/O functions are a set of file operation functions, which provide both user convenience and overall efficiency (GNU I/O on streams 2017; GNU libc 2017; GNU Library Reference Manual 2017).

9.2   Library I/O Functions vs. System Calls

Almost every operating system that supports C programming also provides library functions for file I/O. In Unix/Linux, library I/O functions are built on top of system calls. In order to illustrate their intimate relationship, we first list a few of them for comparison.

© Springer International Publishing AG, part of Springer Nature 2018
K. C. Wang, *Systems Programming in Unix/Linux*, https://doi.org/10.1007/978-3-319-92429-8_9

System Call Functions: open(), read(), write(), lseek(), close();
Library I/O Functions: fopen(), fread(), fwrite(), fseek(), fclose();

From their strong similarities, the reader can almost guess that every library I/O function has its root in a corresponding system call function. This is indeed the case as fopen() relies on open(), fread() relies on read(), etc. The following C programs illustrate their similarities and differences.

Example 9.1: Display File Contents

```
            System Calls                 |       Library I/O Functions
---------------------------------------|---------------------------------------
#include <fcntl.h>                     |  #include <stdio.h>
int main(int argc, char *argv[ ])     |  int main(int argc, char *argv[ ])
{                                     |  {
1. int fd;                            |      FILE *fp;
   int i, n;                          |
   char buf[4096];                    |      int c;   // for EOF of stdin
   if (argc < 2) exit(1);             |      if (argc < 2) exit(1);
2. fd = open(argv[1], O_RDONLY);      |      fp = fopen(argv[1], "r");
   if (fd < 0) exit(2);               |      if (fp==0) exit(2);
3. while (n = read(fd, buf, 4096)){  |      while ((c = fgetc(fp)) != EOF){
     for (i=0; i<n; i++){             |
        write(1, &buf[i], 1);         |         putchar(c);
     }                                |
   }                                  |      }
}                                     |  }
---------------------------------------------------------------------------------
```

The left-hand side shows a program that uses system calls. The right-hand side shows a similar program that uses library I/O functions. Both programs print the contents of a file to the display screen. The two programs look similar but there are fundamental differences between them.

Line 1: In the system call program, the file descriptor fd is an integer. In the library I/O program, fp is a FILE stream pointer.
Line 2: The system call open() opens a file for read and returns an integer file descriptor fd, or -1 if open() fails. The library I/O function fopen() returns a FILE structure pointer, or NULL if fopen() fails.
Line 3: The system call program uses a while loop to read/write the file contents. In each iteration, it issues a read() system call to read up to 4KB chars into a buf[ ]. Then it writes each char from buf[ ] to the file descriptor 1, which is the standard output of the process. As pointed out before, using system calls to write one byte at a time is grossly inefficient. In contrast, the library I/O program simply uses fgetc(fp) to get chars from the FILE stream, output them by putchar() until EOF.

Besides the slight differences in syntax and functions used, there are some fundamental differences between the two programs, which are explained in more detail below.

Line 2: fopen() issues an open() system call to get a file descriptor fd. If the open() call fails, it returns a NULL pointer. Otherwise, it allocates a FILE structure in the program's **heap area.** The FILE structure contains an internal buffer char fbuf[BLKSIZE] and an integer fd field. It records the file descriptor returned by open() in the FILE structure, initializes fbuf[ ] as empty, and returns the address of the FILE structure as fp.

Line 3: fgetc(c, fp) tries to get a char from the file stream fp. If the fbuf[ ] in the FILE structure is empty, it issues a read(fd, fbuf, BLKSIZE) system call to read BLKSIZE bytes from the file, where BLKSIZE matches the file system block size. Then it returns a char from fbuf[ ]. Subsequently, fgetc() returns a char from fbuf[ ] as long as it still has data. Thus, the library I/O read functions issues read() syscalls only to refill the fbuf[ ] and they transfer data from the OS kernel to user space always in BLKSZISE. Similar remarks also apply to library I/O write functions.

Exercise 9.1: In the system call program of Example 9.1, writing each char by a system call is very inefficient. Replace the for loop by a single write() system call.

Example 9.2: Copy files: Again, we list two versions of the program side by side to illustrate their similarities and differences

```
        System Calls                    |        Library I/O Functions
------------------------------------    |-----------------------------------
#include <fcntl.h>                      | #include <stdio.h>
#define BLKSIZE 4096                    | #define BLKSIZE 4096
int fd, gd;                             | FILE *fp, *gp;
char buf[4096];                         | char buf[4096];
                                        |
int main(int argc,char *argv[])         | int main(int argc,char *argv[])
{                                       | {
  int n, total=0;                       |   int n, total=0;
  if (argc < 3) exit(1);                |   if (argc < 3) exit(1);
  // check for same file                |   // check for same file
  fd = open(argv[1], O_RDONLY);         |   fp = fopen(argv[1], "r");
  if (fd < 0) exit(2);                  |   if (fp == NULL) exit(2);
  gd = open(argv[2],O_WRONLY|O_CREAT);  |   gp = fopen(argv[2], "w");
  if (gd < 0) exit(3);                  |   if (gp == NULL) exit(3);
  while(n=read(fd, buf, BLKSIZE))       |   while(n=fread(buf,1,BLKSIZE,fp))
  {                                     |   {
     write(gd, buf, n);                 |      fwrite(buf, 1, n, gp);
     total += n;                        |      total += n;
  }                                     |   }
  printf("total=%d\n",total);           |   printf("total = %d\n", total);
  close(fd); close(gd);                 |   fclose(fp); fclose(gp);
}                                       | }
------------------------------------------------------------------------------
```

Both programs copy a src file to a dest file. Since the system call program was already explained in Chapter 6, we shall only discuss the program that uses library I/O functions.

(1). fopen() uses a string for Mode, where "r" for READ, "w" for WRITE. It returns a pointer to a FILE structure. fopen() first issues an open() system call to open the file to get a file descriptor number fd. If the open() system call fails, fopen() returns a NULL pointer. Otherwise, it allocates a FILE structure in the program's heap area. Each FILE structure contains an internal buffer, fbuf

[BLKSIZE], whose size usually matches the BLKSIZE of the file system. In addition, it also has pointers, counters and status variables for manipulating the fbuf[ ] contents and a fd field, which stores the file descriptor from open(). It initializes the FILE structure and returns fp which points at the FILE structure. It is important to note that the FILE structure is in the process' User mode Image. This means that calls to library I/O functions are ordinary function calls, not system calls.

(2). The programs terminates if any of the fopen() calls has failed. As mentioned above, fopen() returns a NULL pointer on failure, e.g. if the file can not be opened for the indicated mode.

(3). Then it uses a while loop to copy the file contents. Each iteration of the while loop tries to read BLKSIZE bytes from the source file, and write n bytes to the target file, where n is the returned value from fread(). The general forms of fread() and fwrite() are

```
int n = fread(buffer, size, nitems, FILEptr);
int n = fwrite(buffer,size, nitems, FILEptr);
```

where size is the record size in bytes, nitems is the number of records to be read or written, and n is the actual number of records read or written. These functions are intended for read/write structured data objects. For example, assume that the buffer area contains data objects of structured records

```
struct record{.....}
```

We may use

```
n = fwrite(buffer, sizeof(struct record), nitem, FILEptr);
```

to write nitem records to a file. Similarly,

```
n =    fread(buffer, sizeof(struct record), nitem, FILEptr);
```

reads nitem records from a file.

The above program tries to read/write BLKSIZE bytes at a time. So, it has size = 1 and nitems = BLKSIZE. As a matter of fact, any combination of size and nitems such that size*nitems = BLKSIZE would also work. However, using a size > 1 may cause problem on the last fread() because the file may have fewer than size bytes left. In that case, the returned n is zero even if it has read some data. To deal with the "tail" part of the source file, we may add the following lines of code after the while loop:

```
fseek(fp, total, SEEK_SET);  // fseek to byte total
n = fread(buf, 1, size, fp); // read remaining bytes
    fwrite(buf,1, n, gp);    // write to dest file
total += n;
```

fseek() works exactly the same as lseek(). It positions the file's R|W pointer to the byte location total. From there, we read the file as 1-byte objects. This will read all the remaining bytes, if any, and write them to the target file.

(4). After the copying is complete, both files are closed by fclose(FILE *p).

9.3   Algorithms of Library I/O Functions

9.3.1   Algorithm of fread

The algorithm of fread() is as follows:

(1). On the first call to fread(), the FILE structure's buffer is empty. fread() uses the saved file descriptor fd to issue a

```
n = read(fd, fbuffer, BLKSIZE);
```

system call to fill the internal fbuf[ ] with a block of data. Then, it initializes fbuf[ ]'s pointers, counters and status variables to indicate that there is a block of data in the internal buffer. It then tries to satisfy the fread() call from the internal buffer by copying data to the program's buffer area. If the internal buffer does not have enough data, it issues additional read() system call to fill the internal buffer, transfer data from the internal buffer to the program buffer, until the needed number of bytes is satisfied (or the file has no more data). After copying data to the program's buffer area, it updates the internal buffer's pointers, counters, etc. making it ready for next fread() request. It then returns the actual number of data objects read.

(2). On each subsequent call to fread(), it tries to satisfy the call from the FILE structure's internal buffer. It issues a read() system call to refill the internal buffer whenever the buffer becomes empty. Thus, fread() accepts calls from user program on one side and issues read() system calls to the OS kernel on the other. Except for the read() system calls, all processing of fread() are performed inside the user mode image. It enters the OS kernel only when needed and it does so in a way that matches the file system for best efficiency. It provides automatic buffering mechanism so that user programs do not have to worry about such detailed operations.

9.3.2   Algorithm of fwrite

The algorithm of fwrite() is similar to that of fread() except for the data transfer direction. Initially the FILE structure's internal buffer is empty. On each call to fwrite(), it writes data to the internal buffer, and adjusts the buffer's pointers, counters and status variable to keep track of the number of bytes in the buffer. If the buffer becomes full, it issues a write() system call to write the entire buffer to the OS kernel.

9.3.3   Algorithm of fclose

fclose() first flushes the local buffer of the FILE stream if the file was opened for WRITE. Then it issues a close(fd) system call to close the file descriptor in the FILE structure. Finally it frees the FILE structure and resets the FILE pointer to NULL.

9.4   Use Library I/O Function or System Call

Based on the above discussions, we can now answer the question of when to use system calls or library functions to do file I/O. fread() relies on read() to copy data from Kernel to an internal buffer, from which it copies data to the program's buffer area. So it transfers data twice. In contrast, read() copies data from Kernel directly to the program's buffer area, which copies only once. Thus, for read/write data in units of BLKSIZEs, read() is inherently more efficient than fread() because it only needs one copying operation instead of two. Similar remarks are also applicable to write() and fwrite().

It is noted that in some implementations of fread() and fwrite(), e.g. in the GNU libc library, if the requested size is in units of BLKSIZE, they may use system calls to transfer data in BLKSIZE from kernel to user specified buffer directly. Even so, using library I/O functions still require additional function calls. Therefore, in the above example, the program that uses system calls is actually more efficient than the one that uses library I/O functions. However, if the read/write is not in units of BLKSIZE, fread() and fwrite() may be far more efficient. For example, if we insists on R/W one byte at a time, fread() and fwrite() would be far better because they enter the OS kernel only to fill or flush the internal buffer, not on every byte. Here, we have implicitly assumed that entering Kernel mode is more expensive than staying in User mode, which is indeed true.

9.5   Library I/O Modes

The Mode parameter in fopen() may be specified as
"r", "w", "a" :   for READ, WRITE, APPEND.

Each of the mode string may include a + sign, which means for both READ, WRITE, and in the cases of WRITE or APPEND, create the file if it does not exist.
"r+" :   for R/W, without truncating the file.
"w+":   for R/W, but truncate the file first; create if file does not exist.
"a+" :   for R/W by append; create if file does not exist.

9.5.1   Char Mode I/O

```
int fgetc(FILE *fp):          // get a char from fp, cast to int.
int ungetc(int c, FILE *fp);  // push a previously char got by fgetc()
                              //   back to stream
int fputc(int c, FILE *fp);   // put a char to fp
```

Note that fgetc() returns an integer, not a char. This is because it must return EOF on end of file. The EOF symbol is normally an integer -1, which distinguishes it from any char from the FILE stream.

For fp = stdin or stdout, c = getchar(); putchar(c); may be used instead. For run time efficiency, getchar() and putchar() are often not the shortened versions of getc() and putc(). Instead, they may be implemented as macros in order to avoid an extra function call.

Example 9.3: Char Mode I/O

```
(1). /* file copy using getc(), putc() */
    #include <stdio.h>
    FILE *fp,*gp;
    int main()
    {
        int c;   /* for testing EOF */
        fp=fopen("source", "r");
        gp=fopen("target", "w");
        while ( (c=getc(fp)) != EOF )
            putc(c,gp);
        fclose(fp); fclose(gp);
    }
```

Exercise 9.2: Write a C program which converts letters in a text file from lowercase to uppercase.

Exercise 9.3: Write a C program which counts the number of lines in a text file.

Exercise 9.4: Write a C program which counts the number of words in a text file. Words are sequences of chars separated by white spaces.

Exercise 9.5: Linux's man pages are compressed gz files. Use gunzip to uncompress a man page file. The uncompressed man page file is a text file but it is almost unreadable because it contains many special chars and char sequences for the man program to use. Assume ls.1 is the uncompressed man page of ls.1.gz. Analyze the uncompressed ls.1 file to find out what are the special chars. Then write a C program which eliminates all the special chars, making it a pure text file.

9.5.2   Line mode I/O

char *fgets(char *buf, int size, FILE *fp):   read a line (with a \n at end) of at most size chars from fp to buf .

int fputs(char *buf, FILE *fp):   write a line from buf to fp.

Example 9.4: Line Mode I/O

```
#include <stdio.h>
FILE *fp,*gp;
char buf[256]; char *s="this is a string";
int main()
{
  fp = fopen("src",  "r");
  gp = fopen("dest", "w");
  fgets(buf, 256, fp); // read a line of up to 255 chars to buf
  fputs(buf, gp);      // write line to destination file
}
```

When fp is stdin or stdout, the following functions may also be used but they are not shortened versions of fgets() and fputs().

```
gets(char *buf);        // input line from stdin but without checking length
puts(char *buf);        // write line to stdout
```

9.5.3   Formatted I/O

These are perhaps the most commonly used I/O functions.

Foratted Inputs: (FMT=format string)

```
scanf(char *FMT, &items);          // from stdin
fscanf(fp, char *FMT, &items);     // from file stream
```

Formatted Outputs:

```
printf(char *FMT, items);          // to stdout
fprintf(fp, char *FMT, items);     // to file stream
```

9.5.4   In-memory Conversion Functions

```
sscanf(buf, FMT, &items);       // input from buf[ ] in memory
sprintf(buf,FMT, items);        // print to buf[ ] in memroy
```

Note that sscanf() and sprintf() are not I/O functions but in-memory data conversion functions. For example, atoi() is a standard library function, which converts an string of ASCII digits to integer, but most Unix/Linux system do not have an itoa() function because the conversion can be done by sprintf (), so it is not needed.

9.5.5   Other Library I/O Functions

fseek(), ftell(), rewind() :   change read/write byte position in file stream
feof(), ferr(), fileno()   :   test file stream status
fdopen()   :   open a file stream by a file descriptor
freopen()   :   reopen an existing stream by a new name
setbuf(), setvbuf()   :   set buffering scheme
popen()   :   create a pipe, fork a subprocess to invoke the sh

9.5.6   Restriction on Mixed fread-fwrite

When a file stream is for both R|W, there are restrictions on the use of mixed fread() and fwrite() calls. The specification requires at least one fseek() or ftell() between every pair of fread() and fwrite().

Example 9.5: Mixed fread-fwrite: This program yields different results when run under HP-UX and Linux.

```
#include <stdio.h>
FILE fp; char buf[1024];
int main()
{
  fp = fopen("file", "r+");   // for both R/W
  fread(buf, 1, 20, fp);      // read 20 bytes
  fwrite(buf,1, 20, fp);      // write to the same file
}
```

Linux gives the right result, which modifies the bytes from 20 to 39. HP-UX appends 40 bytes to the end of the original file. The difference stems from the non-uniform treatment of R/W pointers in the two systems. Recall that fread()/fwrite() issue read()/write() system calls to fill/flush the internal buffer. While read()/write() use the R/W pointer in the file's OFTE, fread()/fwrite() use the local buffer's R/W pointer in the FILE structure. Without a fseek() to synchronize these two pointers, the results depend on how are they used in the implementations. In order to avoid any inconsistencies, follow the suggestions of the man pages. For the Example 9.5 program, the results become identical (and correct) if we insert a line

```
fseek(fp, (long)20, 0);
```

between the fread() and fwrite() lines.

9.6   File Stream Buffering

Every file stream has a FILE structure, which contains an internal buffer. Read from or write to a file stream goes through the internal buffer of the FILE structure. A file stream may employ one of three kinds of buffering schemes.

. **unbuffered:** characters written to or read from an unbuffered stream are transmitted individually to or from the file as soon as possible. For example, the file stream stderr is usually unbuffered. Any outputs to stderr will appear immediately.
. **line buffered:** characters written to a line buffered stream are transmitted in blocks when a newline char is encountered. For example, the file stream stdout is usually line buffered. It outputs data line by line.
. **fully buffered:** characters written to or read from a fully buffered stream are transmitted to or from the file in block size. This is the normal buffering scheme of file streams.

After creating a file stream by fopen() and before any operation has been performed on it, the user may issue a

```
setvbuf(FILE *stream, char *buf,  int node,  int size)
```

call to set the buffer area (buf), buffer size (size) and buffering scheme (mode), which must be one of the macros

_IONBUF: unbuffered
_IOLBUF: line buffered
_IOFBUF: fully buffered

In addition, there are other setbuf() functions, which are variants of setvbuf(). The reader may consult the man pages of setvbuf for more details.

For line or fully buffered streams, **fflush(stream)** can be used to flush out the stream's buffer immediately. We illustrate the different buffering schemes by an example.

Example 9.6. FILE stream buffering: Consider the following C program

```
#include <stdio.h>
int main()
{
   (1).  // setvbuf(stdout, NULL, _IONBF, 0);
         while(1){
   (2).     printf("hi ");  // not a line yet
   (3).     // fflush(stdout);
            sleep(1);       // sleep for 1 second
          }
}
```

When running the above program, no outputs will appear immediately despite the printf() statement at line (2) on each second. This is because stdout is line buffered. Outputs will appear only when the printed chars fill the internal buffer of stdout, at which time, all the previously printed chars will appear at once. So, if we do not write lines to stdout, it behaves as a fully buffered stream. If we uncomment line (3), which flushes out stdout, each print will appear immediately despite it is not a line yet. If we uncomment line (1), which sets stdout to unbuffered, then the printing will appear on each second.

9.7   Functions with Varying Parameters

Among the library I/O functions, printf() is rather unique in that it can be called with a varying number of parameters of different types. This is permissible because the original C was not a type-checking language. Current C and C++ enforce type-checking but both still allow functions with varying number of parameters for convenience. Such functions must be declared with at least one argument, followed by 3 dots, as in

```
int func(int m, int n . . .)        // n = last specified parameter
```

Inside the function, parameters can be accessed by the C library macros

```
void va_start(va_list ap, last);  // start param list from last parameter
type va_arg(va_list ap, type);    //  type = next parameter type
va_end(va_list ap);               // clear parameter list
```

We illustrate the usage of these macros by an example:

Example 9.7: Access parameter list using stdarg Macros.

```
/******* Example of accessing varying parameter list *******/
#include <stdio.h>
#include <stdarg>      // need this for va_list type

// assume: func() is called with m integers, followed by n strings
int func(int m, int n . . .) // n = last known parameter
{
     int i;
(1). va_list ap;         // define a va_list ap
(2). va_start(ap, n);    // start parameter list from last param n
     for (i=0; i<m; i++)
(3).   printf("%d ", va_arg(ap, int));   // extract int params
     for (i=0; i<n, i++)
(4).   printf("%s ", va_arg(ap, char *)) // extra char* params
(5).   va_end(ap);
}
int main()
{
   func(3, 2, 1, 2, 3, "test", "ok");
}
```

In the example program, we assume that the function func() will be called with 2 known parameters, int m, int n, followed by m integers and n strings.

Line (1) defines a va_list ap variable.
Line (2) starts the parameter list from the last known parameter (n).
Line (3) uses va_arg(ap, **int**) to extract the next m parameters as integers.
Line (4) uses va_arg(ap, char *) to extract the next n parameters as strings.
Line (5) ends the parameter list by resetting the ap list to NULL.

The reader may compile and run the example program. It should print **1 2 3 test OK.**

9.8   Programming Project: Printf-like Function

The programming project is to write a printf()-like function for formatted printing of chars, strings, unsigned integers, signed integers in decimal and unsigned integers in HEX. The objective of the programming project is to let the reader understand how library I/O functions are implemented. In the case of printf(), which can print a varying number of items of different types, the basic operation is to print a single char.

9.8.1   Project Specification

In Linux, putchar(char c) prints a char. Use only putchar() to implement a function

    int myprintf(char *fmt, . . .)

for formatted printing of other parameters, where fmt is a format string containing

    %c : print char
    %s : print string
    %u : print unsigned integer
    %d : print signed integer
    %x : print unsigned integer in HEX

For simplicity, we shall ignore field width and precision. Just print the parameters, if any, as specified in the format string. Note that the number and type of the items to be printed are implicitly specified by the number of % symbols in the format string.

9.8.2   Base Code of Project

(1). The reader should implement a prints(char *s) function for printing strings.

(2). The following shows a printu() function, which prints unsigned integers in decimal.

```
char *ctable = "0123456789ABCDEF";
int BASE = 10; // for printing numbers in decimal
int rpu(unsigned int x)
{
    char c;
    if (x){
        c = ctable[x % BASE];
        rpu(x / BASE);
        putchar(c);
    }
}
int printu(unsigned int x)
{
    (x==0)? putchar('0') : rpu(x);
    putchar(' ');
}
```

The function rpu(x) recursively generates the digits of x % 10 in ASCII and prints them on the return path. For example, if x=123, the digits are generated in the order of '3', 2', '1', which are printed as '1', '2', '3' as they should.

(3). With the printu() function, the reader should be able to implement a printd() function to print signed integers.

(4). Implement a printx() function to print unsigned integers in HEX (for addresses).

(5). Assume that we have printc(), prints(), printd(), printu() and printx() functions. Then implement myprintf(char *fmt, ...) by the following algorithm.

9.8.3   Algorithm of myprintf()

Assume that the format string fmt = "char=**%c** string=**%s** integer=**%d** u32=**%x\n**". It implies that there are 4 additional parameters of char, char *, int, unsigned int, types respectively. The algorithm of myprint() is as follows.

(1). Scan the format string fmt. Print any char that's not %. For each '\n' char, print an extra '\r'char.

(2). When encounter a '%', get the next char, which must be one of 'c', 's', 'u', 'd' or 'x'. Use va_arg (ap, type) to extract the corresponding parameter. Then call the print function by the parameter type.

(3). The algorithm ends when scanning the fmt string ends.

Exercise 9.6:   Assume 32-bit GCC. Implement the myprintf(char *fmt, . . .) function by the following algorithm and explain WHY the algorithm works.

```
int myprintf(char *fmt, . . .)
{
   char *cp = fmt;
   int  *ip = (int *)&fmt + 1;
   // Use cp to scan the format string for %TYPE symbols;
   // Use ip to access and print each item by TYPE;
}
```

9.8.4   Project Refinements

(1). Define tab key as 8 spaces. Add %t to the format string for tab keys.

(2). Modify %u, %d and %x to include a width field, e.g. %8d prints an integer in a space of 8 chars and right-justified, etc.

9.8.5   Project Demonstration and Sample Solutions

Demonstrate the myprintf() function by driver programs. Sample solution to the programming project is available at the book's website for downloading. Source code of the project for instructors is available on request.

9.9   Summary

This chapter covers library I/O functions. It explains the roles of library I/O functions and their advantages over system calls. It uses sample programs to show the relationship between library I/O functions and system calls, and it explains their similarities and fundamental differences. It describes the algorithms of library I/O functions in detail. These include the algorithms of fread, fwrite and fclose, with an emphasis on their interactions with read, write and close system calls. It describes the different modes of library I/O functions, which include char mode, line mode, structured records mode and formatted I/O operations. It explains the buffering schemes of file streams and shows the effects of different buffering schemes by example programs. It explains functions with varying parameters and how to access parameters using stdarg macros.

The programming project is to integrate the principles and programming techniques of the chapter to implement a printf-like function for formatted printing of chars, strings and numbers in different number bases in accordance with a format string. The basis of the printf-like function is putchar() of Linux, but it works exactly the same as the library function printf(). The purpose of the project is to let the reader understand how library I/O functions are implemented.

Problems
1. Given the following C programs

```
---------- System call ---------------- Library I/O -------------
#include <fcntl.h>               |    #include <stdio.h>
char buf[4096];                  |    char buf[4096];
#define SIZE 1                   |    #define SIZE 1
int main()                       |    int main()
{                                |    {
  int i;                         |      int i;
  int fd = open("file", O_RDONLY); |    FILE *fp = fopen("file","r")
  for (i=0; i<100; i++){         |      for (i=0; i<100; i++)
    read(fd, buf, SIZE);         |        fread(buf, SIZE, 1, fp);
  }                              |      }
}                                |    }
-----------------------------------------------------------------
```

    (1). Which program would run faster? WHY?

    (2). Change SIZE to 4096 which is the file block size of Linux. Which program would run faster? WHY?

2. When copying files, we should never copy a file to itself.

    (1). WHY?

    (2). Modify the Example 9.2 programs to prevent copying a file to itself. Note that comparing the file names may not work because two distinct file names could be the same file due to hard links. So the problem is how to tell whether two pathnames are the same file. HINT: stat system call.

3. When copying directories, we should never copy a directory into itself. Assume that /a/b/c/ is a directory. It is permissible to copy /a/b/c into /a, but not /a/b into /a/b/c/.

    (1). WHY?

    (2). How to determine a directory is inside another directory?

    (3). Write C code to determine whether a directory is inside itself.

References

The GNU C Library:I/O on Streams, www.gnu.org/s/libc/manual/html_node/I_002fO-Overview.html, 2017
The GNU C Library (glibc), www.gnu.org/software/libc/, 2017
The GNU C Library Reference Manual, www.gnu.org/software/libc/manual/pdf/libc.pdf, 2017

Sh Programming

10

Abstract

This chapter covers sh programming. It explains sh scripts and different versions of sh. It compares sh scripts with C programs and points out the difference between interpreted and compiled languages. It shows how to write sh scripts in detail. These include sh variables, sh statements, sh built-in commands, regular system commands and command substitution. Then it explains sh control statements, which include test conditions, for loop, while loop, do-until loop, case statements, and it demonstrates their usage by examples. It shows how to write sh functions and invoke sh functions with parameters. It also shows the wide range of applications of sh scripts by examples. These include the installation, initialization and administration of the Linux system.

The programming project is for the reader to write a sh scripts which recursively copies files and directories. The project is organized in a hierarchy of three sh functions; cpf2f() which copies file to file, cpf2d() which copies file into a directory and cpd2d() which recursively copies directories.

10.1 sh Scripts

A sh script (Bourne 1982; Forouzan and Gilberg 2003) is a text file containing sh statements for the command interpreter sh to execute. As an example, we may create a text file, mysh, containing

```
#! /bin/bash
# comment line
echo hello
```

Use **chmod +x mysh** to make it executable. Then run mysh. The first line of a sh script usually begins with the combination of #!, which is commonly called a **shebang.** When the main sh sees the shebang, it reads the program name for which the script is intended and invokes that program. There are many different versions of sh, e.g. bash of Linux, csh of BSD Unix and ksh of IBM AIX, etc. All the sh programs perform essentially the same task but their scripts differ slightly in syntax. The shebang allows the main sh to invoke the proper version of sh to execute the script. If the shebang is not specified, it runs the default sh, which is /bin/bash in Linux. When bash executes the mysh script, it will print hello.

© Springer International Publishing AG, part of Springer Nature 2018

K. C. Wang, *Systems Programming in Unix/Linux*, https://doi.org/10.1007/978-3-319-92429-8_10

10.2   sh Scripts vs. C Programs

sh scripts and C programs have some similarities but they are fundamentally different. The following lists a sh script and a C program side by side in order to compare their syntax form and usage.

```
------------ sh ----------------------- C -----------------
 INTERPRETER: read & execute |    COMPILE-LINKED to a.out
                             |
  mysh a  b  c  d            |    a.out a b c d
   $0  $1 $2 $3 $4           |    main(int argc, char *argv[ ])
---------------------------------------------------------------
```

First, sh is an **interpreter**, which reads a sh script file line by line and executes the lines directly. If a line is an executable command, sh executes the command directly if it's a built-in command. Otherwise, it forks a child process to execute the command and waits for the child to terminate before continuing, exactly as it does a single command line. In contrast, a C program must be compile-linked to a binary executable first. Then run the binary executable by a child process of the main sh. Second, in C programs, every variable must have a type, e.g. char, int, float, derived types like structs, etc. In contrast, in sh scripts, everything is string. So there is no need for types since there is only one type, namely strings. Third, every C program must have a main() function, and each function must define a return value type and arguments, if any. In contrast, sh scripts do not need a main function. In a sh script, the first executable statement is the entry point of the program.

10.3   Command-line parameters

A sh script can be invoked with parameters exactly as running a sh command, as in

mysh one two three

Inside the sh script, the command line parameters can be accessed by the position parameters $0, $1, $2, etc. The first 10 command line parameters can be accessed as $0 to $9. Other parameters must be referenced as ${10} to ${n} for n>=10. Alternatively, they can be brought into view by the shift command, which will be shown later. As usual, $0 is the program name itself and $1 to $n are parameters to the program. In sh the built-in variables $# and $* can be used to count and display the command-line parameters.

$# = the number of command-line parameters $1 to $n
$* = ALL command-line parameters, including $0

In addition, sh also has the following built-in variables related to command executions.

$$ = PID of the process executing the sh
$? = last command execution exit status (0 if success, nonzero otherwise)

Example   Assume the following mysh script is run as

```
       mysh abc   D   E   F   G   H   I   J   K   L   M   N
              #   1   2   3   4   5   6   7   8   9  10  11  12
1. #! /bin/bash
2. echo \$# = $#              #  $# = 12
3. echo \$* = $*              #  $* = abc D E F G H I J K L M N
4. echo $1  $9  $10           #  abc K abc0  (note: $10 becomes abc0)
5. echo $1  $9  ${10}         #  abc K L       (note: ${10} is L)
6. shift                      # replace $1, $2 .. with $2, $3,...
7. echo $1  $9  ${10}         #  D L M
```

In sh, the special char $ means substitution. In order to use $ as is, it must be either single quoted or back quoted by \, similar to \n , \r, \t, etc. in C. In Lines 2 and 3, each \$ is printed as is with no substitution. In Line 4, $1 and $9 are printed correctly but **$10** is printed as **abc0**. This is because sh treats $10 as $1 concatenated with 0. Before echoing, it substitutes $1 with abc, making $10 as abc0. In Line 5, ${10} is printed correctly as L. The reader may try to echo other position parameters ${11} and ${12}, etc. Line 6 shifts the position parameters once to the left, making $2=$1, $3=$2, etc. After a shift, $9 becomes L and ${10} becomes M.

10.4   Sh Variables

Sh has many built-in variables, such as PATH, HOME, TERM, etc. In addition to built-in variables, the user may use any symbol as sh variable. No declaration is necessary. All sh variable values are strings. An unassigned sh variable is the NULL string. A sh variable can be set or assigned a value by

```
     variable=string      # NOTE: no white spaces allowed between tokens
```

If A is a variable, then $A is its value.

Examples

```
echo A      ==>    A
echo $A     ==>    (null if variable A is not set)
A="this is fun" # set A value
echo $A     ==>    this is fun
B=A             # assign "A" to B
echo $B     ==>    A (B was assigned the string "A")
B=$A            (B takes the VALUE of A)
echo $B     ==>    this is fun
```

10.5   Quotes in sh

Sh has many special chars, such as $, /, *, >, <, etc. To use them as ordinary chars, use \ or single quotes to quote them.

Examples:

```
A=xyz
echo \$A      ==> $A        # back quote $ as is
echo '$A'     ==> $A        # NO substitution within SINGLE quotes
echo "see $A" ==> see xyz   # substitute $A in DOUBLE quotes
```

In general, \ is used to quote single chars. Single quotes are used to quote long strings. No substitution occurs within single quotes. Double quotes are used to preserve white spaces in double quoted strings but substitution will occur within double quotes.

10.6   sh Statements

sh statements include all Unix/Linux commands, with possible I/O redirections.

Examples:

```
ls
ls > outfile
date
cp f1 f2
mkdir newdir
cat < filename
```

In addition, the sh programming language also supports statements for testing conditions, loops and cases, etc. which controls the executions of sh programs.

10.7   sh Commands

10.7.1   Built-in Commands

sh has many built-in commands, which are executed by sh without forking a new process. The following lists some of the commonly used built-in sh commands.

. file	:	read and execute file
break [n]	:	exit from the nearest nth nested loop
cd [dirname]	:	change directory
continue [n]	:	restart the nearest nth nested loop
eval [arg . . .]	:	evaluate args once and let sh execute the resulting command(s).
exec [arg . . .]	:	execute command by this sh, which will exit
exit [n]	:	cause sh to exit with exit status n
export [var ..]	:	export variables to subsequently executed commands
read [var . . .]	:	read a line from stdin and assign values to variables
set [arg . . .]	:	set variables in execution environment
shift	:	rename position parameters $2 $3 . . . as $1 $2. . . .
trap [arg] [n]	:	execute arg on receiving signal n
umask [ddd]	:	set umask to octal ddd
wait [pid]	:	wait for process pid, if pid is not given, wait for all active children

The read Command: When sh executes the read command, it waits for an input line from stdin. It divides the input line into tokens, which are assigned to the listed variables. A common usage of read is to allow the user to interact with the executing sh, as shown by the following example.

```
echo -n "enter yes or no : "   # wait for user input line from stdin
read ANS                       # sh reads a line from stdin
echo $ANS                      # display the input string
```

After getting the input, sh may test the input string to decide what to do next.

10.7.2   Linux Commands

sh can execute all Linux commands. Among these, some commands have become almost an integral part of sh because they are used extensively in sh scripts. The following lists and explains some of these commands.

The echo Command: echo simply echoes the parameter strings as lines to stdout. It usually condenses adjacent white spaces into a single space unless quoted.

Examples

```
echo This  is    a   line      # display This is a line
echo "This is    a   line"     # display This is    a   line
echo -n hi                     # display hi without NEWLINE
echo    there                  # display hithere
```

The expr Command: Since all sh variables are strings, we can not change them as numerical value directly. For example,

```
I=123      # I assigned the string "123"
I=I + 1    # I assigned the string "I + 1"
```

Rather than incrementing the numerical value of I by 1, the last statement merely changes I to the string "I + 1", which is definitely not what we hoped (I=124). Changing the (numerical) values of sh variables can be done indirectly by the expr command. Expr is a program, which runs as

```
expr string1 OP string2    # OP = any binary operator on numbers
```

It first converts the two parameter strings to numbers, performs the (binary) operation OP on the numbers and then converts the resulting number back to a string. Thus,

```
I=123
I=$(expr $I + 1)
```

changes I from "123" to "124". Similarly, expr can also be used to perform other arithmetic operations on sh variables whose values are strings of digits.

The pipe Command: Pipes are used very often in sh scripts to act as filters.

Examples:

```
ps -ax | grep httpd
cat file | grep word
```

Utility Commands: In addition to the above Linux commands, sh also uses many other utility programs as commands. These include

awk: data manipulation program.
cmp: compare two files
comm: select lines common to two sorted files
grep: match patterns in a set of files
diff: find differences between two files
join :   compare two files by joining records with identical keys
sed: stream or line editor
sort: sort or merge files
tail: print the lasst n lines of a file
tr: one-to-one char translation
uniq: remove successive duplicated lines from a file

10.8   Command Substitution

In sh, $A is substituted with the value of A. Likewise, when sh sees `cmd` (in grave quotes) or $(cmd), it executes the cmd first and substitutes $(cmd) with the result string of the execution.

Examples

```
echo $(date)      # display the result string of date command
echo $(ls dir)    # display the result string of ls dir command
```

Command substitution is a very powerful mechanism. We shall show its usage throughout the latter part of this chapter.

10.9   Sh Control Statements

Sh is a programming language. It supports many execution control statements, which are similar to those in C.

10.9.1   if-else-fi statement

The syntax of if-else-fi statement is

```
if [ condition ]      # NOTE: must have white space between tokens
   then
        statements
   else                # as usual, the else part is optional
        statements
fi                     # each if must end with a matching fi
```

Each statement must be on a separate line. However, sh allows multiple statements on the same line if they are separated by semi-colon ;. In practice, if-else-fi statements are often written as

```
if [ condition ]; then
     statements
  else
     statements
  fi
```

Examples: By default, all values in sh are strings, so they can be compared as strings by

```
if  [ s1 = s2 ]          # NOTE: white spaces needed between tokens
if  [ s1 != s2 ]
if  [ s1 \< s2 ]         # \< because < is a special char
if  [ s1 \> s2 ] etc.    # \> because > is a special char
```

In the above statements, the left bracket symbol [is actually a **test** program, which is executed as

```
test string1 COMP string2  OR  [ string1 COMP string2 ]
```

It compares the two parameter strings to decide whether the condition is true. It is important to note that in sh **0 is TRUE** and **nonzero is FALSE,** which are exactly opposite of C. This is because when sh executes a command, it gets the exit status of the command execution, which is 0 for success and nonzero otherwise. Since [is a program, its exit status is 0 if the execution succeeds, i.e. the tested condition is true, and nonzero if the tested condition is false. Alternatively, the user may also use the sh built-in variable **$?** to test the exit status of the last command execution.

In contrast, the operators -eq, -ne, -lt, -gt , etc. compare parameters as integer numbers.

```
if [ "123" = "0123" ]        is false since they differ as strings
if [ "123" -eq "0123" ]      is true since they have the same numerical value
```

In addition to comparing strings or numerical values, the TEST program can also test file types and file attributes, which are often needed in file operations.

```
if [ -e name ]     # test whether file name exists
if [ -f name ]     # test whether name is a (REG) file
if [ -d name ]     # test whether name is a DIR
if [ -r name ]     # test whether name is readable; similarly for -w, -x, etc.
if [ f1 -ef f2 ]   # test whether f1, f2 are the SAME file
```

Exercise: How does the test program tests files type and file attributes, e.g. readable, writeable, etc.? In particular, how does it determine whether f1 −ef f2?

HINT: stat system call.

Compound if-elif-else-fi statement: This is similar to if-else if-else in C except sh uses elif instead of else if. The syntax of compound if-elif-else-fi statement is

```
if [ condition1 ]; then
    commands
  elif [ condition2 ]; then
    commands
  # additional elif [ condition3 ]; then etc.
  else
    commands
fi
```

Compound Conditions: As in C, sh allows using **&&** (AND) and ‖ (OR) in compound conditions, but the syntax is more rigid than C. The conditions must be enclosed in a pair of matched double brackets, [[and]].

Examples

```
if [[ condition1 && condition2 ]]; then
if [[ condition1 && condition2 || condition3 ]]; then
```

As in C, compound conditions can be grouped by ( ) to enforce their evaluation orders.

```
if [[ expression1 && (expression2 || expression3) ]]; then
```

10.9.2 for Statement

The for statement in sh behaves as for loop in C.

```
for VARIABLE in string1 string2 .... stringn
  do
    commands
  done
```

On each iteration, the VARIABLE takes on a parameter string value and execute the commands between the keywords do and done.

Examples:

```
for FRUIT in apple orange banana cherry
  do
     echo $FRUIT          # print lines of apple orange banana cherry
  done


for NAME in $*
  do
    echo $NAME           # list all command-line parameter strings
    if [ -f $NAME ]; then
       echo $NAME is a file
    elif [ -d $NAME ]; then
        echo $NAME is a DIR
    fi
  done
```

10.9.3   while Statement

The sh while statement is similar to while loop in C

```
while [ condition ]
  do
    commands
  done
```

sh will repeatedly execute the commands inside the do-done keywords while the condition is true. It is expected that the condition will change so that the loop will exit at some point in time.

Example: The following code segment creates directories dir0, dir1,.., dir10000

```
I=0                    # set I to "0" (STRING)
while [ $I != 10000 ]  # compare as strings; OR while [ $I \< 1000 ] as numbers
  do
    echo $I            # echo current $I value
    mkdir dir$I        # make directories dir0, dir1, etc
    I=$(expr $I + 1)   # use expr to inc I (value) by 1
  done
```

10.9.4   until-do Statement

This is similar to the do-until statement in C.

```
until [ $ANS = "give up" ]
  do
      echo -n "enter your answer : "
      read ANS
  done
```

10.9.5   case Statement

This is similar to the case statement in C also, but it is rarely used in sh programming.

```
case $variable in
     pattern1)    commands;;   # note the double semicolons ;;
     pattern2)    command;;
     patternN)    command;;
esac
```

10.9.6   continue and break Statements

As in C, **continue** restarts the next iteration of the nearest loop and **break** exits the nearest loop. They work exactly the same as in C

10.10   I/O Redirection

When entering a sh command, we may instruct sh to redirect I/O to files other than the default stdin, stdout, sterr. I/O redirections have the following form and meaning:

> file   stdout goes to file, which will be created if non-existing.
>> file   stdout append to file
< file   use file as stdin; file must exist and have r permission.
<< word   take inputs from "here" file until a line containing only "word"

10.11   Here Documents

An output command can be instructed to take inputs from stdin, echo them to stdout until a prearranged keyword is encountered.

Examples:

```
echo << END
    # keep enter and echo lines until a line with only
END
cat << DONE
    # keep enter and echo lines until
DONE
```

These are commonly known as **here documents**. They are typically used in a sh script to generate long blocks of descriptive text without echoing each line individually.

10.12 sh Functions

sh functions are defined as

```
func()
{
   # function code
}
```

Since sh executes commands line by line, all functions in a sh script must be defined **before** any executable statements. Unlike C, there is no way to declare function prototypes in sh scripts. Sh functions are invoked in exactly the same way as executing a sh script file. The sh statement

```
func s1 s2 ... sn
```

calls the sh func, passing as parameters (strings) s1 to sn. Inside the called function, the parameters are referenced as $0, $1 to $n. As usual, $0 is the function name, and $1 to $n are position parameters corresponding to the command-line parameters. When a function execution finishes, $? is its exit status, which is 0 for success and nonzero otherwise. The value of $? can be changed by the explicit return value of a function. However, in order to test $? of the last execution, it must be assigned to a variable and test that variable instead.

Examples of sh functions:

```
#! /bin/bash
testFile()    # test whether $1 is a REG file
{
  if [ -f $1 ]; then
     echo $1 is a REG file
  else
     echo $1 is NOT a REG file
}
testDir()     # test whether $1 is a DIR
{
  if [ -d $1 ]; then
     echo $1 is a DIR
  else
     echo $1 is NOT a DIR
}
echo entry point here # entry point of the program
for A in $*       # for A in command-line parameter list
  do
    testFile $A    # call testFile on each command-line param
    testDir  $A    # call testDir  on each command-line param
  done
```

Exercise: In the following sh program

```
testFile()   # test whether $1 is a REG file; return 0 if yes, 1 if not
{
 if [ -f $1 ]; then
    return 0
 else
    return 1
}
for A in f1 D2      # assume f1 is a REG file, D2 is a DIRectory
 do
    testFile $A     # testFile return $?=0 or 1
    if [ $? = 0 ]; then
       echo $A is a REG file
    else
       echo $A is not a REG file
    fi
 done
```

The result is always "$A is a REG file" even if $A is a directory. Explain why?

Modify the program code to make it work properly.

10.13 Wild Cards in sh

Star Wildcard: The most useful wildcard in sh is the *, which expands to all files in the current directory.

Examples
   file * :   list information of all files in the current directory.
   ls *.c :   list all files ends with .c in the current directory.

? Wildcard: inquires chars in a file name

Examples
   file ??? :   all files names with exactly 3 chars
   ls *.?? :   all file names with 2 chars following a dot.

[ ] Wildcard : Inquire about chars within a pair of [ ] in filenames.

Examples
   file *[ab]* :   all file names containing the chars a or b
   ls *[xyz]* :   list all file names containing x or y or z
   ls *[a-m]* :   list all file names containing chars in the range of a to m

10.14 Command Grouping

In sh scripts, commands can be grouped together by either { } or ( ).

{ ls; mkdir abc; ls; } : execute the list of commands in { } by the current sh. The only usefulness of
command grouping by { } is to execute them in the same environment, e.g. to redirect I/O for all the
commands in the group.
The more useful command grouping is by () which is executed by a subsh (process).

(cd newdir; ls; A=value; mkdir $A): execute commands in ( ) by a subsh process. The subsh process
may change its working directory without affecting the parent sh. Also, any assigned variables in
the subsh will have no effect when the subsh process terminates.

10.15 eval Statement

```
eval [arg1 arg1 .. argn]
```

eval is a built-in command of sh. It is executed by sh itself without forking a new process. It
concatenates the input argument strings into a single string, evaluates it once, i.e. perform variable
and command substitutions, and present the resulting string for sh to execute.

Example:

```
a="cat big.c | more"
$a         # error: because sh would execute the command cat with big.c, |, more as
                    files. cat would fail on | because it's not a file.
eval $a # OK   : eval substitutes $a with "cat big.c | more" first, then let sh
                    execute the resulting command line cat big.c | more.
```

Example: Assume

```
A='$B';  B='abc*';  C=newdir;  CWD=/root;  /root/newdir is a DIR
```

For the command line

```
cp $A `pwd`/$C   # grave quoted command pwd
```

sh evaluates the command line in the following steps before executing it.
(1). **Parameter substation:** Scan the command line, substitute any $x with its value but do it only
once, i.e. no substitutions again for any resulting $ symbols. The line becomes

```
cp $B `pwd`/newdir
```

(2). **Command substitution:** perform `pwd` with substitution. Sh will execute the resulting line

```
cp $B /root/newdir
```

This will result in an error if the current directory does not have any file named $B. However, if we change the original command line to

```
eval cp $A $(pwd)/$C
```

sh will evaluate the command line first before executing it. After eval, the line becomes

```
cp abc* /root/newdir
```

(3). **Wildcard expansion:** When sh executes the line, it expands **new*** to file names that begin with **abc**. This will copy all file names beginning with **abc** to the target directory.

It should be noted that we can always achieve the same effect of eval manually with a few additional statements. Using eval saves a few substitution statements but it may also makes the code hard to understand. Therefore, any unnecessary use of eval should be avoided.

10.16 Debugging sh Scripts

A sh script can be run by a sub sh with the –x option for debugging, as in

```
bash -x mysh
```

The sub sh will show each sh command to be executed, including variable and command substitutions, before executing the command. It allows the user to trace command executions. In case of error, sh will stop at the error line and show the error message.

10.17 Applications of sh scripts

sh scripts are most often used to perform routine work that involves lengthy sequence of commands. We cite some examples where sh scripts are found to be very useful.

Example 1: Most users have the experience of installing Linux to their computers. The Linux installing packages are written in sh scripts. During the installing process, it can interact with the user, find out available hard disks on the users computer, partition and format the disk partitions, download or extract files from the installation media and install the files to their directories until the installation process completes. Attempting to install Linux manually would be very tedious and almost impossible.

Example 2: When a user login to a Linux system, the login process executes a series of sh scripts,

```
.login,  .profile,  .bashrc, etc.
```

to configure the execution environment of the user process automatically. Again, it would be impractical to do all these steps manually.

Example 3: Instead of using Makefiles, simple compile-link tasks can be done by sh scripts containing the compile and link commands. The following shows a sh script which generates a MTX operating system kernel image and user mode command programs on a virtual disk named VFD (Wang 2015).

```
#---------- mk script of the MTX OS -------------
VFD=mtximage
# generate MTX kernel image file
as86 -o ts.o ts.s          # assemble .s file
bcc  -c -ansi t.c          # compile .c files
ld86 -d -o mtx ts.o t.o OBJ/*.o mtxlib 2> /dev/null
# write MTX kernel image to /boot directory of VFD
mount -o loop $VFD /mnt
cp mtx /mnt/boot           # mtx kernel image in /boot directory
umount /mnt
# generate User mode command binaries in /bin of VFD
(cd USER; mkallu)          # command grouping
echo all done
#--------------- end
```

Example 4: Create user accounts for a CS class on a Linux machine. At the author's institution, enrollment in the CS360, Systems Programming, class averages 70 students every semester. It would be too tedious to create all the students accounts on a Linux machine by hand. This is done by the following steps using sh scripts.

(1). The Linux command

```
sudo useradd -m -k DIR -p PASSWORD -s /bin/bash LOGIN
```

creates a new user account with login name LOGIN and password PASSWORD. It creates a user home directory /home/LOGIN, which is populated with files in the -k DIR directory. It creates a line in /etc/passwd for the new user account and adds a line in /etc/shadow for the encrypted PASSWORD. However, the PASSWORD used in the useradd command must be encrypted password, not the original password string. Converting password string to encrypted form can be done by the **crypt** library function. The following C program enc.c also converts a PASS-WORD string into encrypted form.

```
/******* enc.c file *********/
#define _XOPEN_SOURCE
#include <stdio.h>
#include <unistd.h>
int main(int argc, char *argv[ ])
{
  printf("%s\n", crypt(argv[1], "$1$"));
}
# gcc -o enc -lcrypt enc.c   # generate the enc file
```

(2). Assume that roster.txt is a class roster file containing lines of students ID and name

```
ID name                    # name string in lowercase
```

(3). Run the following sh script **mkuser < roster.txt**

```
# --------------- mkuser sh script file --------------------
#! /bin/bash
while read LINE        # read a line of roster file
do
  I=0
  for N in $LINE       # extract ID as NAME0, name as NAME1
  do
    eval NAME$I=$N      # set NAME0, NAME1, etc.
    I=$(expr $I + 1)    # inc I by 1
  done
  echo $NAME0 $NAME1    # echo ID and name
  useradd -m -k h -p $(./enc $NAME0) -s /bin/bash $NAME1
done
```

(4). User home DIR contents: Every user's home directory, /home/name, can be populated with a set of default DIRs and files. For the CS360 class, every user home directory is populated with a public_html directory containing an index.html file as the user's initial Web page for the user to practice Web programming later.

10.18 Programming Project: Recursive File Copy by sh Script

The programming project is for the reader to use most sh facilities to write a meaningful and useful program in sh script. The requirement is to write a sh script

```
myrcp f1 f. .... fn-1 fn
```

which copies f1, f2, .. fn-1 to fn, where each fi may be either a REG/LNK file or a DIR. For simplicity, exclude special files, which are I/O devices. The myrcp program should behave exactly the same as Linux's command **cp –r** command. The following is a brief analysis of the various cases of the program requirements.

(1). n<2: show usage and exit
(2). n>2: fn must be an existing DIR.
(3). n=2: copy file to file or file to DIR or DIR1 to DIR2
(4). Never copy a file or DIR to itself. Also, do not copy if DIR2 is a descendant of DIR1

The above case analysis is incomplete. The reader must complete the case analysis and formulate an algorithm before attempting to write any code.

Hint and Helps: for the command line **myrcp f1 f. .... fn**

```
(1). echo n = $#                              # n = value of n
(2). last = \${$#}; eval echo last = $last    # last = fn
(3). for NAME in $*
        do
          echo $NAME                          # show f1 to fn
        done
(4). Implement the following functions
        cpf2f(): copy $1 to $2 as files, handle symbolic links
        cpf2d(): copy file $1 into an existing DIR $2 as $2/$(basename $1)
        cod2d(): recursively copy DIR $1 to DIR $2
```

```
# Sample solution of myrcp program

cpf2f()        # called as cpf2f  f1  f2
{
   if [ ! -e $1 ]; then
      echo no such source file $1
      return 1
   fi
   if [ $1 -ef  $2 ]; then
      echo "never copy a file to itself"
      return 1
   fi
  if [ -L $1 ]; then
      echo "copying symlink $1"
      link=$(readlink $1)
        ln -s $link $2
        return 0
   fi
   echo "copying $1 to $2"
   cp $1 $2  2> /dev/null
}
cpf2d()        # called as cpf2d file DIR
{
   newfile=$2/$(basename $1)
   cpf2f $1 $newfile
}
cpd2d()        # called as cpd2d dir1 dir2
{
   # reader FINISH cpd2d code
}
# **************** entry point of myrcp ****************
# case analysis;
# for each f1 to fn-1 call cpf2f() or cpf2d() or cpd2d()
```

10.19 Summary

This chapter covers sh programming. It explains sh scripts and different versions of sh. It compares sh scripts with C programs and points out the difference between interpreted and compiled languages. It shows how to write sh scripts in detail. These include sh variables, sh statements, sh built-in commands, regular system commands and command substitution. Then it explains sh control statements, which include test conditions, for loop, while loop, do-until loop, case statements, and it demonstrates their usage by examples. It shows how to write sh functions and invoke sh functions with parameters. It also shows the wide range of applications of sh scripts by examples. These include the installation, initialization and administration of the Linux system.

The programming project is for the reader to write a sh scripts which recursively copies files and directories. The project is organized in a hierarchy of three sh functions; cpf2f() which copies file to file, cpf2d() which copies file into a directory and cpd2d() which recursively copies directories.

References

Bourne, S.R., The Unix System, Addison-Wesley, 1982
Forouzan, B.A., Gilberg, R.F., Unix and Shell Programming, Brooks/Cole, 2003
Wang, K.C., Design and Implementation of the MTX Operating System, Springer International Publishing AG, 2015

EXT2 File System

11

Abstract

This chapter covers EXT2 file system. The goal of this chapter is to lead the reader to implement a complete EXT2 file system that is totally Linux compatible. The premise is that if the reader understands one file system well, it should be easy to adapt to any other file systems. It first describes the historic role of EXT2 file system in Linux and the current status of EXT3/EXT4 file systems. It uses programming examples to show the various EXT2 data structures and how to traverse the EXT2 files system tree. Then it shows how to implement an EXT2 file system which supports all file operations as in the Linux kernel. It shows how to build a base file system by mount_root from a virtual disk. Then it divides the file system implementation into 3 levels. Level-1 expands the base file system to implement the file system tree. Level-2 implements read/write operations of file contents. Level-3 implements mount/umount of file systems and file protection. In each level, it describes the algorithms of the file system functions and demonstrates their implementations by programming examples. Each level is cumulated by a programming project. The final project is to integrate all the programming examples and exercises into a fully functional file system.

11.1 EXT2 File System

For many years, Linux used EXT2 (Card et al. 1995) as the default file system. EXT3 (ETX3, 2014) is an extension of EXT2. The main addition in EXT3 is a journal file, which records changes made to the file system in a journal log. The log allows for quicker recovery from errors in case of a file system crash. An EXT3 file system with no error is identical to an EXT2 file system. The newest extension of EXT3 is EXT4 (Cao et al. 2007). The major change in EXT4 is in the allocation of disk blocks. In EXT4, block numbers are 48 bits. Instead of discrete disk blocks, EXT4 allocates contiguous ranges of disk blocks, called extents. Other than these minor changes, the file system structure and file operations remain the same. The purpose of this book is to teach the principles of file systems. Large file storage capacity is not the primary goal. Principles of file system design and implementation, with an emphasis on simplicity and compatibility with Linux, are the major focal points. For these reasons, we shall use ETX2 as the file system. The goal of this chapter is to lead the reader to implement a complete EXT2

© Springer International Publishing AG, part of Springer Nature 2018
K. C. Wang, *Systems Programming in Unix/Linux*, https://doi.org/10.1007/978-3-319-92429-8_11

file system that is totally Linux compatible. The premise is that if the reader understands one file system well, it should be relatively easy to adapt to any other file systems.

11.2   EXT2 File System Data Structures

11.2.1   Create Virtual Disk by mkfs

Under Linux, the command

```
mke2fs [-b blksize -N ninodes] device nblocks
```

creates an EXT2 file system on a device with nblocks blocks of blksize bytes per block and ninodes inodes. The device can be either a real device or a virtual disk file. If blksize is not specified, the default block size is 1 KB. If ninoides is not specified, mke2fs will compute a default ninodes number based on nblocks. The resulting EXT2 file system is ready for use in Linux. As a specific example, the following commands

```
dd if=/dev/zero of=vdisk bs=1024 count=1440
mke2fs vdisk 1440
```

creates an EXT2 files system on a virtual disk file named vdisk with 1440 blocks of 1 KB block size.

11.2.2   Virtual Disk Layout

The layout of such an EXT2 file system is shown in Fig. 11.1.

To begin with, we shall assume this basic file system layout first. Whenever appropriate, we point out the variations, including those in large EXT2/3 file systems on hard disks. The following briefly explains the contents of the disk blocks.

Block#0: Boot Block: B0 is the boot block, which is not used by the file system. It is used to contain a booter program for booting up an operating system from the disk.

11.2.3   Superblock

Block#1: Superblock: (at byte offset 1024 in hard disk partitions): B1 is the superblock, which contains information about the entire file system. Some of the important fields of the superblock structure are shown below.

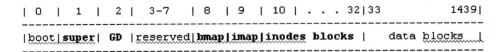

```
| 0   |  1  |  2  |  3-7   |  8  |  9  | 10  | . . . 32|33                1439|
-----------------------------------------------------------------------------
|boot|super|  GD  |reserved|bmap|imap|inodes blocks  |    data blocks       |
-----------------------------------------------------------------------------
```

Fig. 11.1 Simple EXT2 file system layout

```
struct ext2_super_block {
    u32   s_inodes_count;          /* Inodes count */
    u32   s_blocks_count;          /* Blocks count */
    u32   s_r_blocks_count;        /* Reserved blocks count */
    u32   s_free_blocks_count;     /* Free blocks count */
    u32   s_free_inodes_count;     /* Free inodes count */
    u32   s_first_data_block;      /* First Data Block */
    u32   s_log_block_size;        /* Block size */
    u32   s_log_cluster_size;      /* Allocation cluster size */
    u32   s_blocks_per_group;      /* # Blocks per group */
    u32   s_clusters_per_group;    /* # Fragments per group */
    u32   s_inodes_per_group;      /* # Inodes per group */
    u32   s_mtime;                 /* Mount time */
    u32   s_wtime;                 /* Write time */
    u16   s_mnt_count;             /* Mount count */
    s16   s_max_mnt_count;         /* Maximal mount count */
    u16   s_magic;                 /* Magic signature */
    // more non-essential fields
    u16   s_inode_size;            /* size of inode structure */
}
```

The meanings of most superblock fields are obvious. Only a few fields deserve more explanation.

s_first_data_block = 0 for 4KB block size and 1 for 1KB block size. It is used to determine the start block of group descriptors, which is s_first_data_block + 1.

s_log_block_size determines the file block size, which is 1KB*(2**s_log_block_size), e.g.. 0 for 1KB block size, 1 for 2KB block size and 2 for 4KB block size, etc. The most often used block size is 1KB for small file systems and 4KB for large file systems.

s_mnt_count= number of times the file system has been mounted. When the mount count reaches the **max_mnt_count**, a fsck session is forced to check the file system for consistency.

s_magic is the magic number which identifies the file system type. For EXT2/3/4 files systems, the magic number is **0xEF53**.

11.2.4 Group Descriptors

Block#2: Group Descriptor Block (s_first_data_block+1 on hard disk): EXT2 divides disk blocks into groups. Each group contains 8192 (32 K on HD) blocks. Each group is described by a group descriptor structure.

```
struct ext2_group_desc {
    u32   bg_block_bitmap;      // Bmap block number
    u32   bg_inode_bitmap;      // Imap block number
    u32   bg_inode_table;       // Inodes begin block number
    u16   bg_free_blocks_count; // THESE are OBVIOUS
    u16   bg_free_inodes_count;
    u16   bg_used_dirs_count;
    u16   bg_pad;               // ignore these
    u32   bg_reserved[3];
};
```

Since a virtual floppy disk (FD) has only 1440 blocks, B2 contains only 1 group descriptor. The rest are 0's. On hard disks with a large number of groups, group descriptors may span many blocks. The most important fields in a group descriptor are bg_block_bitmap, bg_inode_bitmap and bg_inode_table, which point to the group's blocks bitmap, inodes bitmap and inodes start block, respectively. For the Linux formatted EXT2 file system, blocks 3 to 7 are reserved. So bmap=8, imap=9 and inode_table = 10.

11.2.5 Block and Inode Bitmaps

Block#8: Block Bitmap (Bmap): (bg_block_bitmap): A bitmap is a sequence of bits used to represent some kind of items, e.g. disk blocks or inodes. A bitmap is used to allocate and deallocate items. In a bitmap, a 0 bit means the corresponding item is FREE, and a 1 bit means the corresponding item is IN_USE. A FD has 1440 blocks but block#0 is not used by the file system. So the Bmap has only 1439 valid bits. Invalid bits are treated as IN_USE and set to 1's.

Block#9: Inode Bitmap (Imap): (bg_inode_bitmap): An **inode** is a data structure used to represent a file. An EXT2 file system is created with a finite number of inodes. The status of each inode is represented by a bit in the Imap in B9. In an EXT2 FS, the first 10 inodes are reserved. So the Imap of an empty EXT2 FS starts with ten 1's, followed by 0's. Invalid bits are again set to 1's.

11.2.6 Inodes

Block#10: Inodes (begin) Block: (bg_inode_table): Every file is represented by a unique inode structure of 128 (256 in EXT4) bytes. The essential inode fields are listed below.

```
struct ext2_inode {
  u16  i_mode;           // 16 bits = |tttt|ugs|rwx|rwx|rwx|
  u16  i_uid;            // owner uid
  u32  i_size;           // file size in bytes
  u32  i_atime;          // time fields in seconds
  u32  i_ctime;          // since 00:00:00,1-1-1970
  u32  i_mtime;
  u32  i_dtime;
  u16  i_gid;            // group ID
  u16  i_links_count;    // hard-link count
  u32  i_blocks;         // number of 512-byte sectors
  u32  i_flags;          // IGNORE
  u32  i_reserved1;      // IGNORE
  u32  i_block[15];      // See details below
  u32  i_pad[7];         // for inode size = 128 bytes
}
```

In the inode structure, i_mode is a u16 or 2-byte unsigned integer.

```
              |  4  | 3 |   9      |
i_mode =  |tttt|ugs|rwxrwxrwx|
```

In the i_mode field, the leading 4 bits specify the file type, e.g. tttt=1000 for REG file, 0100 for DIR, etc. The next 3 bits ugs indicate the file's special usage. The last 9 bits are the rwx permission bits for file protection.

The i_size field is the file size in bytes. The various time fields are number of seconds elapsed since 0 hr 0 min, 0 s of January 1, 1970. So each time filed is a very large unsigned integer. They can be converted to calendar form by the library function

```
char *ctime(&time_field)
```

which takes a pointer to a time field and returns a string in calendar form. For example,

```
printf("%s", ctime(&inode.i_atime); // note: pass & of time field prints i_atime
in calendar form.
```

The i_block[15] array contains pointers to disk blocks of a file, which are

Direct blocks:	i_block[0] to i_block[11], which point to direct disk blocks.
Indirect blocks:	i_block[12] points to a disk block, which contains 256 (for 1KB BLKSIZE) block numbers, each points to a disk block.
Double Indirect blocks:	i_block[13] points to a block, which points to 256 blocks, each of which points to 256 disk blocks.
Triple Indirect blocks:	i_block[14] is the triple-indirect block. We may ignore this for "small" EXT2 file systems.

The inode size (128 or 256) is designed to divides block size (1 KB or 4 KB) evenly, so that every inode block contains an integral number of inodes. In the simple EXT2 file system, the number of inodes is (a Linux default) 184. The number of inodes blocks is equal to $184/8 = 23$. So the inodes blocks include B10 to B32. Each inode has a unique **inode number**, which is the inode's position in the inode blocks plus 1. Note that inode positions count from 0, but inode numbers count from 1. A 0 inode number means no inode. The root directory's inode number is 2. Similarly, disk block numbers also count from 1 since block 0 is never used by a file system. A zero block number means no disk block.

11.2.7   Data Blocks

Data Blocks Immediately after the inodes blocks are data blocks for file storage. Assuming 184 inodes, the first real data block is B33, which is i_block[0] of the root directory /.

11.2.8   Directory Entries

EXT2 Directory Entries A directory contains dir_entry structures, which is

```
struct ext2_dir_entry_2{
    u32 inode;              // inode number; count from 1, NOT 0
    u16 rec_len;           // this entry's length in bytes
```

```
    u8   name_len;              // name length in bytes
    u8   file_type;             // not used
    char name[EXT2_NAME_LEN]; // name: 1-255 chars, no ending NULL
};
```

The dir_entry is an open-ended structure. The name field contains 1 to 255 chars without a terminating NULL. So the dir_entry's rec_len also varies.

11.3   Mailman's Algorithm

In computer systems, a problem which arises very often is as follows. A city has M blocks, numbered 0 to M-1. Each block has N houses, numbered 0 to N-1. Each house has a unique block address, denoted by (block, house), where $0 <= block < M, 0 <= house < N$. An alien from outer space may be unfamiliar with the block addressing scheme on Earth and prefers to address the houses linearly as 0,1,..N-1,N, N + 1 ....., etc. Given a block address BA = (block, house), how to convert it to a linear address LA, and vice versa? If everything counts from 0, the conversion is very simple.

```
    Linear_address LA = N*block + house;
    Block_address  BA = (LA / N, LA % N);
```

Note that the conversion is valid only if everything counts from 0. If some of the items do not count from 0, they can not be used in the conversion formula directly. The reader may try to figure out how to handle such cases in general. For ease of reference, we shall refer to the conversion method as the Mailman's algorithm. The following shows applications of the Mailman's algorithm.

11.3.1   Test-Set-Clear Bits in C

(1) Test, Set and Clear bits in C: In standard C programs, the smallest addressable unit is a char or byte. It is often necessary to manipulate bits in a bitmap, which is a sequence of bits. Consider char buf [1024], which has 1024 bytes, denoted by buf[i], i = 0, 1,...., 1023. It also has 8192 bits numbered 0,1,2,....8191. Given a bit number BIT, e.g. 1234, which byte i contains the bit, and which bit j is it in that byte? Solution:

```
    i = BIT / 8;   j = BIT % 8;   // 8 = number of bits in a byte.
```

This allows us to combine the Mailman's algorithm with bit masking to do the following bit operations in C.

```
    .TST a bit for 1 or 0 :  if (buf[i] &   (1 << j))
    .SET a bit to 1       :      buf[i] |=  (1 << j);
    .CLR a bit to 0       :      buf[i] &= ~(1 << j);
```

It is noted that some C compilers allow specifying bits in a structure, as in.

```
struct bits{
   unsigned int bit0      :  1;  // bit0 field is a single bit
   unsigned int bit123    :  3;  // bit123 field is a range of 3 bits
   unsigned int otherbits : 27;  // other bits field has 27 bits
   unsigned int bit31     :  1;  // bit31 is the highest bit
}var;
```

The structure defines var. as an unsigned 32-bit integer with individual bits or ranges of bits. Then, var.bit0 = 0; assigns 1 to bit 0, and var.bit123 = 5; assigns 101 to bits 1 to 3, etc. However, the generated code still relies on the Mailman's algorithm and bit masking to access the individual bits. The Mailman's algorithm allows us to manipulate bits in a bitmap directly without defining complex C structures.

11.3.2   Convert INODE Number to INODE on Disk

(2) In an EXT2 file system, each file has a unique INODE structure. On the file system disk, inodes begin in the **inode_table** block. Each disk block contains

```
INODES_PER_BLOCK = BLOCK_SIZE/sizeof(INODE)
```

inodes. Each inode has a unique inode number, ino = 1, 2, ..., counted linearly from 1. Given an ino, e.g. 1234, determine which disk block contains the inode and which inode is it in that block? We need to know the disk block number because read/write a real disk is by blocks. Solution:

```
block = (ino - 1)  /  INODES_PER_BLOCK + inode_table;
inode = (ino - 1) % INODES_PER_BLOCK;
```

Similarly, converting double and triple indirect logical block numbers to physical block numbers in an EXT2 file system also depends on the Mailman's algorithm.

(3) Convert linear disk block number to CHS = (cylinder, head, sector) format: Floppy disk and old hard disk use CHS addressing but file systems always use linear block addressing. The algorithm can be used to convert a disk block number to CHS when calling BIOS INT13.

11.4   Programming Examples

In this section, we shall show how to access and display the contents of EXT2 file systems by example programs. In order to compile and run these programs, the system must have the **ext2fs.h** header file installed, which defines the data structures of EXT2/3/4 file systems. Ubuntu Linux user may get and install the ext2fs development package by

```
sudo apt-get install ext2fs-dev
```

11.4.1   Display Superblock

The following C program displays the superblock of an EXT2 file system. The basic technique is as follows.

(1) Open vdisk for READ: int fd = open("vdisk", O_RDONLY);

(2) Read the superblock (block #1 or 1 KB at offset 1024) into a char buf[1024].

```
char buf[1024];
lseek(fd, 1024, SEEK_SET); // seek to byte offset 1024
int n = read(fd, buf, 1024);
```

(3) Let a struct ext2_super_block *sp point to buf[ ]. Then use sp- > field to access the various fields of the superblock structure.

```
struct ext2_super_block *sp = (struct ext2_super_block *)buf;
printf("s_magic = %x\n", sp->s_magic)              // print s_magic
printf("s_inodes_count = %d\n", sp->s_inodes_count); // print s_inodes_
count
etc.
```

The same technique is also applicable to any other data structures in a real or virtual disk.

Example 11.1 superblock.c program: display superblock information of an EXT2 file system.

```
/*********** superblock.c program ************/
#include <stdio.h>
#include <stdlib.h>
#include <fcntl.h>
#include <ext2fs/ext2_fs.h>

// typedef u8, u16, u32 SUPER for convenience
typedef unsigned char   u8;
typedef unsigned short u16;
typedef unsigned int   u32;
typedef struct ext2_super_block SUPER;

SUPER *sp;
char buf[1024];
int fd, blksize, inodesize;

int print(char *s, u32 x)
{
  printf("%-30s = %8d\n", s, x);
}
```

```
int super(char *device)
{
  fd = open(device, O_RDONLY);
  if (fd < 0){
    printf("open %sfailed\n", device); exit(1);
  }
  lseek(fd, (long)1024*1, 0);   // block 1 on FD, offset 1024 on HD
  read(fd, buf, 1024);
  sp = (SUPER *)buf;            // as a super block structure

  // check EXT2 FS magic number:
  printf("%-30s = %8x ", "s_magic", sp->s_magic);
  if (sp->s_magic != 0xEF53){
    printf("NOT an EXT2 FS\n");
    exit(2);
  }
  printf("EXT2 FS OK\n");
  print("s_inodes_count",     sp->s_inodes_count);
  print("s_blocks_count",     sp->s_blocks_count);
  print("s_r_blocks_count",   sp->s_r_blocks_count);
  print("s_free_inodes_count", sp->s_free_inodes_count);
  print("s_free_blocks_count", sp->s_free_blocks_count);
  print("s_first_data_block", sp->s_first_data_block);
  print("s_log_block_size",   sp->s_log_block_size);
  print("s_blocks_per_group", sp->s_blocks_per_group);
  print("s_inodes_per_group", sp->s_inodes_per_group);
  print("s_mnt_count",        sp->s_mnt_count);
  print("s_max_mnt_count",    sp->s_max_mnt_count);
  printf("%-30s = %8x\n", "s_magic", sp->s_magic);
  printf("s_mtime = %s", ctime(&sp->s_mtime));
  printf("s_wtime = %s", ctime(&sp->s_wtime));
  blksize = 1024 * (1 << sp->s_log_block_size);
  printf("block size = %d\n", blksize);
  printf("inode size = %d\n", sp->s_inode_size);
}

char *device = "mydisk";       // default device name
int main(int argc, char *argv[])
{
  if (argc>1)
    device = argv[1];
  super(device);
}
```

Figure 11.2 shows the outputs of running the superblock.c program.

```
s_magic                =      ef53  EXT2 FS OK
s_inodes_count         =       184
s_blocks_count         =      1440
s__r_blocks_count      =        72
s_free_inodes_count    =       173
s_free_blocks_count    =      1393
s_first_data_blcok     =         1
s_log_block_size       =         0
s_blocks_per_group     =      8192
s_inodes_per_group     =       184
s_mnt_count            =         1
s_max_mnt_count        =        -1
s_magic                =      ef53
s_mtime = Sun Oct  8 14:22:03 2017
s_wtime = Sun Oct  8 14:22:07 2017
block size = 1024
inode size = 128       _
```

Fig. 11.2 Superblock of Ext2 file system

Exercise 11.1 Write a C program to display the group descriptor of an EXT2 file system on a device. (See Problem 1).

11.4.2 Display Bitmaps

The program in Example 11.2 displays the inodes bitmap (imap) in HEX.

Example 11.2 imap.c program: display inodes bitmap of an EXT2 file system.

```c
/*************** imap.c program *************/
#include <stdio.h>
#include <stdlib.h>
#include <fcntl.h>
#include <ext2fs/ext2_fs.h>
typedef struct ext2_super_block SUPER;
typedef struct ext2_group_desc  GD;
#define BLKSIZE 1024
SUPER *sp;
GD    *gp;
char buf[BLKSIZE];
int fd;

// get_block() reads a disk block into a buf[ ]
int get_block(int fd, int blk, char *buf)
{
  lseek(fd, (long)blk*BLKSIZE, SEEK_SET);
  return read(fd, buf, BLKSIZE);
}

int imap(char *device)
{
  int i, ninodes, blksize, imapblk;
```

```
  fd = open(dev, O_RDONLY);
  if (fd < 0){printf("open %s failed\n", device); exit(1);}
  get_block(fd, 1, buf);              // get superblock
  sp = (SUPER *)buf;
  // check magic number to ensure it's an EXT2 FS
  ninodes = sp->s_inodes_count;    // get inodes_count
  printf("ninodes = %d\n", ninodes);
  get_block(fd, 2, buf);              // get group descriptor
  gp = (GD *)buf;
  imapblk = gp->bg_inode_bitmap;  // get imap block number
  printf("imapblk = %d\n", imapblk);
  get_block(fd, imapblk, buf);     // get imap block into buf[ ]
  for (i=0; i<=nidoes/8; i++){     // print each byte in HEX
      printf("%02x ", (u8)buf[i]);
  }
  printf("\n");
}

char * dev="mydisk";               // default device
int main(int argc, char *argv[ ] )
{
  if (argc>1) dev = argv[1];
  imap(dev);
}
```

The program prints each byte of the inodes bitmap as 2 HEX digits. The outputs look like the following.

```
|<-------------- niodes = 184 bits (23 bytes)--------------------|
ff 07 00 00 00 00 00 00 00 00 00 00 00 00 00 00 00 00 00 00 00 00 ff
```

In the imap, bits are stored linearly from low to high address. The first 16 bits (from low to high) are b'11111111 11100000', but they are printed as ff 07 in HEX, which is not very informative since the bits in each byte are printed in reverse order, i.e. from high to low address.

Exercise 11.2 Modify the imap.c program to print the inodes bitmap in char map form, i.e. for each bit, print a '0' if the bit is 0, print a '1' if the bit is 1. (see Problem 2).

The outputs of the modified program should look like Fig. 11.3, in which each char represents a bit in the imap.

Exercise 11.3 Write a C program to display the blocks bitmap of an Ext2 file system, also in char map form.

```
ninodes = 184  imapblk = 9
11111111 11100000 00000000 00000000 00000000 00000000 00000000 00000000
00000000 00000000 00000000 00000000 00000000 00000000 00000000 00000000
00000000 00000000 00000000 00000000 00000000 00000000 00000000 11111111
```

Fig. 11.3 Inodes Bitmap of an EXT2 file system

11.4.3   Display Root Inode

In an EXT2 file system, the number 2 (count from 1) inode is the inode of the root directory /. If we read the root inode into memory, we should be able to display its various fields such as mode, uid, gid, file size, time fields, hard links count and data block numbers, etc. The program in Example 11.3 displays the INDOE information of the root directory of an EXT2 file system.

Example 11.3 inode.c program: display root inode information of an EXT2 file system.

```
/*********** inode.c file **********/
#include <stdio.h>
#include <stdlib.h>
#include <fcntl.h>
#include <ext2fs/ext2_fs.h>
#define BLKSIZE 1024
typedef struct ext2_group_desc  GD;
typedef struct ext2_super_block SUPER;
typedef struct ext2_inode       INODE;
typedef struct ext2_dir_entry_2 DIR;
SUPER *sp;
GD    *gp;
INODE *ip;
DIR   *dp;
char buf[BLKSIZE];
int fd, firstdata, inodesize, blksize, iblock;
char *dev = "mydisk";

int get_block(int fd, int blk, char *buf)
{
  lseek(fd, blk*BLKSIZE, SEEK_SET);
  return read(fd, buf, BLKSIZE);
}

int inode(char *dev)
{
  int i;
  fd = open(dev, O_RDONLY);
  if (fd < 0){
    printf("open failed\n"); exit(1);
  }
  /*************************************
   same code as before to check EXT2 FS
  *************************************/
  get_block(fd, 2, buf);   // get group descriptor
  gp = (GD *)buf;
  printf("bmap_block=%d imap_block=%d inodes_table=%d ",
         gp->bg_block_bitmap,
         gp->bg_inode_bitmap,
         gp->bg_inode_table,
  iblock = gp->bg_inode_table;
```

```
   printf("---- root inode information ----\n");
   get_block(fd, iblock, buf);
   ip = (INODE *)buf;
   ip++;    // ip point at #2 INODE
   printf("mode = %4x ", ip->i_mode);
   printf("uid = %d  gid = %d\n", ip->i_uid, ip->i_gid);
   printf("size = %d\n", ip->i_size);
   printf("ctime = %s", ctime(&ip->i_ctime));
   printf("links = %d\n", ip->i_links_count);
   for (i=0; i<15; i++){       // print disk block numbers
     if (ip->i_block[i])       // print non-zero blocks only
        printf("i_block[%d] = %d\n", i, ip->i_block[i]);
   }
}


int main(int argc, char *argv[ ])
{
   if (argc>1) dev = argv[1];
   inode(dev);
}
```

Figure 11.4 shows the root inode of an EXT2 file system.

In Fig. 11.4, i_mode = 0x41ed or b'0100 0001 1110 1101' in binary. The first 4 bits 0100 is the file type (DIRectory). The next 3 bits 000 = ugs are all 0's, meaning the file has no special usage, e.g. it is not a setuid program. The last 9 bits can be divided into 3 groups 111,101,101, which are the rwx permission bits of the file's owner, same group as owner and others. For regular files, x bit = 1 means the file is executable. For directories, x bit = 1 means access to (i.e. cd into) the directory is allowed; a 0 x bit means no access to the directory.

11.4.4 Display Directory Entries

Each data block of a directory INODE contains dir_entries, which are.

```
   struct ext2_dir_entry_2 {
      u32 inode;                // inode number; count from 1, NOT 0
      u16 rec_len;              // this entry's length in bytes
      u8  name_len;             // name length in bytes
      u8  file_type;            // not used
      char name[EXT2_NAME_LEN]; // name: 1-255 chars, no ending NULL
   };
```

```
        bmap = 8 imap = 9 iblock = 10
        ---- root inode information ----
        mode = 41ed uid = 0  gid = 0
        size = 1024
        ctime = Mon Oct  9 16:11:44 2017
        links = 3
        i_block[0] = 33
```

Fig. 11.4 Root Inode of EXT2 file system

The contents of each data block of a directory has the form

```
[inode rec_len name_len NAME] [inode rec_len name_len NAME] ......
```

where NAME is a sequence of name_len chars without a terminating NULL byte. Each dir_entry has a record length rec_len. The rec_len of the last entry in a block covers the remaining block length, i.e. from where the entry begins to the end of block. The following algorithm shows how to step through the dir_entries in a directory data block.

```
/******** Algorithm to step through entries in a DIR data block ********/
struct ext2_dir_entry_2 *dp;           // dir_entry pointer
char *cp;                              // char pointer
int blk = a data block (number) of a DIR (e.g. i_block[0]);
char buf[BLKSIZE], temp[256];
get_block(fd, blk, buf);               // get data block into buf[ ]

dp = (struct ext2_dir_entry_2 *)buf;   // as dir_entry
cp = buf;
while(cp < buf + BLKSIZE){
  strncpy(temp, dp->name, dp->name_len); // make name a string
  temp[dp->name_len] = 0;                // ensure NULL at end
  printf("%d %d %d %s\n", dp->inode, dp->rec_len, dp->name_len, temp);
  cp += dp->rec_len;                     // advance cp by rec_len
  dp = (struct ext2_dir_entry_2 *)cp;    // pull dp to next entry
}
```

Exercise 11.4 Write a C program to print the dir_entries of a directory. For simplicity, we may assume a directory INODE has at most 12 direct blocks, i_block[0] to i_block[11]. This assumption is reasonable. With 1 KB block size and an average file name length of 16 chars, a single disk block can contain up to $1024/(8 + 16) = 42$ dir_entries. With 12 disk blocks, a directory can contain more than 500 entries. We may safely assume that no user would put that many files in any directory. For an empty EXT2 file system, the program output should look like Fig. 11.5. (see Problem 4).

```
check ext2 FS : OK
GD info: 8 9 10 1393 173 2
inodes begin block=10
******* root inode info ********
mode=41ed  uid=0  gid=0
size=1024
ctime=Sun Oct  8 14:04:52 2017
links=3
i_block[0]=33
*******************************
inode# rec_len name_len name
  2       12      1     .
  2       12      2     ..
 11     1000     10 _   lost+found
```

Fig. 11.5 Entries of a directory

```
******* root inode info ********
mode=41ed  uid=0  gid=0
size=1024
ctime=Sun Oct  8 17:19:15 2017
links=7
i_block[0]=33
*******************************
inode# rec_len name_len name
   2      12       1    .
   2      12       2    ..
  11      20      10    lost+found
  12      12       1    a
  13      16       8    shortDir
  14      20      12    longNamedDir
  15      28      17    aVeryLongNamedDir
  16      16       7    super.c
  17      16       6    bmap.c
  18      16       6    imap.c
  19     856       5    dir.c
```

Fig. 11.6 List entries of a directory

Exercise 11.5 Mount mydisk under Linux. Create new directories and copy files to the mounted file system, then umount it (See Problem 5). Run the dir.c program on mydisk again to see the outputs, which should look like Fig. 11.6. The reader may verify that the name_len of each entry is the exact number of chars in the name field, and every rec_len is a multiple of 4 (for alignment), which is (8 + name_len) raised to the next multiple of 4, except the last entry, whose rec_len covers the remaining block length.

Exercise 11.6 Given an INODE pointer to a DIRectory inode. Write a

```
int  search(INODE *dir, char *name)
```

function which searches for a dir_entry with a given name. Return its inode number if found, else return 0. (see Problem 6).

11.5 Traverse EXT2 File System Tree

Given an EXT2 file system and the pathname of a file, e.g. /a/b/c, the problem is how to find the file. To find a file amounts to finding its inode. The algorithm is as follows.

11.5.1 Traversal Algorithm

(1) Read in the superblock. Check the magic number s_magic (0xEF53) to verify it's indeed an EXT2 FS.
(2) Read in the group descriptor block (1 + s_first_data_block) to access the group 0 descriptor. From the group descriptor's bg_inode_table entry, find the inodes begin block number, call it the InodesBeginBlock.
(3) Read in InodeBeginBlock to get the inode of /, which is INODE #2.

(4) Tokenize the pathname into component strings and let the number of components be n. For example, if pathname=/a/b/c, the component strings are "a", "b", "c", with n = 3. Denote the components by name[0], name[1], ..,name[n-1].

(5) Start from the root INODE in (3), search for name[0] in its data block(s). For simplicity, we may assume that the number of entries in a DIR is small, so that a DIR inode only has 12 direct data blocks. With this assumption, it suffices to search 12 (non-zero) direct blocks for name[0]. Each data block of a DIR INODE contains dir_entry structures of the form

```
[ino rec_len name_len NAME] [ino rec_len name_len NAME] ......
```

where NAME is a sequence of nlen chars without a terminating NULL. For each data block, read the block into memory and use a dir_entry *dp to point at the loaded data block. Then use name_len to extract NAME as a string and compare it with name[0]. If they do not match, step to the next dir_entry by

```
dp = (dir_entry *)((char *)dp + dp->rec_len);
```

and continue the search. If name[0] exists, we can find its dir_entry and hence its inode number.

(6) Use the inode number, ino, to locate the corresponding INODE. Recall that ino counts from 1. Use Mailman's algorithm to compute the disk block containing the INODE and its offset in that block.

```
blk    = (ino - 1)  /   INODES_PER_BLOCK  + InodesBeginBlock;
offset = (ino - 1) % INODES_PER_BLOCK;
```

Then read in the INODE of /a, from which we can determine whether it's a DIR. If /a is not a DIR, there can't be /a/b, so the search fails. If it's a DIR and there are more components to search, continue for the next component name[1]. The problem now becomes: search for name[1] in the INODE of /a, which is exactly the same as that of Step (5).

(7) Since Steps 5–6 will be repeated n times, it's better to write a search function

```
u32 search(INODE *inodePtr, char *name)
{
    // search for name in the data blocks of current DIR inode
    // if found, return its ino; else return 0
}
```

Then all we have to do is to call search() n times, as sketched below.

```
Assume: n,  name[0],  ...., name[n-1] are globals
INODE *ip points at INODE of /
for (i=0; i<n; i++){
    ino = search(ip, name[i])
    if (!ino){ // can't find name[i], exit;}
    use ino to read in INODE and let ip point to INODE
}
```

If the search loop ends successfully, ip must point at the INODE of pathname. Traversing large EXT2/3 file systems with many groups is similar. The reader may consult Chap. 3 of [Wang, 2015] for details.

11.5.2   Convert Pathname to INODE

Given a device containing an EXT2 file system and a pathname, .e.g. /a/b/c/d, write a C function.

```
INODE *path2inode(int fd, char *pathname)   // assume fd=file descriptor
```

which returns an INODE pointer to the file's inode or 0 if the file in inaccessible (see Problem 7).
     As will be seen shortly, the path2inode() function is the most important function in a file system.

11.5.3   Display INODE Disk Blocks

Write a C program, showblock, which prints all disk block (numbers) of a file (see Problem 8).

11.6   Implementation of EXT2 File System

The objective of this section is to show how to implement a complete file system. First, we show the overall organization of a file system, and the logical steps of the implementation. Next, we present a base file system to help the reader get started. Then we organize the implementation steps as a series of programming projects for the reader to complete. It is believed that such an experience would be beneficial to any computer science student.

11.6.1   File System Organization

Figure 11.7 shows the internal organization of an EXT2 file system. The organization diagram is explained by the labels (1) to (5).

(1) is the PROC structure of the current running process. As in a real system, every file operation is due to the current executing process. Each PROC has a cwd, which points to the in-memory INODE of the PROC's Current Working Directory (CWD). It also has an array of file descriptors, fd[], which point to opened file instances.

(2) is the root pointer of the file system. It points to the in-memory root INODE. When the system starts, one of the devices is chosen as the root device, which must be a valid EXT2 file system. The root INODE (inode #2) of the root device is loaded into memory as the root (/) of the file system. This operation is known as **"mount root file system"**

(3) is an openTable entry. When a process opens a file, an entry of the PROC's fd array points to an openTable, which points to the in-memory INODE of the opened file.

(4) is an in-memory INODE. Whenever a file is needed, its INODE is loaded into a minode slot for reference. Since INODEs are unique, only one copy of each INODE can be in memory at any time. In the minode, (dev, ino) identify where the INODE came from, for writing the INODE back to disk if modified. The refCount field records the number of processes that are using the minode.

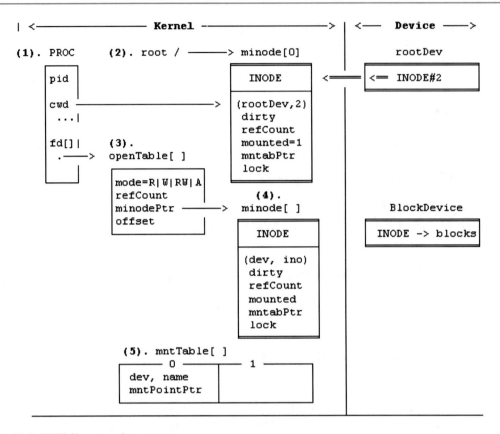

Fig. 11.7 EXT2 file system data structures

The dirty field indicates whether the INODE has been modified. The mounted flag indicates whether the INODE has been mounted on and, if so, the mntabPtr points to the mount table entry of the mounted file system. The lock field is to ensure that an in-memory INODE can only be accessed by one process at a time, e.g. when modifying the INODE or during a read/write operation.
(5) is a table of mounted file systems. For each mounted file system, an entry in the mount table is used to record the mounted file system information, e.g. the mounted file system device number. In the in-memory INODE of the mount point, the mounted flag is turned on and the mntabPtr points to the mount table entry. In the mount table entry, mntPointPtr points back to the in-memory INODE of the mount point. As will be shown later, these doubly-linked pointers allow us to cross mount points when traversing the file system tree. In addition, a mount table entry may also contain other information of the mounted file system, such as values from the superblock, group descriptor, bitmaps and inodes start block, etc. for quick access. If any of these cached items are modified, they must be written back to the device when the device is umounted.

11.6.2   Files System Levels

Implementation of the file system is divided into three levels. Each level deals with a distinct part of the file system. This makes the implementation process modular and easier to understand. In the file system implementation, the FS directory contains files which implement the EXT2 file system. The files are organized as follows.

```
----------------- Common files of FS ----------------------------
  type.h  : EXT2 data structure types
  global.c: global variables of FS
  util.c   : common utility functions: getino(), iget(), iput(), search
  (), etc.
  allocate_deallocate.c : inodes/blocks management functions
```

Level-1 implements the basic file system tree. It contains the following files, which implement the indicated functions.

```
----------------- Level-1 of FS ----------------------------
mkdir_creat.c          : make directory, create regular file
ls_cd_pwd.c            : list directory, change directory, get CWD path
rmdir.c                : remove directory
link_unlink.c          : hard link and unlink files
symlink_readlink.c     : symbolic link files
stat.c                 : return file information
misc1.c                : access, chmod, chown, utime, etc.
----------------------------------------------------------------
```

User command programs which use the level-1 FS functions include

mkdir, creat, mknod, rmdir, link, unlink, symlink, rm, ls, cd and pwd, etc.

Level-2 implements functions for reading/writing file contents.

```
-------------------- Level-2 of FS -----------------------------
open_close_lseek.c    : open file for READ|WRITE|APPEND, close file and lseek
read.c                : read from file descriptor of an opened regular file
write.c               : write to file descriptor of an opened regular file
opendir_readdir.c     : open and read directory
```

Level-3 implements mount, umount file systems and file protection.

```
-------------------- Level-3 of FS -----------------------------
mount_umount.c        : mount/umount file systems
file protection       : access permission checking
file-locking          : lock/unlock files
----------------------------------------------------------------
```

11.7   Base File System

11.7.1   type.h file

This file contains the data structure types of the EXT2 file system, such as superblock, group descriptor, inode and directory entry structures. In addition, it also contains the open file table, mount table, PROC structures and constants of the file system.

```
/***** type.h file for EXT2 FS *****/
#include <stdio.h>
#include <stdlib.h>
#include <fcntl.h>
#include <linux/ext2_fs.h>
#include <libgen.h>
#include <string.h>
#include <sys/stat.h>
// define shorter TYPES for convenience
typedef struct ext2_group_desc  GD;
typedef struct ext2_super_block SUPER;
typedef struct ext2_inode        INODE;
typedef struct ext2_dir_entry_2 DIR;
#define BLKSIZE        1024

// Block number of EXT2 FS on FD
#define SUPERBLOCK        1
#define GDBLOCK           2
#define ROOT_INODE        2

// Default dir and regular file modes
#define DIR_MODE          0x41ED
#define FILE_MODE         0x81AE
#define SUPER_MAGIC       0xEF53
#define SUPER_USER        0
// Proc status
#define FREE              0
#define BUSY              1

// file system table sizes
#define NMINODE           100
#define NMTABLE           10
#define NPROC             2
#define NFD               10
#define NOFT              40

// Open File Table
typedef struct oft{
  int   mode;
  int   refCount;
  struct minode *minodePtr;
  int    offset;
}OFT;

// PROC structure
typedef struct proc{
  struct Proc *next;
  int   pid;
  int   uid;
  int   gid;
```

```
  int    ppid;
  int    status;
  struct minode *cwd;
  OFT    *fd[NFD];
}PROC;

// In-memory inodes structure
typedef struct minode{
  INODE INODE;                 // disk inode
  int   dev, ino;
  int   refCount;              // use count
  int   dirty;                 // modified flag
  int   mounted;               // mounted flag
  struct mount *mntPtr;        // mount table pointer
  // int lock;                 // ignored for simple FS
}MINODE;

// Open file Table           // opened file instance
typedef struct oft{
  int  mode;                   // mode of opened file
  int  refCount;               // number of PROCs sharing this instance
  MINODE *minodePtr;           // pointer to minode of file
  int  offset;                 // byte offset for R|W
}OFT;

// Mount Table structure
typedef struct mtable{
  int    dev;                  // device number; 0 for FREE
  int    ninodes;              // from superblock
  int    nblocks;
  int    free_blocks           // from superblock and GD
  int    free_inodes
  int    bmap;                 // from group descriptor
  int    imap;
  int    iblock;               // inodes start block
  MINODE *mntDirPtr;           // mount point DIR pointer
  char   devName[64];          //device name
  char   mntName[64];          // mount point DIR name
}MTABLE;
```

(2). global.c file: This file contains global variables of the file system. Examples of global variables are

```
  MINODE minode[NMINODE];      // in memory INODEs
  MTABLE mtable[NMTABLE];      // mount tables
  OFT    oft[NOFT];            // Opened file instance
  PROC   proc[NPROC]           // PROC structures
  PROC   *running;             // current executing PROC
```

When the file system starts, we initializes all the global data structures and let running point at PROC[0], which is process P0 of the superuser (uid = 0). As in a real file system, every operation is due to the current running process. We begin with a superuser process because it does not need any file protection. File protection by permission checking will be enforced later in Level 3 of the FS implementation.

```
int fs_init()
{
  int i,j;
  for (i=0; i<NMINODE; i++)     // initialize all minodes as FREE
      minode[i].refCount = 0;
  for (i=0; i<NMTABLE; i++)     // initialize mtables as FREE
      mtable[i].dev = 0;
  for (i=0; i<NOFT; i++)        // initialize ofts as FREE
      oft[i].refCount = 0;
  for (i=0; i<NPROC; i++){      // initialize PROCs
      proc[i].status = READY;   // ready to run
      proc[i].pid = i;          // pid = 0 to NPROC-1
      proc[i].uid = i;          // P0 is a superuser process
      for (j=0; j<NFD; j++)
          proc[i].fd[j] = 0;    // all file descriptors are NULL
      proc[i].next = &proc[i+1]; // link list
  }
  proc[NPROC-1].next = &proc[0]; // circular list
  running = &proc[0];            // P0 runs first
}
```

During file system operation, global data structures are regarded as system resources, which are used and released dynamically. Each set of resources is managed by a pair of allocate and deallocate functions. For example, mialloc() allocates a FREE minode for use, and midalloc() releases a used minode. Other resource management functions are similar, which will be shown later when they are actually needed.

```
MINODE *mialloc()          // allocate a FREE minode for use
{
   int i;
   for (i=0; i<NMINODE; i++){
     MIONDE *mp = &minode[i];
     if (mp->refCount == 0){
        mp->refCount = 1;
        return mp;
     }
   }
   printf("FS panic: out of minodes\n");
   return 0;
}
int midalloc(MINODE *mip) // release a used minode
{
  mip->refCount = 0;
}
```

11.7.2 Utility Functions

(3). util.c file: This file contains commonly used utility functions of the file system. The most important utility functions are read/write disk block functions, iget(), iput() and getino(), which are explained in more detail.

(3).1. get_block/put_block functions: We assume that a block device, e.g. a real or virtual disk, can only be read or written in unit of block size. For real disks, this is due to hardware constraints. For virtual disks, we assume that read/write is also by block size, so that the code can be ported to real disks if desired. For a virtual disk, we first open it for R|W mode and use the file descriptor as the device number. The following functions read/write a virtual disk block into/from a buffer area in memory.

```
int get_block(int dev, int blk, char *buf)
{
    lseek(dev, blk*BLKSIZE, SEEK_SET);
    int n = read(dev, buf, BLKSIZE);
    if (n<0) printf("get_block [%d %d] error\n", dev, blk);
}
int put_block(int dev, int blk, char *buf)
{
    lseek(dev, blk*BLKSIZE, SEEK_SET);
    int n = write(dev, buf, BLKSIZE);
    if (n != BLKSIZE)
        printf("put_block [%d %d] error\n", dev, blk);
}
```

(3).2. iget(dev, ino) function: This function returns a pointer to the in-memory minode containing the INODE of (dev, ino). The returned minode is unique, i.e. only one copy of the INODE exists in memory. In a real file system, the returned minode is locked for exclusive use until it is either released or unlocked. For simplicity, we shall assume that minode locking is unnecessary, which will be explained later.

```
MINODE *iget(int dev, int ino)
{
  MINODE *mip;
  MTABLE *mp;
  INODE  *ip;
  int i, block, offset;
  char buf[BLKSIZE];

  // serach in-memory minodes first
  for (i=0; i<NMINODES; i++){
    MINODE *mip = &MINODE[i];
    if (mip->refCount && (mip->dev==dev) && (mip->ino==ino)){
      mip->refCount++;
      return mip;
    }
  }
```

```
// needed INODE=(dev,ino) not in memory
mip = mialloc();                     // allocate a FREE minode
mip->dev = dev; mip->ino = ino;   // assign to (dev, ino)
block = (ino-1)/8 + iblock;          // disk block containing this inode
offset= (ino-1)%8;                   // which inode in this block
get_block(dev, block, buf);
ip = (INODE *)buf + offset;
mip->INODE = *ip;                    // copy inode to minode.INODE
// initialize minode
mip->refCount = 1;
mip->mounted = 0;
mip->dirty = 0;
mip->mountptr = 0;
return mip;
}
```

(3).3. The iput(INODE *mip) function: This function releases a used minode pointed by mip. Each minode has a refCount, which represents the number of users that are using the minode. iput() decrements the refCount by 1. If the refCount is non-zero, meaning that the minode still has other users, the caller simply returns. If the caller is the last user of the minode (refCount = 0), the INODE is written back to disk if it is modified (dirty).

```
int iput(MINODE *mip)
{
  INODE  *ip;
  int i, block, offset;
  char buf[BLKSIZE];

  if (mip==0) return;
  mip->refCount--;                   // dec refCount by 1
  if (mip->refCount > 0) return;   // still has user
  if (mip->dirty == 0)   return;   // no need to write back

  // write INODE back to disk
  block  = (mip->ino - 1) / 8 + iblock;
  offset = (mip->ino - 1) % 8;

  // get block containing this inode
  get_block(mip->dev, block, buf);
  ip = (INODE *)buf + offset;       // ip points at INODE
  *ip = mip->INODE;                  // copy INODE to inode in block
  put_block(mip->dev, block, buf); // write back to disk
  midalloc(mip);                     // mip->refCount = 0;
}
```

(3).4. getino() function: The getino() function implements the file system tree traversal algorithm. It returns the INODE number (ino) of a specified pathname. To begin with, we assume that in the level-1 file system implementation, the file system resides on a single root device, so that there are no mounted devices and mounting point crossings. Mounted file systems and mounting point crossing will be considered later in level-3 of the file system implementation. Thus, the getino() function essentially returns the (dev, ino) of a pathname. The function first uses the tokenize() function to break up pathname into component strings. We assume that the tokenized strings are in a global data area, each pointed by a name[i] pointer and the number of token strings is nname. Then it calls the search() function to search for the token strings in successive directories. The following shows the tokenize() and search() functions.

```
char *name[64];   // token string pointers
char gline[256];  // holds token strings, each pointed by a name[i]
int  nname;       // number of token strings

int tokenize(char *pathname)
{
  char *s;
  strcpy(gline, pathname);
  nname = 0;
  s = strtok(gline, "/");
  while(s){
    name[nname++] = s;
    s = strtok(0, "/");
  }
}

int search(MINODE *mip, char *name)
{
   int i;
   char *cp, temp[256], sbuf[BLKSIZE];
   DIR *dp;
   for (i=0; i<12; i++){ // search DIR direct blocks only
     if (mip->INODE.i_block[i] == 0)
        return 0;
     get_block(mip->dev, mip->INODE.i_block[i], sbuf);
     dp = (DIR *)sbuf;
     cp = sbuf;
     while (cp < sbuf + BLKSIZE){
        strncpy(temp, dp->name, dp->name_len);
        temp[dp->name_len] = 0;
        printf("%8d%8d%8u %s\n",
               dp->inode, dp->rec_len, dp->name_len, temp);
        if (strcmp(name, temp)==0){
           printf("found %s : inumber = %d\n", name, dp->inode);
           return dp->inode;
        }
        cp += dp->rec_len;
        dp = (DIR *)cp;
     }
   }
   return 0;
}
```

```
int getino(char *pathname)
{
  MINODE *mip;
  int i, ino;
  if (strcmp(pathname, "/")==0){
      return 2;                    // return root ino=2
  }
  if (pathname[0] == '/')
      mip = root;                  // if absolute pathname: start from root
  else
      mip = running->cwd;   // if relative pathname: start from CWD
  mip->refCount++;               // in order to iput(mip) later

  tokenize(pathname);            // assume: name[ ], nname are globals

  for (i=0; i<nname; i++){    // search for each component string
      if (!S_ISDIR(mip->INODE.i_mode)){  // check DIR type
         printf("%s is not a directory\n", name[i]);
         iput(mip);
         return 0;
      }
      ino = search(mip, name[i]);
      if (!ino){
         printf("no such component name %s\n", name[i]);
         iput(mip);
         return 0;
      }
      iput(mip);                    // release current minode
      mip = iget(dev, ino);     // switch to new minode
  }
  iput(mip);
  return ino;
}
```

(3).5. Use of getino()/iget()/iput(): In a file system, almost every operation begins with a pathname, e.g. mkdir pathname, cat pathname, etc. Whenever a pathname is specified, its inode must be loaded into memory for reference. The general pattern of using an inode is

```
. ino  = getino(pathname);
. mip = iget(dev, ino);
.    use mip->INODE, which may modify the INODE;
. iput(mip);
```

There are only a few exceptions to this usage pattern. For instance,

chdir :   iget the new DIR minode but iput the old DIR minode.
open :   iget the minode of a file, which is released when the file is closed.
mount: iget the minode of mountPoint, which is released later by umount.

In general, iget and iput should appear in pairs, like a pair of matched parentheses. We may rely on this usage pattern in the implementation code to ensure that every INODE is loaded and then released properly.

(4). Minodes Locking: In a real file system, each minode has a lock field, which ensures that the minode can only be accessed by one process at a time, e.g. when modifying the INODE. Unix kernel uses a busy flag and sleep/wakeup to synchronize processes accessing the same minode. In other systems, each minode may have a mutex lock or a semaphore lock. A process is allowed to access a minode only if it holds the minode lock. The reason for minodes locking is as follows.

Assume that a process Pi needs the inode of (dev, ino), which is not in memory. Pi must load the inode into a minode entry. The minode must be marked as (dev, ino) to prevent other processes from loading the same inode again. While loading the inode from disk Pi may wait for I/O completion, which switches to another process Pj. If Pj needs exactly the same inode, it would find the needed minode already exists. Without the lock, Pj would proceed to use the minode before it is even loaded in yet. With the lock, Pj must wait until the minode is loaded, used and then released by Pi. In addition, when a process read/write an opened file, it must lock the file's minode to ensure that each read/write operation is atomic. For simplicity, we shall assume that only one process runs at a time, so that the lock is unnecessary. However, the reader should beware that minodes locking is necessary in a real file system.

Exercise 11.7 Design and implement a scheme, which uses the minode[ ] area as a cache memory for in-memory INODES. Once an INODE is loaded into a minode slot, try to keep it in memory for as long as possible even if no process is actively using it.

11.7.3   Mount-Root

(5). mount_root.c file: This file contains the mount_root() function, which is called during system initialization to mount the root file system. It reads the superblock of the root device to verify the device is a valid EXT2 file system.Then it loads the root INODE (ino = 2) of the root device into a minode and sets the root pointer to the root minode. It also sets the CWD of all PROCs to the root minode. A mount table entry is allocated to record the mounted root file system. Some key information of the root device, such as the number of inodes and blocks, the starting blocks of the bitmaps and inodes table, are also recorded in the mount table for quick access.

```
/************ FS1.1.c file ************/
#include "type.h"
#include "util.c"

// global variables
MINODE minode[NMINODES], *root;
MTABLE mtable[NMTABLE];
PROC proc[NPROC], *running;
int ninode, nblocks, bmap, imap, iblock;
int dev;
char gline[25], *name[16];   // tokenized component string strings
int  nname;                  // number of component strings
char *rootdev = "mydisk";    // default root_device
```

```
int fs_init()
{
  int i,j;
  for (i=0; i<NMINODES; i++)  // initialize all minodes as FREE
      minode[i].refCount = 0;
  for (i=0; i<NMOUNT; i++)    // initialize mtable entries as FREE
      mtable[i].dev = 0;
  for (i=0; i<NPROC; i++){    // initialize PROCs
      proc[i].status = READY; // reday to run
      proc[i].pid = i;        // pid = 0 to NPROC-1
      proc[i].uid = i;        // P0 is a superuser process
      for (j=0; j<NFD; j++)
          proc[i].fd[j] = 0;  // all file descriptors are NULL
      proc[i].next = &proc[i+1];
  }
  proc[NPROC-1].next = &proc[0];   // circular list
  running = &proc[0];              // P0 runs first
}


int mount_root(char *rootdev)  // mount root file system
{
  int i;
  MTABLE *mp;
  SUPER  *sp;
  GD     *gp;
  char buf[BLKSIZE];

  dev = open(rootdev, O_RDWR);
  if (dev < 0){
     printf("panic : can't open root device\n");
     exit(1);
  }
  /* get super block of rootdev */
  get_block(dev, 1, buf);
  sp = (SUPER *)buf;
  /* check magic number */
  if (sp->s_magic != SUPER_MAGIC){
     printf("super magic=%x : %s is not an EXT2 filesys\n",
            sp->s_magic, rootdev);
     exit(0);
  }
  // fill mount table mtable[0] with rootdev information
  mp = &mtable[0];     // use mtable[0]
  mp->dev = dev;
  // copy super block info into mtable[0]
  ninodes = mp->ninodes = sp->s_inodes_count;
  nblocks = mp->nblocks = sp->s_blocks_count;
  strcpy(mp->devName, rootdev);
  strcpy(mp->mntName, "/");
```

```
   get_block(dev, 2, buf);
   gp = (GD *)buf;
   bmap = mp->bmap = gp->bg_blocks_bitmap;
   imap = mp->imap = gp->bg_inodes_bitmap;
   iblock = mp->iblock = gp->bg_inode_table;
   printf("bmap=%d imap=%d iblock=%d\n", bmap, imap iblock);

   // call iget(), which inc minode's refCount
   root = iget(dev, 2);              // get root inode
   mp->mntDirPtr = root;             // double link
   root->mntPtr = mp;
   // set proc CWDs
   for (i=0; i<NPROC; i++)           // set proc's CWD
       proc[i].cwd = iget(dev, 2); // each inc refCount by 1
   printf("mount : %s  mounted on / \n", rootdev);
   return 0;
}

int main(int argc, char *argv[ ])
{
   char line[128], cmd[16], pathname[64];
   if (argc > 1)
      rootdev = argv[1];
   fs_init();
   mount_root(rootdev);
   while(1){
      printf("P%d running: ", running->pid);
      printf("input command : ");
      fgets(line, 128, stdin);
      line[strlen(line)-1] = 0;
      if (line[0]==0)
         continue;
      sscanf(line, "%s %s", cmd, pathname);
      if (!strcmp(cmd, "ls"))
         ls(pathname);
      if (!strcmp(cmd, "cd"))
         chdir(pathname);
      if (!strcmp(cmd, "pwd"))
         pwd(running->cwd);
      if (!strcmp(cmd, "quit"))
         quit();
   }
}

int quit() // write all modified minodes to disk
{
   int i;
   for (i=0; i<NMINODES; i++){
     MINODE *mip = &minode[i];
     if (mip->refCount && mip->dirty){
```

```
        mip->refCount = 1;
        iput(mip);
     }
   }
   exit(0);
}
```

How to ls: ls [pathname] lists the information of either a directory or a file. In Chap. 5 (Sect. 5.4), we showed an ls program, which works as follows.

(1) ls_dir(dirname): use opendir() and readdir() to get filenames in the directory. For each filename, call ls_file(filename).

(2) ls_file(filename): stat the filename to get file information in a STAT structure. Then list the STAT information.

Since the stat system call essentially returns the same information of a minode, we can modify the original ls algorithm by using minodes directly. The following shows the modified ls algorithm

```
/*********************** Algorithm of ls ******************************/
(1). From the minode of a directory, step through the dir_entries in the data
blocks of the minode.INODE. Each dir_entry contains the inode number, ino, and
name of a file. For each dir_entry, use iget() to get its minode, as in
        MINODE *mip = iget(dev, ino);
Then, call ls_file(mip, name).
(2). ls_file(MINODE *mip, char *name): use mip->INODE and name to list the file
information.
```

How to chdir [pathname]: The algorithm of chdir is as follows.

```
/*************** Algorithm of chdir ***************/
(1). int ino = getino(pathname);            // return error if ino=0
(2). MINODE *mip = iget(dev, ino);
(3). Verify mip->INODE is a DIR        // return error if not DIR
(4). iput(running->cwd);                         // release old cwd
(5). running->cwd = mip;                      // change cwd to mip
```

HOW TO pwd: The following shows the algorithm of pwd, which uses recursion on the directory minodes.

```
/*************** Algorithm of pwd ***************/
   rpwd(MINODE *wd){
    (1). if (wd==root) return;
    (2). from wd->INODE.i_block[0], get my_ino and parent_ino
    (3). pip = iget(dev, parent_ino);
    (4). from pip->INODE.i_block[ ]: get my_name string by my_ino as LOCAL
    (5). rpwd(pip);  // recursive call rpwd(pip) with parent minode
    (6). print "/%s", my_name;
   }
```

```
pwd(MINODE *wd){
    if (wd == root)    print "/"
    else                       rpwd(wd);
}
// pwd start:
pwd(running->cwd);
```

Exercise 11.8 Implement step (2) of the pwd algorithm as a utility function.

```
                    int get_myino(MINODE *mip, int *parent_ino)
```

which returns the inode number of . and that of .. in parent_ino.

Exercise 11.9 Implement step (4) of the pwd algorithm as a utility function.

```
          int get_myname(MINODE *parent_minode, int my_ino, char *my_name)
```

which returns the name string of a dir_entry identified by my_ino in the parent directory.

11.7.4   Implementation of Base File System

The programming task here is to complete the above mount_root.c program as the base file system. Run it with a virtual disk containing an EXT2 file system. The outputs of the base file system should look like Fig. 11.8. The figure only shows the results of the ls command. It should also support the cd and pwd commands.

```
checking EXT2 FS ....OK
bmp = 8 imap = 9 inodes_start = 10
init()
mount_root()
creating P0 as running process
mydisk mounted on / OK
input command : [ls|cd|pwd|quit] ls
drwxr-xr-x   5   0   0   Oct 21 09:02    1024    .
drwxr-xr-x   5   0   0   Oct 21 09:02    1024    ..
drwx------   2   0   0   Oct 21 09:01   12288    lost+found
drwxr-xr-x   4   0   0   Oct 21 09:03    1024    dir1
drwxr-xr-x   2   0   0   Oct 21 09:02    1024    dir2
-rw-r--r--   1   0   0   Oct 21 09:02       0    file1
-rw-r--r--   1   0   0   Oct 21 09:02       0    file2
input command : [ls|cd|pwd|quit] █
```

Fig. 11.8 Sample outputs of mount_root

11.8   File System Level-1 Functions

1. mkdir: The command

```
mkdir pathname
```

makes a new directory with pathname. The permission bits of the new directory are set to the default value 0755 (owner can access and rw, others can access but can only READ).

11.8.1   Algorithm of mkdir

mkdir creates an empty directory with a data block containing the default . and .. entries. The algorithm of mkdir is

```
/********* Algorithm of mkdir pathname*********/
(1). divide pathname into dirname and basename, e.g. pathname=/a/b/c, then
           dirname=/a/b;   basename=c;
(2). // dirname must exist and is a DIR:
           pino = getino(dirname);
           pmip = iget(dev, pino);
           check pmip->INODE is a DIR
(3). // basename must not exist in parent DIR:
           search(pmip, basename) must return 0;
(4). call kmkdir(pmip, basename) to create a DIR;

         kmkdir() consists of 4 major steps:
         (4).1. Allocate an INODE and a disk block:
                ino = ialloc(dev);
                blk = balloc(dev);
         (4).2. mip = iget(dev, ino) // load INODE into a minode
                initialize mip->INODE as a DIR INODE;
                mip->INODE.i_block[0] = blk; other i_block[ ] = 0;
                mark minode modified (dirty);
                iput(mip);   // write INODE back to disk
         (4).3. make data block 0 of INODE to contain . and .. entries;
                write to disk block blk.
         (4).4. enter_child(pmip, ino, basename); which enters
                (ino, basename) as a dir_entry to the parent INODE;

(5). increment parent INODE's links_count by 1 and mark pmip dirty;
     iput(pmip);
```

Most steps of the mkdir algorithm are self-explanatory. Only step (4) needs more explanation. We illustrate step (4) in more detail by example code. In order to make a directory, we need to allocate an inode from the inodes bitmap, and a disk block from the blocks bitmap, which rely on test and set bits in the bitmaps. In order to maintain file system consistency, allocating an inode must decrement the free inodes count in both superblock and group descriptor by 1. Similarly, allocating a disk block must decrement the free blocks count in both superblock and group descriptor by 1. It is also worth noting that bits in the bitmaps count from 0 but inode and block numbers count from 1. The following code segments show the detailed steps of (4).

(4).1 Allocate Inode and Disk Block:

```
// tst_bit, set_bit functions
int tst_bit(char *buf, int bit){
    return buf[bit/8] & (1 << (bit % 8));
}
int set_bit(char *buf, int bit){
    buf[bit/8] |= (1 << (bit % 8));
}
int decFreeInodes(int dev)
{
  // dec free inodes count in SUPER and GD
  get_block(dev, 1, buf);
  sp = (SUPER *)buf;
  sp->s_free_inodes_count--;
  put_block(dev, 1, buf);
  get_block(dev, 2, buf);
  gp = (GD *)buf;
  gp->bg_free_inodes_count--;
  put_block(dev, 2, buf);
}
int ialloc(int dev)
{
 int i;
 char buf[BLKSIZE];
 // use imap, ninodes in mount table of dev
 MTABLE *mp = (MTABLE *)get_mtable(dev);
 get_block(dev, mp->imap, buf);
 for (i=0; i<mp->ninodes; i++){
   if (tst_bit(buf, i)==0){
      set_bit(buf, i);
      put_block(dev, mp->imap, buf);
      // update free inode count in SUPER and GD
      decFreeInodes(dev);
      return (i+1);
   }
 }
 return 0; // out of FREE inodes
}
```

Allocation of disk blocks is similar, except it uses the blocks bitmap and it decrements the free blocks count in both superblock and group descriptor. This is left as an exercise.

Exercise 11.10 Implement the function

```
int balloc(int dev)
```

which allocates a free disk block (number) from a device.

(4).2. Create INODE: The following code segment creates an INODE=(dev, ino) in a minode, and writes the INODE to disk.

```
MINODE *mip = iget(dev, ino);
INODE *ip = &mip->INODE;
ip->i_mode = 0x41ED;        // 040755: DIR type and permissions
ip->i_uid  = running->uid; // owner uid
ip->i_gid  = running->gid; // group Id
ip->i_size = BLKSIZE;       // size in bytes
ip->i_links_count = 2;      // links count=2 because of . and ..
ip->i_atime = ip->i_ctime = ip->i_mtime = time(0L);
ip->i_blocks = 2;           // LINUX: Blocks count in 512-byte chunks
ip->i_block[0] = bno;       // new DIR has one data block
ip->i_block[1] to ip->i_block[14] = 0;
mip->dirty = 1;             // mark minode dirty
iput(mip);                  // write INODE to disk
```

(4).3. Create data block for new DIR containing . and .. entries

```
char buf[BLKSIZE];
bzero(buf, BLKSIZE); // optional: clear buf[ ] to 0
DIR *dp = (DIR *)buf;
// make . entry
dp->inode = ino;
dp->rec_len = 12;
dp->name_len = 1;
dp->name[0] = '.';
// make .. entry: pino=parent DIR ino, blk=allocated block
dp = (char *)dp + 12;
dp->inode = pino;
dp->rec_len = BLKSIZE-12;   // rec_len spans block
dp->name_len = 2;
dp->name[0] = d->name[1] = '.';
put_block(dev, blk, buf);   // write to blk on diks
```

(4).4. Enter new dir_entry into parent directory: The function

```
            int enter_name(MINODE *pip,  int ino,  char *name)
```

enters a [ino, name] as a new dir_entry into a parent directory. The enter_name algorithm consists of several steps.

```
/****************** Algorithm of enter_name ******************/
 for each data block of parent DIR do  // assume: only 12 direct blocks
 {
        if (i_block[i]==0) BREAK;      // to step (5) below
    (1). Get parent's data block into a buf[ ];
    (2). In a data block of the parent directory, each dir_entry has an ideal
    length
```

```
         ideal_length = 4*[ (8 + name_len + 3)/4 ]        // a multiple of 4

         All dir_entries rec_len = ideal_length, except the last entry. The
         rec_len of the LAST entry is to the end of the block, which may be
         larger than its ideal_length.
      (3). In order to enter a new entry of name with n_len, the needed length is

         need_length = 4*[ (8 + n_len + 3)/4 ]            // a multiple of 4

      (4). Step to the last entry in the data block:

         get_block(parent->dev, parent->INODE.i_block[i], buf);
         dp = (DIR *)buf;
         cp = buf;
         while (cp + dp->rec_len < buf + BLKSIZE){
            cp += dp->rec_len;
            dp = (DIR *)cp;
         }
         // dp NOW points at last entry in block
         remain = LAST entry's rec_len - its ideal_length;

         if (remain >= need_length){
            enter the new entry as the LAST entry and
            trim the previous entry rec_len to its ideal_length;
         }
         goto step (6);
      }
```

The following diagrams show the block contents before and after entering [ino, name] as a new entry.

```
Before                     |          LAST entry                 |
|-4---2----2--|----|----|------- rlen to end of block ----------|
|ino rlen nlen NAME|.....|ino rlen nlen|NAME                     |
 ------------------------------------------------------------------


After                      |   Last entry   |     NEW entry      |
|-4---2----2--|----|----|----ideal_len-----|---- rlen=remain ----|
|ino rlen nlen NAME|....|ino rlen nlen|NAME|ino rlen nlen name    |
 ------------------------------------------------------------------
}
```

(5). If no space in existing data block(s):

Allocate a new data block; increment parent size by BLKSIZE;
Enter new entry as the first entry in the new data block with rec_len=BLKSIZE.

The following diagrams shows the new data block containing only one entry.

```
|------------------ rlen = BLKSIZE ----------------------------
|ino rlen=BLKSIZE nlen name                                    |
----------------------------------------------------------------

(6).Write data block to disk;
}
```

2. creat: Creat creates an empty regular file. The algorithm of creat is

11.8.2   Algorithm of creat

```
/************** Algorithm of creat   ************/
creat(char * pathname)
{
   This is similar to mkdir() except
   (1). the INODE.i_mode field is set to REG file type, permission bits set to
               0644 = rw-r--r--, and
   (2). no data block is allocated for it, so the file size is 0.
   (3). links_count = 1; Do not increment parent INODE's links_count
}
```

It is noted that the above creat algorithm differs from Unix/Linux in that it does not open the file for WRITE mode and return a file descriptor. In practice, creat is rarely used as a stand-alone function. It is used internally by the open() function, which may create a file, open it for WRITE and return a file descriptor. The open operation will be implemented later in level-2 of the file system.

11.8.3   Implementation of mkdir-creat

The programming task here is to implement **mkdir-creat** functions and add the corresponding mkdir and creat commands to the base file system. Demonstrate the system by testing the mkdir and creat functions. Figure 11.9 shows the sample outputs of the resulting file system. It shows the detailed steps of executing the command **mkdir dir1,** as described in the mkdir Algorithm.

3. rmdir: The command

```
        rmdir dirname
```

removes a directory. As in Unix/Linux, in order to remove a DIR, the directory must be empty, for the following reasons. First, removing a non-empty directory implies the removal of all the files and subdirectories in the directory. Although it is possible to implement a recursive rmdir operation, which removes an entire directory tree, the basic operation is still remove one directory at a time. Second, a non-empty directory may contain files that are actively in use, e.g. files opened for read/write, etc. Removing such a directory is clearly unacceptable. Although it is possible to check whether there are any active files in a directory, doing this would incur too much overhead. The simplest way out is to require that a directory must be empty in order to be removed. The algorithm of rmdir is.

```
fs_init()
mount_root
checking EXT2 FS : OK
bmp = 8 imap = 9 iblock = 10
mydisk mounted on / OK
root refCount = 3
input command : [ls|cd|pwd|mkdir|creat|quit] mkdir dir1
mkdir dir1
parent=.  child=dir1
getino: pathname=.
===========================================
getino: i=0 name[0]=.
search for . in MINODE = [3, 2]
. found . : ino = 2
search for dir1 in MINODE = [3, 2]
. .. lost+found : dir1 not yet exits
ialloc: ino=12 balloc: bno=47
making INODE
iput: dev=3 ino=12
making data block
writing data block 47 to disk
enter name: parent=(3 2) name=dir1
enter name: dir1 need_len=12
parent data blk[0] = 33
step to LAST entry in data block 33
. .. lost+found
found space: name=lost+found ideal=20 rlen=1000 remain=980
write parent data block[0]=33
-------------------------------------------
input command : [ls|cd|pwd|mkdir|creat|quit] ls
i_block[0] = 33
drwxr-xr-x  4  0  0  Oct 22 10:32   1024    .
drwxr-xr-x  4  0  0  Oct 22 10:32   1024    ..
drwx------  2  0  0  Oct 22 10:32   12288   lost+found
drwxr-xr-x  2  0  0  Oct 22 10:33   1024    dir1
i_block[1] = 0
input command : [ls|cd|pwd|mkdir|creat|quit] █
```

Fig. 11.9 Sample outputs of project #2

11.8.4 Algorithm of rmdir

```
/************ Algorithm of rmdir ************/
  (1). get in-memory INODE of pathname:
        ino = getino(pathanme);
        mip = iget(dev, ino);

  (2). verify INODE is a DIR (by INODE.i_mode field);
        minode is not BUSY (refCount = 1);
        verify DIR is empty (traverse data blocks for number of entries = 2);

  (3). /* get parent's ino and inode */
        pino = findino();  //get pino from .. entry in INODE.i_block[0]
        pmip = iget(mip->dev, pino);

  (4). /* get name from parent DIR's data block
        findname(pmip, ino, name); //find name from parent DIR
```

```
    (5).  remove name from parent directory */
          rm_child(pmip, name);

    (6). dec parent links_count by 1; mark parent pimp dirty;
          iput(pmip);

    (7). /* deallocate its data blocks and inode */
          bdalloc(mip->dev, mip->INODE.i_blok[0];
          idalloc(mip->dev, mip->ino);
          iput(mip);
```

In the rmdir algorithm, most steps are simple and self-explanatory. We only need to explain the following steps in more detail.

1. **How to test DIR empty:** Every DIR's links_count starts with 2 (for the . and .. entries). Each subdirectory increments its links_count by 1 but regular files do not increment the links_count of the parent directory. So, if a DIR's links_count is greater than 2, it is definitely not empty. However, if links_count = 2, the DIR may still contain regular files. In that case, we must traverse the DIR's data blocks to count the number of dir_entries, which must be greater than 2. This can be done by the same technique of stepping through dir_entris in the data blocks of a DIR INODE.

2. **How to deallocate inode and data block**: When removing a DIR, we must deallocate its inode and data block (numbers). The function

$$idalloc(dev, ino)$$

deallocates an inode (number). It clears the ino's bit in the device's inodes bitmap to 0. Then it increments the free inodes count in both superblock and group descriptor by 1.

```
int clr_bit(char *buf, int bit) // clear bit in char buf[BLKSIZE]
{   buf[bit/8] &= ~(1 << (bit%8)); }

int incFreeInodes(int dev)
{
  char buf[BLKSIZE];
  // inc free inodes count in SUPER and GD
  get_block(dev, 1, buf);
  sp = (SUPER *)buf;
  sp->s_free_inodes_count++;
  put_block(dev, 1, buf);
  get_block(dev, 2, buf);
  gp = (GD *)buf;
  gp->bg_free_inodes_count++;
  put_block(dev, 2, buf);
}
int idalloc(int dev, int ino)
{
  int i;
  char buf[BLKSIZE];
  MTABLE *mp = (MTABLE *)get_mtable(dev);
```

```
   if (ino > mp->ninodes){ // niodes global
      printf("inumber %d out of range\n", ino);
      return;
   }
   // get inode bitmap block
   get_block(dev, mp->imap, buf);
   clr_bit(buf, ino-1);
   // write buf back
   put_block(dev, mp->imap, buf);
   // update free inode count in SUPER and GD
   incFreeInodes(dev);
}
```

Deallocating a disk block number is similar, except it uses the device's blocks bitmap and it increaments the free blocks count in both superblock and groupdescriptor. This is left as an exercise.

Exercise 11.11 Implement a **bdalloc(int dev, int bno)** function which deallocates a disk block (number) bno.

3. **Remove dir_entry form parent DIR**: The function

```
        rm_child(MINODE *pmip, char *name)
```

removes the dir_entry of name from a parent directory minode pointed by pmip. The algorithm of rm_child is as follows.

```
/*************** Algorithm of rm_child ***************/
(1). Search parent INODE's data block(s) for the entry of name
(2). Delete name entry from parent directory by
(2).1. if (first and only entry in a data block){
       In this case, the data block looks like the following diagram.


       ---------------------------------------------
       |ino rlen=BLKSIZE nlen NAME                 |
       ---------------------------------------------


       deallocate the data block; reduce parent's file size by BLKSIZE;
       compact parent's i_block[ ] array to eliminate the deleted entry if it's
       between nonzero entries.
          }
(2).2. else if LAST entry in block{
       Absorb its rec_len to the predecessor entry, as shown in the following diagrams.


       Before                          |remove this entry   |
       -----------------------------------------------------
       xxxxx|INO rlen nlen NAME |yyy   |zzz rec_len         |
       -----------------------------------------------------
       After
       -----------------------------------------------------
```

```
       xxxxx|INO rlen nlen NAME |yyy (add rec_len to yyy)   |
       -----------------------------------------------------

       }
```

(2).3. **else:** entry is first but not the only entry or in the middle of a block:
```
       {
           move all trailing entries LEFT to overlay the deleted entry;
           add deleted rec_len to the LAST entry; do not change parent's file
           size;

           The following diagrams illustrate the block contents before and after
           deleting such an entry.

           Before:  | delete this entry |<= move these LEFT  |
                    ------------------------------------------------
               xxxxx|ino rlen nlen NAME |yyy|...|zzz           |
               -----|------------------|------ size ---------
                      dp                cp
       After:
               -----|---- after move LEFT ------------------
               xxxxx|yyy|...|zzz (rec_len += rlen)           |
               ------------------------------------------------

           How to move trailing entries LEFT? Hint: memcpy(dp, cp, size);
       }
```

11.8.5   Implementation of rmdir

The programming task here is to implement the rmdir function and add the rmdir command to the file
system. Compile and run the resulting program to demonstrate rmdir operation. Figure 11.10 shows the
sample outputs of the resulting file system. The figure shows the detailed steps of removing a directory.

4. **link:** The command

```
        link old_file   new_file
```

creates a hard link from new_file to old_file. Hard links can only be applied to regular files, not to
DIRs, because linking to DIRs may create loops in the file system name space. Hard link files share the
same inode. Therefore, they must be on the same device. The algorithm of link is as follows.

11.8.6   Algorithm of link

```
/******************* Algorithm of link *******************/
(1). // verify old_file exists and is not a DIR;
        oino = getino(old_file);
        omip = iget(dev, oino);
        check omip->INODE file type (must not be DIR).
```

```
fs_init()
mount_root
checking EXT2 FS : OK
bmp = 8 imap = 9 iblock = 10
mydisk mounted on / OK
root refCount = 3
input command : [ls|cd|pwd|mkdir|creat|rmdir|quit] ls
i_block[0] = 33
drwxr-xr-x   5   0   0   Oct 22 10:39   1024    .
drwxr-xr-x   5   0   0   Oct 22 10:39   1024    ..
drwx------   2   0   0   Oct 22 10:39   12288   lost+found
drwxr-xr-x   2   0   0   Oct 22 10:39   1024    dir1
drwxr-xr-x   2   0   0   Oct 22 10:39   1024    dir2
i_block[1] = 0
input command : [ls|cd|pwd|mkdir|creat|rmdir|quit] rmdir dir1
getino: pathname=dir1
tokenize dir1
dir1
===========================================
getino: i=0 name[0]=dir1
search for dir1 in MINODE = [3, 2]
search: i=0  i_block[0]=33
    i_number  rec_len  name_len    name
       2        12        1          .
       2        12        2          ..
      11        20        10        lost+found
      12        12        4         dir1
found dir1 : ino = 12
[3 12] refCount=1
last entry=[13 968] last entry=[13 980]
input command : [ls|cd|pwd|mkdir|creat|rmdir|quit] ls
i_block[0] = 33
drwxr-xr-x   4   0   0   Oct 22 10:39   1024    .
drwxr-xr-x   4   0   0   Oct 22 10:39   1024    ..
drwx------   2   0   0   Oct 22 10:39   12288   lost+found
drwxr-xr-x   2   0   0   Oct 22 10:39   1024    dir2
i_block[1] = 0
input command : [ls|cd|pwd|mkdir|creat|rmdir|quit] ▮
```

Fig. 11.10 Sample outputs of project #3

(2). // new_file must not exist yet:
        getino(new_file) must return 0;
(3). creat new_file with the same inode number of old_file:
        parent = dirname(new_file);   **child** = basename(new_file);
        pino = getino(parent);
        pmip = iget(dev, pino);
        // creat entry in new parent DIR with same inode number of old_file
        enter_name(**pmip, oino, child**);
(4). omip->INODE.i_links_count++;   // inc INODE's links_count by 1
     omip->dirty = 1;   // for write back by iput(omip)
     iput(omip);
     iput(pmip);

We illustrate the link operation by an example. Consider.

                    link /a/b/c   /x/y/z

The following diagrams show the outcome of the link operation. It adds an entry z to the data block of /x/y. The inode number of z is the same ino of a/b/c, so they share the same INODE, whose links_count is incremented by 1.

```
     link    /a/b/c                        /x/y/z
              /a/b/  datablock              /x/y    datablock
     ------------------------      ---------------------------
     |....|ino rlen nlen c|...|    |....|ino rlen nlen z .... |
     -----|-|------------------    -----|-|-------------------
          |                             |
          INODE <-- same INODE <----------
          i_links_count=1 <=== increment i_links_count to 2
```

5. **unlink:** The command

```
            unlink filename
```

unlinks a file. It decrements the file's links_count by 1 and deletes the file name from its parent DIR. When a file's links_count reaches 0, the file is truly removed by deallocating its data blocks and inode. The algorithm of unlink is

11.8.7   Algorithm of unlink

```
/************** Algorithm of unlink *************/
(1). get filenmae's minode:
        ino = getino(filename);
        mip = iget(dev, ino);
        check it's a REG or symbolic LNK file; can not be a DIR
(2). // remove name entry from parent DIR's data block:
        parent = dirname(filename); child = basename(filename);
        pino = getino(parent);
        pimp = iget(dev, pino);
        rm_child(pmip, ino, child);
        pmip->dirty = 1;
        iput(pmip);
(3). // decrement INODE's link_count by 1
         mip->INODE.i_links_count--;
(4).     if (mip->INODE.i_links_count > 0)
             mip->dirty = 1;  // for write INODE back to disk
(5).     else{  // if links_count = 0: remove filename
             deallocate all data blocks in INODE;
             deallocate INODE;
         }
         iput(mip);                    // release mip
```

6. **symlink:** The command

```
symlink old_file  new_file
```

creates a symbolic link from new_file to old_file. Unlike hard links, symlink can link to anything, including DIRs, even files not on the same device. The algorithm of symlink is

11.8.8   Algorithm of symlink

```
/********* Algorithm of symlink old_file new_file ********/
(1). check: old_file must exist and new_file not yet exist;
(2). creat new_file; change new_file to LNK type;
(3). // assume length of old_file name <= 60 chars
        store old_file name in newfile's INODE.i_block[ ] area.
        set file size to length of old_file name
        mark new_file's minode dirty;
        iput(new_file's minode);
(4). mark new_file parent minode dirty;
        iput(new_file's parent minode);
```

7. **readlink:** The function

```
int readlink(file, buffer)
```

reads the target file name of a symbolic file and returns the length of the target file name. The algorithm of readlink() is.

11.8.9   Algorithm of readlink

```
/************* Algorithm of readlink (file, buffer) *************/
(1). get file's INODE in memory; verify it's a LNK file
(2). copy target filename from INODE.i_block[ ] into buffer;
(3). return file size;
```

11.8.10 Other Level-1 Functions

Other level-1 functions include access, chmod, chown, change file's time fields, etc. The operations of all such functions are of the same pattern:

```
(1). get the in-memory INODE of a file by
        ino = getino(pathname);
        mip = iget(dev,ino);
(2). get information from INODE or modify the INODE;
(3). if INODE is modified, set mip->dirty to zonzero for write back;
(4). iput(mip);
```

```
root@wang:~/abc/360/F17/TEST4# a.out
checking EXT2 FS ....OK
bmp=8 imap=9 inode_start = 10
init()
mount_root()
mydisk mounted on / OK
creating P0 as running process
input command: [ls|cd|pwd|mkdir|creat|rmdir|link|unlink|symlink|readlink|chmod|utime|quit] ls
cmd=ls path= param=
i_block[0] = 33
drwxr-xr-x   3   0   0   Apr 21 19:50    1024    .
drwxr-xr-x   3   0   0   Apr 21 19:50    1024    ..
drwx------   2   0   0   Apr 21 19:50   12288    lost+found
drwxr-xr-x   2   0   0   Apr 21 19:50    1024    dir2
drwxr-xr-x   2   0   0   Apr 26 16:03    1024    dir1
-rw-r--r--   1   0   0   Apr 26 16:03       0    file1
lrwxrwxrwx   1   0   0   Dec 23 07:18       4    hi -> dir1
i_block[1] = 0
input command: [ls|cd|pwd|mkdir|creat|rmdir|link|unlink|symlink|readlink|chmod|utime|quit] █
```

Fig. 11.11 Sample outputs of file system level-1

Examples of Other Level-1 Operations

1. **chmod oct filename:** Change filename's permission bits to octal value
2. **utime filename**: change file's access time to current time:

11.8.11 Programming Project #1: Implementation of File System Level-1

The programming project #1 is to complete the level-1 implementation of the file system and demonstrate the file system. Figure 11.11 shows the sample outputs of running the Level 1 implementation of the file system. The ls command shows that hi is a symbolic link to the directory dir1.

11.9   File System Level-2 Functions

Level-2 of the file system implements read and write operations of file contents. It consists of the following functions: open, close, lseek, read, write, opendir and readdir.

1. Open Operation
In Unix/Linux, the **system call**

```
int open(char *filename, int flags);
```

opens a file for read or write, where flags is one of O_RDONLY, O_WRONLY, O_RDWR, which may be bitwise or-ed with O_CREAT, O_APPEND, O_TRUNC, etc. These symbolic constants are defined in the **fcntl.h** file. On success, open() returns a file descriptor (number), which is used in subsequent system calls, such as read(), write(), lseek() and close(), etc. For simplicity, we shall assume the parameter flags = 0|1|2|3 or RD|WR|RW|AP for READ|WRITE| RDWR|APEND, respectively. The algorithm of open() is.

11.9.1   Algorithm of open

```
/******************  Algorithm of open  ********************/
(1). get file's minode:
        ino = getino(filename);
        if (ino==0){  // if file does not exist
            creat(filename);          // creat it first, then
            ino = getino(filename);   // get its ino
        }
        mip = iget(dev, ino);

(2). allocate an openTable entry OFT; initialize OFT entries:
        mode = 0(RD) or 1(WR) or 2(RW) or 3(APPEND)
        minodePtr = mip;             // point to file's minode
        refCount = 1;
        set offset = 0 for RD|WR|RW; set to file size for APPEND mode;

(3). Search for the first FREE fd[index] entry with the lowest index in PROC;
        fd[index] = &OFT;            // fd entry points to the openTable entry;

(4). return index as file descriptor;
```

Figure 11.12 shows the data structure created by open. In the figure, (1) is the PROC structure of the process that calls open(). The returned file descriptor, fd, is the index of the fd[ ] array in the PROC structure. The contents of fd[fd] points to an OFT, which points to the minode of the file. The OFT's refCount represents the number of processes that share the same instance of an opened file. When a process opens a file, the refCount in the OFT is set to 1. When a process forks a child process, the child process inherits all the opened file descriptors of the parent, which increments the refCount of every shared OFT by 1. When a process closes a file descriptor, it decrements OFT.refCount by 1. When OFT.refCount reaches 0, the file's minode is released and the OFT is deallocated. The OFT's offset is a conceptual pointer to the current byte position in the file for read/write. It is initialized to 0 for RD|WR| RW mode or to file size for APPEND mode.

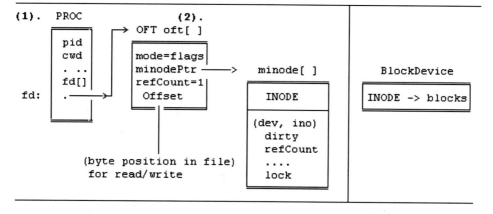

Fig. 11.12 Data structures of open

11.9.2   lseek

In Linux, the system call.

```
lseek(fd, position, whence); // whence=SEEK_SET or SEEK_CUR
```

sets the offset in the OFT of an opened file descriptor to the byte **position** either from the file beginning (**SEEK_SET**) or relative to the current position (**SEEK_CUR**). For simplicity, we shall assume that the new position is always from the file beginning. Once set, the next read/write begins from the current offset position. The algorithm of lseek is trivial. It only needs to check the requested position value is within the bounds of [0, fileSize-1]. We leave the implementation of lseek as an exercise.

Exercise 11.12   Write C code for the lseek function **int lseek(int fd, int position)**.

2. Close Operation
The **close(int fd)** operation closes a file descriptor. The algorithm of close is

11.9.3   Algorithm of close

```
/**************** Algorithm of close ***************/
(1). check fd is a valid opened file descriptor;
(2). if (PROC's fd[fd] != 0){        // points to an OFT
    .      OFT.refCount--;           // dec OFT's refCount by 1
         if (refCount == 0)          // if last process using this OFT
             iput(OFT.minodePtr);    // release minode
     }
(4). PROC.fd[fd] = 0;                // clear PROC's fd[fd] to 0
```

11.9.4   Read Regular Files

In Unix/Linux, the system call

```
int read(int fd, char *buf, int nbytes);
```

reads nbytes from an opened file descriptor into a buffer area in user space. The read system call is routed to the read function in the OS kernel. For regular files, the algorithm of read is.

```
/********* Algorithm of read(int fd,  char *buf,  int nbytes) *********/
(1). count = 0;               // number of bytes read
    offset = OFT.offset;      // byte offset in file to READ
    compute bytes available in file: avil = fileSize - offset;
(2). while (nbytes && avil){
         compute logical block: lbk  = offset  /  BLKSIZE;
         start byte in block:        start = offset % BLKSIZE;
(3).     convert logical block number, lbk, to physical block number, blk,
         through INODE.i_block[ ] array;
```

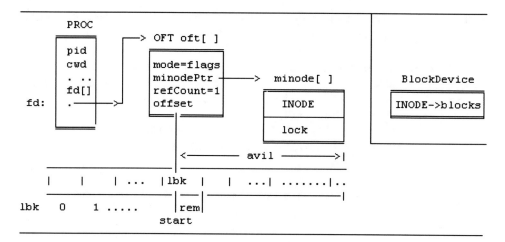

Fig. 11.13 Data structures for read

```
(4).      get_block(dev, blk, kbuf);    // read blk into char kbuf[BLKSIZE];
          char *cp = kbuf + start;
          remain = BLKSIZE - start;
(5).      while (remain){    // copy bytes from kbuf[ ] to buf[ ]
              *buf++ = *cp++;
              offset++; count++;              // inc offset, count;
              remain--; avil--; nbytes--;    // dec remain, avail, nbytes;
              if (nbytes==0 || avil==0)
                  break;
          } // end of while(remain)
      }      //  end of while(nbytes && avil)
(6). return count;
```

The algorithm of read() can be best explained in terms of Fig. 11.13. Assume that fd is opened for READ. The offset in the OFT points to the current byte position in the file from where we wish to read nbytes. To the file system in kernel, a file is just a sequence of contiguous bytes, numbered from 0 to fileSize-1. As Fig. 11.13 shows, the current byte position, offset, falls in a logical block.

$$\textbf{lbk} = \text{offset} ~/~ \text{BLKSIZE},$$

the byte to start read is.

$$\textbf{start} = \text{offset} ~\%~ \text{BLKSIZE}$$

and the number of bytes remaining in the logical block is.

$$\textbf{remain} = \text{BLKSIZE} - \text{start}.$$

At this moment, the file has.

$$\textbf{avil} = \text{fileSize} - \text{offset}$$

bytes still available for read. These numbers are used in the read algorithm.

For small EXT2 files systems, the block size is 1 KB and files have at most double indirect blocks. For read, the algorithm of converting logical blocks to physical blocks is.

```
/* Algorithm of Converting Logical Blocks to Physical Blocks */
  int map(INODE, lbk){                       // convert lbk to blk via INODE
      if (lbk < 12)                          // direct blocks
          blk = INODE.i_block[lbk];
      else if (12 <= lbk < 12+256){          // indirect blocks
          read INODE.i_block[12] into int ibuf[256];
          blk = ibuf[lbk-12];
      }
      else{    // doube indirect blocks; see Exercise 11.13 below.
      }
       return blk;
  }
```

Exercise 11.13 Complete the algorithm for converting double indirect logical blocks to physical blocks. Hint: Mailman's algorithm.

Exercise 11.14 For simplicity and clarity, step (5) of the read algorithm transfers data one byte at a time and updates the control variable on each byte transfer, which are not very efficient. Optimize the code by transferring a maximal sized chunk of data at a time.

11.9.5   Write Regular Files

In Unix/Linux, the system call

```
        int write(int fd, char buf[ ], int nbytes);
```

writes nbytes from buf in user space to an opened file descriptor and returns the actual number of bytes written. The write system call is routed to the write function in the OS kernel. For regular files, the algorithm of write is

```
/******* Algorithm of write(int fd, char *buf, int nbytes) *******/
(1). count = 0;          // number of bytes written
(2). while (nbytes){
       compute logical block: lbk = oftp->offset  / BLOCK_SIZE;
       compute start byte:     start = oftp->offset % BLOCK_SIZE;
(3).   convert lbk to physical block number, blk, through the i_block[ ] array;
(4).   read_block(dev, blk, kbuf); // read blk into kbuf[BLKSIZE];
       char *cp = kbuf + start;  remain = BLKSIZE - start;
(5)    while (remain){                    // copy bytes from buf[ ] to kbuf[ ]
          *cp++ = *buf++;
          offset++;  count++;      // inc offset, count;
          remain --; nbytes--;     // dec remain, nbytes;
          if (offset > fileSize)  fileSize++; // inc file size
          if (nbytes <= 0) break;
```

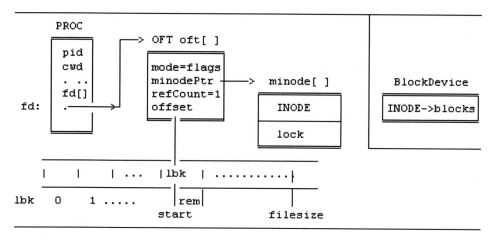

Fig. 11.14 Data structures for write

```
        } // end while(remain)
(6).    write_block(dev, blk, kbuf);
    } // end while(nbytes)
(7). set minode dirty = 1;   // mark minode dirty for iput() when fd is closed
    return count;
```

The algorithm of write can be best explained in terms of Fig. 11.14. In the figure, the offset in the OFT is the current byte position in the file to write, which falls in a logical block. It uses offset to compute the logical block number, lbk, the start byte position and the number of bytes remaining in the logical block. It then converts the logical block to physical block through the file's INODE.i_block array.Then it reads the physical block into a kbuf and transfer data from buf into kbuf, which may increase the file size if offset exceeds the current file size. After transferring data to kbuf, it writes the buffer back to disk. The write algorithm stops when all nbytes are written. The return value is nbtyes unless write fails.

The algorithm of converting logical block to physical block for write is similar to that of read, except for the following difference. During write, the intended data block may not exist. If a direct block does not exist, it must be allocated and recorded in the INODE. If the indirect block i_block [12] does not exist, it must be allocated and initialized to 0. If an indirect data block does not exist, it must be allocated and recorded in the indirect block. Simliarly, if the double indirect block i_block [13] dose not exist, it must be allocated and initialized to 0. If an entry in the double indirect block does not exist, it must be allocated and initialized to zero. If a double indirect block does not exist, it must be allocated and recorded in a double indirect block entry, etc.

Exercise 11.15 In the write algorithm, a file opened for WRITE mode may start with no data blocks at all. Complete the algorithm for coverting logical block numbers to physical blocks, including direct, indirect and double indirect blocks.

Exercise 11.16 For simplicity and clarity, step (5) of the write algorithm transfers data one byte at a time and updates the control variable on each byte transfer. Optimize the code by transferring a maximal sized chunk of data at a time.

Exercise 11.17 With open() and read(), implement the command cat filename, which displays the contents of a file.

Exercise 11.18 With open(), read() and write(), implement the command cp src dest, which copies a src file src to a dest file.

Exercise 11.19 Implement the command function mv file1 file2.

11.9.6   Opendir-Readdir

Unix considers everything as a file. Therefore, we should be able to open a DIR for read just like a regular file. From a technical point of view, there is no need for a separate set of opendir() and readdir() functions. However, different Unix systems may have different file systems. It may be difficult for users to interpret the contents of a DIR file. For this reason, POSIX specifies **opendir** and **readdir** operations, which are independent of file systems. Support for opendir is trivial; it's the same open system call, but readdir() has the form.

```
struct dirent *ep = readdir(DIR *dp);
```

which returns a pointer to a dirent structure on each call. This can be implemented in user space as a library I/O function. Instead, we shall implement opendir() and readir() directly.

```
int opendir(pathaname)
{   return open(pathname, RD|O_DIR); }
```

where O_DIR is a bit pattern for opening the file as a DIR. In the open file table, the mode field contains the O_DIR bit.

```
int readdir(int fd, struct udir *udirp) // struct udir{DIR udir;};
{
    // same as read() except:
    use the current byte offset in OFT to read the next dir_entry;
    copy the dir_entry into *udirp;
    advance offset by dir_entry's rec_len for reading next dir_entry;
}
```

11.9.7   Programming Project #2: Implementation of File System Level-2

The programming project #2 is to complete the implementation of File System Level-2 and demonstrate read, write, cat, cp and mv operations in the file system. The reader may consult earlier Chapters for cat and cp operations. For the mv operation, see Problem 12. Figure 11.15 show the sample outputs of running the complete Level 2 file system.

```
root@wang:~/abc/360/F17/TEST5# a.out
checking EXT2 FS ....OK
bmp=8 imap=9 inode_start = 10
init()
mount_root()
root refCount = 1
creating P0 as running process
root refCount = 2
input command: [ls|cd|pwd|mkdir|creat|rmdir|link|symlink|unlink
               |open|close|lseek|read|write|cat|cp|mv|quit] : ls
cmd=ls path= param=
i_block[0] = 33
drwxr-xr-x   3   0   0   Nov  9 12:54    1024   .
drwxr-xr-x   3   0   0   Nov  9 12:54    1024   ..
drwx------   2   0   0   Nov  3 09:07   12288   lost+found
-rw-r--r--   1   0   0   Nov  9 12:54      42   f1
drwxr-xr-x   2   0   0   Apr 21 18:49    1024   dir2
-rw-r--r--   1   0   0   Apr 10 08:48       0   file2
i_block[1] = 0
input command: [ls|cd|pwd|mkdir|creat|rmdir|link|symlink|unlink
               |open|close|lseek|read|write|cat|cp|mv|quit] : █
```

Fig. 11.15 File system level-2

11.10   File System Level-3

File system level-3 supports mount, umount of file systems and file protection.

Mount Operation
The command

```
            mount filesys mount_point
```

mounts a file system to a mount_point directory. It allows the file system to include other file systems as parts of the existing file system. The data structures used in mount are the MOUNT table and the in-memory minode of the mount_point directory. The algorithm of mount is

11.10.1   Algorithm of mount

```
/********* Algorithm of mount *********/
1. If no parameter, display current mounted file systems;
2. Check whether filesys is already mounted:
   The MOUNT table entries contain mounted file system (device) names
   and their mounting points. Reject if the device is already mounted.
   If not, allocate a free MOUNT table entry.
3. Open the filesys virtual disk (under Linux) for RW; use (Linux) file
   descriptor as new dev. Read filesys superblock to verify it is an EXT2 FS.
```

4. Find the ino, and then the minode of mount_point:
```
       ino = getino(pathname);      // get ino:
       mip = iget(dev, ino);        // load its inode into memory;
```
5. Check mount_point is a DIR and not busy, e.g. not someone's CWD.
6. Record new dev and filesys name in the MOUNT table entry, store its
   ninodes, nblocks, bmap, imap and inodes start block, etc. for quick
   access.
7. Mark mount_point minode as mounted on (mounted flag = 1) and let it point
   at the MOUNT table entry, which points back to the mount_point minode.

Umount Operation:

The operation **umount filesys**

un-mounts a mounted file system. It detaches a mounted file system from the mounting point, where filesys may be a virtual diak name or a mounting point directory name. The algorithm of umount is

11.10.2 Algorithm of umount

```
/****************** Algorithm of umount ********************/
 1. Search the MOUNT table to check filesys is indeed mounted.
 2. Check whether any file is active in the mounted filesys; If so, reject;
 3. Find the mount_point in-memory inode, which should be in memory while
    it's mounted on. Reset the minode's mounted flag to 0; then iput() the
    minode.
```

   To check whether a mounted file system contains any files that are actively in use, search the in-memory minodes for any entry whose dev matches the dev number of the mounted file system.

11.10.3 Cross Mounting Points

While it is easy to implement mount and umount, there are implications. With mount, we must modify the getino(pathname) function to support crossing mount points. Assume that a file system, newfs, has been mounted on the directory /a/b/c/. When traversing a pathname, mount point crossing may occur in both directions.

(1) **Downward traversal:** When traversing the pathname /a/b/c/x, once we reach the minode of /a/b/c, we should see that the minode has been mounted on (mounted flag=1). Instead of searching for x in the INODE of /a/b/c, we must

   - Follow the minode's mntPtr pointer to locate the mount table entry.
   - From the mount table's dev number, get its root (ino=2) INODE into memory.
   - Then continue search for x under the root INODE of the mounted device.

(2) **Upward traversal:** Assume that we are at the directory /a/b/c/x/ and traversing upward, e.g. cd ../ ../, which will cross the mount point /a/b/c. When we reach the root INODE of the mounted file system, we should see that it is a root directory (ino=2) but its dev number differs from that of the

real root, so it is not the real root yet. Using its dev number, we can locate its mount table entry, which points to the mounted minode of /a/b/c/. Then, we switch to the minode of /a/b/c/ and continue the upward traversal. Thus, crossing mount point is like a monkey or squirrel hoping from one tree to another and then back.

Since crossing mounting points changes the device number, a single global device number becomes inadequate. We must modify the getino() function as

```
int getino(char *pathname, int *dev)
```

and modify calls to getino() as

```
int dev;                      // local in function that calls getino()
if (pathnme[0]=='/')
    dev = root->dev;          // absolute pathname
else
    dev = running->cwd->dev;  // relative pathname

int ino = getino(pathname, &dev);  // pass &dev as an extra parameter
```

In the modified getino() function, change *dev whenever the pathname crosses a mounting point. Thus, the modified getino() function essentially returns (**dev**, ino) of a pathname with **dev** being the final device number.

11.10.4 File Protection

In Unix/Linux, file protection is by permission bits in the file's INODE. Each file's INODE has an i_mode field, in which the low 9 bits are permissions. The 9 permission bits are

```
owner      group      other
-------    -------    -------
r w x      r w x      r w x
```

The first 3 bits apply to the owner of the file, the second 3 bits apply to users in the same group as the owner, and the last 3 bits apply to all others. For directories, the x bit indicates whether a process is allowed to go into the directory. Each process has a uid and a gid. When a process tries to access a file, the file system checks the process uid and gid against the file's permission bits to determine whether it is allowed to access the file with the intended mode of operation. If the process does not have the right permission, the access will be denied. For the sake of simplicity, we may ignore process gid and use only the process uid to check access permission.

11.10.5 Real and Effective uid

In Unix/Linux, each process has a **real uid** and an **effective uid**. The file system checks the access rights of a process by its effective uid. Under normal conditions, the effective uid and real uid of a process are identical. When a process executes a **setuid** program, which has the **setuid** bit in the file's i_mode field turned on, the process' effective uid becomes the uid of the program. While executing a **setuid program**, the process effectively becomes the owner of the program file. For example, when a process executes the mail program, which is a setuid program owned by the superuser, it can write to the mail file of another user. When a process finishes executing a setuid program, it reverts back to the real uid. For simplicity, we shall ignore effective uid also.

11.10.6 File Locking

File locking is a mechanism which allows a process to set locks on a file, or parts of a file to prevent race conditions when updating files. File locks can be either shared, which allows concurrent reads, or exclusive, which enforces exclusive write. File locks can also be mandatory or advisory. For example, Linux supports both shared and exclusive files locks but file locking is only advisory. In Linux, file locks can be set by the fcntl() system call and manipulated by the flock() system call. For simplicity, we shall assume only a very simple kind of file locking. When a process tries to open a file, the intended mode of operation is checked for compatibility. The only compatible modes are READs. If a file is already opened for updating mode, i.e. WR|RW|APPEND, it cannot be opened again. However, this does not prevent related processes, e.g. a parent process and a child process, from modifying the same file that's opened by the parent, but this is also true in Unix/Linux. In that case, the file system can only guarantee each write operation is atomic but not the writing order of the processes, which depends on process scheduling.

11.10.7 Programming Project #3: Implementation of Complete File System

Programming Project #3 is to complete the file system implementation by including functions in the Level-3 of the file system. Sample solution of the file system is available for download at the book's website. Source code of the complete file system is available for instructors upon request.

11.11 Extensions of File System Project

The simple EXT2 file system uses 1 KB block size and has only 1 disk block group. It can be extended easily as follows.

(1) Multiple groups: The size of group descriptor is 32 bytes. With 1 KB block size, a block may contain 1024/32 = 32 group descriptors. With 32 groups, the file system size can be extended to 32*8 = 256 MB.
(2) 4 KB block size: With 4 KB block size and only one group, the file system size would be 4*8 = 32 MB. With one group descriptor block, the file system may have 128 groups, which extend the file system size to 128*32 = 4GB. With 2 group descriptor blocks, the file system size would be 8GB, etc. Most of the extensions are straightforward, which are suitable topics for programming projects.
(3) Pipe files: It's possible to implement pipes as regular files, which obey the read/write protocol of pipes. The advantages of this scheme are: it unifies pipes and file inodes and it allows named pipes, which can be used by unrelated processes. In order to support fast read/write operations, pipe contents should be in memory, such as a RAMdisk. If desired, the reader may implement named pipes as FIFO files.

(4) I/O Buffering: In the Programming Project, every disk block is read in or written out directly. This would incur too much physical disk I/O operations. For better efficiency, a real file system usually uses a set of I/O buffers as a cache memory for disk blocks. File system I/O buffering is covered in Chap. 12, but it may be incorporated into the file system project.

11.12 Summary

This chapter covers EXT2 file system. The goal of this chapter is to lead the reader to implement a complete EXT2 file system that is totally Linux compatible. The premise is that if the reader understands one file system well, it should be easy to adapt to any other file systems. It first describes the historic role of EXT2 file system in Linux and the current status of EXT3/EXT4 file systems. It uses programming examples to show the various EXT2 data structures and how to traverse the EXT2 files system tree. Then it shows how to implement an EXT2 file system which supports all file operations as in the Linux kernel. It shows how to build a base file system by mount_root from a virtual disk. Then it divides the file system implementation into 3 levels. Level-1 expands the base file system to implement the file system tree. Level-2 implements read/write operations of file contents. Level-3 implements mount/umount of file systems and file protection. In each level, it describes the algorithms of the file system functions and demonstrates their implementations by programming examples. Each level is cumulated by a programming project. The final project is to integrate all the programming examples and exercises into a fully functional file system. The programming project has been used as the class project in the CS360, Systems Programming, course at EECS, WSU for many years, and it has proved to be very effective and successful.

Problems

1. Write a C program to display the group descriptor of an EXT2 file system on a device.
2. Modify the imap.c program to print the inodes bitmap in char map form, i.e. for each bit, print a '0' if the bit is 0, print a '1' if the bit is 1.
3. Write a C program to display the blocks bitmap of an Ext2 file system, also in char map form.
4. Write a C program to print the dir_entries of a directory.
5. A virtual disk can be mounted under Linux as a loop device, as in

```
sudo mount -o loop mydisk /mnt      # mount mydisk to /mnt
mkdir /mnt/newdir                   # create new dirs and copy files to /mnt
sudo umount /mnt                    # umount when finished
```

Run the dir.c program on mydisk again to verify the newly created dirs and files still exist.
6. Given an INODE pointer to a DIRectory inode. Write a

```
int  search(INODE *dir, char *name)
```

function which searches for a dir_entry with a given name. Return its inode number if found, else return 0.
7. Given a device containing an EXT2 file system and a pathname, .e.g. /a/b/c/d, write a C function

```
INODE *path2inode(int fd, char *pathname)  // assume fd=file descriptor
```

which returns an INODE pointer to the file's inode, or 0 if the file in inaccessible.

8. Assume: a small EXT2 file system with 1 KB block size and only one blocks group.

   1. Prove that a file may only have some double-indirect blocks but no triple-indirect blocks.
   2. Given the pathname of a file, e.g. /a/b/c/d, write a C program, showblock, which prints all disk block numbers of the file. Hint: use Mailman's algorithm for double indirect blocks, if any.

9. In the Programming Project #1, an in-memory minode is released as FREE when its refCount reaches 0. Design and implement a scheme, which uses the minode[ ] area as a cache memory for in-memory INODES. Once an INODE is loaded into a minode slot, try to keep it in memory for as long as possible even if no process is actively using it. Whenever a process finds a needed INODE in memory, count it as a cache hit. Otherwise, it's a cache miss. Modify the iget(dev, ino) function to count the number of cache hits.

10. Implement step (2) of the pwd algorithm as a utility function

```
int get_myino(MINODE *mip, int *parent_ino)
```

which returns the inode number of . and that of .. in parent_ino.

11. Implement step (4) of the pwd algorithm as a utility function

```
int get_myname(MINODE *parent_minode, int my_ino, char *my_name)
```

which returns the name string of a dir_entry identified by my_ino in the parent directory.

12. Implement the **mv file1 file2** operation, which moves file1 to file2. For files on the same device, mv should just rename file1 as file2 without copying file contents. Hints: link-unlink. How to implement mv if the files are on different devices?

References

Card, R., Theodore Ts'o, T., Stephen Tweedie, S., "Design and Implementation of the Second Extended Filesystem", web.mit.edu/tytso/www/linux/ext2intro.html, 1995
Cao, M., Bhattacharya, S, Tso, T., "Ext4: The Next Generation of Ext2/3 File system", IBM Linux Technology Center, 2007.
EXT2: http://www.nongnu.org/ext2-doc/ext2.html, 2001
EXT3: http://jamesthornton.com/hotlist/linux-filesystems/ext3-journal, 2015

Block Device I/O and Buffer Management

12

Abstract

This chapter covers block device I/O and buffer management. It explains the principles of block device I/O and advantages of I/O buffering. It discusses the buffer management algorithm of Unix and points out its shortcomings. Then it uses semaphores to design new buffer management algorithms to improve the efficiency and performance of the I/O buffer cache. It is shown that the simple PV algorithm is easy to implement, has good cache effect and is free of deadlock and starvation. It presents a programming project to compare the performances of the Unix buffer management algorithm and the PV algorithm. The programming project should also help the reader to better understand I/O operations in file systems.

12.1 Block Device I/O Buffers

In Chap. 11, we showed the algorithms of read/write regular files. The algorithms rely on two key operations, get_block and put_block, which read/write a disk block to/from a buffer in memory. Since disk I/O are slow in comparison with memory access, it is undesirable to do disk I/O on every read/write file operation. For this reason, most file systems use I/O buffering to reduce the number of physical I/O to/from storage devices. A well designed I/O buffering scheme can significantly improve file I/O efficiency and increase system throughput.

The basic principle of I/O buffering is very simple. The file system uses a set of I/O buffers as a cache memory for block devices. When a process tries to read a disk block identified by (dev, blk), it first searches the buffer cache for a buffer already assigned to the disk block. If such a buffer exists and contains valid data, it simply reads from the buffer without reading the block from disk again. If such a buffer does not exist, it allocates a buffer for the disk block, reads data from disk into the buffer, then reads data from the buffer. Once a block is read in, the buffer will be kept in the buffer cache for the next read/write requests of the same block by any process. Similarly, when a process writes to a disk block, it first gets a buffer assigned to the block. Then it writes data to the buffer, marks the buffer as dirty for delay write and releases it to the buffer cache. Since a dirty buffer contains valid data, it can be used to satisfy subsequent read/write requests for the same block without incurring real disk I/O. Dirty buffers will be written to disk only when they are to be reassigned to different blocks.

© Springer International Publishing AG, part of Springer Nature 2018

K. C. Wang, *Systems Programming in Unix/Linux*, https://doi.org/10.1007/978-3-319-92429-8_12

Before discussing buffer management algorithms, we first introduce the following terms. In read_file/write_file, we have assumed that they read/write from/to a dedicated buffer in memory. With I/O buffering, the buffer will be allocated dynamically from a buffer cache. Assume that BUFFER is the structure type of buffers (defined below) and getblk(dev, blk) allocates a buffer assigned to (dev, blk) from the buffer cache. Define a bread(dev, blk) function, which returns a buffer (pointer) containing valid data.

```
BUFFER *bread(dev,blk) // return a buffer containing valid data
{
    BUFFER *bp = getblk(dev,blk); // get a buffer for (dev,blk)
    if (bp data valid)
        return bp;
    bp->opcode = READ;              // issue READ operation
    start_io(bp);                   // start I/O on device
    wait for I/O completion;
    return bp;
}
```

After reading data from a buffer, the process releases the buffer back to the buffer cache by brelse(bp). Similarly, define a write_block(dev, blk, data) function as

```
write_block(dev, blk, data)        // write data from U space
{
    BUFFER *bp = bread(dev,blk);   // read in the disk block first
    write data to bp;
    (synchronous write)? bwrite(bp) : dwrite(bp);
}
```

where bwrite(bp) is for synchronous write and dwrite(bp) is for delay-write, as shown below.

```
-----------------------------------------------------------------
bwrite(BUFFER *bp){              |   dwrite(BUFFER *bp){
    bp->opcode = WRITE;          |      mark bp dirty for delay_write;
    start_io(bp);                |      brelse(bp); // release bp
    wait for I/O completion;     |   }
    brelse(bp); // release bp    |
}                                |
-----------------------------------------------------------------
```

Synchronous write waits for the write operation to complete. It is used for sequential or removable block devices, e.g. USB drives. For random access devices, e.g. hard disks, all writes can be delay writes. In delay write, dwrite(bp) marks the buffer as dirty and releases it to the buffer cache. Since dirty buffers contain valid data, they can be used to satisfy subsequent read/write requests of the same block. This not only reduces the number of physical disk I/O but also improves the buffer cache effect. A dirty buffer will be written to disk only when it is to be reassigned to a different disk block, at which time the buffer is written out by

```
awrite(BUFFER *bp)
{
    bp->opcode = ASYNC;      // for ASYNC write;
    start_io(bp);
}
```

awrite() calls start_io() to start I/O operation on the buffer but does not wait for the operation to complete. When an ASYNC write operation completes, the disk interrupt handler will release the buffer.

Physical block device I/O: Each device has an I/O queue which contains buffers of pending I/O. The start_io() operation on a buffer is

```
start_io(BUFFER *bp)
{
    enter bp into device I/O queue;
    if (bp is first buffer in I/O queue)
        issue I/O command for bp to device;
}
```

When an I/O operation completes, the device interrupt handler finishes the I/O operation on the current buffer and starts I/O for the next buffer in the I/O queue if it is non-empty. The algorithm of the device interrupt handler is

```
InterruptHandler()
{
    bp = dequeue(device I/O queue); // bp = remove head of I/O queue
    (bp->opcode == ASYNC)? brelse(bp) : unblock process on bp;
    if (!empty(device I/O queue))
        issue I/O command for first bp in I/O queue;
}
```

12.2 Unix I/O Buffer Management Algorithm

Unix I/O buffer management algorithm first appeared in V6 Unix (Ritchie and Thompson 1978; Lion 1996). It is discussed in detail in Chapter 3 of Bach (Bach 1990). The Unix buffer management subsystem consists of the following components.

(1). I/O buffers: A set of NBUF buffers in kernel is used as a buffer cache. Each buffer is represented by a structure.

```
typdef struct buf{
    struct buf *next_free;     // freelist pointer
    struct buf *next_dev;      // dev_list pointer
    int dev,blk;               // assigned disk block;
```

```
      int opcode;                 // READ|WRITE
      int dirty;                  // buffer data modified
      int async;                  // ASYNC write flag
      int valid;                  // buffer data valid
      int busy;                   // buffer is in use
      int wanted;                 // some process needs this buffer
      struct semaphore lock=1;    // buffer locking semaphore; value=1
      struct semaphore iodone=0;  // for process to wait for I/O completion;
      char buf[BLKSIZE];          // block data area
    } BUFFER;
    BUFFER buf[NBUF], *freelist; // NBUF buffers and free buffer list
```

The buffer structure consists of two parts; a header part for buffer management and a data part for a block of data. To conserve kernel memory, the status fields may be defined as a bit vector, in which each bit represents a unique status condition. They are defined as int here for clarity and ease of discussion.

(2). Device Table: Each block device is represented by a device table structure.

```
    struct devtab{
      u16  dev;               // major device number
      BUFFER *dev_list;       // device buffer list
      BUFFER *io_queue;       // device I/O queue
    } devtab[NDEV];
```

Each devtab has a dev_list, which contains I/O buffers currently assigned to the device, and an io_queue, which contains buffers of pending I/O operations on the device. The I/O queue may be organized for optimal I/O operations. For instance, it may implement the various disk scheduling algorithms, such as the elevator algorithm or the linear-sweep algorithm, etc. For the sake of simplicity, Unix uses FIFO I/O queues.

(3). Buffer Initialization: When the system starts, all I/O buffers are in the freelist and all device lists and I/O queues are empty.

(4). Buffer Lists: When a buffer is assigned to a (dev, blk), it is inserted into the devtab's dev_list. If the buffer is currently in use, it is marked as BUSY and removed from the freelist. A BUSY buffer may also be in the I/O queue of a devtab. Since a buffer cannot be free and busy at the same time, the device I/O queue is maintained by using the same next_free pointer. When a buffer is no longer BUSY, it is released back to the freelist but remains in the dev_list for possible reuse. A buffer may change from one dev_list to another only when it is reassigned. As shown before, read/write disk blocks can be expressed in terms of bread, bwrite and dwrite, all of which depend on getblk and brelse. Therefore, getblk and brelse form the core of the Unix buffer management scheme. The algorithm of getblk and brelse is as follows.

(5). Unix getblk/brelse algorithm: (Lion 1996; Chapter 3 of (Bach 1990)).

```
      /* getblk: return a buffer=(dev,blk) for exclusive use */
      BUFFER *getblk(dev,blk){
        while(1){
          (1). search dev_list for a bp=(dev, blk);
```

```
    (2). if (bp in dev_lst){
           if (bp BUSY){
              set bp WANTED flag;
              sleep(bp);      // wait for bp to be released
              continue;       // retry the algorithm
           }
           /* bp not BUSY */
           take bp out of freelist;
           mark bp BUSY;
           return bp;
         }
    (3). /* bp not in cache; try to get a free buf from freelist */
         if (freelist empty){
            set freelist WANTED flag;
            sleep(freelist); // wait for any free buffer
            continue;        // retry the algorithm
         }
    (4). /* freelist not empty */
         bp = first bp taken out of freelist;
         mark bp BUSY;
         if (bp DIRTY){          // bp is for delayed write
            awrite(bp);          // write bp out ASYNC;
            continue;            // from (1) but not retry
         }
    (5). reassign bp to (dev,blk); // set bp data invalid, etc.
         return bp;
}


/** brelse: releases a buffer as FREE to freelist **/
brelse(BUFFER *bp){
  if (bp WANTED)
     wakeup(bp);        // wakeup ALL proc's sleeping on bp;
  if (freelist WANTED)
     wakeup(freelist); // wakeup ALL proc's sleeping on freelist;
  clear bp and freelist WANTED flags;
  insert bp to (tail of) freelist;
}
```

It is noted that in (Bach 1990), buffers are maintained in hash queues. When the number of buffers is large, hashing may reduce the search time. If the number of buffers is small, hashing may actually increases the execution time due to additional overhead. Furthermore, studies (Wang 2002) have shown that hashing has almost no effect on the buffer cache performance. In fact, we may consider the device lists as hash queues by the simple hashing function hash(dev, blk) = dev. So there is no loss of generality by using the device lists as hash queues. The Unix algorithm is very simple and easy to understand. Perhaps because of its extreme simplicity, most people are not very impressed by it at first sight. Some may even consider it naive because of the repeated retry loops. However, the more you look at it, the more it makes sense. This amazingly simple but effective algorithm attests to the ingenuity of the original Unix designers. Some specific comments about the Unix algorithm follow.

(1). Data Consistency: In order to ensure data consistency, getblk must never assign more than one buffer to the same (dev, blk). This is achieved by having the process re-execute the "retry loops" after waking up from sleep. The reader may verify that every assigned buffer is unique. Second, dirty buffers are written out before they are reassigned, which guarantees data consistency.

(2). Cache effect: Cache effect is achieved by the following means. A released buffer remains in the device list for possible reuse. Buffers marked for delay-write do not incur immediate I/O and are available for reuse. Buffers are released to the tail of freelist but allocated from the front of freelist. This is based on the LRU ((Least-Recent-Used) principle, which helps prolong the lifetime of assigned buffers, thereby increasing their cache effect.

(3). Critical Regions: Device interrupt handlers may manipulate the buffer lists, e.g. remove a bp from a devtab's I/O queue, change its status and call brelse(bp). So in getblk and brelse, device interrupts are masked out in these critical regions. These are implied but not shown in the algorithm.

12.2.1   Shortcomings of Unix Algorithm

The Unix algorithm is very simple and elegant, but it also has the following shortcomings.

(1). Inefficiency: the algorithm relies on retry loops. For example, releasing a buffer may wake up two sets of processes; those who want the released buffer, as well as those who just need a free buffer. Since only one process can get the released buffer, all other awakened processes must go back to sleep again. After waking up from sleep, every awakened process must re-execute the algorithm again from beginning because the needed buffer may already exist. This would cause excessive process switches.

(2). Unpredictable cache effect: In the Unix algorithm, every released buffer is up for grabs. If the buffer is obtained by a process which needs a free buffer, the buffer would be reassigned, even though there may be processes which still need the buffer.

(3). Possible starvation: The Unix algorithm is based on the principle of "free economy", in which every process is given chances to try but with no guarantee of success. Therefore, process starvation may occur.

(4). The algorithm uses sleep/wakeup, which is only suitable for uniprocessor systems.

12.3   New I/O Buffer Management Algorithm

In this section, we shall show a new algorithm for I/O buffer management. Instead of using sleep/wakeup, we shall use P/V on semaphores for process synchronization. The main advantages of semaphores over sleep/wakeup are

(1). Counting semaphores can be used to represent the number of available resources, e.g. the number of free buffers.

(2). When many processes wait for a resource, the V operation on a semaphore unblocks only one waiting process, which does not have to retry since it is guaranteed to have the resource.

These semaphore properties can be used to design more efficient algorithms for buffer management. Formally, we specify the problem as follows.

12.3.1   Buffer Management Algorithm using Semaphores

Assume a uniprocessor kernel (one process runs at a time). Use P/V on counting semaphores to design new buffer management algorithms which meet the following requirements:

(1). Guarantee data consistency.
(2). Good cache effect.
(3). High efficiency: No retry loops and no unnecessary process "wakeups".
(4). Free of deadlocks and starvation.

It is noted that merely replacing sleep/wakeup in the Unix algorithm by P/V on semaphores is not an acceptable solution because doing so would retain all the retry loops. We must redesign the algorithm to meet all the above requirements and justify that the new algorithm is indeed better than the Unix algorithm. First, we define the following semaphores.

```
BUFFER buf[NBUF];         // NBUF I/O buffers
SEMAPHORE free = NBUF;    // counting semaphore for FREE buffers
SEMAPHORE buf[i].sem = 1; // each buffer has a lock sem=1;
```

To simplify the notations, we shall refer to the semaphore of each buffer by the buffer itself. As in the Unix algorithm, initially all buffers are in the freelist and all device lists and I/O queues are empty. The following shows a simple buffer management algorithm using semaphores.

12.4   PV Algorithm

```
BUFFER *getblk(dev, blk)
{
     while(1){
(1).     P(free);              // get a free buffer first
(2).     if (bp in dev_list){
(3).         if (bp not BUSY){
                 remove bp from freelist;
                 P(bp);        // lock bp but does not wait
                 return bp;
             }
             // bp in cache but BUSY
             V(free);          // give up the free buffer
(4).         P(bp);            // wait in bp queue
             return bp;
         }
         // bp not in cache, try to create a bp=(dev, blk)
```

```
  (5).    bp = frist buffer taken out of freelist;
          P(bp);                 // lock bp, no wait
  (6).    if (bp dirty){
              awrite(bp);        // write bp out ASYNC, no wait
              continue;          // continue from (1)
          }
  (7).    reassign bp to (dev,blk); // mark bp data invalid, not dirty
          return bp;
       }                         // end of while(1)
}


brelse(BUFFER *bp)
{
  (8). if (bp queue has waiter){ V(bp); return; }
  (9). if (bp dirty && free queue has waiter){ awrite(bp); return; }
  (10). enter bp into (tail of) freelist; V(bp); V(free);
}
```

Next, we show that the PV algorithm is correct and meets the requirements.

1. **Buffer uniqueness:** In getblk(), if there are free buffers, the process does not wait at (1). Then it searches the dev_list. If the needed buffer already exits, the process does not create the same buffer again. If the needed buffer does not exist, the process creates the needed buffer by using a free buffer, which is guaranteed to have. If there are no free buffers, it is possible that several processes, all of which need the same buffer, are blocked at (1). When a free buffer is released at (10), it unblocks only one process to create the needed buffer. Once a buffer is created, it will be in the dev_list, which prevents other processes from creating the same buffer again. Therefore, every assigned buffer is unique.

2. **No retry loops:** The only place a process re-executes the while(1) loop is at (6), but that is not a retry because the process is continually executing.

3. **No unnecessary wakeups:** In getblk(), a process may wait for a free buffer at (1) or a needed buffer at (4). In either case, the process is not woken up to run again until it has a buffer. Furthermore, at (9), when a dirty buffer is to be released as free and there are waiters for free buffers at (1), the buffer is not released but written out directly. This avoids an unnecessary process wakeup.

4. **Cache effect:** In the Unix algorithm, every released buffer is up for grabs. In the new algorithm, a buffer with waiters is always kept for reuse. A buffer is released as free only if it has no waiters. This should improve the buffer's cache effect.

5. **No deadlocks and starvation:** In getblk(), the semaphore locking order is always unidirectional, i.e. P(free), then P(bp), but never the other way around, so deadlock cannot occur. If there are no free buffers, all requesting processes will be blocked at (1). This implies that while there are processes waiting for free buffer, all buffers in use cannot admit any new users. This guarantees that a BUSY buffer will eventually be released as free. Therefore, starvation for free buffers cannot occur.

Although we have shown that the new algorithm is correct, whether it can perform better than the Unix algorithm remains an open question, which can only be answered by real quantitative data. For this purpose, we have designed a programming project to compare the performances of the buffer management algorithms. The programming project should also help the reader to better understand I/O operations in file systems.

12.5   Programming Project: Comparison of I/O Buffer Management Algorithms

The programming project is to implement a simulation system to compare the performances of the Unix I/O buffer management algorithms and the PV algorithm using semaphores. Although the immediate goal is I/O buffer performance, the real goal is for the reader to understand I/O operations of file systems. The following describes the project.

12.5.1   System Organization

Figure 12.1 shows the organization of the simulation system.

(1). Box#1: User Interface: This is the user interface part of the simulation system. It prompts for input commands, show command executions, displays system status and execution results, etc. During development, the reader may input commands manually for tasks to execute. During final testing, tasks should have their own sequence of input commands. For example, each task may read an input file containing commands. After a task switch, task inputs will be read from a different file.

Fig. 12.1 System Organization Diagram

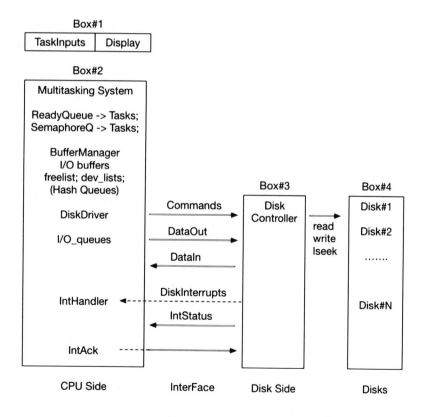

12.5.2   Multitasking System

(2). Box#2: This is the CPU side of a multitasking system, which simulates the kernel mode of a uniprocessor (single CPU) file system. It is essentially the same multitasking system described in Chap. 4 for user-level threads, except for the following modifications. When the system starts, it creates and runs a main task with the lowest priority, but it creates ntask working tasks, all with priority 1, and enters them into the readyQueue. Then the main task executes the following code, which switches task to run working tasks from the readyQueue.

```
/******* Main Task Code *******/
// after system initialization
while(1){
  while(task && readyQ == 0);   // loop if no task runnable
  if (readyQ)                   // if readyQueue nonempty
     kswitch();                 // switch to run a working task
  else
     end_task();                // all working tasks have ended
}
```

Since the main task has the lowest priority, it will run again if there are no runnable tasks or if all tasks have ended. In the latter case, the main task execute end_task(), in which it collects and displays the simulation results and terminates, thus ending the simulation run.

All working tasks execute the same body() function, in which each task reads commands from an input file to execute read or write disk block operations until end of the command file.

```
#define CMDLEN 10
int cmdfile[NTASK]; // opened command file descriptors
int task = ntask;   // number of active tasks
int body()
{
   int dev, blk;
   char opcode, cmd[CMDLEN];
   while(1){
      if (read(cmdfile[running->pid], cmd, CMDLEN)==0){
         running->status = DEAD; // task ends
         task--;                 // dec task count by 1
         tswtich();
      }
      sscanf(cmd, "%c%4d%5d", &opcode, &dev, &blk);
      if (opcode=='r')           // read (dev, blk)
         readBlk(dev, blk);
      if (opcode=='w')
         writeBlk(dev, blk);   // write (dev, blk)
   }
}
```

The commands of each task are generated randomly by the rand() function modulo a limit value. Each command is a triple of the form

```
[r xxx yyyy] or [w xxx yyyy], where xxx=dev, yyyy=blkno;
```

For a [r dev blk] command, the task calls

$$BUFFER\ *bread(dev,\ blk)$$

to get a buffer (pointer) containing valid data. After reading data from the buffer, it releases the buffer back to the buffer cache for reuse. In bread(), the task may wait for a buffer in getblk() or until the buffer data become valid. If so, it sleeps (in Unix algorithm) or becomes blocked (in PV algorithm), which switches task to run the next task from the readyQueue.

For a [w dev blk] command, the task tries to get a buffer for (dev, blk). If it has to wait for a buffer in getblk(), it will sleep or become blocked and switch task to run the next task. After writing data to a buffer, it marks the buffer as DIRTY for delayed write and releases the buffer to the buffer cache. Then it tries to execute the next command, etc.

12.5.3   Buffer Manager

The Buffer Manager implements buffer management functions, which consist of

```
BUFFER *bread(dev, blk)
         dwrite(BUFFER *bp)
         awrite(BUFFER *bp)
BUFFER *getblk(dev, blk)
         brelse(BUFFER *bp)
```

These functions may invoke the Disk Driver to issue physical disk I/O.

12.5.4   Disk Driver

The Disk Driver consists of two parts:

(1). **start_io():** maintain device I/O queues and issue I/O operation for buffers in I/O queue.
(2). **Interrupt Handler:** At the end of each I/O operation the Disk Controller interrupts the CPU. Upon receiving an interrupt, the Interrupt Handler first reads the Interrupt Status from IntStatus, which contains

```
[dev  | R|W |  StatusCode]
|<----- e.g.10 chars---->|
```

where dev identifies the device. The Interrupt Handler removes the buffer from the head of the device I/O queue and processes the interrupt for the buffer. For a disk READ interrupt, the Interrupt Handler first moves the block of data from DataIn into the buffer's data area. Then it marks the buffer data valid and wakes up or unblocks the task that's waiting on the buffer for valid data. The awakened process will read data from the buffer and release the buffer back to the buffer cache. For a disk WRITE interrupt, there is no process waiting on the buffer for I/O completion. Such an ASYNC write buffer is handled by the Interrupt handler. It turns off the buffer's ASYNC write flag and releases the buffer to the buffer cache. Then, it examines the device I/O queue. If the I/O queue is nonempty, it issues I/O commands for the first buffer in the I/O queue. Before issuing a disk WRITE operation, it copies the buffer's data to DataOut for the Disk Controller to get. Finally, it writes an ACK to IntAck to acknowledge the current interrupt, allowing the Disk Controller to continue When the Interrupt Handler finishes processing the current interrupt, normal task execution resumes from the last interrupted point.

12.5.5   Disk Controller

(3). Box#3: This is the Disk Controller, which is a **child process** of the **main process**. As such, it operates independently with the CPU side except for the communication channels between them, which are shown as the **Interface** between CPU and Disk Controller. The communication channels are implemented by pipes between the main process and the child process.

Commands: I/O commands from CPU to Disk Controller
DataOut   :   data out from CPU to Disk Controller in write operations
DataIn   :   data in from Disk Controller to CPU in read operations
IntStatus :   interrupt status from Disk Controller to CPU
IntAck   :   interrupt ACK from CPU to Disk Controller

12.5.6   Disk Interrupts

Interrupts from Disk Controller to CPU are implemented by the SIGUSR1 (#10) signal. At the end of each I/O operation, the Disk Controller issues a kill(ppid, SIGUSR1) system call to send a SIGUSR1 signal to the parent process, which acts as an interrupt to the virtual CPU. As usual, the virtual CPU may mask out/in disk interrupts (signals) in Critical Regions. To prevent race condition, the Disk Controller must receive an interrupt ACK from the CPU before it can interrupt again.

12.5.7   Virtual Disks

(4). Box#4: These are virtual disks, which are simulated by Linux files. Using the Linux system calls lseek(), read() and write(), we may support any block I/O operations on the virtual disks. For simplicity, the disk block size is set to 16 bytes. Since the data contents do not matter, they can be set to a fixed sequence of 16 chars.

12.5.8   Project Requirements

Implement two versions of buffer management algorithms:

```
        Unix algorithm using sleep/wakeup
        New algorithm using semaphores.
```

Compare their performances in terms of buffer cache hit-ratio, numbers of actual I/O operations, task switches, retries and total run time, etc. under different task/buffer ratios.

12.5.9 Sample Base Code

For the sake of brevity, we only show the main.c file of the CPU side and the controller.c file of the Disk Controller. The functions of other included files are only explained briefly. Also, not shown are the code segments used to collect performance statistics, but they can be added easily to the base code.

```c
/************ CPU side: main.c file **********/
#include <stdio.h>
#include <stdlib.h>
#include <sys/time.h>
#include <signal.h>
#include <string.h>
#include "main.h"             // constants, PROC struct pipes
struct itimerval itimer;      // for timer interrupt
struct timeval tv0, tv1, tv2; // count running time
sigset_t sigmask;             // signal mask for critical regions
int stack[NTASK][SSIZE];      // task stacks
int pd[5][2];                 // 5 pipes for communication
int cmdfile[NTASK];           // task command file descriptors
int record[NTASK+2][13];      // record each task use buff status
int task;                     // count alive task
int ntask;                    // number of tasks
int nbuffer;                  // number of buffers
int ndevice;                  // number of devices
int nblock;                   // number of blocks per device
int sample;                   // number of per task inputs
int timer_switch;             // count time switch
char cmd[CMLEN];              // command=[r|w dev blkno]
char buffer[BLOCK];           // save command to commuicate with device
char dev_stat[CMLEN];         // device status
PROC proc[NTASK], MainProc;   // NTASK tasks and main task
PROC *running;                // pointer to current running task
PROC *readyQ, *freeQ, *waitQ; // process link lists
FILE *fp;                     // record simulation results file
int body();                   // task body function
void catcher();               // signal catcher (interrupt handler)

#include "proc.c"             // PROC init, queue functions
#include "buf.c"              // buffer struct, link lists
#include "utility.c"          // generate cmds, end_task()
#include "manager.c"          // getblk,brelse, bread,dwrite,awrite

int main(int argc, char *argv[ ])
{
    if(argc != 6){
        printf("usage: a.out ntask nbuffer ndevice nblock nsample\n");
        exit(0);
    }
```

```
   task = ntask  = atoi(argv[1]);
   nbuffer= atoi(argv[2]);
   ndevice= atoi(argv[3]);
   nblock = atoi(argv[4]);
   sample = atoi(argv[5]);
   if(ntask>NTASK||nbuffer>NBUFFER||ndevice>NDEVICE||nblock>NBLOCK)
      exit(1) ;
   fp = fopen("record", "a"); // record task activities
   printf("Welcome to UNIX Buffer Management System\n");
   printf("Initialize proc[] & buff[] & signal\n");
   initproc();              // build tasks to compete for buffers
   initbuf();               // build buffer link lists
   initsig();               // set sigmask & init itimer for timing
   printf("Install signal handler\n");
   signal(SIGUSR1, catcher); // install catcher for SIGUSR1 signal
   printf("Open pipes for communication\n");
   open_pipe();             // create communication pipes
   printf("fork(): parent as CPU child as Disk Controller\n");
   switch(fork()){
      case -1: perror("fork call"); exit(2); break;
      case  0: // child process as disk controller
         close_pipe(0);  // configure pipes at child side
         sprintf(buffer,"%d %d %d %d %d",\
                 CMDIN, WRITEIN, READOUT, STATOUT, ACKIN);
         execl("controller","controller",buffer,argv[3],argv[4],0);
         break;
      default:              // parent process as virtual CPU
         close_pipe(1);  // configure pipes at parent side
         printf("MAIN: check device status\n");
         check_dev();    // wait for child has created devices
         printf("Generate command file for each task\n");
         gencmd();       // generate command files of tasks
         gettimeofday(&tv0,0);  // start record run time
         while(1){
            INTON                 // enable interrupts
            while(tasks && readyQ == 0); // wait for ready tasks
            if(readyQ)
             kswitch();           // switch to run ready task
            else
              end_task();        // end processing
         }
      }
}

/******* task body function **********/
int body(int pid)
{
   char rw;             // opcode in command: read or write
   int dev, blk;        // dev, blk in command
   int n, count=0;      // task commands count
```

```
   while(1){
      n = read(cmdfile[running->pid], cmd, CMLEN);
      if (n==0){                    // if end of cmd file
         running->status = DEAD;    // mark task dead
         task--;                    // number of active task -1
         kswitch();                 // switch to next task
      }
      count++;                      // commands count++
      sscanf(cmd, "%c%5d%5d",&rw,&dev,&blk);
      if (rw == 'r')
         readBlk(dev, blk);         // READ (dev, blk)
      else
         writeBlk(dev, blk);        // WRITE (dev, blk)
   }
}
int kswitch()
{
  INTOFF        // disable interrupts
    tswitch();  // switch task in assembly code
  INTON         // enable interrupts

}
```

The main.c file includes the following files, which are only explained briefly.

(1). **main.h:** This file defines system constants, PROC structure type and symbolic constants. It also defines the macros

```
        #define INTON  sigprocmask(SIG_UNBLOCK, &sigmask, 0);
        #define INTOFF sigprocmask(SIG_BLOCK,   &sigmask, 0);
```

for masking in/out interrupts, where sigmask is a 32-bit vector with SIGUSR1 bit (10)=1.

(2). **proc.c:** This file initializes the multitasking system. It creates ntask tasks to do disk I/O operations through the buffer cache.

(3). **buf.c:** This file defines semaphore, buffer and device structures. It initializes the buffer and device data structures, and it contains code for buffer link lists operations.

(4). **utility.c:** This file contains functions common to both the CPU side and the Disk Controller side. Examples are creation and configuration of pipes, generation of input commands files and data files for simulated disks, etc. It also implements the end_task() function which collects and display simulation statistics when all tasks have ended.

(5). **manager.c:** This file implements the actual buffer management functions, such as readBlk(dev, blk), writeBlk(dev, blk), getblk() and brelse() which are the core functions of buffer management.

In the simulator, all the files are identical except the manager.c file, which has two versions; one version implements the Unix algorithm and the other one implements the PV algorithm using semaphores.

The following shows the Disk Controller source file, which is executed by a child process of the main process. The information needed by the child process are passed in via command-line parameters in argv[]. After initialization, the Disk Controller process executes an infinite loop until it gets the 'END' command from the CPU, indicating all tasks on the CPU side have ended. Then it closes all the virtual disk files and terminates.

```
/******* Pseudo Code of Disk Controller *******/
initialization;
while(1){
    read command from CMDIN
    if  command = "END", break;
    decode and execute the command
    interrupt CPU;
    read ACK from ACKIN
}
close all virtual disk files and exit
```

```c
/******** Disk Controller: controller.c file: ******/
#include <stdio.h>
#include <fcntl.h>
#include <signal.h>
#include <string.h>

#define DEVICE  128      // max number of devices
#define BLOCK    16      // disk BLOCK size
#define CMLEN    10      // command record length
int main(int argc, char *argv[ ])
{
    char opcode, cmd[CMLEN], buf[BLOCK], status[CMLEN];
    int CMDIN,READIN,WRITEOUT,STATOUT,ACKIN;  // PIPEs
    int i, ndevice, dev, blk;
    int CPU = getppid();  // ppid for sending signal
    int fd[DEVICE];       // files simulate n devices
    char datafile[8];     // save file name
    // get command line parameters
    sscanf(argv[1], "%d %d %d %d %d",\
        &CMDIN, &READIN, &WRITEOUT, &STATOUT, &ACKIN);
    ndevice = atoi(argv[2]);
    printf("Controller: ndevice=%d\n", ndevice);
    gendata(ndevice);      // generate data files as virtual disks
    for (i=0; i<ndevice i++){  // open files to simulate devices
      sprintf(datafile,"data%d", i%128);
      if(( fd[i] = open(datafile, O_RDWR)) < 0)
        sprintf(status, "%dfail",i) ;
      else
        sprintf(status, " %d ok",i) ;
      write(STATOUT, status, CMLEN);  // send device status to CPU
    }
```

```
// Disk Controller Processing loop
while(1){
    read(CMDIN, cmd, CMLEN);            // read command from pipe
    if (!strcmp(cmd, "END"))            // end command from CPU, break
        break;
    sscanf(cmd,"%c%4d%5d", &opcode, &dev, &blk);
    if (opcoe == 'r'){
        read(fd[dev], buf, BLOCK);      // read data of (dev, blk)
        write(WRITEOUT, buf, BLOCK);    // write data to WRITEOUT pipe
    }
    else if (opcode == 'w'){            // write cmd
        read(READIN, buf, BLOCK);       // read data from READIN pipe
        write(fd[dev], buf, BLOCK);     // write data to (dev, blk)
    }
    else
        strcpy(status, "IOerr");
    write(STATOUT, cmd, CMLEN);         // write INTstatus to STATOUT
    kill(CPU, SIGUSR1);                 // interrupt CPU by SIGUSR1
    read(ACKIN, buf, CMLEN);            // read ACK from CPU
}
// Disk controller end processing
for (i=0; i < ndevice;i++)
    close(fd[i]);
}


int gendata(int ndev) // generate data file as virtual disks
{
  char cmd[2048], name[8];
  int fd[128], i, j;
  printf("generate data files\n");
  for(i=0; i<ndev; i++){
    sprintf(name,"data%d", i);
    fd[i]=creat(name, 0644);  // create data files
    for (j=0; j<2048; j++){   // 2 K bytes of '0'-'9' chars
        cmd[j]= i%10 +'0';
    }
    write(fd[i],cmd,2048);
    close(fd[i]);
  }
}
```

The simulator system is compiled and linked into two binary executables, a.out as the CPU side and controller as the Disk Controller side.

```
cc main.c s.s            # a.out as the CPU side
cc -o controller controller.c  # controller as Disk Controller
```

Then run the simulator system as

```
a.out  ntask nbuffer ndevice nblock nsample
```

In order to run the simulator with different input parameters, a sh script can be used, as in

```
# run: sh script to run the simulator systems
#! /bin/bash
for TASK in 4 8 16 64; do
  For BUF in 4 16 64 128; do
    a.out $TASK $BUF 16 64 1000    # ndev=16,nblk=64,sample=1000
  done
  echo -----------------------
done
```

12.5.10 Sample Solutions

Figure 12.2 shows the outputs of the simulator using the Unix algorithm with

4 tasks, 4 buffers, 4 devices, 16 blocks per device and 100 input samples per task.
In the figure, the performance metrics are shown as

```
run-time = total running time
rIO  = number of actual read operations
wIO = number of actual write operations
intr = number of disk interrupts
hits = number of buffer cache hits
swtch = number of task switches
dirty = number of delay write buffers
retry = number of task retries in getblk()
```

The last row of the outputs shows the percentages of the various metrics. The most important performance metrics are the total run time of the simulation and the buffer cache hit ratio. Other metrics may be used as guidance to justify the performance of the algorithms.

Fig. 12.2 Sample Outputs
of Unix Algorithm

```
-----------------------------------------------------------------
ntask:4      nbuffer = 4        ndevice = 4        nblock = 16
run-time=29 msec
CMD  read  write  rIO   wIO  hits  intr swtch dirty retry
--0----1-----2-----3-----4----5-----6-----7-----8-----9--
100    52    48    51    44    3    93    57    43    48
100    51    49    50    55    4   106    59    55    63
100    44    56    44    50    1    94    51    50    56
100    55    45    54    44    3    98    59    44    48
-------------------- percentages ----------------------------
100    50    49    49    48    2    97    56    48    53
-----------------------------------------------------------------
```

Fig. 12.3 Sample Outputs
of PV Algorithm

```
-------------------------------------------------------------------
ntask:4        nbuffer = 4         ndevice = 4          nblock = 16
run-time=24 msec
CMD  read  write  rIO   wIO   hits  intr swtch dirty retry
--0----1-----2--  ---3----4-----5-----6-----7-----8-----9--
100    52    48    49    47    5     91    52    46     0
100    51    49    47    53    5    100    52    53     0
100    44    56    42    55    5     99    47    55     0
100    55    45    49    40   10     85    57    40     0
--------------------- percentages ---------------------------
100    50    49    46    48    6     95    53    48     0
-------------------------------------------------------------------
```

Figure 12.3 shows the outputs of the simulator using the PV algorithm with the same input parameters as in the Unix algorithm. It shows that the run-time (24 msec) is shorter than the Unix algorithm (29 msec) and the buffer cache hit ratio (6%) is higher than the Unix algorithm (2%). It also shows that, whereas the Unix algorithm has a large number of task retries, there are no task retries in the PV algorithm, which may account for the differences in performance between the two algorithms.

12.6   Refinements of Simulation System

The simulation system can be refined in several ways to make it a better model of real file systems.

(1). Instead of a single disk controller, the simulation system can be extended to support a multiple number of disk controllers, which relives I/O congestions through a single data channel.
(2). The input commands can be generated with non-uniform distributions to better model file operations in a real system. For example, they can be generated with more read commands over write commands, and with heavier I/O demands on some devices, etc.

12.7   Refinements of PV Algorithm

The simple PV algorithm is very simple and easy to implement, but it does has the following two weaknesses. First, its cache effect may not be optimal. This is because as soon as there is no free buffer, all requesting processes will be blocked at (1) in getblk(), even if their needed buffer may already exist in the buffer cache. Second, when a process wakes up from the freelist semaphore queue, it may find the needed buffer already exists but BUSY, in which case it will be blocked again at (4). Strictly speaking, the process has been woken up unnecessarily since it gets blocked twice. The reader may consult (Wang 2015) for an improved algorithm, which is optimal in terms of process switches and its cache performance is also better.

12.8   Summary

This chapter covers block device I/O and buffer management. It explains the principles of block device I/O and the advantages of I/O buffering. It discusses the buffer management algorithm of Unix and points out its shortcomings. Then it uses semaphores to design a new buffer management algorithm to improve the efficiency and performance of the I/O buffer cache. It is shown that the simple PV algorithm is easy to implement, has good cache effect and is free of deadlock and starvation. The programming project is for the reader to implement and compare the performances of the buffer management algorithms in a simulation system. The programming project should help the reader better understand I/O operations and interrupts processing in file systems.

References

Bach, M.J., "The Design of the Unix operating system", Prentice Hall, 1990
Lion, J., "Commentary on UNIX 6th Edition, with Source Code", Peer-To-Peer Communications, ISBN 1-57398-013-7, 1996.
Ritchie, D.M., Thompson, K., "The UNIX Time-Sharing System", Bell System Technical Journal, Vol. 57, No. 6, Part 2, July, 1978,
Wang, X., "Improved I/O Buffer Management Algorithms for Unix Operating System", M.S. thesis, EECS, WSU, 2002
Wang, K. C., Design and Implementation of the MTX Operating system, Springer A.G, 2015

TCP/IP and Network Programming

13

Abstract

This chapter covers TCP/IP and network programming. The chapter consists of two parts. The first part covers the TCP/IP protocol and its applications. These include the TCP/IP stack, IP address, hostname, DNS, IP data packets and routers. It describes the UDP and TCP protocols, port number and data flow in TCP/IP networks. It explains the server-client computing model and the socket programming interface. It demonstrates network programming by examples using both UDP and TCP sockets. The first programming project is to implement a pair of TCP server-client to do file operations across the Internet. It allows the user to define additional communication protocols for reliable transfer of file contents.

The second part of the chapter covers Web and CGI programming. It explains the HTTP programming model, Web pages and Web browsers. It shows how to configure the Linux HTTPD server to support user Web pages, PHP and CGI programming. It explains both client side and server side dynamic Web pages. It shows how to create server side dynamic Web pages by both PHP and CGI. The second programming project is for the reader to implement server-side dynamic Web pages by CGI programming on a Linux HTTPD server machine.

13.1 Introduction to Network Programming

Nowadays, accessing the Internet has become a necessity in daily life. While most people may only use the Internet as a tool for information gathering, on-line shopping and social media, etc. computer science students must have some understanding of the Internet technology, as well as some skills in network programming. In this chapter, we shall cover the basics of TCP/IP networks and network programming. These include the TCP/IP protocol, UDP and TCP protocols, server-client computing, HTTP and Web pages, PHP and CGI programming for dynamic Web pages.

13.2 TCP/IP Protocol

TCP/IP (Comer 1988, 2001; RFC1180 1991) is the backbone of Internet. TCP stands for Transmission Control Protocol. IP stands for Internet Protocol. Currently there are 2 versions of IPs, known as IPv4

© Springer International Publishing AG, part of Springer Nature 2018

K. C. Wang, *Systems Programming in Unix/Linux*, https://doi.org/10.1007/978-3-319-92429-8_13

and IPv6. IPv4 uses 32-bit address and IPv6 uses 128-bit address. The discussion here is based on IPv4, which is still the predominant version of IP in use. TCP/IP is organized in several layers, usually referred to as the **TCP/IP stack**. Figure 13.1 shows the TCP/IP layers, representative components in each layer and their functions.

At the top layer are applications which use TCP/IP. Application such as ssh for login to remote hosts, mail for exchanging e-mails, http for Web pages, etc. require reliable data transfer. Such applications typically use TCP in the transport layer. On the other hand, there are applications, e.g. the **ping** command, which is used to query other hosts, do not need reliability. Such applications may use UDP (RFC 768 1980; Comer 1988) in the transport layer for better efficiency. The transport layer is responsible for send/receive application data as packets to/from IP hosts. Data transfer at or above the transport layer between processes and hosts are only logical. Actual data transfer occurs in the **internet** (IP) and Link layers, which divide data packets into data frames for transmission across physical networks. Figure 13.2 shows the data flow paths in TCP/IP networks.

Fig. 13.1 TCP/IP layers

```
---------- Layer ----------   Components ---------- Functions --------------
| Application Layer       |   ssh    ping  |  Application commands          |
--------------------------------------------------------------------------
| Transport Layer         |   TCP    UCP   |  Connection      Datagram      |
--------------------------------------------------------------------------
| Internet Layer          |        IP      |  send/receive  data frames     |
--------------------------------------------------------------------------
| Link Layer              |     Ethernet   |  send/receive  data frames     |
--------------------------------------------------------------------------
```

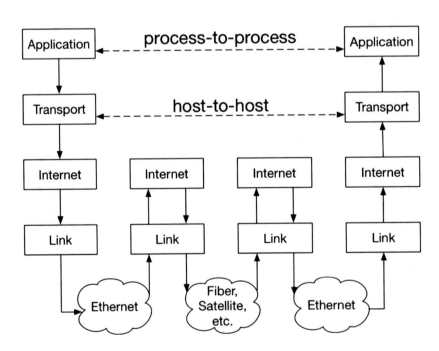

Fig. 13.2 Data flow paths in TCP/IP networks

13.3   IP Host and IP address

A host is a computer or device that supports the TCP/IP protocol. Every host is identified by a 32-bit number called the **IP address**. For convenience, the 32-bit IP address number is usually expressed in a dot notation, e.g.134.121.64.1, in which the individual bytes are separated by dots. A host is also known by a **host name**, e.g. dns1.eecs.wsu.edu. In practice, applications usually use host names rather than IP addresses. Host name and IP address are equivalent in the sense that, given one, we can find the other by **DNS** (Domain Name System) (RFC 134 1987; RFC 1035 1987) servers, which translate IP address into host name and vice versa.

An IP address is divided into two parts: a NetworkID field and a HostID field. Depending on the division, IP addresses are classified into classes A to E. For example, a class B IP address is divided into a 16-bit NetworkID, in which the leading 2 bits are 10, followed by a 16-bit HostID field. Data packets intended for an IP address are first sent to a **router** with the same networkID. The router will forward the packets to a specific host in that network by HostID. Every host has a local host name **localhost** with a default IP address **127.0.0.1.** The Link layer of localhost is a loop-back virtual device, which routes every data packet back to the same localhost. This special feature allows us to run TCP/IP applications on the same computer without actually connecting to the Internet.

13.4   IP Protocol

IP is a protocol for sending/receiving data packets between IP hosts. IP operates in a best-effort manner. An IP host just sends data packets to a receiving host, but it does not guarantee the data packets will be delivered to their destinations, nor in order. This means that IP is not a reliable protocol. If needed, reliability must be implemented above the IP layer.

13.5   IP Packet Format

An IP packet consists of an IP header, sender and receiver IP addresses, followed by data. The maximum size of each IP packet is 64 KB. The IP header contains more information about the data packet, e.g. total length, whether the packet uses TCP or UDP, time-to-live (TTL) count, check-sum for error detection, etc. Figure 13.3 shows the IP header format.

0	4	8	15	16		31
Version	IHL	Type of Service		Total Length		
Identification			Flags		Fragment Offset	
Time to Live		Protocol		Header Checksum		
Source IP Address						
Destination IP Address						
Options					Padding	

Fig. 13.3 IP header format

Fig. 13.4 TCP/IP network
topology

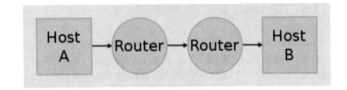

13.6   Routers

IP hosts may be located far apart. It is usually not possible to send data packets from one host to the other directly. Routers are special IP hosts which receive and forward packets. An IP packet may go through many routers, or hops, before arriving at a destination, if at all. Figure 13.4 shows the topology of a TCP/IP network.

Each IP packet has an 8-bit Time-To-Live (TTL) count in the IP header, which has a maximum value of 255. At each router, the TTL is reduced by 1. If the TTL reduces to 0 and the packet still has not reached the destination, it is simply dropped. This prevents any packets from circulating around indefinitely in the IP network.

13.7   UDP User Datagram Protocol

UDP (RFC 768 1980; Comer 1988) operates on top of IP. It is used to send/receive datagrams. Like IP, UDP does not guarantee reliability but it is fast and efficient. It is used in situations where reliability is not essential. For example, a user may use the ping command to probe a target host, as in

ping hostname   OR   ping IPaddress

Ping is an application program which sends a UDP packet with a timestamp to a target host. Upon receiving a pinging packet, the target host echoes the UDP packet with a timestamp back to the sender, allowing the sender to compute and display the round-trip time. If the target host does not exist or is down, the pinging UDP packets would be dropped by routers when its TTL reduces to 0. In that case, the user would notice the absence of any response from the target host. The user may either try to ping it again or conclude that the target host is down. In this case, using UDP is preferred since reliability is not essential.

13.8   TCP Transmission Control Protocol

TCP is a connection-oriented protocol for sending/receiving streams of data. TCP also operates on top of IP but it guarantees reliable data transfers. A common analogy is that UDP is similar to USPS of sending mails and TCP is similar to telephone connections.

13.9   Port Number

At each host, many applications (processes) may be using TCP/UDP at the same time. Each application is uniquely identified by a triple

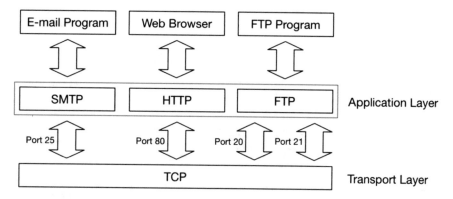

Fig. 13.5 Applications using TCP

Application = (HostIP, Protocol, PortNumber)

where Protocol is either TCP or UDP, PortNumber is a unique unsigned short integer assigned to the application. In order to use UDP or TCP, an application (process) must choose or obtain a PortNumber first. The first 1024 port numbers are reserved. Other port numbers are available for general use. An application may either choose an available port number or let the OS kernel assign a port number. Figure 13.5 shows some of the applications that use TCP in the transport layer and their default port numbers.

13.10 Network and Host Byte Orders

Computers may use either big-endian or little-endian byte order. On the Internet, data are always in network order, which is big-endian. For little-endian machines, such as Intel x86 based PCs, a set of library functions, htons(), htonl(), ntohs(), ntohl(), are available for converting data between host order and network order. For example, a port number 1234 in a PC is an unsigned short integer in host (little-endian) byte order. It must be converted to network order by htons(1234) before using. Conversely, a port number received from the Internet must be converted to host order by ntohs(port).

13.11 Data Flow in TCP/IP Networks

Figure 13.6 shows the data formats of the various layers in a TCP/IP network. It also shows the data flow paths among the different layers.

In Fig. 13.6, data from application layer is passed to the transport layer, which adds a TCP or UDP header to identify the transport protocol used. The combined data is passed on to the IP internet layer, which adds an IP header containing IP addresses to identify the sending and receiving hosts. The combined data is then passed on to the Network Link layer, which divides the data into frames, adding the addresses of the sending and receiving networks for transmission across physical networks. Mapping of IP addresses to network addresses is performed by the Address Resolution Protocol (**ARP**) (ARP 1982). At the receiving end, the data encoding process is reversed. Each layer unpacks the received data by stripping off the headers, reassembles them and delivers the data to a layer above. The original data of an application at a sending host is ultimately delivered to the corresponding application at the receiving host.

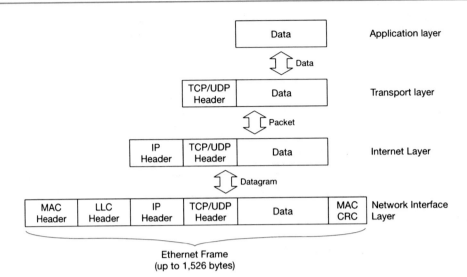

Fig. 13.6 Data format in TCP/IP layers

13.12 Network Programming

All Unix/Linux systems provide TCP/IP support for network programming. In this section, we shall explain the platforms and the server-client computing model for network programming.

13.12.1 Network Programming Platforms

In order to do network programming, the reader must have access to a platform that supports network programming. Such a platform is available in several ways.

(1). User Account on Server Machines: Nowadays, almost all educational institutions provide network access, often in the form of wireless connections, to their faculty, staff and students. Every member of the institution should be able to login to a server machine to access the Internet. Whether the server machine allows general network programming depends on the policy of the local network administration. Here, we describe the setup of a network programming platform at the author's institution, EECS of Washington State University. The author maintains a private server machine

cs360.eecs.wsu.edu

The server machine runs Slackware Linux version 14.2, which comes with a full compliment of support for network programming. The server machine is registered with the DNS server of EECS of WSU. When the server machine boots up, it uses **DHCP** (Dynamic Host Configuration Protocol) to obtain a private IP address from the DHCP server (RFC 2131 1997). Although not a public IP address, it can be accessed on the Internet through **NAT** (Network Address Translation). Then the author creates user accounts for students in the CS360 class for them to login. Students typically connect their laptops to the Internet via the WSU wireless network. Once on the Internet, they can login to the cs360 server machine.

(2). Standalone PCs or Laptops: Even if the reader does not have access to a server machine, it is still possible to do network programming on a standalone computer by using the localhost of the computer. In this case, the reader may have to download and install some of the network components. For example, Ubuntu Linux users may have to install and configure the Apache server for HTTP and CGI programming, which will be described later in Sect. 13.17.

13.12.2 Server-Client Computing Model

Most network programming tasks are based on the **Server-Client** computing model. In the Server-Client computing model, we run a server process at a server host first. Then we run a client from a client host. In UDP, the server waits for datagram from a client, processes the datagram and generates a response to the client. In TCP, the server waits for a client to connect. The client first connects to the server to establish a virtual circuit between the client and the server. After the connection is made, the server and client can exchange continuous streams of data. In the following, we shall show how to do network programming using both UDP and TCP.

13.13 Socket Programming

In network programming, user interface to TCP/IP is through a set of C library functions and system calls, which are collectively known as the **sockets API** (Rago 1993; Stevens et al. 2004). In order to use the socket API, we need the socket address structure, which is used to identify both the server and the client. The socket address structure is defined in netdb.h and sys/socket.h.

13.13.1 Socket Address

```
struct sockaddr_in {
        sa_family_t sin_family;   // AF_INET for TCP/IP
        in_port_t   sin_port;     // port number
        struct in_addr sin_addr;  // IP address
};
struct in_addr {                  // internet address
        uint32_t    s_addr;       // IP address in network byte order
};
```

In the socket address structure,
   sin_family is always set to **AF_INET** for TCP/IP networks.
   sin_port contains the port number in network byte order.
   sin_addr is the host IP address in network byte order.

13.13.2 The Socket API

A server must create a socket and bind it with a sockaddr containing the server's IP address and port number. It may use either a fixed port number, or let the OS kernel choose a port number if sin_port is 0. In order to communicate with a server, a client must create a socket. For UPD sockets, binding the socket to a server address is optional. If the socket is not bound to any specific server, it must provide a socket address containing the IP and port number of the server in subsequent sendto()/recvfrom() calls. The following shows the socket() system call, which creates a socket and returns a file descriptor

(1). int socket(int domain, int type, int protocol)
   Examples:

      int udp_sock = socket(AF_INET, SOCK_DGRAM, 0);

This creates a socket for sending/receiving UDP datagrams.

      int tcp_sock = socket(AF_INET, SOCK_STREAM, 0);

This creates a connect-oriented TCP socket for sending/receiving data streams.
   A newly created socket does not have any associated address. It must be bound with a host address and port number to identify either the receiving host or the sending host. This is done by the bind() system call.

(2). int bind(int sockfd**, struct sockaddr** *addr**, socklen_t** addrlen**);**
   The bind() system call assigns the address specified by addr to the socket referred to by the file descriptor sockfd, addrlen specifies the size in bytes of the address structure pointed to by addr. For a UDP socket intended for contacting other UDP server hosts, it must be bound to the address of the client, allowing the server to send reply back. For a TCP socket intended for accepting client connections, it must be bound to the server host address first.

(3). UDP Sockets
   UDP sockets use sendto()/recvfrom() to send/receive datagrams.

```
ssize_t sendto(int sockfd, const void *buf, size_t len, int flags,
               const struct sockaddr *dest_addr, socklen_t addrlen);

ssize_t recvfrom(int sockfd, void *buf, size_t len, int flags,
                 struct sockaddr *src_addr, socklen_t *addrlen);
```

   sendto() sends len bytes of data in buf to a destination host identified by dest_addr, which contains the destination host IP and port number. Recvfrom() receives data from a client host. In addition to data, it also fills src_addr with client's IP and port number, allowing the server to send reply back to the client.

(4). TCP Sockets
   After creating a socket and binding it to the server address, a TCP server uses **listen**() and **accept**() to accept connections from clients

      int listen(int sockfd, int backlog);

listen() marks the socket referred to by sockfd as a socket that will be used to accept incoming connection The backlog argument defines the maximum queue length of pending connections.

int accept(int sockfd, struct sockaddr *addr, socklen_t *addrlen);

The accept() system call is used with connection-based sockets. It extracts the first connection request on the queue of pending connections for the listening socket, sockfd, creates a new connected socket, and returns a new file descriptor referring to that socket., which is connected with the client host. When executing the accept() system call, the TCP server blocks until a client has made a connection through connect().

int connect(int sockfd, const struct sockaddr *addr, socklen_t addrlen);

The connect() system call connects the socket referred to by the file descriptor sockfd to the address specified by addr, and the addrlen argument specifies the size of addr. The format of the address in addr is determined by the address space of the socket sockfd;

If the socket sockfd is of type **SOCK_DGRAM**, i.e. UDP socket, addr is the address to which datagrams are sent by default, and the only address from which datagrams are received. This restricts a UDP socket to communicate with a specific UDP host, but it is rarely used in practice. So for UDP sockets, connection is either optional or unnecessary. If the socket is of type **SOCK_STREAM**, i.e. TCP socket, the connect() call attempts to make a connection to the socket that is bound to the address specified by addr.

(5). send()/read() and recv/write()

After establishing a connection, both TCP hosts may use send() /write() to send data, and recv()/ read() to receive data. Their only difference is the flag parameter in send() and recv(), which can be set to 0 for simple cases.

```
ssize_t send(int sockfd, const void *buf, size_t len, int flags);
ssize_t write(sockfd, void *buf, size_t, len)

ssize_t recv(int sockfd, void *buf, size_t len, int flags);
ssize_t read(sockfd, void *buf, size_t len);
```

13.14 UDP Echo Server-Client Program

In this section, we show a simple echo server/client program using UDP. For ease of reference, the program is denoted by C13.1. The following chart lists the algorithms of the server and client.

```
---------- UDP Server ---------------- UDP Client -------------
1. create a UDP socket         | 1. create a UDP socket
2. set addr = server [IP,port] | 2. set addr = server [IP,port]
3. bind socket to addr         |    while(1){
   while(1){                    | 3.    ask user for an input line
4.    recvfrom() from client    | 4.    sendto() line to server
5.    sendto() reply to client  | 5.    recvfrom() reply from server
   }                           |    }
--------------------------------------------------------------
```

For simplicity, we assume that both the server and client run on the same computer. The server runs on the default localhost with IP = 127.0.0.1, and it uses a fixed port number 1234. This simplifies the program code. It also allows the reader to test run the server and client programs in different xterms on the same computer. The following shows the server and client program code using UDP.

```c
/*  C13.1.a: UDP server.c file */
#include <stdio.h>
#include <stdlib.h>
#include <string.h>
#include <sys/socket.h>
#include <netinet/ip.h>

#define BUFLEN  256  // max length of buffer
#define PORT    1234  // fixed server port number

char line[BUFLEN];
struct sockaddr_in me, client;
int sock, rlen, clen = sizeof(client);

int main()
{
  printf("1. create a UDP socket\n");
  sock = socket(AF_INET, SOCK_DGRAM, IPPROTO_UDP);

  printf("2. fill me with server address and port number\n");
  memset((char *)&me, 0, sizeof(me));
  me.sin_family = AF_INET;
  me.sin_port = htons(PORT);
  me.sin_addr.s_addr = htonl(INADDR_ANY); // use localhost

  printf("3. bind socket to server IP and port\n");
  bind(sock, (struct sockaddr*)&me, sizeof(me));

  printf("4. wait for datagram\n");
  while(1){
    memset(line, 0, BUFLEN);
    printf("UDP server: waiting for datagram\n");
    // recvfrom() gets client IP, port in sockaddr_in clinet
    rlen=recvfrom(sock,line,BUFLEN,0,(struct sockaddr *)&client,&clen);
    printf("received a datagram from [host:port] = [%s:%d]\n",
            inet_ntoa(client.sin_addr), ntohs(client.sin_port));
    printf("rlen=%d: line=%s\n", rlen, line);
    printf("send reply\n");
    sendto(sock, line, rlen, 0, (struct sockaddr*)&client, clen);
  }
}
```

```
/***** C13.1.b: UDP client.c file *****/
#include<stdio.h>
#include<stdlib.h>
#include<string.h>
#include<sys/socket.h>
#include <netinet/ip.h>

#define SERVER_HOST "127.0.0.1" // default server IP: localhost
#define SERVER_PORT  1234       // fixed server port number
#define BUFLEN         256      // max length of buffer

char line[BUFLEN];
struct sockaddr_in server;
int sock, rlen, slen=sizeof(server);

int main()
{
  printf("1. create a UDP socket\n");
  sock = socket(AF_INET, SOCK_DGRAM, IPPROTO_UDP);

  printf("2. fill in server address and port number\n");
  memset((char *) &server, 0, sizeof(server));
  other.sin_family = AF_INET;
  other.sin_port = htons(SERVER_PORT);
  inet_aton(SERVER_HOST, &server.sin_addr);

  while(1){
     printf("Enter a line : ");
     fgets(line, BUFLEN, stdin);
     line[strlen(line)-1] = 0;
     printf("send line to server\n");
     sendto(sock,line,strlen(line),0,(struct sockaddr *)&server,slen);
     memset(line, 0, BUFLEN);
     printf("try to receive a line from server\n");
     rlen=recvfrom(sock,line,BUFLEN,0,(struct sockaddr*)&server,&slen);
     printf("rlen=%d: line=%s\n", rlen, line);
  }
}
```

Figure 13.7 shows the sample outputs of running the UDP server-client program C13.1.

13.15 TCP Echo Server-Client Program

This section presents a simple echo server-client program using TCP. The program is denoted by C13.2. For simplicity, we assume that both the server and client run on the same computer, and the server port number is hard coded as 1234. The following chart shows the algorithms and sequence of actions of the TCP server and client.

```
root@wang:~/NET# server
1. create a UDP socket
2. fill in server address with port number
3. bind socket to port
4. wait for datagram loop
UDP server: waiting for datagram
received a datagram from [host:port] = [127.0.0.1:46349]
rlen=9: line=test line
send reply
UDP server: waiting for datagram
█
```

```
root@wang:~/NET# client
1. create a UDP socket
2. fill in server address and port number
Enter a line : test line
send line to server
try to receive a line from server
rlen=9: line=test line
Enter a line : []
```

Fig. 13.7 Outputs of UDP server-client program

```
---------- TCP Server -----------  | ---------- TCP Client ----------
1. create a TCP socket             |  1. create a TCP socket sock
2. fill server_addr = [IP, port]   |  2. fill server_addr = [IP, port]
3. bind socket to server_addr      |
4. listen at socket by listen()    |
5. int csock = accept()      <==|= 3. connect() to server via sock
   ----------------------------|--------------------------------
                                   4. while(gets() line){
6. while(read()line from csock){<-|--5.  write() line   to  sock
      write() reply   to   csock  --|--->    read()  reply from sock
   }                               |     }
7. close newsock;                  |  6. exit
8. loop to 5 to accept new client  |
---------------------------------------------------------------------
```

```c
/******** C13.2.a: TCP server.c file ********/
#include <stdio.h>
#include <stdlib.h>
#include <string.h>
#include <sys/socket.h>
#include <netdb.h>

#define MAX          256
#define SERVER_HOST  "localhost"
#define SERVER_IP    "127.0.0.1"
#define SERVER_PORT  1234

struct sockaddr_in  server_addr, client_addr;
int  mysock, csock;        // socket descriptors
int  r, len, n;            // help variables
```

```
int server_init()
{
  printf("================= server init =====================\n");
  //  create a TCP socket by socket() syscall

  printf("1 : create a TCP STREAM socket\n");
  mysock = socket(AF_INET, SOCK_STREAM, 0);
  if (mysock < 0){
     printf("socket call failed\n"); exit(1);
  }

  printf("2 : fill server_addr with host IP and PORT# info\n");
  // initialize the server_addr structure
  server_addr.sin_family = AF_INET;              // for TCP/IP
  server_addr.sin_addr.s_addr = htonl(INADDR_ANY); // This HOST IP
  server_addr.sin_port = htons(SERVER_PORT);   // port number 1234

  printf("3 : bind socket to server address\n");
  r = bind(mysock,(struct sockaddr*)&server_addr,sizeof(server_addr));
  if (r < 0){
     printf("bind failed\n"); exit(3);
  }
  printf("   hostname = %s port = %d\n", SERVER_HOST, SERVER_PORT);
  printf("4 : server is listening ....\n");
  listen(mysock, 5); // queue length = 5
  printf("================= init done =====================\n");
}

int main()
{
  char line[MAX];
  server_init();
  while(1){  // Try to accept a client request
    printf("server: accepting new connection ....\n");
    // Try to accept a client connection as descriptor newsock
    len = sizeof(client_addr);
    csock = accept(mysock, (struct sockaddr *)&client_addr, &len);
    if (csock < 0){
       printf("server: accept error\n"); exit(1);
    }
    printf("server: accepted a client connection from\n");
    printf("---------------------------------------------\n");
    printf("Clinet: IP=%s  port=%d\n",
                  inet_ntoa(client_addr.sin_addr.s_addr),
                  ntohs(client_addr.sin_port));
    printf("---------------------------------------------\n");
```

```
    // Processing loop: client_sock <== data ==> client
    while(1){
        n = read(csock, line, MAX);
        if (n==0){
            printf("server: client died, server loops\n");
            close(csock);
            break;
        }
        // show the line string
        printf("server: read  n=%d bytes; line=%s\n", n, line);
        // echo line to client
        n = write(csock, line, MAX);
        printf("server: wrote n=%d bytes; ECHO=%s\n", n, line);
        printf("server: ready for next request\n");
    }
  }
}


/******** C13.2.b: TCP client.c file TCP ********/
#include <stdio.h>
#include <stdlib.h>
#include <string.h>
#include <sys/socket.h>
#include <netdb.h>

#define MAX          256
#define SERVER_HOST "localhost"
#define SERVER_PORT  1234
struct sockaddr_in  server_addr;
int sock, r;

int client_init()
{
  printf("======= clinet init ==========\n");
  printf("1 : create a TCP socket\n");
  sock = socket(AF_INET, SOCK_STREAM, 0);
  if (sock<0){
    printf("socket call failed\n"); exit(1);
  }

  printf("2 : fill server_addr with server's IP and PORT#\n");
  server_addr.sin_family = AF_INET;
  server_addr.sin_addr.s_addr = htonl(INADDR_ANY); // localhost
  server_addr.sin_port = htons(SERVER_PORT); // server port number

  printf("3 : connecting to server ....\n");
  r = connect(sock,(struct sockaddr*)&server_addr, sizeof(server_addr));
  if (r < 0){
    printf("connect failed\n");  exit(3);
  }
```

```
    printf("4 : connected OK to\n");
    printf("-----------------------------------------------------\n");
    printf("Server hostname=%s PORT=%d\n", SERVER_HOST, SERVER_PORT);
    printf("-----------------------------------------------------\n");
    printf("========= init done ==========\n");
}


int main()
{
  int n;
  char line[MAX], ans[MAX];
  client_init();
  printf("********  processing loop  ********\n");
  while (1){
    printf("input a line : ");
    bzero(line, MAX);            // zero out line[ ]
    fgets(line, MAX, stdin);     // get a line from stdin
    line[strlen(line)-1] = 0;    // kill \n at end
    if (line[0]==0)              // exit if NULL line
        exit(0);
    // Send line to server
    n = write(sock, line, MAX);
    printf("client: wrote n=%d bytes; line=%s\n", n, line);
    // Read a line from sock and show it
    n = read(sock, ans, MAX);
    printf("client: read  n=%d bytes; echo=%s\n", n, ans);
  }
}
```

Figure 13.8 shows the sample outputs of running the TCP server-client program C13.2.

13.16 Hostname and IP Address

So for, we have assumed that both the server and client run on the same computer using localhost or IP=127.0.0.1, and the server uses a fixed port number. If the reader intends to run the server and client on different hosts with a server port number assigned by the OS kernel, it is necessary to know server's host name or IP address and its port number. If a computer runs TCP/IP, its hostname is usually recorded in the /etc/hosts file. The library function

gethostname(char *name, sizeof(name))
returns the machine's hostname string in a name array, but it may not be the full official name in dot notation, nor its IP address. The library function

struct hostent *gethostbyname(void *addr, socklen_t len, int typo)
can be used to get the full name of the machine, as well as its IP address. It returns a pointer to a hostent structure in <netdb.h>, which is

```
root@wang:~/NET# server
================== server init =====================
1 : create a TCP STREAM socket
2 : fill server_addr with host IP and PORT# info
3 : bind socket to server address
    hostname = localhost port = 1234
4 : server is listening ....
================== init done ====================
server: accepting new connection ....
server: accepted a client connection from
---------------------------------------------------
Clinet: IP=127.0.0.1  port=43580
---------------------------------------------------
server: read  n=256 bytes; line=test line
server: wrote n=256 bytes; ECHO=test line
server: ready for next request
[]
```

```
root@wang:~/NET# client
======= clinet init ==========
1 : create a TCP socket
2 : fill server_addr with server's IP and PORT#
3 : connecting to server ....
4 : connected OK to
---------------------------------------------------
Server hostname=localhost PORT=1234
---------------------------------------------------
========= init done ==========
******** processing loop  *********
input a line : test line
client: wrote n=256 bytes; line=test line
client: read  n=256 bytes; echo=test line
input a line : []
```

Fig. 13.8 Sample outputs of TCP server-client program

```
struct hostent {
    char  *h_name;          // official name of host
    char **h_aliases;       // alias list
    int    h_addrtype;      // host address type
    int    h_length;        // length of address
    char **h_addr_list;     // list of addresses
}
#define h_addr h_addr_list[0] // for backward compatibility
```

Note that h_addr is defined as a char *, but it points at a 4-byte IP address in network byte order. The contents of h_addr can be accessed as

```
u32 NIP = *(u32 *)h_addr is the host IP address in network byte order.
u32 HIP = ntohl(NIP) is NIP in host byte order.
inet_ntoa(NIP) converts NIP to a string in DOT notation.
```

The following code segments show how to use gethostbyname() and getsockname() to get the server IP address and port number if it is dynamically assigned. The server must publish its hostname or IP address and port number for clients to connect.

```
/********* TCP server code *********/
char myname[64];
struct sockaddr_in server_addr, sock_addr;

// 1. gethostname(), gethostbyname()
  gethostname(myname,64);
  struct hostent *hp = gethostbyname(myname);
  if (hp == 0){
     printf("unknown host %s\n", myname); exit(1);
  }

// 2. initialize the server_addr structure
  server_addr.sin_family = AF_INET;     // for TCP/IP
  server_addr.sin_addr.s_addr = *(long *)hp->h_addr;
  server_addr.sin_port = 0; // let kernel assign port number

// 3. create a TCP socket
  int mysock = socket(AF_INET, SOCK_STREAM, 0);

// 4. bind socket with server_addr
  bind(mysock,(struct sockaddr *)&server_addr, sizeof(server_addr));

// 5. get socket addr to show port number assigned by kernel
  getsockname(mysock, (struct sockaddr *)&name_addr, &length);

// 6. show server host name and port number
  printf("hostname=%s IP=%s port=%d\n", hp->h_name,
          inet_ntoa(*(long *)hp->h_addr), ntohs(name_addr.sin_port));

/********* TCP client code *********/
// run as client server_name server_port
  struct sockaddr_in server_addr, sock_addr;
// 1.  get server IP by name
  struct hostent *hp = gethostbyname(argv[1]);
  SERVER_IP   = *(long *)hp->h_addr;
  SERVER_PORT = atoi(argv[2]);

// 2. create TCP socket
  int sock = socket(AF_INET, SOCK_STREAM, 0);

// 3. fill server_addr with server IP and PORT#
  server_addr.sin_family = AF_INET;
  server_addr.sin_addr.s_addr = SERVER_IP;
  server_addr.sin_port = htons(SERVER_PORT);

// 4. connect to server
  connect(sock,(struct sockaddr *)&server_addr, sizeof(server_addr));
```

Incorporating hostname and IP address into the TCP server-client program is left as exercises in the problem section.

13.17 TCP Programming Project: File Server on Internet

The above TCP server-client program can be used as a basis for TCP-based network programming. It can be adapted to different applications by simply changing the data contents and the ways they process the data. For example, instead of numbers, the client may send file operation commands to the server, which processes the commands and send results back to the client. This programming project is to develop a pair of TCP server and client to do file operations across the Internet. The project specification is as follows.

13.17.1 Project Specification

Design and implement a TCP server and a TCP client to do file operations across the Internet. The following charts depict the algorithms of the server and the client.

-------------------------- **Server** -------------------------
(1). Set virtual root to Current Working Directory (CWD)
(2). Advertise server hostname and port number
(3). Accept a connection from client
(4). Get a **command line** = **cmd pathname** from client
(5). Perform **cmd** on **pathname**
(6). Send results to client
(7). Repeat (4) until client disconnects
(8). Repeat (3) to accept new client connection

-------------------------- **Client** -------------------------
(1). Connect to server at server hostname and port number
(2). Prompt user for a **command line** = **cmd pathname**
(3). Send command line to server
(4). Receive results from server
(5). Repeat (2) until command line is NULL or quit command

In a command line, depending on the command, pathname may be either a file or a directory. Valid commands are

mkdir: make a directory with pathname
rmdir: remove directory named pathname
rm: remove file named pathname
cd :   change Current Working Directory (CWD) to pathname
pwd: show absolute pathname of CWD
ls: list CWD or pathname in the same format as ls –l of Linux
get: download the pathname file from server
put: upload the pathname file to server

13.17.2 Helps and Hints

(1). When running on an Internet host, the server must publish its hostname or IP address and port number to allow clients to connect. For security reasons, the server should set the **virtual root** to CWD of the server process to prevent the client from accessing files above the virtual root.

(2). Most commands are simple to implement. For example, each of the first 5 commands requires only a single Linux system call, as shown below.

```
mkdir  pathname:   int r = mkdir(pathname, 0755);  // default permissions
rmdir  pathname:   int r = rmdir(pathname);
rm     pathname:   int r = unlink(pathname);
cd     pathname:   int r = chdir(pathname);
pwd :  char buf[SIZE]; char *getcwd(buf, SIZE);
```

For the ls command, the reader may consult the ls.c program in Section 8.6.7 of Chapter 8. For the get filename command, it is essentially the same as a file copy program split into two parts. The server opens the file for READ, read the file contents and send them to the client. The client opens a file for WRITE, receives data from the server and writes the received data to the file. For the put filename command, simply reverse the roles of the server and client.

(3). When using TCP, data are continuous streams. To ensure the client and server can send/receive commands and simple replies, it is better for both sides to write/read lines of fixed size, e.g. 256 bytes.

(4). The reader must design user-level protocols to ensure correct data transfer between the server and client. The following describes the commands which need user-level data transfer protocols

For the ls command, the server has two options. In the first option, for each entry in a directory, the server generates a line of the form

```
-rw-r--r--  link gid uid size date name
```

and saves the line into a temporary file. After accumulating all the lines, the server sends the entire temporary file to the client. In this case, the server must be able to tell the client where the file begins and where it ends. Since the ls command generates only text lines, the reader may use special ASCII chars as file begin and end marks.

In the second option, the server may generate a line and send it immediately to the client before generating and sending the next line. In this case, the server must be able to tell the client when it starts to send lines and also when there are no more lines to come.

For the get/put commands, which transfer file contents, it is not possible to use special ASCII chars as file begin and end marks. This is because a binary file may contain any ASCII code. The standard solution to this problem is by bit stuffing [SDLC, IBM, 1979]. In this scheme, while sending data, the sender inserts an extra 0 bit after each sequence of 5 or more consecutive 1 bits, so that the transmitted data never contains any 6 or more consecutive 1's. At the receiving end, the receiver strips off the extra 0 bit after every sequence of 5 consecutive 1's. This allows both sides to use the special flag bits pattern 01111110 as file begin and end marks. Bit-stuffing is inefficient without hardware assistance. The reader must think of other ways to synchronize the server and the client.

Hint: by file size.

(5). The project is suitable for 2-person team work. During development, the team members may discuss how to design user-level protocols and divide the implementation work between them. During testing, one member can run the server on an Internet host while the other runs the client on a different host.

```
root@wang:~/NET# server wang             root@E4200:~/NET# client wang.eecs.wsu.edu 56809
================== server init =========== ====== clinet init =========
1 : get and show server host info         1 : get server info
    hostname=wang.eecs.wsu.edu  IP=69.166.48.131  2 : create a TCP socket
2 : create a socket                       3 : fill server_addr with server's IP and PORT#
3 : fill server_addr with host IP and PORT# info  4 : connecting to server ....
4 : bind socket to host info              5 : connected OK to
5 : find out Kernel assigned PORT# and show it  ...............................................
    Port=56809                                  host=wang.eecs.wsu.edu  IP=69.166.48.131  PORT=56809
6 : server listening ....                 ...............................................
================== init done ============= ========= init done ===========
server : chroot to /root/NET
server: accepting new connection ....
server: accepted a client connection from ****************** menu *******************
------------------------------------------- * get   put  ls   cd   pwd   mkdir  rmdir   rm  *
        IP=172.19.160.221  port=48774      * lcat       lls  lcd  lpwd  lmkdir lrmdir  lrm  *
-------------------------------------------  ****************************************************
server ready for next request ....        input a command : █
```

Fig. 13.9 TCP server-client for file operations

Figure 13.9 shows the sample outputs of running the project program.

As the figure shows, the server runs on the host **wang.eecs.wsu.edu** at port **56809**. The client runs on a different host with **IP=172.19.160.221** at port **48774**. In addition to the specified commands, the client side also implements local file operation commands, which are performed by the client directly.

13.17.3 Multi-threaded TCP Server

In the TCP server-client programming project, the server can only serve one client at a time. In a multi-threaded server, it can accept connections from multiple clients and serve them at the same time or concurrently. This can be done either by fork-exec of new server processes or by multiple threads in the same server process. We leave this extension as another possible programming project.

13.18 Web and CGI Programming

The World Wide Web (**WWW**), or the **Web**, is a combination of resources and users on the Internet that uses the Hypertext Transfer Protocol (**HTTP**) (RFC 2616 1999), for information exchange. Since its debut in the early 90's, coupled with the ever-expanding capability of the Internet, the Web has become an indispensable part of daily lives of people all over the world. It is therefore important for Computer Science students to have some understanding of this technology. In this section, we shall cover the basics of HTTP and Web programming. Web programming in general includes the writing, markup and coding involved in Web development, which includes Web content, Web client and server scripting and network security. In a narrower sense, Web programming refers to creating and maintaining Web pages. The most common languages used in Web programming are HTML, XHTML, JavaScript, Perl 5 and PHP.

13.18.1 HTTP Programming Model

HTTP is a server-client based protocol for applications on the Internet. It runs on top of TCP since it requires reliable transfer of files. Figure 13.10 shows the HTTP programming model.

Fig. 13.10 HTTP
programming model

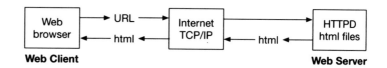

In the HTTP programming model, a HTTP server runs on a Web server host. It waits for requests from a HTTP client, which is usually a Web browser. At the HTTP client side, the user enters a **URL** (Uniform Resource Locator) of the form

http://hostname[/filename]

to send a request to a HTTP server, requesting for a file. In the URL, http identifies the HTTP protocol, hostname is the host name of the HTTP server and filename is the requested file. If filename is not specified, the default file is **index.html**. The client first connects to the server to send the request. Upon receiving a request, the server sends the requested file back to the client. Requested files are usually Web page files written in the HTML language for the browser to interpret and display, but it may also be files in other formats, such as video, audio or even binary files.

In HTTP, a client may issue URLs to send requests to different HTTP servers. It is unnecessary, nor desirable, for a client to maintain a permanent connection with a specific server. A client connects to a server only to send a request, after which the connection is closed. Likewise, a server connects to a client only to send a reply, after which the connection is again closed. Each request or reply requires a separate connection. This means that HTTP is a stateless protocol since there are no information maintained across successive requests or replies. Naturally, this would cause a lot of overhead and inefficiency. In order to remedy this lack of state information problem, HTTP server and client may use **cookies**, which are small piece of data imbedded in requests and replies, to provide and maintain some state information between them.

13.18.2 Web Pages

Web pages are files written in the HTML markup language. A Web file specifies the layout of a Web page by a series of HTML elements for a Web browser to interpret and display. Popular Web browsers include Internet Explorer, Firefox, Google Chrome, etc. To create a Web page amounts to creating a text file using HTML elements as building blocks. It is more a clerical type work than programming. For this reason, we shall not discuss how to create Web pages. Instead, we shall only use an example HTML file to illustrate the essence of Web pages. The following shows a simple Web page file in HTML.

```
1.   <html>
2.   <body>
3.   <h1>H1 heading: A Simple Web Page</h1>
4.   <P>This is a paragraph of text</P>
5.   <!---- this is a comment line ---->
6.   <P><img src="firefox.jpg" width=16></P>
7.   <a href="http://www.eecs.wsu.edu/~cs360">link to cs360 web page</a>
     <P>
8.   <font color="red">red</font>
9.   <font color="blue">blue</font>
10.  <font color="green">green</font>
```

```
      </P>
      <!--- a table ---->
11.   <table>
12.       <tr>
13.           <th>name</th>
14.           <th>ID</th>
15.       </tr>
16.       <tr>
17.            <th>kwang</th>
18.            <th>12345</th>
19.       </tr>
20.   </table>
      <!---- a FORM ---->
21.   <FORM>
22.    Enter command:  <INPUT NAME="command"><P>
23.    Submit command: <INPUT TYPE="submit" VALUE="Click to Submit">
24.   </FORM>
25.   </body>
26.   </html>
```

Explanations of HTML File Contents

A HTML file comprises HTML elements. Each HTML element is specified by a matched pair of open and close tags.

```
      <tag>contents</tag>
```

In fact, a HTML file itself may be regarded as a HTML element specified by a matched pair of <html> tags.

```
      <html>HTML file</html>
```

Lines 1 to 26 specify a HTML file. A HTML file includes a body specified by a matched pair of <body> tags

```
      <body>body of HTML file</body>
```

Lines 2 to 25 specify the body of the HTML file.
A HTML file may use the tags <H1> to <H7> to display head lines of different font sizes.
Line 3 specifies a <H1> head line.
Each matched pair of <P> tags specifies a paragraph, which is displayed on a new line.
Line 4 specifies a paragraph of text.
Line 5 specifies a comment line, which will be ignored by the browser.
Line 6 specifies an image file, which will be displayed with width pixels per row.
Line 7 specifies a link element

```
          <a HREF="link_URL">link</a>
```

Fig. 13.11 Web page
from a HTML file

A Simple Web page

this is a paragraph of text

link to cs360 web page

red blue green

NAME   ID

kwang 12345

Enter command :

Submit command : Click to Submit

in which the attribute HREF specifies a link_URL and a text string describing the link. The browser usually displays link texts in dark blue color. If the user clicks on a link, it will direct the request to a Web server identified by the link_URL. This is perhaps the most powerful feature of Web pages. It allows the user to navigate to anywhere in the Web by following the links.

Lines 8 to 10 use <font> elements to display texts in different colors. The <font> element can also specify text in different font sizes and styles.

Lines 11 to 20 specify a table with <tr> as rows, and <th> as columns in each row.

Lines 21 to 24 specify a form for collecting user inputs and submitting them to a Web server for processing. We shall explain and demonstrate HTML forms in more detail in the next section on CGI programming.

Figure 13.11 shows the Web page of the above HTML file.

13.18.3 Hosting Web Pages

Now that we have a HTML file. It must be placed in a Web server. When a Web client requests the HTML file by a URL, the Web server must be able to locate the file and send it back to the client for display. There are several ways to host Web pages.

(1). Sign up with a commercial Web hosting service provider with a monthly fee. For most casual users, this may not be an option at all.

(2). User account on an institutional or departmental server. If the reader has a user account on a server machine running Linux, it's very easy to create a private website in the user's home directory by the following steps

  . login to the user account on the server machine.

  . in the user's home directory, create a public_html directory with permissions 0755.

  . in the public_html directory, create an index.html file and other HTML files.

As an example, from a Web browser on the Internet, entering the URL

http://cs360.eecs.wsu.edu/~kcw

will access the author's website on the server machine **cs360.eecs.wsu.edu**.

(3.) Standalone PC or laptop: The steps described here are for standalone PCs or laptops running standard Linux, but it should be applicable to other Unix platforms as well. For some reason, Ubuntu Linux chooses to do things differently, deviating from the standard setups of Linux. Ubuntu users may consult the HTTPD-Apache2 Web Server Web page of Official Ubuntu Documentation for details.

13.18.4 Configure HTTPD for Web Pages

(3).1. Download and install the Apache Web server. Most Linux distributions, e.g. Slackware Linux 14.2, come with the Apache Web server installed, which is known as HTTPD.

(3).2. Enter ps –x | grep httpd to see whether httpd is running. If not, enter

```
sudo chmod  +x  /etc/rc.d/rc.httpd
```

to make the rc.httpd file executable. This would start up httpd during next booting. Alternatively, httpd can also be started up manually by entering

```
sudo /usr/sbin/httpd –kstart.
```

(3).3. Configure httpd.conf file: Operations of the HTTPD server are governed by a httpd.conf file in the /etc/httpd/ directory. To allow individual user websites, edit the httpd.conf file as follows.

```
. Uncomment these lines if they are commented out
    Loadmodule dir_module MODULE_PATH
    Include /etc/httpd/extra/httpd-userdir.conf

. In the first Directory block
        <Directory />
          Require all denied    # deny requests for all files in /
        </Directory>
Change the line Require all denied to Require all granted.

. All user home directories are in the /home directory. Change the line
        DocumentRoot  /srv/httpd/htdocs to DocumentRoot  /home

. The default directory for all HTML file is htdoc. Change the line
        <Directory /srv/httpd/htdocs> to <Directory /home>

After  editing  the  httpd.conf  file,  restart  the  httpd  server  or  enter  the
commands
        ps –x | grep httpd   # to see httpd PID
        sudo kill –s 1 httpdPID
```

The kill command sends a number 1 signal to httpd, causing it to read the updated httpd.conf file without restarting the httpd server.

(3).4. Create a user account by **adduser user_name**. login to the user account by

```
ssh user_name@localhost
```

Create public_html directory and HTML files as before.
Then open a Web browser and enter http://localhost/~user_name to access the user's Web pages.

13.18.5 Dynamic Web Pages

Web pages written in standard HTML are all static. When fetched from a server and displayed by a browser, the web page contents do not change. To display a Web page with different contents, a different Web page file must be fetched from the server again. Dynamic Web pages are those whose contents can vary. There are two kinds of dynamic Web pages, known as **client-side** and **server-side** dynamic Web pages, respectively. Client-side dynamic Web page files contain code written in JavaScripts, which are executed by a JavaScripts interpreter on the Client machine. It can respond to user inputs, time events, etc. to modify the Web page locally without any interaction with the server. Server-side dynamic Web pages are truly dynamic in the sense that they are generated dynamically in accordance with user inputs in the URL request. The heart of server-side dynamic Web pages lies in the server's ability to either execute PHP code inside HTML files or CGI programs to generate HTML files by user inputs.

13.18.6 PHP

PHP (Hypertext Preprocessor) (PHP 2017) is a script language for creating server-side dynamic Web pages. PHP files are identified by the .php suffix. They are essentially HTML files containing PHP code for the Web server to execute. When a Web client request a PHP file, the Web server will process the PHP statements first to generate a HTML file, which is sent to the requesting client. All Linux systems running the Apache HTTPD server support PHP, but it may have to be enabled. To enable PHP, only a few modifications to the httpd.conf file are needed, which are shown below.

(1).	DirectoryIndex **index.php**	# default Web page is index.php
(2).	AddType application/x-httpd-php **.php**	# add .php extension type
(3).	Include /etc/httpd/**mod_php.conf**	# load php5 module

After enabling PHP in httpd.conf, restart the httpd server, which will load the PHP module into Linux kernel. When a Web client requests a .php file, the httpd server will fork a child process to execute the PHP statements in the .php file. Since the child process has the PHP module loaded in its image, it can execute the PHP code fast and efficiently. Alternatively, the httpd server can also be configured to execute php as CGI, which is slower since it must use fork-exec to invoke the PHP interpreter. For better efficiency, we assume that .php files are handled by the PHP module. In the following, we shall show basic PHP programming by examples.

(1). PHP statements in HTML files

In a .php file, PHP statements are included inside a pair of PHP tags

```
<?php
  // PHP statements
?>
```

The following shows a simple PHP file, p1.php.

```
<html>
<body>
<?php
   echo "hello world<br>";      // hello world<br>
   print "see you later<br>";   // see you later<br>
?>
</body>
</html>
```

Similar to C programs, each PHP statement must end with a semicolon. It may include comment blocks in matched pairs of /* and */, or use //, # for single comment lines. For outputs, PHP may use either echo or print. In an echo or print statement, multiple items must be separated by the dot (string concatenation) operator, not by white spaces, as in

```
echo "hello world<br> . "see you later<br>";
```

When a Web client requests the p1.php file, the httpd server's PHP preprocessor will execute the PHP statements first to generate HTML lines (shown at the right hand side of PHP lines). It then sends the resulting HTML file to the client.

(2). PHP Variables:

In PHP, variables begins with the $ sign, followed by variable name. PHP variable values may be strings, integers or float point numbers. Unlike C, PHP is a loosely typed language. Users do not need to define variables with types. Like C, PHP allows typecast to change variable types. For most parts, PHP can also convert variables to different types automatically.

```
<?php
  $PID = getmypid();         // return an integer
  echo "pid = $PID <br>";    // pid = php Process PID
  $STR = "hello world!";     // a string
  $A = 123; $B = "456";      // integer 123, string "456"
  $C = $A + $B;              // type conversion by PHP
  echo "$STR Sum=$C<br>";    // hello world! Sum=579<br>
?>
```

Like variables in C or sh scripts, PHP variables may be local, global or static.

(3). PHP Operators

In PHP, variables and values may be operated by the following operators.

Arithmetic operators
Assignment operators

Comparison operators
Increment/Decrement operators
Logical operators
String operators
Array operators

Most PHP operators are similar to those in C. We only show some special string and array operators in PHP.

(3).1. String operations: Most string operations, e.g. strlen(), strcmp(), etc. are the same as in C. PHP also supports many other string operations, often in slightly different syntax form. For example, instead of strcat(), PHP uses the dot operator for string concatenation, as in "string1" . "string2"

(3).2. PHP Arrays: PHP arrays are defined by the array() keyword. PHP supports both indexed arrays and multi-dimensional arrays. Indexed arrays can be stepped through by an array index, as in

```php
<?php
$name  = array('name0", "name1", "name2", "name3");
$value = array(1,2,3,4);   // array of values
$n = count($name);         // number of array elements
for ($i=0; $i<n; $i++){    // print arrays by index
    echo $name[$i]; echo " = ";
    echo $value[$i];
}
?>
```

In addition, PHP arrays can be operated on as sets by operators, such as union (+) and comparisons, or as lists, which can be sorted in different orders, etc.

Associative Arrays: Associative arrays consist of name-value pairs.

```php
$A = array('name"=>1, "name1"=>2, "name2"=>3, "name"=>4);
```

An associative array allows accessing element value by name, rather than by index, as in

```php
echo "value of name1 = " . $A['name1'];
```

(4). PHP Conditional Statements: PHP supports conditions and test conditions by if, if-else, if-elseif-else and switch-case statements, which are exactly the same as in C, but with slight difference in syntax.

```php
<?php
  if (123 < 456){           // test a condition
     echo "true<br>";       // in matched pair of {  }
  } else {
     echo "not true<br>";   // in matched pair of {  }
  }
?>
```

(5). PHP Loop Statements: PHP supports while, do-while, for loop statements, which are the same as in C. The foreach statement may be used to step through an array without an explicit index variable.

```php
<?php
  $A = array(1,2,3,4);
  for ($i=0; $i<4; $i++){     // use an index variable
      echo "A[$i] = $A[$i]<br>";
  }
  foreach ($A as $value){     // step through array elements
      echo "$value<br>";
  }
?>
```

(6). PHP Functions: In PHP, functions are defined using the function keyword. Their formats and usage are similar to functions in C.

```php
<?php
  function nameValue($name, $value) {
     echo "$name . " has value " . $value <br>";}
  nameValue("abc", 123); // call function with 2 parameters
  nameValue("xyz", 456);
?>
```

(7). PHP Date and Time Functions: PHP has many built-in functions, such as date() and time().

```php
<?php
   echo date("y-m-d");   // time in year-month-day format
   echo date("h:i:sa");  // time in hh:mm:ss format
?>
```

(8). File Operations in PHP: One of the great strengths of PHP is its integrated support for file operations. File operations in PHP includes functionalities of both system calls, e.g. mkdir(), link(), unlink(), stat(), etc. and standard library I/O functions of C, e.g. fopen(), fread(), fwrite() and fclose(), etc. The syntax of these functions may differ from that in the I/O library functions in C. Most functions do not need a specific buffer for data since they either take string parameters or return strings directly. As usual, for write operations, the Apache process must have write permissions to the user directory. The reader may consult PHP file operation manuals for details. The following PHP code segments show how to display the contents of a file and copy files by fopen(), fread() and fwrite().

```php
<?php
  readfile("filename");              // same as cat filename
  $fp = fopen("src.txt", "r");       // fopen() a file for READ
  $gp = fopen("dest.txt", "w");      // fopen a file for WRITE
  while(!feof($fp){                  // feof() same as in C
      $s = fread($fp, 1024);         // read nbytes from $fp
      fwrite($gp, $s, strlen($s));// write string to  $gp
  }
?>
```

(9). Forms in PHP: In PHP, forms and form submission are identical to those in HTML. Form processing is by a PHP file containing PHP code, which is executed by the PHP preprocessor. The PHP

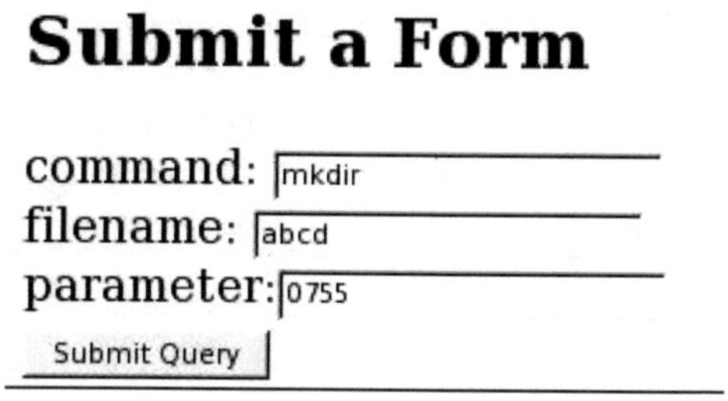

Fig. 13.12 PHP
submitting form

Submit a Form

command: mkdir

filename: abcd

parameter: 0755

Submit Query

Fig. 13.13 PHP form
processing

process PID = 30256
user_name = root
you submitted the following name-value pairs
command = mkdir
filename = abcd
parameter= 0755

code can get inputs from the submitted form and handle them in the usual way. We illustrate form processing in PHP by an example.

(9).1. A form.php file: This .php file displays a form, collects user inputs and submits the form with METHOD="post" and ACTION="action.php" to the httpd server. Figure 13.12 shows the Web page of the form.php file. When the user clicks on Submit, it sends the form inputs to the HPPTD server for processing.

```
<!------- form.php file ------->
<html><body>
<H1>Submit a Form</H1>
<form METHOD="post" ACTION="action.php">
  command:  <input type="text" name="command"><br>
  filename: <input type="text" name="filename"><br>
  parameter:<input type="text" name="parameter"><br>
  <input type="submit">
</form>
</body></html>
```

(9).2. Action.php file: The action.php file contains PHP code to process user inputs. Form inputs are extracted from the global _POST associative array by keywords. For simplicity, we only echo the user submitted input name-value pairs. Figure 13.13 shows the returned Web page of action.php. As the figure shows, it was executed by an Apache process with PID=30256 at the server side.

```
<!------- action.php file ------->
<html><body>
<?php
  echo "process PID = " . getmypid() . "<br>";
  echo "user_name = " . get_current_user() . "<br>";
  $command  = $_POST["command"];
  $filename = $_POST["filename"];
```

```
  $parameter= $_POST["parameter"];
  echo "you submitted the following name-value pairs<br>";
  echo "command  = " . $command .   "<br>";
  echo "filename = " . $filename .  "<br>";
  echo "parameter= " . $parameter . " <br>";
?>
</body></html>
```

Summary on PHP

PHP is a versatile script language for developing applications on the Internet. From a technical point view, PHP may have nothing new, but it represents the evolution of several decades of efforts in Web programming. PHP is not a single language but an integration of many other languages. It includes features of many earlier script languages, such as sh and Perl. It includes most of the standard features and functions of C, and it also provides file operations in the standard I/O library of C. In practice, PHP is often used as the front-end of a Web site, which interacts with a database engine at the back-end for storing and retrieving data online through dynamic Web pages. Interface PHP with MySQL databases will be covered the Chap. 14.

13.18.7 CGI Programming

CGI stands for **Common Gateway Interface** (RFC 3875 2004). It is a protocol which allows a Web server to execute programs to generate Web pages dynamically in accordance with user inputs. With CGI, a Web server does not have to maintain millions of static Web page files to satisfy client requests. Instead, it creates Web pages to satisfy client requests by generate them dynamically. Figure 13.14 shows the CGI programming model.

In the CGI programming model, a client sends a request, which is typically a HTML form containing both inputs and the name of a CGI program for the server to execute. Upon receiving the request, the httpd server forks a child process to execute the CGI program. The CGI program may use user inputs to query a database system, such as MySQL, to generate a HTML file based on user inputs. When the child process finishes, the httpd server sends the resulting HTML file back to the client. CGI program can be written in any programming language, such as C, sh scripts and Perl.

13.18.8 Configure HTTPD for CGI

In HTTPD, the default directory of CGI programs is /srv/httpd/cgi-bin. This allows the network administrator to control and monitor which users are allowed to execute CGI programs. In many institutions, user-level CGI programs are usually disabled for security reasons. In order to allow

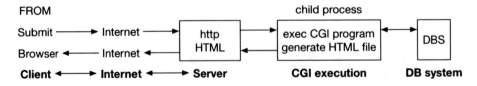

Fig. 13.14 CGI programming model

user-level CGI programming, the httpd server must be configured to enable user-level CGI. Edit the /etc/httpd/httpd.conf file and change the CGI directory settings to

```
<Directory "/home/*/public_html/cgi-bin">
    Options +ExecCGI
    AddHandler cgi-script .cgi .sh .bin .pl
    Order allow,deny
    Allow from all
</Directory>
```

The modified CGI Directory block sets the CGI directory to public_html/cgi-bin/ in the user home directory. The **cgi-script** setting specifies file with suffix .cgi, .sh, .bin and .pl (for Perl scripts) as executable CGI programs.

13.19 CGI Programming Project: Dynamic Webpage by CGI

This programming project is intended for readers to practice CGI programming. It combines remote file operations, CGI programming and server-side dynamic Web pages into a single package. The organization of the project is as follows.

(1). User website: On the cs360.eecs.wsu.edu server machine, each user has an account for login. The user's home directory has a public_html directory containing an index.html file, which can be accessed from a Web browser on the Internet by the URL

http://cs360.eecs.wsu.edu/~username

The following shows the index.html file of the user kcw.

```
<!---------- index.html file ---------->
<html>
<body bgcolor="#00FFFF"
<H1>Welcome to KCW's Web Page</H1><P>
<img src="kcw.jpg" width=100><P>

<FORM METHOD="POST" ACTION=\
  "http://cs360.eecs.wsu.edu/~kcw/cgi-bin/mycgi.bin">
  Enter command: <INPUT NAME="command"> (mkdir|rmdir|rm|cat|cp|ls)<P>
  Enter filename1: <INPUT NAME="filename1"> <P>
  Enter filename2: <INPUT NAME="filename2"> <P>
  Submit command: <INPUT TYPE="submit" VALUE="Click to Submit"> <P>
</FORM>

</body>
</html>
```

Figure 13.15 shows the Web page corresponding to the above index.html file.

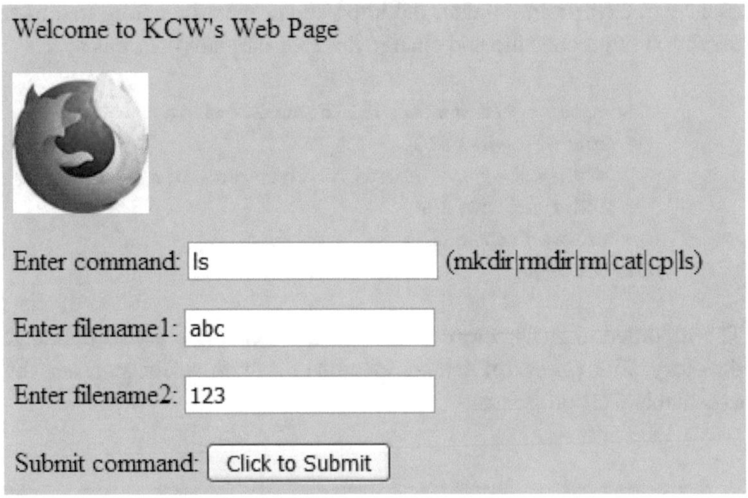

Fig. 13.15 HTML
form page

Welcome to KCW's Web Page

Enter command: ␣ls␣   (mkdir|rmdir|rm|cat|cp|ls)

Enter filename1: ␣abc␣

Enter filename2: ␣123␣

Submit command: [Click to Submit]

(2). HTML Form: The index.html file contains a HTML form.

```
<FORM METHOD="POST" ACTION=\
  "http://cs360.eecs.wsu.edu/~kcw/cgi-bin/mycgi.bin">
  Enter command: <INPUT NAME="command"> (mkdir|rmdir|rm|cat|cp|ls)<P>
  Enter filename1: <INPUT NAME="filename1"> <P>
  Enter filename2: <INPUT NAME="filename2"> <P>
  Submit command: <INPUT TYPE="submit" VALUE="Click to Submit"> <P>
</FORM>
```

In a HTML form, METHOD specifies how to submit the form inputs, ACTION specifies the Web server and the CGI program to be executed by the Web server. There are two kinds of form submission methods. In the **GET method**, user inputs are included in the submitted URL, which makes them directly visible and the amount of input data is also limited. For these reasons, GET method is rarely used. In the **POST method**, user inputs are (URL) encoded and transmitted via data streams, which are more secure and the amount of input data is also unlimited. Therefore, most HTML forms use the POST method. A HTML form allows the user to enter inputs in the prompt boxes. When the user clicks on the Submit button, the inputs will be sent to a Web server for processing. In the example HTML file, the form inputs will be sent to the HTTP server at cs360.eecs.wsu.edu, which will execute the CGI program mycgi.bin in the user's cgi-bin directory.

(3). CGI Directory and CGI Programs: The HTTPD server is configured to allow user-level CGI. The following diagram shows the user-lever CGI setup.

```
/home/username:  public_html
                        | ----   index.html
                        | ----   cgi-bin
                                | ---- mycgi.c
                                | ---- util.o
                                | ---- mycgi.bin, sample.bin
```

In the cgi-bin directory, mycgi.c is a C program, which gets and shows user inputs in a submitted HTML form. It echoes user inputs and generates a HTML file containing a FORM, which is sent back to the Web client to display. The following shows the mycgi.c program code.

```c
/************* mycgi.c file ************/
#include <stdio.h>
#include <stdlib.h>
#include <string.h>
#define MAX 1000
typedef struct{
    char *name;
    char *value;
}ENTRY;
ENTRY entry[MAX];
extern int getinputs(); // in util.o
int main(int argc, char *argv[])
{
  int i, n;
  char cwd[128];
  n = getinputs();       // get user inputs name=value into entry[ ]
  getcwd(cwd, 128);      // get CWD pathname
  // generate a HTML file containing a HTML FORM
  printf("Content-type: text/html\n\n"); // NOTE: 2 new line chars
  printf("<html>");
  printf("<body bgcolor=\"#FFFF00\"); // background color=YELLOW
  printf("<p>pid=%d uid=%d cwd=%s\n", getpid(), getuid(), cwd);
  printf("<H2>Echo Your Inputs</H2>");
  printf("You submitted the following name/value pairs:<p>");
  for(i=0; i<=n; i++)
     printf("%s = %s<P>", entry[i].name, entry[i].value);
  printf("<p>");
  // create a FORM webpage for user to submit again
  printf("---------- Send Back a Form Again ------------<P>");
  printf("<FORM METHOD=\"POST\"
  ACTION=\"http://cs360.eecs.wsu.edu/~kcw/cgi-bin/mycgi.bin\">");
  printf("<font color=\"RED\">");
  printf("Enter command : <INPUT NAME=\"command\"> <P>");
  printf("Enter filename1: <INPUT NAME=\"filename1\"> <P>");
  printf("Enter filename2: <INPUT NAME=\"filename2\"> <P>");
  printf("Submit command: <INPUT TYPE=\"submit\" VALUE=\"Click to \
          Submit\"> <P>");
  printf("</form>");
  printf("</font>");
  printf("-------------------------------------------------<p>");
  printf("</body>");
  printf("</html>");
}
```

Figure 13.16 shows the Web page generated by the above CGI program.

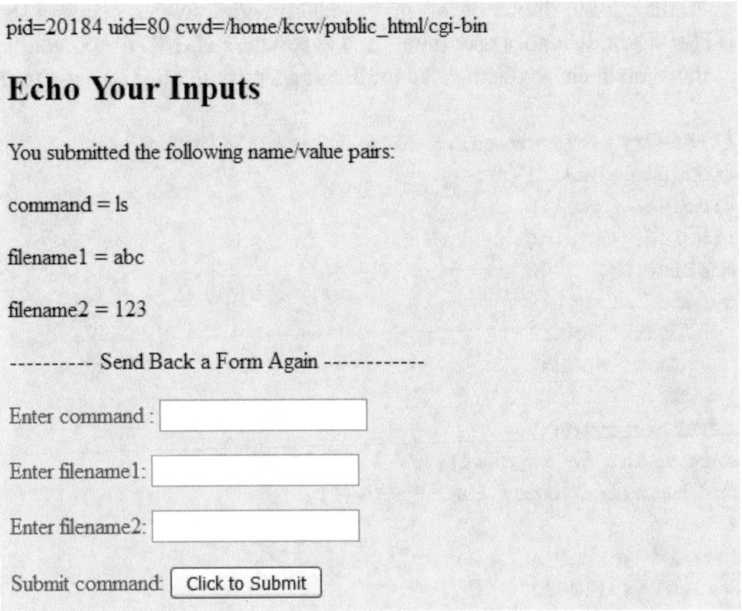

Fig. 13.16 Web page of
CGI program

pid=20184 uid=80 cwd=/home/kcw/public_html/cgi-bin

Echo Your Inputs

You submitted the following name/value pairs:

command = ls

filename1 = abc

filename2 = 123

---------- Send Back a Form Again ------------

Enter command :

Enter filename1:

Enter filename2:

Submit command: Click to Submit

(4). CGI Programs: When the HTTPD server receives a CGI request, it forks a child process with UID 80 to execute the CGI program. The form submission method, inputs encoding and input data length are in the environment variables REQUEST_METHOD, CONETENT_TYPE and CONTENT_LENGTH of the process, and the input data are in stdin. The input data are typically URL-encoded. Decoding the inputs into name-value pairs is straightforward but fairly tedious. For this reason, a pre-compiled util.o file is provided. It contains a function

```
int getinputs()
```

which decodes user inputs into pairs of name-value strings. The CGI program is generated by the Linux commands

```
gcc -o mycgi.bin mycgi.c util.o
```

(5). Dynamic Web Pages: After getting user inputs, the CGI program can process the user inputs to generate output data. In the example program it only echoes the user inputs. Then it generates a HTML file by writing HTML statements as lines to stdout. To qualify the lines as a HTML file, the first line must be

```
printf("Content-type: text/html\n\n");
```

with 2 new line chars. The rest lines can be any HTML statements. In the example program, it generates a FORM identical to the submitted form, which is used to get new user inputs in the next submission.

(6). SETUID Programs: Normally, a CGI program only uses user inputs to read from a database on the server side to generate a HTML file. For security reasons, it may not allow CGI programs to modify the server side database. In the programming project, we shall allow uses requests to do file operations, such as mkdir, rmdir, cp files, etc. which require writing permissions into the user's directory. Since the CGI process has a UID=80, it should not be able to write into the user's directory. There are two options to allow the CGI process to write in the user's directory. In the first option, the user may set the cgi-bin directory permissions to 0777, but this is undesirable because it would allow anyone to be able to write in its directory. The second option is to make the CGI program a SETUID program by

```
chmod u+s mycgi.bin
```

When a process executes a SETUID program, it temporarily assumes the UID of the program owner, allowing it to write in the user's directory.

(7). User Requests for File Operations: Since the objective of the project is CGI programming, we only assume the following simple file operations as user requests:

```
ls        [directory]        // list directory in ls -l form of Linux
mkdir dirname permission     // make a directory
rmdir   dirname              // rm director y
unlink  filename             // rm file
cat       filename           // show file contents
cp        file1 file2        // copy file1 to file2
```

(8) Sample Solution: In the cgi-bin directory, sample.bin is a sample solution of the project. The reader may replace mycgi.bin in the index.html file with sample.bin to test user requests and observe the results.

13.20 Summary

This chapter covers TCP/IP and network programming. The chapter consists of two parts. The first part covers the TCP/IP protocol and its applications. These include the TCP/IP stack, IP address, hostname and DNS, IP data packets and routers. It describes the UDP and TCP protocols, port number, network byte order and data flow in TCP/IP networks. It explains the server-client computing model and the socket programming interface. It demonstrates network programming by examples using both UDP and TCP sockets. The first programming project is to implement a pair of TCP server-client to do file operations across the Internet. It also allows the user to define additional communication protocols for reliable transfer of file contents.

The second part of the chapter covers Web and CGI programming. It explains the HTTP programming model, Web pages and Web browsers. It shows how to configure the Linux HTTPD server to support user Web pages, PHP and CGI programming. It explains both client side and server side dynamic Web pages. It shows how to create server side dynamic Web pages by both PHP and CGI. The second programming project is for the reader to implement server-side dynamic Web pages by CGI programming on a Linux HTTPD server machine.

Problems
1. Modify the UDP client code of Program C13.1 to append a timestamp in usec to the datagram. Modify the UDP server code to append a timestamp, also in usec, to the received datagram before sending it back. In the client code, compute and display the round-trip time of the datagram in msec.
2. Modify the UDP client code of Program 13.1 to add timeout and resend. For each datagram sent, start a REAL mode interval timer with a timeout value. If the client receives a reply from the server

before the timeout expires, cancel the timer. If the timeout expires and the client has not received any reply, resend the datagram.

3. Modify the TCP client code of Program C13.2 to send two integer numbers separated by white spaces, e.g. 1 2, to the server. Modify the TCP server code to send back the sum of the two numbers, e.g. 1 2 sum=3.

4. Modify the TCP server code of Program 13.2 to use gethostbyname() and kernel assigned port number. Modify the TCP client code to find server IP by name.

5. Instead of gethostbyname(), POSIX recommends using the new function getaddrinfo() to get the name and IP address of a host. Read Linux man pages on getaddrinfo() and re-implement the TCP server and client in Program 13.2 using getaddrinfo().

6. Modify the TCP/IP Programming Project of Sect. 13.7 to implement bit-stuffing in both the server and client.

7. Implement a multi-threaded server in the TCP/IP Programming Project of Sect. 13.7 to support multiple clients.

References

ARP, RFC 826, 1982
Apache, HTTP Server Project,https://httpd.apache.org, 2017
Comer, D., "Internetworking with TCP/IP Principles, Protocols, and Architecture", Prentice Hall, 1988.
Comer, D., "Computer Networks and Internets with Internet Applications", 3rd edition, Pretence Hall, 2001
IBM Synchronous Data Link Control, IBM, 1979
PHP: History of PHP and Related Projects, www, php.net, 2017
Rago, Stephen A, "Unix System V Network Programming". Addision Wesley, 1993
RFC 134, Domain Names-Concepts and facilities, 1987
RFC 768, User Datagram Protocol, 1980
RFC 826, An Ethernet address Resolution protocol, 1982
RFC 1035, Domain Names-Implementation and Specification, 1987
RFC1180, A TCP/IP Tutorial, January 1991
RFC 2131, Dynamic Host Configuration Protocol, 1997
RFC 2616, Hypertext Transfer Protocol - HTTP/1.1, June 1999
RFC 3875, The Common Gateway Interface (CGI) Version 1.1, Oct. 2004
Stevens, Richard W., Fenner, Bill, Ruddof Andrew M., "UNIX Network Programming", Volume 1, 3rd edition, Addison Wesley, 2004

MySQL Database System

14

Abstract

This chapter covers the MySQL relational database system. It introduces MySQL and points out its importance. It shows how to install and run MySQL on Linux machines. It shows how to use MySQL to create and manage databases in both command mode and batch mode using SQL scripts. It shows how to interface MySQL with C programming. It also shows how to integrate MySQL with PHP to create and manage databases by dynamic Web pages.

14.1 Introduction to MySQL

MySQL (MySQl 2018) is a relational database system (Codd 1970). In a relational database, data are stored in tables. Each table consists of rows and columns. Data in a table are related to each other. Tables may also be related to other tables. The relational structure makes it possible to run queries on the tables to retrieve information as well as to modify data in the database. The standard query language for relational database systems is SQL (Structured Query Language), including MySQL.

MySQL is an open source database management system. It consists of server and a client. After connecting a client to a server, users may enter SQL commands to the server, allowing them to create databases, delete databases, store, organize, and retrieve data in the database. MySQL has a wide range of applications. In addition to providing standard database system services, MySQL combined with PHP (PHP 2018) have formed the backbone of most Web sites for data management as well as for online commerce. This chapter provides an introduction to MySQL. We shall cover the basics of MySQL. These include how to install/configure MySQL in Linux, how to use MySQL to create and manage simple databases and how to interface with MySQL form both C and PHP programming environments.

14.2   Install MySQL

14.2.1   Ubuntu Linux

For Ubuntu 16.04 and later, install MySQL by

sudo apt-get install mysql-server

The mysql-server package includes both a MySQL server and a client. While installing MySQL, it will ask for a root user password. You may use the same login password of Ubuntu. After installing MySQL, it may be configured for better security by running the script

mysql_secure_installation

For simple and standard security setup, the reader may press Y and then ENTER to accept the defaults for all the questions.

14.2.2   Slackware Linux

Slackware Linux comes with MySQL preinstalled but it still needs to be configured. Otherwise, Slackware will show an error message for the mysql database when it starts up. In Slackware 14.0 or earlier, configure MySQL by the following steps.

(1). Setup my.cnf: MySQL loads a config file called my.cnf at startup. This file needs to be created when you first set up MySQL. In the /etc directory there are a few sample my.cnf files named my-small.cnf, my-large.cnf, etc. Select a desired version to create a my.cnf file, as in
      cp /etc/my-small.cnf /etc/my.cnf
(2). Install Required Databases: Mysql has a required database set which it needs. These are used for user identification etc. To install them use mysql user as superuser and install the initial required databases with the following command.
      mysql_install_db
(3). Setup Required System Permissions: This step ensures that the mysql user has ownership of the mysql system.
      chown -R mysql.mysql /var/lib/mysql
(4). Make /etc/rc.d/rc.mysqld executable by
      chmod 755 /etc/rc.d/rc.mysqld
This will start up the MySQL daemon mysqld automatically on subsequent system boots.

   Slackware 14.2 use MariaDB in place of MySQL. MariaDB is basically the same database as MySQL except it is not tied to Oracle. In fact, it still uses mysqld as its daemon name. In Slackware 14.2, MySQL already has a default .cnf file, so Step 1 is no longer needed. Configure MySQL by Steps (2) to (4) listed above. After configuration, start up the MySQL daemon mysqld manually by

/etc/rc.d/rc.mysqld -start

14.3   Use MySQL

Assume that the MySQL server is already set up and running on either a Ubuntu or Slackware Linux machine. The MySQL server may be set up to support different users. For simplicity, we shall only assume the root user. In order to use MySQL, the user must run a MySQL client to connect to the server. MySQL supports client connections from remote IP hosts. For simplicity, we shall run both the server and client on the same machine, i.e. the default localhost. The following sections show to use MySQL to manage databases.

14.3.1   Connect to MySQL Server

The first step of using MySQL is to run the MySQL client program. From an X-Window terminal, enter the MySQL client command, mysql, which connects to the MySQL server on the default localhost on the same computer.

```
mysql -u root -p              # specify the root user with password
Enter password:               #  enter the MySQL root user password
mysql>                        # mysql prompt
```

After connecting to the MySQL server, you will be accessing the MySQL shell, as indicated by a mysql> prompt. The MySQL shell behaves like a regular shell. It shows a mysql promt >, asking the user to enter SQL commands for the MySQL server to execute. Like regular sh, it also maintains a command history, which allows the user to recall and modify previous commands by arrow keys. However, it only accepts mysql commands or mysql scripts, but not regular sh commands. When entering MySQL commands, the reader should note the following.

.All MySQL command lines must end with a semicolon. For long commands, you may enter the command phrases on separate lines (by pressing the ENTER key). mysql will continue to prompt for more inputs by a -> symbol until it sees an ending semicolon.
.MySQL command line is not case sensitive. Although not required, it is a common practice to write MySQL commands in uppercase and databases, tables, usernames, or text in lowercase for clarity and easier identification.

14.3.2   Show Databases

The command SHOW DATABASES shows the current databases in MySQL.

Example:

```
mysql> SHOW DATABASES;
+--------------------+
| Database           |
+--------------------+
| information_schema |
| mysql              |
```

```
| performance_schema |
| test               |
+--------------------+
4 rows in set (0.01 sec)
```

14.3.3   Create New database

The command CREATE DATABASE dbname creates a new database named dbname, if it does not yet exist. The command can be qualified by an optional IF NOT EXISTS clause to avoid an error message if the database already exists.

Example:

```
mysql> CREATE DATABASE testdb
Query OK; 1 row affected (0.02 sec)   # mysql response
```

After creating a new database, enter SHOW DATABASES to see the result.

```
mysql> SHOW DATABASES;
+--------------------+
| Database           |
+--------------------+
| information_schema |
| mysql              |
| performance_schema |
| test               |
| testdb             |
+--------------------+
5 rows in set (0.00 sec)
```

14.3.4   Drop Database

The command DROP DATABASE dbname drops or deletes a named database if it exists. The command may be qualified with an optional IF EXIST clause. Beware that the DROP operation is irreversible. Once a database is dropped or deleted, it can not be undone or restored. So be careful about its usage.

Example:

```
mysql> DROP DATABASE testdb;
Query OK; one row affected (0.04 sec)

mysql> SHOW DATABASES;
+--------------------+
| Database           |
+--------------------+
```

```
| information_schema |
| mysql              |
| performance_schema |
| test               |
+--------------------+
4 rows in set (0.01 sec)
```

14.3.5   Choose Database

Assume that MySQL already has several databases. In order to operate on a specific database, the user must choose a database by the USE dbname command.

Example:

```
mysql> CREATE DATABASE cs360;
Query OK, 1 row affected (0.00 sec)

mysql> use cs360;
Database changed
```

14.3.6   Create Tables

This section shows how to create tables in MySQL databases. Assume that a **cs360** database contains the following student records.

```
struct students{
    int student_id;  # an integer ID number must exist
    char name[20];   # name string of 20 chars
    int score;       # an integer exam score, which may not exist
}
```

The command CREATE TABLE table_name creates a table in the current database. The command syntax is

```
CREATE TABLE [IF NOT EXISTS] tableName (
   columnName columnType columnAttribute, ...
   PRIMARY KEY(columnName),
   FOREIGN KEY (columnNmae) REFERENCES tableName (columnNmae)
)
```

For a single table case, the FOREIGN KEY clause is not needed.

Example:

```
mysql> CREATE TABLE students (
       student_id INT NOT NULL PRIMARY KEY AUTO_INCREMENT,
```

```
        name CHAR(20),
        score INT );
Query OK, 0 rows affected (0.00 sec)
```

```
mysql> SHOW TABLES;
+--------------------+
| Tables_in_cs360    |
+--------------------+
| students           |
+--------------------+
1 row in set (0.00 sec)
```

The DESCRIBE or DESC command shows the table format and column attributes.

```
mysql> DESCRIBE students
+------------+----------+------+-----+---------+----------------+
| Field      | Type     | Null | Key | Default | Extra          |
+------------+----------+------+-----+---------+----------------+
| student_id | int(11)  | NO   | PRI | NULL    | auto_increment |
| name       | char(20) | YES  |     | NULL    |                |
| score      | int(11)  | YES  |     | NULL    |                |
+------------+----------+------+-----+---------+----------------+
3 rows in set (0.00 sec)
```

It shows that the students table has 3 fields or columns, where

"student_id" is an integer, which can not be NULL, used as the primary key and its value will be incremented automatically when new rows are added.
"name" is a fixed length string of 20 chars long, **which may be NULL**.
"score" is an integer.

In a table, a **primary key** is a column or a set of columns which can be used to uniquely identify a row. A primary key is **unique** by default. As shown, the name column may be NULL, which could result in a row with a valid student_id but without a name. In order to avoid this, it should be declared with the **not null** attribute.

14.3.7   Drop Tables

The DROP TABLE table_name command drops or deletes a table.

Example:

```
mysql> CREATE TABLE dummy (
        id INT PRIMARY KEY, name CHAR(20));
Query OK, 0 rows affected (0.00 sec)
```

```
mysql> SHOW TABLES;
+-------------------+
| Tables_in_cs360   |
+-------------------+
| students          |
+-------------------+
| dummy             |
+-------------------+
1 row in set (0.00 sec)

mysql> DROP TABLE dummy;
mysql> SHOW TABLES;
+-------------------+
| Table_in_cs360    |
+-------------------+
| students          |
+-------------------+
1 rows in set (0.01 sec)
```

14.3.8   Data Types in MySQL

Before continuing, it is necessary to know the basic data types used in MySQL, which include mainly 3 categories; numeric, strings, date and time. We only show some of the commonly used data types in each category.

Numeric Types:
   INT: integer (4 bytes), **TINYINT:** (1 byte), **SMALLINT:** (2 bytes), etc.
   FLOAT: floating pointers number.
String Types:
   CHAR(size): fixed length string of 1-255 chars.
   VARCHAR(size): variable length strings, but may not use all the space.
   TEXT: variable length strings
Date and Time Types:
   DATE – Date in YYYY-MM-DD format
   TIME – Stores the time in HH:MM:SS format.

14.3.9   Insert Rows

To add rows to a table, use the INSERT command, which has the syntax form
   INSERT INTO table_name VLAUES (columnValue1, columnValue2, ...);

Example:

```
mysql> INSERT INTO students VALUES (1001, 'Baker', '50');
Query OK, 1 row affected (0.01 sec)
```

```
mysql> SELECT * FROM students;
+------------+-------+-------+
| student_id | name  | score |
+------------+-------+-------+
|       1001 | Baker |    50 |
+------------+-------+-------+
1 row in set (0.00 sec)
```

Similarly, we may insert more student records into the table. Since it is tedious to insert many entries by individual command lines manually, we may create a MySQL script file containing many INSERT command lines and use it as an input source file to mysql. Assume that we have edited a .sql script file as shown below.

```
/********  insert.sql script file *********/
INSERT INTO students VALUES (NULL, "Miller", 65);
INSERT INTO students VALUES (2001, "Smith",  76);
INSERT INTO students VALUES (NULL, "Walton", 85);
```

Enter the SOURCE command to let mysql use the sql script as input file, as in

```
mysql> SOURCE insert.sql;    # use insert.sql as input source file
(Query OK, rows affected, etc)

mysql> SELECT * FROM students;
+------------+--------+-------+
| student_id | name   | score |
+------------+--------+-------+
|       1001 | Baker  |    50 |
|       1002 | Miller |    65 |
|       2001 | Smith  |    76 |
|       2002 | Walton |    85 |
+------------+--------+-------+
4 rows in set (0.00 sec)
```

Note that, when inserting a new row, if an ID number is NULL, it will be assigned the next value (from the last entered ID value) by auto_increment.

14.3.10 Delete Rows

Use the DELETE command to delete row(s) from a table, which has the syntax form

```
DELETE FROM table_name;                    # delete all rows of a table
DELETE FROM table_name WHERE condition;  # delete row by condition
```

Example To demonstrate the delete operation, we first add a new row and then delete it from the table.

```
mysql> INSERT INTO students VALUES (NULL, 'Zach', '45');
```

```
mysql> SELECT * from students;
+------------+--------+-------+
| student_id | name   | score |
+------------+--------+-------+
|       1001 | Baker  |    50 |
|       1002 | Miller |    65 |
|       2001 | Smith  |    76 |
|       2002 | Walton |    85 |
|       2003 | Zach   |    45 |
+------------+--------+-------+
5 rows in set (0.00 sec)

mysql> DELETE FROM students WHERE name = 'Zach';
Query OK, 1 row affected (0.00 sec)

mysql> SELECT * FROM students;
+------------+--------+-------+
| student_id | name   | score |
+------------+--------+-------+
|       1001 | Baker  |    50 |
|       1002 | Miller |    65 |
|       2001 | Smith  |    76 |
|       2002 | Walton |    85 |
+------------+--------+-------+
4 rows in set (0.00 sec)
```

14.3.11 Update Table

The UPDATE command is used to modify existing records (columns) in a table. It has the syntax form

> **UPDATE** table_name **SET** col1 = value1, col2 = value2, ... **WHERE** condition;

Example Assume that we want to change Walton's score to 92.

```
mysql> UPDATE students SET score = 92 WHERE name = 'Walton';

mysql> SELECT * FROM students;
+------------+--------+-------+
| student_id | name   | score |
+------------+--------+-------+
|       1001 | Baker  |    50 |
|       1002 | Miller |    65 |
|       2001 | Smith  |    76 |
|       2002 | Walton |    92 |
+------------+--------+-------+
4 rows in set (0.00 sec)
```

Similarly, we may update the values of other columns by changing the **WHERE** condition.

14.3.12 Alter Table

The **ALTER TABLE** command is used to add, delete, or modify columns in an existing table. It is also used to add and drop various constraints on an existing table.

(1). **Change table name:**

```
ALTER TABLE table_name RENAME TO new_name;
```

(2). **Add Column:** To add a column in a table, use the following command:

```
ALTER TABLE table_name ADD column_name datatype;
```

(3). **Drop Column:** To drop a column, use the following command:

```
ALTER TABLE table_name DROP column_name datatype;
```

(4). **Alter/Modify Column:** To change the data type of a column in a table, use the following command:

```
ALTER TABLE table_name ALTER COLUMN column_name datatype;
```

Examples   Assume that we want to add a column named **grade** to the **students** table, and then assign letter grades of A to D to the students by their exam scores.

```
mysql> ALTER TABLE students ADD grade CHAR(2); // for 'A', 'B+', etc.
(Quert OK, 4 rows affected (0,01 sec)

mysql> SELECT * FROM students;
+------------+--------+-------+-------+
| student_id | name   | score | grade |
+------------+--------+-------+-------+
|       1001 | Baker  |    50 | NULL  |
|       1002 | Miller |    65 | NULL  |
|       2001 | Smith  |    76 | NULL  |
|       2002 | Walton |    92 | NULL  |
+------------+--------+-------+-------+
4 rows in set (0.00 sec)
```

After adding the **grade** column, all the entry values are initially NULL. We may assign a letter grade to students by the **UPDATE table_name** command.

Example:

```
mysql> UPDATE students SET grade = 'A' WHERE name = 'Walton';
Query OK, 1 row affected (0.00 sec)
Rows matched: 1  Changed: 1  Warnings: 0
```

```
mysql> SELECT * FROM students;
+------------+--------+-------+-------+
| student_id | name   | score | grade |
+------------+--------+-------+-------+
|       1001 | Baker  |    50 | NULL  |
|       1002 | Miller |    65 | NULL  |
|       2001 | Smith  |    76 | NULL  |
|       2002 | Walton |    92 | A     |
+------------+--------+-------+-------+
4 rows in set (0.00 sec)
```

Alternatively, we can also assign letter grades by using ranges of scores in the WHERE condition clause.

Examples:

```
mysql> UPDATE students SET grade = 'A' WHERE score > 80;

select * from students;
+------------+--------+-------+-------+
| student_id | name   | score | grade |
+------------+--------+-------+-------+
|       1001 | Baker  |    50 | NULL  |
|       1002 | Miller |    65 | NULL  |
|       2001 | Smith  |    76 | NULL  |
|       2002 | Walton |    92 | A     |
+------------+--------+-------+-------+
4 rows in set (0.00 sec)
```

Assume that we have executed the following commands:

```
mysql> UPDATE students SET grade = 'B' WHERE score >= 70 AND score < 80;
mysql> UPDATE students SET grade = 'C' WHERE score >= 60 and score < 70;
mysql> UPDATE students SET grade = 'D' WHERE score < 60;

mysql> SELECT * FROM students;
+------------+--------+-------+-------+
| student_id | name   | score | grade |
+------------+--------+-------+-------+
|       1001 | Baker  |    50 | D     |
|       1002 | Miller |    65 | C     |
|       2001 | Smith  |    76 | B     |
|       2002 | Walton |    92 | A     |
+------------+--------+-------+-------+
4 rows in set (0.00 sec)
```

14.3.13 Related Tables

So far, we have shown databases with only a single table. A real database may consist of many tables, which are related to one another. In MySQL, table relationships are defined by using **Primary Key-Foreign Key** constraints. A link is created between two tables where the primary key of one table is associated with the foreign key of another table. In MySQL, tables may be related in several ways, which include

(1). One-to-One (1-1) Relation

One-to-One (1-1) relation is defined as the relationship between two tables where the tables are associated with each other based on only one matching row. This kind of relationship can be created using the **Primary key-Unique foreign key constraints**. Assume that in the **cs360** database, each student has a unique email address. We may include the email address of each student in the **students table**, but that would require an additional column in the students table. Instead, we can create a separate **email table** containing only student email addresses, and define a 1-1 relation between the two tables by a unique **foreign key** in the email table, which references the **primary key** in the **students table.**

Example:

```
mysql> CREATE TABLE email (id INT PRIMARY KEY AUTO_INCREMENT,
        student_id INT UNIQUE NOT NULL, email CHAR (40),
        FOREIGN KEY (student_id) REFERENCES students(student_id));
Query OK, 0 rows affected (0.00 sec)
```

```
mysql> DESC email;
```

Field	Type	Null	Key	Default	Extra
id	int(11)	NO	PRI	NULL	auto_increment
student_id	int(11)	NO	UNI	NULL	
email	char(40)	YES		NULL	

```
3 rows in set (0.00 sec)
```

Next, we insert student email addresses into the **email table**. Then we query the email table and show the table contents.

```
mysql> INSERT INTO email VALUES (NULL, 2002, 'walton@wsu.edu');
mysql> INSERT INTO email VALUES (NULL, 2001, 'smith@gmail.com');
mysql> INSERT INTO email VALUES (NULL, 1002, 'miller@hotmail.com');
mysql> INSERT INTO email VALUES (NULL, 1001, 'baker@gmail.com');
```

```
mysql> SELECT * FROM email;
```

id	student_id	email
1	2002	walton@wsu.edu

```
|  2 |        2001 | smith@gmail.com    |
|  3 |        1002 | miller@hotmail.com |
|  4 |        1001 | baker@gmail.com    |
+----+------------+--------------------+
4 rows in set (0.00 sec)
```

Note that in the email table the student_id can be in any order as long as they are all unique. Each student_id is a foreign key which references a primary key in the students table.

```
mysql> SELECT a.name, b.email FROM students a, email b WHERE
        a.student_id = b.student_id;
+--------+--------------------+
| name   | email              |
+--------+--------------------+
| Walton | walton@wsu.edu     |
| Smith  | smith@gmail.com    |
| Miller | miller@hotmail.com |
| Baker  | baker@gmail.com    |
+--------+--------------------+
4 rows in set (0.00 sec)
```

(2). One-to-Many (1-M) Relations

In a database, One-to-Many or 1-M relations are more common and useful than 1-1 relations. The One-to-Many relation is defined as a relationship between two tables where a row from one table can have multiple matching rows in another table. This relation can be created using **Primary key-Foreign key relationship**. Suppose that the course **cs360** has a required textbook and also a reference book. Students may order the books through the book store, which uses a **book_order** table to keep track of student book orders. Each book order belongs to a unique student, but each student may order one or several books, including none as most of them do. So the relation between the students table and the book_order table is one-to-many. As in the one-to-one relation case, we may use a foreign key in the book_order table to reference the primary key in the students table. With the two tables related to each other, we can run queries on the tables to check which student has not ordered the required textbook, etc.

Example In this example, we first create a **book_order** table, add a foreign key to it and populate the table with book orders from students.

```
mysql> CREATE TABLE book_order
        (order_no INT PRIMARY KEY AUTO_INCREMENT,
         student_id INT NOT NULL,
         book_name char(20),
         date DATE
        );
Query OK, 0 rows affected (0.01 sec)
```

```
mysql> DESC book_order;
+------------+----------+------+-----+---------+----------------+
| Field      | Type     | Null | Key | Default | Extra          |
+------------+----------+------+-----+---------+----------------+
| order_no   | int(11)  | NO   | PRI | NULL    | auto_increment |
| student_id | int(11)  | NO   |     | NULL    |                |
| book_name  | char(20) | YES  |     | NULL    |                |
| date       | date     | YES  |     | NULL    |                |
+------------+----------+------+-----+---------+----------------+
4 rows in set (0.00 sec)

mysql> ALTER TABLE book_order ADD FOREIGN KEY (student_id)
       REFERENCES students(student_id);
Query OK, 0 rows affected (0.03 sec)
Records: 0  Duplicates: 0  Warnings: 0

mysql> DESC book_order;
+------------+----------+------+-----+---------+----------------+
| Field      | Type     | Null | Key | Default | Extra          |
+------------+----------+------+-----+---------+----------------+
| order_no   | int(11)  | NO   | PRI | NULL    | auto_increment |
| student_id | int(11)  | NO   | MUL | NULL    |                |
| book_name  | char(20) | YES  |     | NULL    |                |
| date       | date     | YES  |     | NULL    |                |
+------------+----------+------+-----+---------+----------------+
4 rows in set (0.00 sec)

mysql> INSERT INTO book_order VALUES (   1, 1001, 'reference',
       '2018-04-16');
mysql> INSERT INTO book_order VALUES (NULL, 1001, 'textbook',
       '2018-04-16');
mysql> INSERT INTO book_order VALUES (NULL, 1002, 'textbook',
       '2018-04-18');
mysql> INSERT INTO book_order VALUES (NULL, 1002, 'reference',
       '2018-04-18');
mysql> INSERT INTO book_order VALUES (NULL, 2001, 'textbookd',
       '2018-04-20');
mysql> INSERT INTO book_order VALUES (NULL, 2002, 'reference',
       '2018-04-21');

mysql> SELECT * FROM book_order;
+----------+------------+-----------+------------+
| order_no | student_id | book_name | date       |
+----------+------------+-----------+------------+
|        1 |       1001 | reference | 2018-04-16 |
|        2 |       1001 | textbook  | 2018-04-16 |
|        3 |       1002 | textbook  | 2018-04-18 |
|        4 |       1002 | reference | 2018-04-18 |
|        5 |       2001 | textbookd | 2018-04-20 |
|        6 |       2002 | reference | 2018-04-21 |
+----------+------------+-----------+------------+
6 rows in set (0.00 sec)
```

(3). Many-to-Many (M-M) Relations

Two tables have a M-M relation if multiple records in one table are related to multiple records in another table. For instance, each student may take several classes and each class usually has many students. So the relation between a students table and a class enrollment table is M-M. A standard way of handling M-M relations is to create a **join table** between the two tables. The join table uses foreign keys to reference the primary keys in both tables, thus creating a bridge between the two tables.

(4). Self-Referencing Relation

A table can relate to itself by some columns. We shall not discuss this type of self-referencing relations.

14.3.14 Join Operations

In MySQL, JOIN operations are used to retrieve data from multiple tables. There are 4 different types of JOIN operations.

(INNER) JOIN table1, table2: retrieve items that are common in both tables.
LEFT   JOIN table1, table2: retrieve items in table1 and items common in both tables.
RIGHT   JOIN table1, table2: retrieve items in table2 and items common in both tables.
OUTER JOIN tabel1, table2: retrieve items in both tables; **uncommon and not useful.**

In terms of regular set operations, JOIN operations in MySQL can be interpreted as follows. Denote + as **union** of two sets and ^ as **intersection** of two sets. Then

```
(INNER) JOIN t1, t2 = t1 ^ t2
LEFT    JOIN t1, t2 = t1 + (t1 ^ t2)
RIGHT   JOIN t1, t2 = t2 + (t1 ^ t2)
OUTER   JOIN t1, t2 = t1 + t2;
```

We illustrate JOIN operations on the tables in the **cs360** database by examples.

```
mysql> select * from students JOIN email ON
       students.student_id = email.student_id;
+------------+--------+-------+-------+----+------------+------------------+
| student_id | name   | score | grade | id | student_id | email            |
+------------+--------+-------+-------+----+------------+------------------+
|       1001 | Baker  |    50 | D     | 1  |       1001 | baker@wsu.edu    |
|       1002 | Miller |    65 | C     | 2  |       1002 | miller@gmail.com |
|       2002 | Walton |    92 | A     | 3  |       2002 | smith@yahoo.com  |
|       2002 | Walton |    92 | A     | 4  |       2002 | walton@wsu.edu   |
+------------+--------+-------+-------+----+------------+------------------+
4 rows in set (0.00 sec)
```

```
mysql> SELECT * FROM students JOIN book_order ON
       students.student_id = book_order.student_id;
+----------+------+-----+-------+----------+----------+----------+------------+
|student_id|name  |score| grade | order_no |student_id| book_name | date       |
+----------+------+-----+-------+----------+----------+----------+------------+
|     1001|Baker  |   50| D     |     1 |      1001| reference | 2018-04-16 |
|     1001|Baker  |   50| D     |     2 |      1001| textbook  | 2018-04-16 |
|     1002|Miller |   65| C     |     3 |      1002| textbook  | 2018-04-18 |
|     1002|Miller |   65| C     |     4 |      1002| reference | 2018-04-18 |
|     2001|Smith  |   76| B     |     5 |      2001| textbookd | 2018-04-20 |
|     2002|Walton |   92| A     |     6 |      2002| reference | 2018-04-21 |
+----------+------+-----+-------+----------+----------+----------+------------+
6 rows in set (0.00 sec)

mysql> SELECT * FROM students RIGHT JOIN book_order ON
       students.student_id = book_order.student_id;
+----------+------+-----+-------+----------+----------+----------+------------+
|student_id|name  |score| grade | order_no |student_id| book_name | date       |
+----------+------+-----+-------+----------+----------+----------+------------+
|     1001|Baker  |   50| D     |     1 |      1001| reference | 2018-04-16 |
|     1001|Baker  |   50| D     |     2 |      1001| textbook  | 2018-04-16 |
|     1002|Miller |   65| C     |     3 |      1002| textbook  | 2018-04-18 |
|     1002|Miller |   65| C     |     4 |      1002| reference | 2018-04-18 |
|     2001|Smith  |   76| B     |     5 |      2001| textbookd | 2018-04-20 |
|     2002|Walton |   92| A     |     6 |      2002| reference | 2018-04-21 |
+----------+------+-----+-------+----------+----------+----------+------------+
6 rows in set (0.00 sec)

mysql> SELECT * FROM students LEFT JOIN book_order ON
       students.student_id = book_order.student_id;
+----------+------+-----+-------+----------+----------+----------+------------+
|student_id|name  |score| grade | order_no |student_id| book_name | date       |
+----------+------+-----+-------+----------+----------+----------+------------+
|     1001|Baker  |   50| D     |     1 |      1001| reference | 2018-04-16 |
|     1001|Baker  |   50| D     |     2 |      1001| textbook  | 2018-04-16 |
|     1002|Miller |   65| C     |     3 |      1002| textbook  | 2018-04-18 |
|     1002|Miller |   65| C     |     4 |      1002| reference | 2018-04-18 |
|     2001|Smith  |   76| B     |     5 |      2001| textbookd | 2018-04-20 |
|     2002|Walton |   92| A     |     6 |      2002| reference | 2018-04-21 |
+----------+------+-----+-------+----------+----------+----------+------------+
6 rows in set (0.00 sec)

mysql> SELECT * FROM book_order JOIN students ON
       students.student_id = book_order.student_id;
+----------+----------+----------+------------+----------+------+------+------+
| order_no |student_id|book_name | date       |student_id|name  | score| grade|
+----------+----------+----------+------------+----------+------+------+------+
|       1 |     1001 | reference | 2018-04-16 |     1001|Baker  |   50 | D    |
|       2 |     1001 | textbook  | 2018-04-16 |     1001|Baker  |   50 | D    |
|       3 |     1002 | textbook  | 2018-04-18 |     1002|Miller |   65 | C    |
```

```
|      4 |          1002 | reference | 2018-04-18 |     1002|Miller|   65 | C    |
|      5 |          2001 | textbookd | 2018-04-20 |     2001|Smith |   76 | B    |
|      6 |          2002 | reference | 2018-04-21 |     2002|Walton|   92 | A    |
+--------+---------------+---------- +------------+---------+------+------+------+
6 rows in set (0.00 sec)
```

14.3.15 MySQL Database Diagram

In MySQL as well as in all relational data base systems, it is very useful to depict the relationships among the tables by a database diagram. Such diagrams are usually called ERD (Entity Relationship Diagram) or EERD (Enhanced/Extended ERD). They provide a visual representation of the various components in a database and their relationships. For the simple **cs360 database** used in this chapter, it can be represented by the database diagram shown below.

```
       email                                     book_order
    -----------          students            -------------
   |id         |      -------------          |order_no    |
   |student_id |<-->|student_id  |<=======<<|student_id  |
   |email      |      |name        |          |book_name   |
    -----------       |score       |          |date        |
                      |grade       |           -------------
                       -------------
```

In the database diagram, arrow lines depict the relations between tables by connecting the **foreign key** in one table to its referenced **primary key** in another table. Lines with a single arrow mark at both ends denote 1-1 relations and lines with multiple arrow marks at one end denote 1-M relations.

14.3.16 MySQL Scripts

Like regular Unix/Linux sh, the MySQL shell can also accepts and executes scripts files. MySQL script files have the suffix .sql. They contain MySQL commands for the MySQL server to execute. Instead of entering command lines by hand, we may use MySQL scripts to create database, create tables in the database, insert table entries and alter the table contents, etc. This section shows how to use MySQL scripts.

First, we create a do.sql file as shown below. For convenience, all MySQL commands are shown in lowercase but highlighted for clarity.

```
-- Comments: do.sql script file
drop database if exists cs360;

-- 1. create database cs360
create database if not exists cs360;
show databases;
use cs360;
show tables;
```

```
-- 2. create table students
create table students (id INT not null primary key auto_increment,
             name char (20) NOT NULL, score INT);
desc students;

-- 3. insert student records into students table
insert into students values (1001, 'Baker',  92);
insert into students values (NULL, 'Miller', 65);
insert into students values (2001, 'Smith',  76);
insert into students values (NULL, 'Walton', 87);
insert into students values (NULL, 'Zach',   50);

-- 4. show students table contents
select * from students;

-- 5 add grade column to students table
alter table students add grade char(2);
select * from students;

-- 6. Assign student grades by score ranges
update students set grade = 'A' where score >= 90;
update students set grade = 'B' where score >= 80 and score < 90;
update students set grade = 'C' where score >= 70 and score < 80;
update students set grade = 'D' where score >= 60 and score < 70;
update students set grade = 'F' where score < 60;

-- 7. Show students table contents
select * from students;
-- end of script file
```

There are two ways to run the mysql client using sql scripts. The first method is to use the **SOURCE** command to let mysql take inputs from a script file. The following shows the MySQL outputs with added comments to identify the results of the commands in the script file.

```
mysql> source do.sql;
Query OK, 0 rows affected, 1 warning (0.00 sec)
// create database cs360 and show it
Query OK, 1 row affected (0.00 sec)
+--------------------+
| Database           |
+--------------------+
| information_schema |
| cs360              |
| mysql              |
+--------------------+
3 rows in set (0.00 sec)


// use cs360
Database changed
Empty set (0.00 sec)
```

// create students table
Query OK, 0 rows affected (0.01 sec)

// describe students table
```
+-------+----------+------+-----+---------+----------------+
| Field | Type     | Null | Key | Default | Extra          |
+-------+----------+------+-----+---------+----------------+
| id    | int(11)  | NO   | PRI | NULL    | auto_increment |
| name  | char(20) | NO   |     | NULL    |                |
| score | int(11)  | YES  |     | NULL    |                |
+-------+----------+------+-----+---------+----------------+
3 rows in set (0.00 sec)
```

// insert student records
Query OK, 1 row affected (0.00 sec)
Query OK, 1 row affected (0.00 sec)
Query OK, 1 row affected (0.00 sec)
Query OK, 1 row affected (0.00 sec)
Query OK, 1 row affected (0.00 sec)

// select * from students
```
+------+--------+-------+
| id   | name   | score |
+------+--------+-------+
| 1001 | Baker  |    92 |
| 1002 | Miller |    65 |
| 2001 | Smith  |    76 |
| 2002 | Walton |    87 |
| 2003 | Zach   |    50 |
+------+--------+-------+
5 rows in set (0.00 sec)
```

// add grade column to table
Query OK, 5 rows affected (0.01 sec)
Records: 5 Duplicates: 0 Warnings: 0

// select * from students
```
+------+-------+-------+-------+
| id   | name  | score | grade |
+------+-------+-------+-------+
| 1001 | Baker |    92 | NULL  |
| 1002 | Miller|    65 | NULL  |
| 2001 | Smith |    76 | NULL  |
| 2002 | Walton|    87 | NULL  |
| 2003 | Zach  |    50 | NULL  |
+------+-------+-------+-------+
5 rows in set (0.00 sec)
```

// assign grades by scores
Query OK, 1 row affected (0.00 sec)
Rows matched: 1 Changed: 1 Warnings: 0
Query OK, 1 row affected (0.00 sec)
Rows matched: 1 Changed: 1 Warnings: 0
Query OK, 1 row affected (0.00 sec)
Rows matched: 1 Changed: 1 Warnings: 0
Query OK, 1 row affected (0.00 sec)
Rows matched: 1 Changed: 1 Warnings: 0
Query OK, 1 row affected (0.00 sec)
Rows matched: 1 Changed: 1 Warnings: 0

// show table with grades

```
+------+--------+-------+-------+
| id   | name   | score | grade |
+------+--------+-------+-------+
| 1001 | Baker  |    92 | A     |
| 1002 | Miller |    65 | D     |
| 2001 | Smith  |    76 | C     |
| 2002 | Walton |    87 | B     |
| 2003 | Zach   |    50 | F     |
+------+--------+-------+-------+
5 rows in set (0.00 sec)
```

The second method is to run mysql in batch mode using sql script as inputs.

root@wang:~/SQL# mysql -u root -p < do.sql
Enter password:
Database
information_schema
cs360
mysql

// after creating students table and desc table
```
Field   Type    Null    Key     Default Extra
id      int(11) NO      PRI     NULL    auto_increment
name    char(20)        NO      NULL
score   int(11) YES             NULL
```

// after inserting rows and select * from students
```
id      name    score
1001    Baker   92
1002    Miller  65
2001    Smith   76
2002    Walton  87
2003    Zach    50
```

// after altering table with grade column
```
id      name    score   grade
1001    Baker   92      NULL
1002    Miller  65      NULL
2001    Smith   76      NULL
2002    Walton  87      NULL
```

```
2003     Zach    50      NULL
// after assigning grades
id       name    score   grade
1001     Baker   92      A
1002     Miller  65      D
2001     Smith   76      C
2002     Walton  87      B
2003     Zach    50      F
```

As can be seen, the outputs in batch mode are much terser than those in interactive or command mode.

14.4   MySQL Programming in C

MySQL works well with many programming languages, such as C, Java and python, etc. This section shows how to program MySQL in C. Interface between C programs and MySQL is supported by a set of MySQL C API functions (C API 2018a, b) in the mysqlclient library.

14.4.1   Build MySQL Client Program in C

Consider the following C program, which prints the libmysqlclient library version.

```
// client.c file
#include <stdio.h>
#include <my_global.h>
#include <mysql.h>
int main(int argc, char *argc[])
{
  printf("MySQL client version is : %s\n", mysql_get_client_info());
}
```

To compile the program, enter

```
gcc client.c -I/usr/include/mysql/ -lmysqlclient
```

Note that the –I option specifies the include file path as **/usr/include/mysql** and the –l option specifies the **mysqlclient** library. Then, run a.out. It should print

```
MySQL client version is : version_number, e.g. 5.5.53
```

14.4.2   Connect to MySQL Server in C

The following C program C14.2 shows how to connect to a MySQL server.

```
// c14.2.c file: connect to MySQL server
#include <stdio.h>
```

```
#include <stdlib.h>
#include <my_global.h>
#include <mysql.h>

int main(int argc, char *argv[ ])
{
    // 1. define a connection object
    MYSQL con;
    // 2. Initialize the connection object
    if (mysql_init(&con)) { // return object address printf("Connection handle
        initialized\n");
    } else {
        printf("Connection handle initialization failed\n");
        exit(1);
    }
    // 3. Connect to MySQL server on localhost
    if (mysql_real_connect(&con, "localhost", "root", "root_password",
                           "cs360", 3306, NULL, 0)) {
        printf("Connection to remote MySQL server OK\n");
    }
    else {
            printf("Connection to remote MySQL failed\n");
            exit(1);
    }
    // 4. Close the connection when done
    mysql_close(&con);
}
```

The program consists of 4 steps.

(1). Define a MYSQL object **con** as the connection handle. Its role is similar to a socket in network programming. Almost all mysql C API functions needs this object pointer as a parameter.

(2). Call **mysql_init**(&con) to initialize the con object, which is required. It returns the address of the initialized object. Most other mysql API functions return 0 for success and nonzero for error. In case of error, the functions

> unsigned int **mysql_errno**(&con) returns an error number,
> constant char ***mysql_error**(&con) returns a string describing the error.

(3). Call **mysql_real_connect**() to connect to a remote server. The general syntax is mysql_real_connect() is

```
MYSQL *mysql_real_connect(MYSQL *mysql,
        const char *host,           // server hostname or IP
        const char *user,           // MySQL user name
        const char *passwd,         // user password
        const char *db,             // database name
        unsigned int port,          // 3306
        const char *unix_socket,    // can be NULL
        unsigned long client_flag); // 0
```

It can be used to connect to any MySQL server on the Internet, provided that the user has access to that MySQL server. For simplicity, we assume that both the MySQL client and server are on the same localhost. After connecting to the server, the client program can start to access the database, which will be shown next.

(4). The client program should close the connection before exits.

14.4.3   Build MySQL Database in C

This section shows how to build MySQL databases in C programs. The following C program C14.3 builds the **students** table in a database **cs360** exactly the same way as in previous sections using MySQL commands or scripts.

```
// C14.1.c: build MySQL database in C
#include <stdio.h>
#include <stdlib.h>
#include <my_global.h>
#include <mysql.h>

MYSQL *con;        // connection object pointer
void error()
{
  printf("errno = %d %s\n", mysql_errno(con), mysql_error(con));
  mysql_close(con);
  exit(1);
}


int main(int argc, char *argv[ ])
{
  con =  mysql_init(NULL); // will allocate and initialize it
  if (con == NULL)
     error();
  printf("connect to mySQL server on localhost using database cs360\n");
  if (mysql_real_connect(con, "localhost", "root", NULL,
         "cs360", 0, NULL, 0) == NULL)
     error();
  printf("connection to server OK\n");

  printf("drop students table if exists\n");
  if (mysql_query(con, "DROP TABLE IF EXISTS students"))
     error();

  printf("create students tables in cs360\n");
  if (mysql_query(con, "CREATE TABLE students(Id INT NOT NULL
    PRIMARY KEY AUTO_INCREMENT, name CHAR(20) NOT NULL, score INT)"))
     error();
```

```
   printf("insert student records into students table\n");
   if (mysql_query(con, "INSERT INTO students VALUES(1001,'Baker',50)"))
      error();
   if (mysql_query(con, "INSERT INTO students VALUES(1002,'Miller',65)"))
      error();
   if (mysql_query(con, "INSERT INTO students VALUES(2001,'Miller',75)"))
      error();
   if (mysql_query(con, "INSERT INTO students VALUES(2002,'Smith',85)"))
      error();
   printf("all done\n");
   mysql_close(con);
}
```

After connecting to the MySQL server, the program uses the **mysql_query**() function to operate on the database. The second parameter of the mysql_query() function is exactly the same as an ordinary MySQL command. It can be used for simple MySQL commands but not for commands if the parameter contains binary values or null bytes. To execute commands that may contain binary data, the program must use the **mysql_real_query**() function, as shown in the next program.

```
// C14.2 Program: build MySQL database with mysql_real_query()
#include <stdio.h>
#include <stdlib.h>
#include <string.h>
#include <my_global.h>
#include <mysql.h>

#define N 5
int id[ ] =          { 1001,    1002,    2001,    2002,    2003};
char name[ ][20] = {"Baker", "Miller", "Smith", "Walton", "Zach"};
int score[ ] =       {  65,      50,      75,      95,      85};
MYSQL *con;
void error()
{
  printf("errno = %d %s\n", mysql_errno(con), mysql_error(con));
  mysql_close(con);
  exit(1);
}
int main(int argc, char *argv[ ])
{
  int i;
  char buf[1024];           // used to create commands for MySQL
  con = mysql_init(NULL); // MySQL server will allocate and init con
  if (con == NULL)
     error();
  printf("connect to mySQL server on localhost using database cs360\n");
  if (mysql_real_connect(con, "localhost", "root", NULL,
          "cs360", 0, NULL, 0) == NULL)
     error();
  printf("connected to server OK\n");
```

```
  printf("drop students table if exists\n");
  if (mysql_query(con, "DROP TABLE IF EXISTS students"))
     error();
  printf("create students tables in cs360\n");
  if (mysql_query(con, "CREATE TABLE students(Id INT NOT NULL PRIMARY
     KEY AUTO_INCREMENT, name CHAR(20) NOT NULL, score INT)"))
     error();
  printf("insert student records into students table\n");
  for (i=0; i<N; i++){
    printf("id=%8d name=%10s, score=%4d\n",id[i],name[i],score[i]);
    sprintf(buf, "INSERT INTO students VALUES (%d, '%s', %d);",
                  id[i], name[i], score[i]);
    if (mysql_real_query(con, buf, strlen(buf)))
       error();
  }
  printf("all done\n");
  mysql_close(con);
}
```

For comparison purpose, we have highlighted the new features in the C14.3 program. In order to insert a large number of rows into the **students** table, it is better to issue the INSERT commands in a loop over the number of rows to be inserted. Since the simple mysql_query() function can not take binary data, we must use the **mysql_real_query**() function. First, we define id[], name[] and score[] as arrays with initialized student data. For each student record, we use **sprinf**() to create a MySQL INSERT command line in a char buf[ ], and calls mysql_real_query(), passing the string in buf[] as a parameter. In practice, student records are usually from a data file. In that case, the C program can open the data file for read, read each student record, perform some preprocessing on the data before issuing commands to the MySQL server. We leave this as a programming exercise in the problem section.

14.4.4   Retrieve Results of MySQL Queries in C

MySQL queries may return results, e.g. SELECT, DESCRIBE, etc. A result is a set of columns and rows. The MySQL C API provides two ways of fetching a result set from the MySQL server: all rows at once or row by row.

The function **mysql_store_result**() is used to fetch the set of rows from the MySQL server all at once and store it in memory locally. Its usage is

```
  MYSQL_RES *mysql_store_result(MYSQL *mysql);
```

The function **mysql_use_result**() is used to initiate a row-by-row result set retrieval.

```
  MYSQL_RES *mysql_use_result(MYSQL *mysql);
```

After each invocation of mysql_query() or mysql_real_query() with MySQL statements that return results, call one of these functions to retrieve the result set. Both functions return the result set represented by an object of type **MYSQL_RES**. The returned result set object is used by other API functions to fetch the set of columns and rows. When the result set is no longer needed, the function

mysql_free_result() is used to free the result object resource. The following program C14.3 shows how to retrieve the result sets and display the columns or rows of a table

```
// C14.3 file: Retrieve MySQL query results
#include <my_global.h>
#include <mysql.h>
#include <string.h>

#define N 5
int id[ ] =          { 1001,    1002,    2001,    2002,     2003};
char name[ ][20] = {"Baker", "Miller", "Smith", "Walton", "Zach"};
int score[ ] =     {  65,     50,      75,      95,       85};
int grade[ ] =     {  'D',    'F',     'C',     'A',      'B'};

MYSQL *con;
void error()
{
  printf("errno = %d %s\n", mysql_errno(con), mysql_error(con));
  mysql_close(con);
  exit(1);
}

int main(int argc, char **argv)
{
  int i, ncols;
  MYSQL_ROW row;
  MYSQL_RES *result;
  MYSQL_FIELD *column;
  char buf[1024];

  con =  mysql_init(NULL);
  if (con == NULL)
     error();

  printf("connect to mySQL server on localhost using database cs360\n");
  if (mysql_real_connect(con, "localhost", "root", NULL,
          "cs360", 0, NULL, 0) == NULL)
     error();
  printf("connected to server OK\n");

  printf("drop students table if exists\n");
  if (mysql_query(con, "DROP TABLE IF EXISTS students"))
     error();

  printf("create students tables in cs360\n");
  if (mysql_query(con, "CREATE TABLE students(Id INT NOT NULL
                  PRIMARY KEY AUTO_INCREMENT, name CHAR(20) NOT NULL,
                  score INT, grade CHAR(2))"))
     error();
```

```
  printf("insert student records into students table\n");
  for (i=0; i<N; i++){
    printf("id =%4d name =%-8s score =%4d  %c\n",
              id[i], name[i], score[i], grade[i]);
    sprintf(buf, "INSERT INTO students VALUES (%d, '%s', %d, '%c');",
              id[i], name[i], score[i], grade[i]);
    if (mysql_real_query(con, buf, strlen(buf)))
       error();
  }
  printf("retrieve query results\n");
  mysql_query(con, "SELECT * FROM students");
  result = mysql_store_result(con); // retrieve result

  ncols = mysql_num_fields(result); // get number of columns in row
  printf("number of columns = %d\n", ncols);
  for (i=0; i<ncols; i++){
    column = mysql_fetch_field(result); // get each column
    printf("column no.%d name = %s\n", i+1, column->name);
  }

  mysql_query(con, "SELECT * FROM students");
  result = mysql_store_result(con);

  ncols = mysql_num_fields(result);
  printf("columns numbers = %d\n", ncols);
  while( row = mysql_fetch_row(result) ){
      for (i=0; i<ncols; i++)
        printf("%-8s ", row[i]);
      printf("\n");
  }
  printf("all done\n");
  mysql_close(con);
}
```

In the C14.3 program, the lines of code that focus on retrieving results are highlighted for clarity. In addition to the **mysql_store_result()** function, it also uses the following functions.

MYSQL_FIELD *mysql_fetch_field(MYSQL_RES *result): Returns the definition of one column of a result set as a MYSQL_FIELD structure. Call this function repeatedly to retrieve information about all columns in the result set. It returns NULL when no more fields are left.

unsigned int mysql_num_fields(MYSQL_RES *result): Returns the number of columns in a result set.

MYSQL_ROW mysql_fetch_row(MYSQL_RES *result): Retrieves the next row of a result set. Returns NULL when there are no more rows to retrieve.

The following shows the outputs of running the C14.3 program

```
connect to mySQL server on localhost using database cs360
connected to server OK
drop students table if exists
```

```
create students tables in cs360
insert student records into students table
id =1001 name =Baker     score =  65  D
id =1002 name =Miller    score =  50  F
id =2001 name =Smith     score =  75  C
id =2002 name =Walton    score =  95  A
id =2003 name =Zach      score =  85  B
retrieve query results
number of columns = 4
column no.1 name = Id
column no.2 name = name
column no.3 name = score
column no.4 name = grade
columns numbers = 4
1001     Baker     65          D
1002     Miller    50          F
2001     Smith     75          C
2002     Walton    95          A
2003     Zach      85          B
all done
```

In summary, accessing MySQL through C programming is fairly simple. It only requires the user to learn how to use a few MySQL API functions in C. In general, running compiled binary executables of C programs is faster and more efficient than interpretive script programs. Running compiled C programs are more suitable for handling large amounts of data processing. Perhaps the main drawback of running C programs is the lack of a GUI interface. For that purpose, we turn to the GUI based programming environment of PHP.

14.5   MySQL Programming in PHP

PHP (PHP 2018) is often used as the front-end of a Web site, which interacts with a database engine, such as MySQL, at the back-end for storing and retrieving data online through dynamic Web pages. The combination of PHP and MySQL provides a wide range of options to create all kinds of Web pages, from small personal contact forms to large corporate portals. This section covers basic programming of MySQL in PHP.

In order to do MySQL programming through PHP, the reader must have access to both a HTTPD server, which can interface with a MySQL server. For Linux users, this is not a problem at all since both HTTPD and MySQL are available on the same Linux machine. Although the HTTPD server and the MySQL server do not have to be on the same IP host, for convenience we shall assume that they are on the same computer, i.e. the same localhost. The following discussions assume the following.

1. The reader's Linux machine has both HTTPD and MySQL server running, and the HTTPD server is configured to support PHP. The reader may consult Chap. 13 for how to configure HTTPD for PHP.
2. The reader has a user account and can host Web pages, which can be accessed as http://localhost/ ~user_name

    If not, consult Chap. 13 for how to set up personal Web pages.
3. A Web browser which can access Web pages on the Internet.

14.5.1   Connect to MySQL Server in PHP

When programming PHP with MySQL, the first step is to connect to a MySQL server. For convenience, we shall assume that the MySQL server is on the same Linux machine. The following program P14.1 shows a PHP script, which connects to a MySQL server to create a new database **cs362**.

```
// P14.1: PHP script, connect to a MySQL Server
<html>
<head>
  <title>Creating MySQL Database</title>
</head>
<body>
  <?php
       $dbhost = 'localhost:3036';
       $dbuser = 'root';
       $dbpass = "; // replace with YOUR MySQL root password
       $con = mysql_connect($dbhost, $dbuser, $dbpass);
       if(! $con ) {
          die('Can not connect: ' . mysql_error());
       }
       echo 'Connected successfully<br />';

       $sql = 'DROP DATABASE IF EXISTS cs362';
       $retval = mysql_query( $sql, $con );
       if ($retval)
          echo "dropped database cs362 OK<br>";

       $sql = 'CREATE DATABASE cs362';
       $retval = mysql_query( $sql, $con );
       if(! $retval ) {
          die('Could not create database: ' . mysql_error());
       }
       echo "Database cs362 created successfully\n";
       mysql_close($con);
    ?>
    </body>
</html>
```

As in C, interface between PHP and MySQL is supported by a set of MySQL PHP API functions (MySQL PHP API 2018). The PHP API functions are usually simpler in syntax than their C counterparts. When calling mysql functions in PHP, it is customary to define PHP variables with values, rather than using hard coded strings or numbers as parameters. As shown, the program uses **mysql_connect**() to connect to the MySQL server. Since creating/deleting databases in MySQL requires the root user privilege, the program connects to the MySQL server as the root user. As in C programming, the standard PHP query function is also **mysql_query**(). When the program ends, it issues **mysql_close**() to close the connection.

14.5.2   Create Database Tables in PHP

The next program shows how to create tables in an existing database. For ease of identification, the PHP code which drops a table (if it exists) and creates a new table are highlighted.

```
// P14.2 : PHP program Create Table
<html>
<head>
    <title>Creating MySQL Tables</title>
</head>
<body>
    <?php
        $dbhost = 'localhost:3036';
        $dbuser = 'root';
        $dbpass = ";
        $con = mysql_connect($dbhost, $dbuser, $dbpass);
        if(! $con ) {
            die('Could not connect: ' . mysql_error());
        }
        echo 'Connected to MySQL Server OK<br>';

        mysql_select_db( 'cs362' ); // use cs362 created earlier

        $sql = "DROP TABLE IF EXISTS students";
        $retval = mysql_query( $sql, $conn );

        echo "create table in cs362<br>";
        $sql = "CREATE TABLE students( ".
            "student_id INT NOT NULL PRIMARY KEY AUTO_INCREMENT, ".
            "name CHAR(20) NOT NULL, ".
            "score INT, ".
            "grade CHAR(2)); ";
        $retval = mysql_query( $sql, $conn );
        if(! $retval ) {
            die('Could not create table: ' . mysql_error());
        }
        echo "Table created successfully\n";
        mysql_close($conn);
    ?>
</body>
</html
```

Figure 14.1 shows the results of running the P14.1 program from a Web browser.

14.5.3   Insert Records into Table in PHP

The following program, P14.2 shows how to insert records into a table in a database using PHP.

Fig. 14.1 Connect to MySQL server in PHP

```
// P14.2: Insert records into table
<html>
<head>
  <title>Insert Record to MySQL Database</title>
</head>
<body>
<?php
 if ( isset($_POST['submit']) ){ // if user has submitted data
    $dbhost = 'localhost:3036';
    $dbuser = 'root';
    $dbpass = ";
    $con = mysql_connect($dbhost, $dbuser, $dbpass);

    if(! $con ) {
      die('Could not connect: ' . mysql_error());
    }
    echo "Connected to server OK<br>";
    mysql_select_db('cs362');      // use cs362 database

    $student_id = $_POST['student_id'];
    $name       = $_POST['name'];
    $score      = $_POST['score'];
    echo "ID=" . $student_id . " name=" . $name .
        " score=".$score."<br>";
    if ($student_id == NULL || $name == NULL || $score == NULL){
       echo "ID or name or score can not be NULL<br>";
    }
    else{
       $sql = "INSERT INTO students ".
              "(student_id, name, score) "."VALUES ".
              "('$student_id','$name','$score')";
       $retval = mysql_query( $sql, $con );

       if(! $retval ) {
         echo "Error " . mysql_error() . "<br>";
       }
       else{
```

```
            echo "Entered data OK\n";
            mysql_close($con);
        }
      }
   }
 ?>


<br>
// a FORM for user to enter and submit data
<form method = "post" action = "<?php $_PHP_SELF ?>">
  ID number : <input name="student_id" type="text" id=student_id"><br>
  name    : <input name="name" type="text" id="name"><br>
  score   : <input name="score" type="text"
                      id="score"><br><br>
  <input name="submit" type="submit" id="submit" value="Submit">
</form>
</body>
</html>
```

Figure 14.2 shows the FORM generated by PHP for user to input data and submit request.

Figure 14.3 shows the results of the insert operation. If the operation is successful, it returns another form for the user to enter and submit more insertion requests

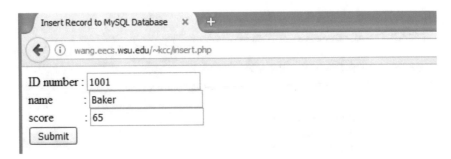

Fig. 14.2 PHP form for insert

Fig. 14.3 Results of insert operation

14.5.4   Retrieve Results of MySQL Queries in PHP

The following program P14.3 shows how to retrieve and display query results in PHP.

```
// P14.3: Select query and display results
<html>
<head>
 <title>Select Records from MySQL Database</title>
</head>
<body>
<?php
   $dbhost = 'localhost:3036';
   $dbuser = 'root';
   $dbpass = ";
   $conn = mysql_connect($dbhost, $dbuser, $dbpass);

   if(! $con ) {
      die('Could not connect: ' . mysql_error());
   }


   mysql_select_db('cs362');

   echo "select 1 row<br>";
   $sql = 'SELECT student_id, name, score FROM students
           WHERE name="Baker"';
   $retval = mysql_query( $sql, $con );

   if(! $retval ) {
      die('Could not retrieve data: ' . mysql_error());
   }
   while($row = mysql_fetch_array($retval, MYSQL_ASSOC)) {
      echo "student_id = {$row['student_id']}  ".
        "name = {$row['name']}  ".
        "score = {$row['score']} <br> ".
        "----------------------------<br>";
   }

   echo "select all rows<br>";
   $sql = 'SELECT * FROM students';
   $retval = mysql_query( $sql, $con );

   if(! $retval ) {
      die('Could not retrieve data: ' . mysql_error());
   }
   while($row = mysql_fetch_assoc($retval)) {
      echo "student_id = {$row['student_id']}  ".
        "name = {$row['name']}  ".
        "score = {$row['score']}<br>  ";
   }
```

```
    echo "--------------------------<br>";

    echo "selected data successfully\n";
    mysql_close($con);
?>
</body>
</html>
```

The program P14.3 shows how to select one row from a database. It retrieves the row by the **mysql_fetch_assoc()** function as an **associative array** $row, and displays the contents of $row by name. It also shows how to select all rows and retrieves the rows by the same **mysql_fetch_assoc()** function and display the contents of each row as an associative array. Associative arrays are standard features in PHP and Perl but they are not available in C.

14.5.5   Update Operation in PHP

The next program P14.4 shows how to update MySQL tables in PHP.

```
// P14.4: Update operations in PHP
<html>
<head> <title>Update tables in NySQL Database</title></head>
<body>
<?php
     $dbhost = 'localhost:3036';
     $dbuser = 'root';
     $dbpass = ";
     $conn = mysql_connect($dbhost, $dbuser, $dbpass);
     if(! $con ) {
       die('Could not connect: ' . mysql_error());
     }
     echo 'connected to Server OK<br>';
     mysql_select_db('cs362');
     $sql = 'UPDATE students SET grade = \'A\'
             WHERE score >= 90';
     $retval = mysql_query( $sql, $conn );
     if(! $retval ) {
        die('Could not update data: ' . mysql_error());
     }
     echo "Updated data successfully\n";
     mysql_close($conn);
?>
</body>
</html>
```

Exercise Modify the C14.4 program to assign letter grades 'B' to 'F' based on student score ranges. After updating the grades, run the PHP program P14.3 to verify the results.

14.5.6   Delete Rows in PHP

The following PHP program P14.5 deletes a row from a MySQL table.

```php
<?php
   $dbhost = 'localhost:3036';
   $dbuser = 'root';
   $dbpass = ";
   $conn = mysql_connect($dbhost, $dbuser, $dbpass);

   if(! $con ) {
      die('Could not connect: ' . mysql_error());
   }
   mysql_select_db('cs362');

   $sql = 'DELETE FROM students WHERE name=\'Zach\";
   $retval = mysql_query( $sql, $con );

   if(! $retval ) {
      die('Could not delete data: ' . mysql_error());
   }
   echo "Deleted data OK\n";
   mysql_close($conn);
?>
```

14.6   Summary

This chapter covers the MySQL relational database system. It introduces MySQL and points out its importance. It shows how to install and run MySQL on Linux machines. It shows how to use MySQL to create and manage databases in both command mode and batch mode using SQL scripts. It shows how to interface MySQL with C programming. It also shows how to integrate MySQL with PHP to create and manage databases by dynamic Web pages.

Problems

1. Assume that the CS360 class list is a file contains one student record per line. Each student record is a C structure

```
struct student_record{
        int  ID;
        char name[20];
        int  score;
        char email[40];   // email address
        struct book_order{
          char [20];       // "text" or "reference"
          date [10];       // yyyy-mm-dd
    }
}
```

Write a C program to build a **cs360** class database for the students. The database should have 3 tables; **students, email and book_order**. The students table should contain a grade column for letter grade. The email table contains student email address and a foreign key that references the student ID in the student table. The book_order table's foreign key also references the ID in the students table.

After building the cs360 class database, run UPDATE commands to assign letter grades and also run JOIN queries on the tables and show the query results.

2. The same assumptions and requirements as in Problem 1. Write PHP scripts to build a cs360 database in PHP. Test the resulting database via Web pages.

3. For simplicity, all the example databases in this chapter use only 1-1 and 1-M relations between tables. Design other students information tables with M-M relations, e.g. classes taken by students and class enrollment tables. Then create a database to support the M-M related tables.

References

C API Functions, MySQL 5.7 Reference Manual::27.8.6 C API Function OverView, https://dev.mysql.com/doc/refman/5.7/en/c-api-function-overview.html, 2018a

C API Functions, MySQL 5.7 Reference Manual:: 27.8.7 C API Function Descriptions, https://dev.mysql.com/doc/refman/5.7/en/c-api-functions.html, 2018b

Codd, E.F. A relational model for data for large shared data banks, communications of the ACM, 13, 1970

MySQL, https://dev.mysql.com/doc/refman/8.0/en/history.html, 2018

MySQL PHP API, https://dev.mysql.com/doc/apis-php/en/, 2018

MySQL Functions, https://dev.mysql.com/doc/apis-php/en/apis-php-ref.mysql.html, 2018.

PHP: History of PHP and Related Projects, www.php.net, 2018

Index

© Springer International Publishing AG, part of Springer Nature 2018   449
K. C. Wang, *Systems Programming in Unix/Linux*, https://doi.org/10.1007/978-3-319-92429-8

Printed in the United States
By Bookmasters